THAT TIME I GOT REINCARNATED AS A SLIME

9

Author: FUSE
Artist: TAIKI KAWAKAMI
Character design: MITZ VAH

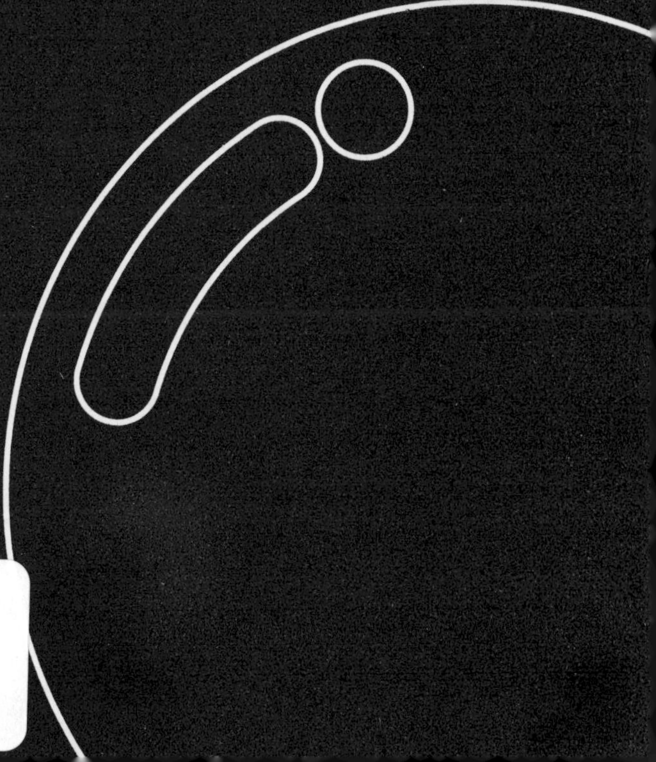

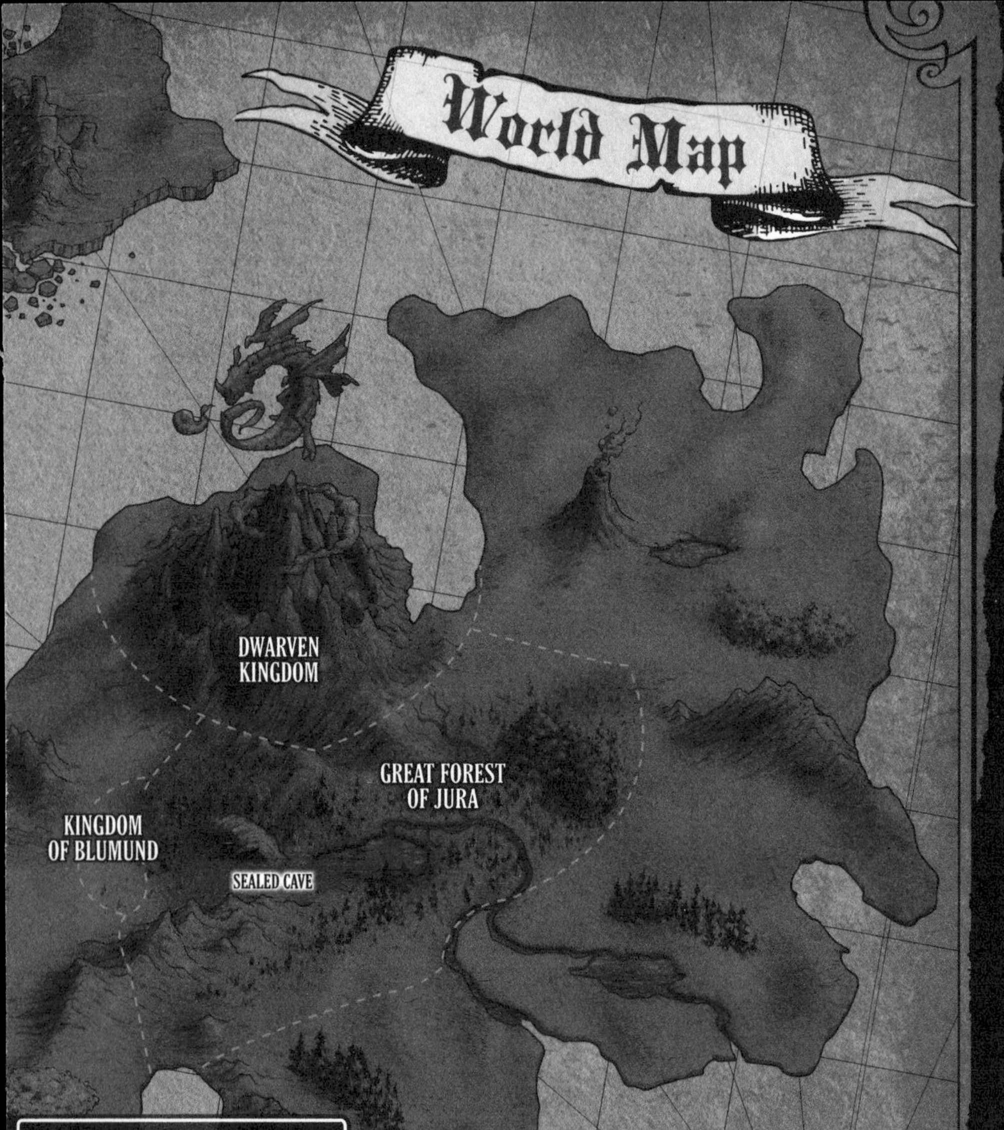
World Map
DWARVEN KINGDOM
GREAT FOREST OF JURA
KINGDOM OF BLUMUND
SEALED CAVE

PLOT SUMMARY

Phobio, who was left with unresolved anger after being defeated by Demon Lord Milim, is lured by Footman and Tear of the Harlequin Alliance into becoming the vessel for Charybdis, a calamity-class monster. Despite the revival of this dread beast, Milim's overwhelming power won out, and with some quick thinking, Rimuru was able to save Phobio. This had the bonus effect of earning him the favor of Carrion, Phobio's demon lord master. And before long, Carrion sends a proposal to carry out a diplomatic mission between Tempest and Eurazania, the kingdom of lycanthropes. ▼

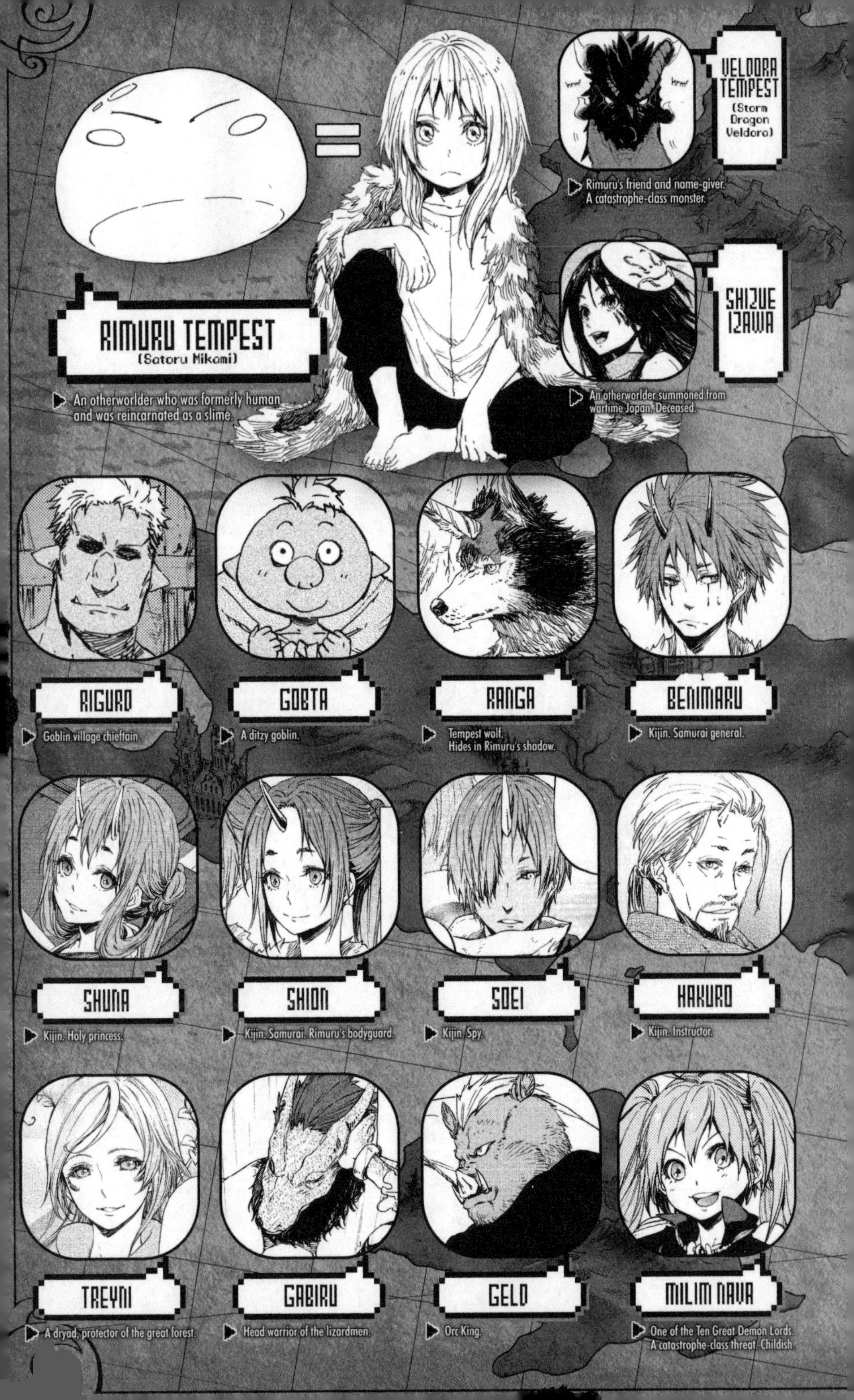

VELDORA TEMPEST
(Storm Dragon Veldora)
Rimuru's friend and name-giver. A catastrophe-class monster.
SHIZUE IZAWA
An otherworlder summoned from wartime Japan. Deceased.
RIMURU TEMPEST
(Satoru Mikami)
An otherworlder who was formerly human and was reincarnated as a slime.
BENIMARU
Kijin. Samurai general.
RANGA
Tempest wolf. Hides in Rimuru's shadow.
GOBTA
A ditzy goblin.
RIGURD
Goblin village chieftain.
HAKURO
Kijin. Instructor.
SOEI
Kijin. Spy.
SHION
Kijin. Samurai. Rimuru's bodyguard.
SHUNA
Kijin. Holy princess.
MILIM NAVA
One of the Ten Great Demon Lords. A catastrophe-class threat. Childish.
GELD
Orc King.
GABIRU
Head warrior of the lizardmen.
TREYNI
A dryad, protector of the great forest.

CONTENTS

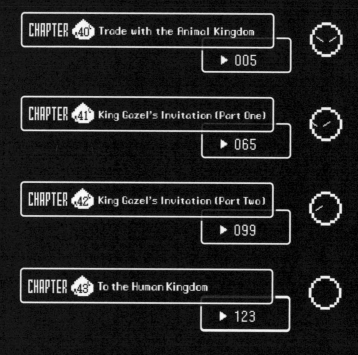

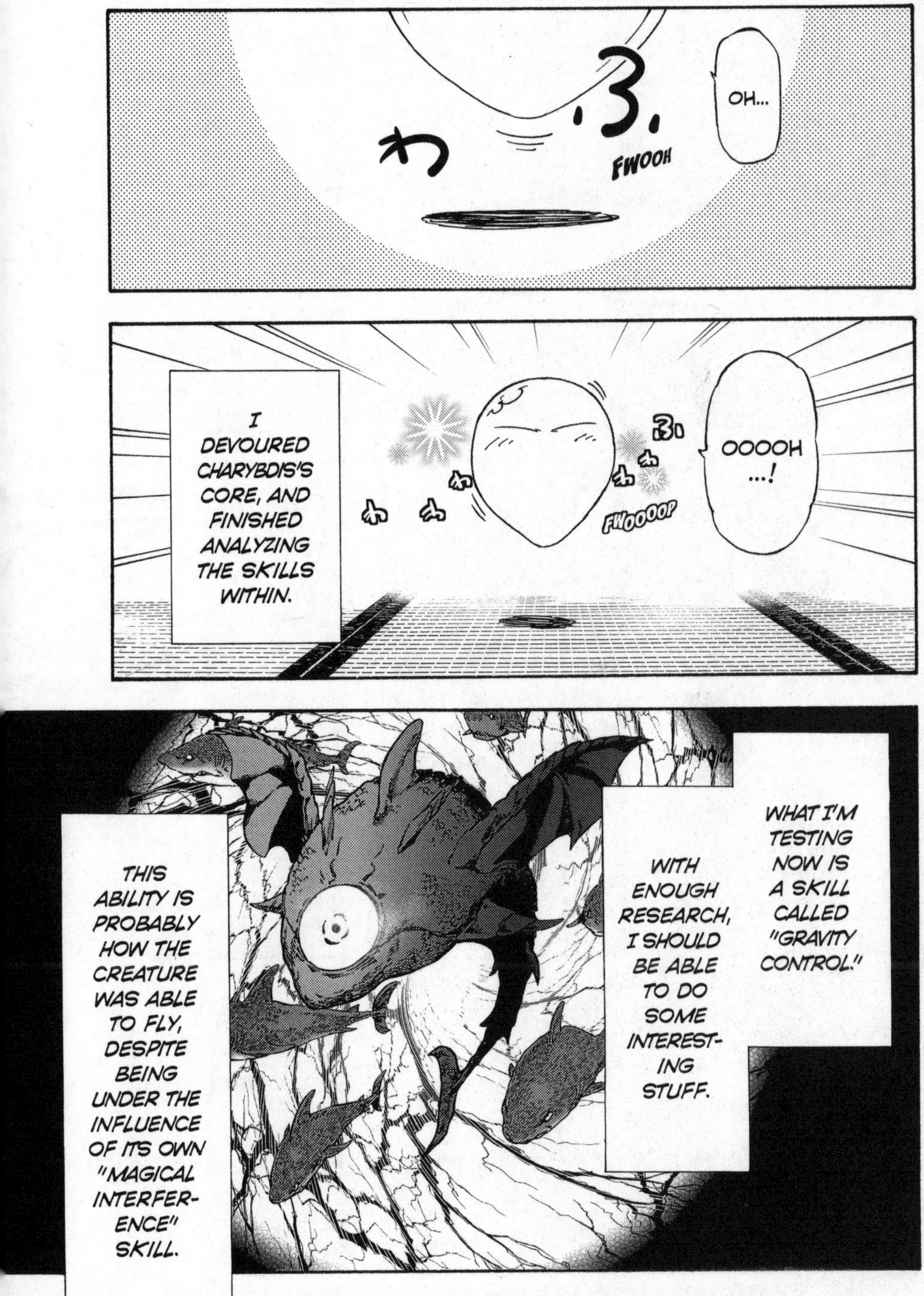
OH...
FWOOH
OOOOH ...!
FWOOOP
I DEVOURED CHARYBDIS'S CORE, AND FINISHED ANALYZING THE SKILLS WITHIN.
WHAT I'M TESTING NOW IS A SKILL CALLED "GRAVITY CONTROL."
WITH ENOUGH RESEARCH, I SHOULD BE ABLE TO DO SOME INTEREST-ING STUFF.
THIS ABILITY IS PROBABLY HOW THE CREATURE WAS ABLE TO FLY, DESPITE BEING UNDER THE INFLUENCE OF ITS OWN "MAGICAL INTERFER-ENCE" SKILL.

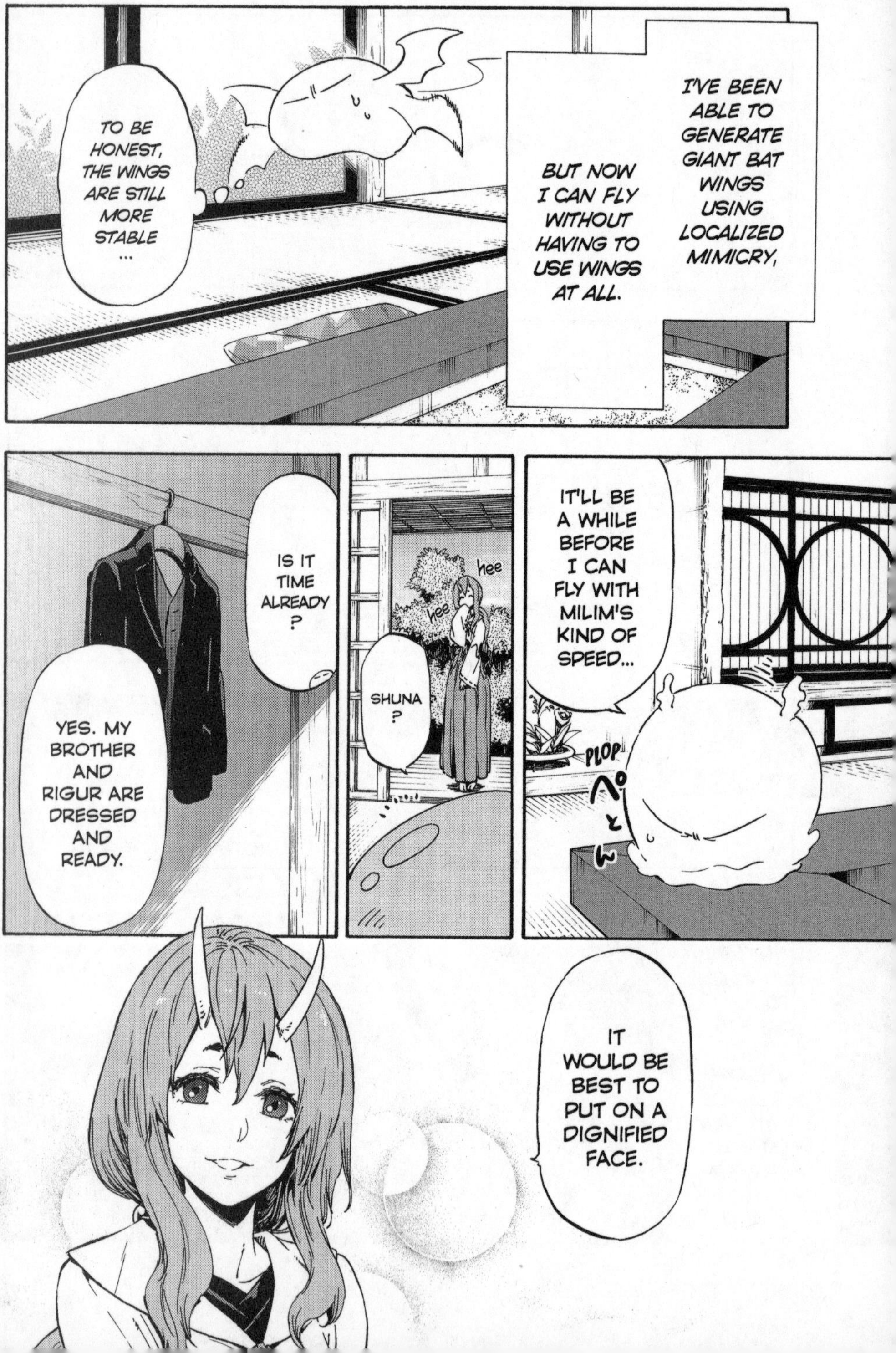
I'VE BEEN ABLE TO GENERATE GIANT BAT WINGS USING LOCALIZED MIMICRY,
BUT NOW I CAN FLY WITHOUT HAVING TO USE WINGS AT ALL.
TO BE HONEST, THE WINGS ARE STILL MORE STABLE ...
IT'LL BE A WHILE BEFORE I CAN FLY WITH MILIM'S KIND OF SPEED...
PLOP
hee
hee
SHUNA ?
IS IT TIME ALREADY ?
YES. MY BROTHER AND RIGUR ARE DRESSED AND READY.
IT WOULD BE BEST TO PUT ON A DIGNIFIED FACE.

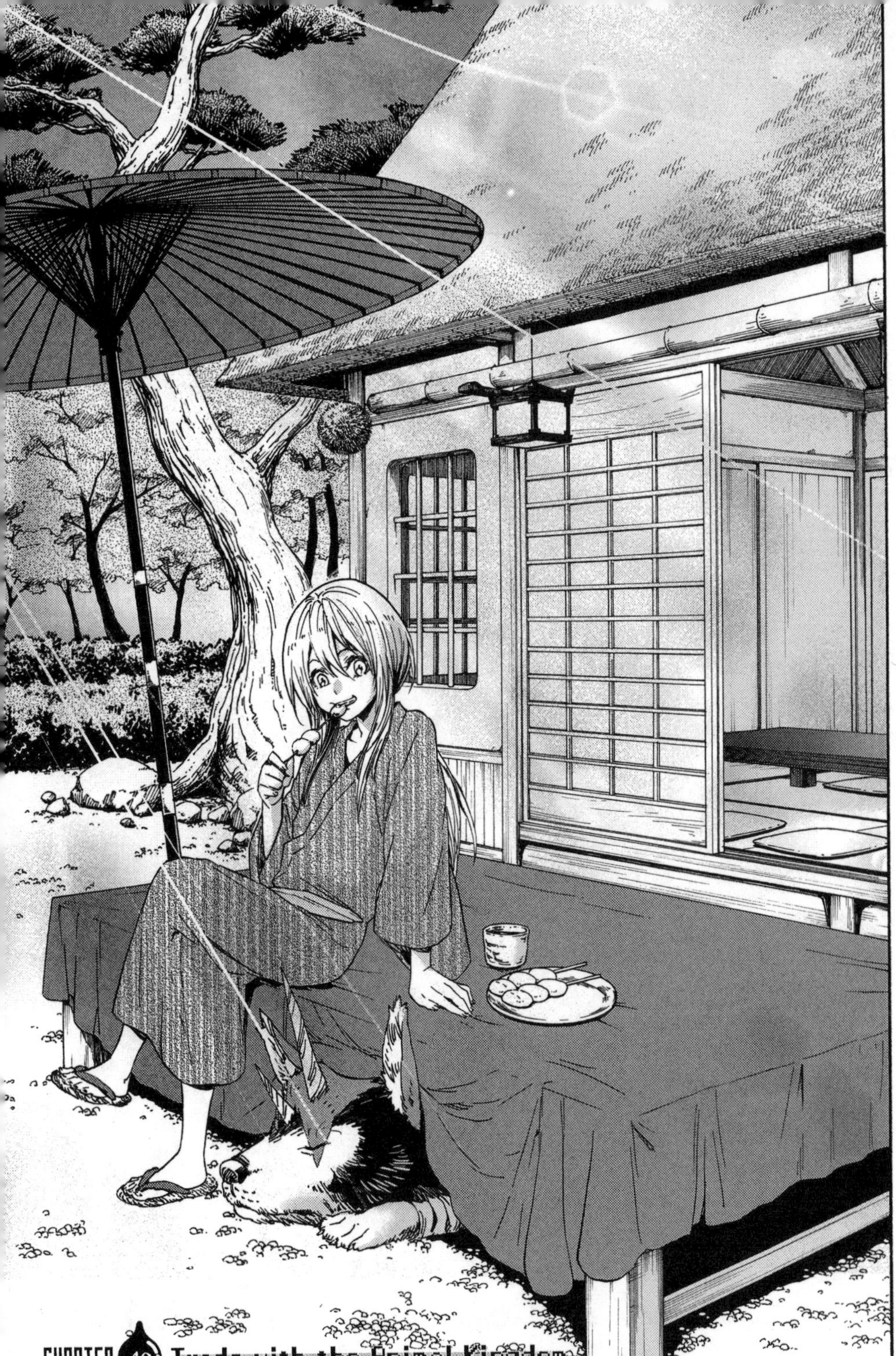

CHAPTER 40 Trade with the Animal Kingdom

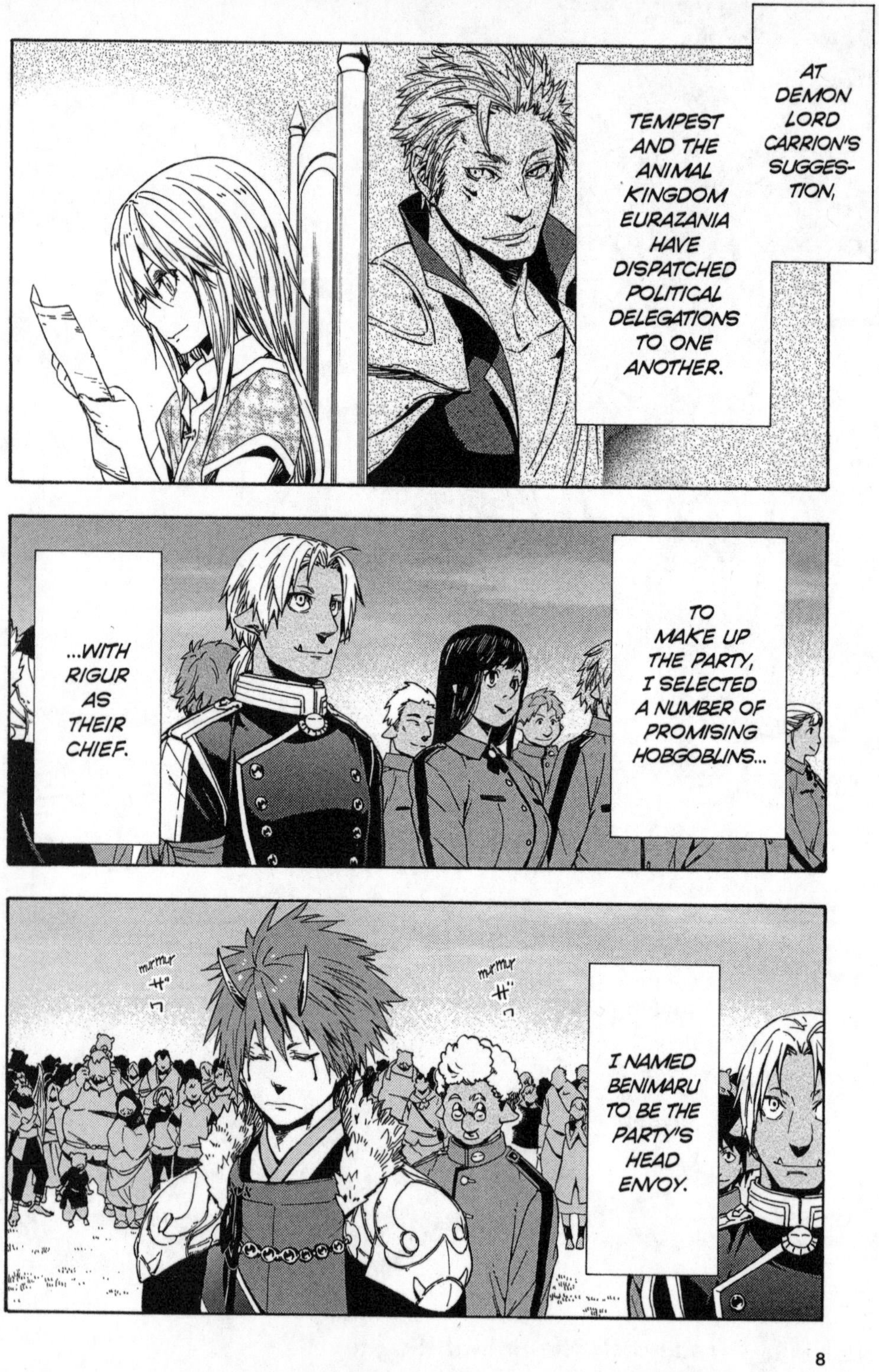
AT DEMON LORD CARRION'S SUGGES-TION,
TEMPEST AND THE ANIMAL KINGDOM EURAZANIA HAVE DISPATCHED POLITICAL DELEGATIONS TO ONE ANOTHER.
TO MAKE UP THE PARTY, I SELECTED A NUMBER OF PROMISING HOBGOBLINS...
...WITH RIGUR AS THEIR CHIEF.
I NAMED BENIMARU TO BE THE PARTY'S HEAD ENVOY.
murmur
murmur

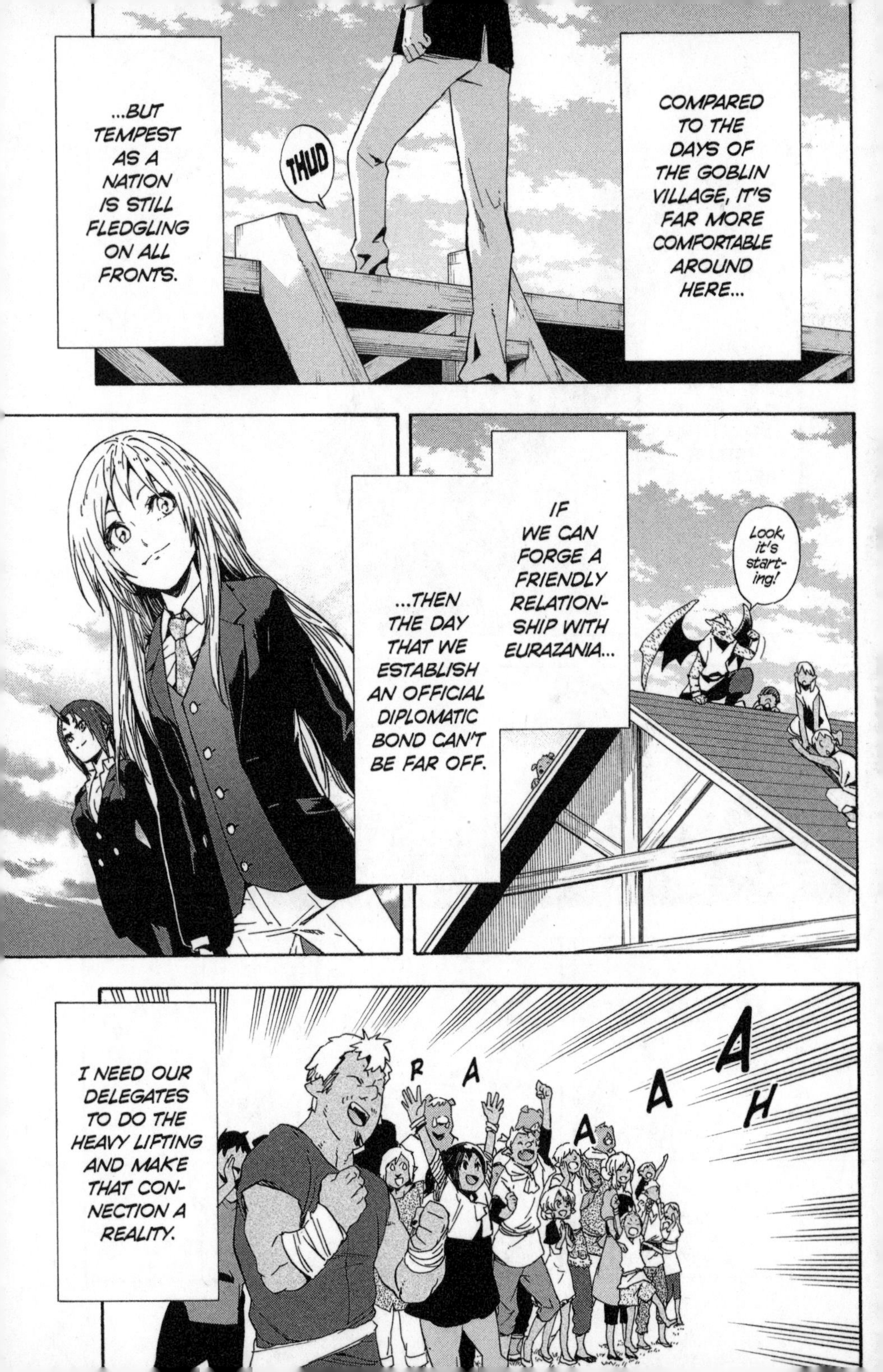
COMPARED TO THE DAYS OF THE GOBLIN VILLAGE, IT'S FAR MORE COMFORTABLE AROUND HERE...
THUD
...BUT TEMPEST AS A NATION IS STILL FLEDGLING ON ALL FRONTS.
Look, it's start-ing!
IF WE CAN FORGE A FRIENDLY RELATION-SHIP WITH EURAZANIA...
...THEN THE DAY THAT WE ESTABLISH AN OFFICIAL DIPLOMATIC BOND CAN'T BE FAR OFF.
RAAAAH
I NEED OUR DELEGATES TO DO THE HEAVY LIFTING AND MAKE THAT CON-NECTION A REALITY.

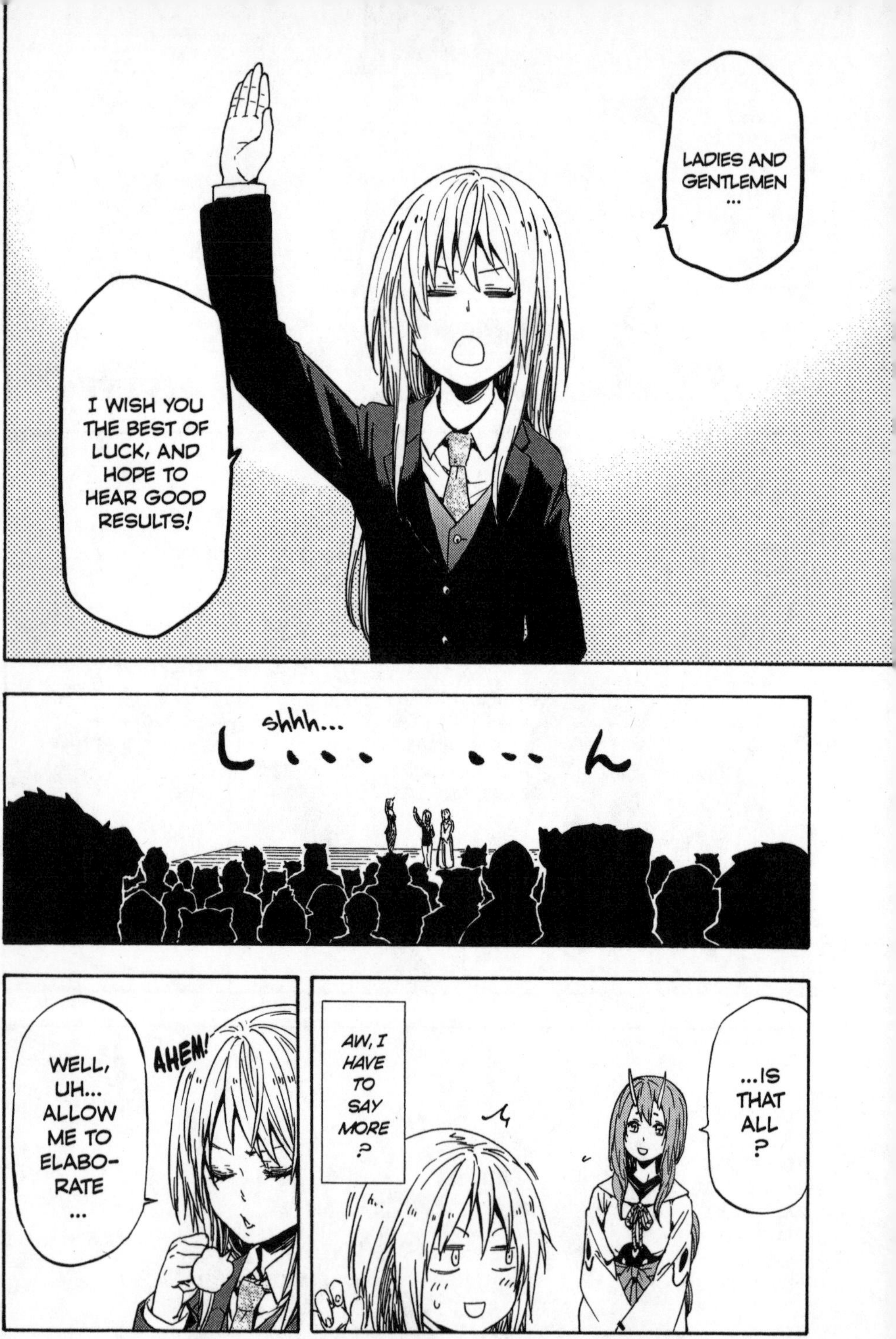
LADIES AND GENTLEMEN ...
I WISH YOU THE BEST OF LUCK, AND HOPE TO HEAR GOOD RESULTS!
shhh...
し・・・ ・・・ん
...IS THAT ALL?
AW, I HAVE TO SAY MORE?
AHEM!
WELL, UH... ALLOW ME TO ELABO-RATE ...

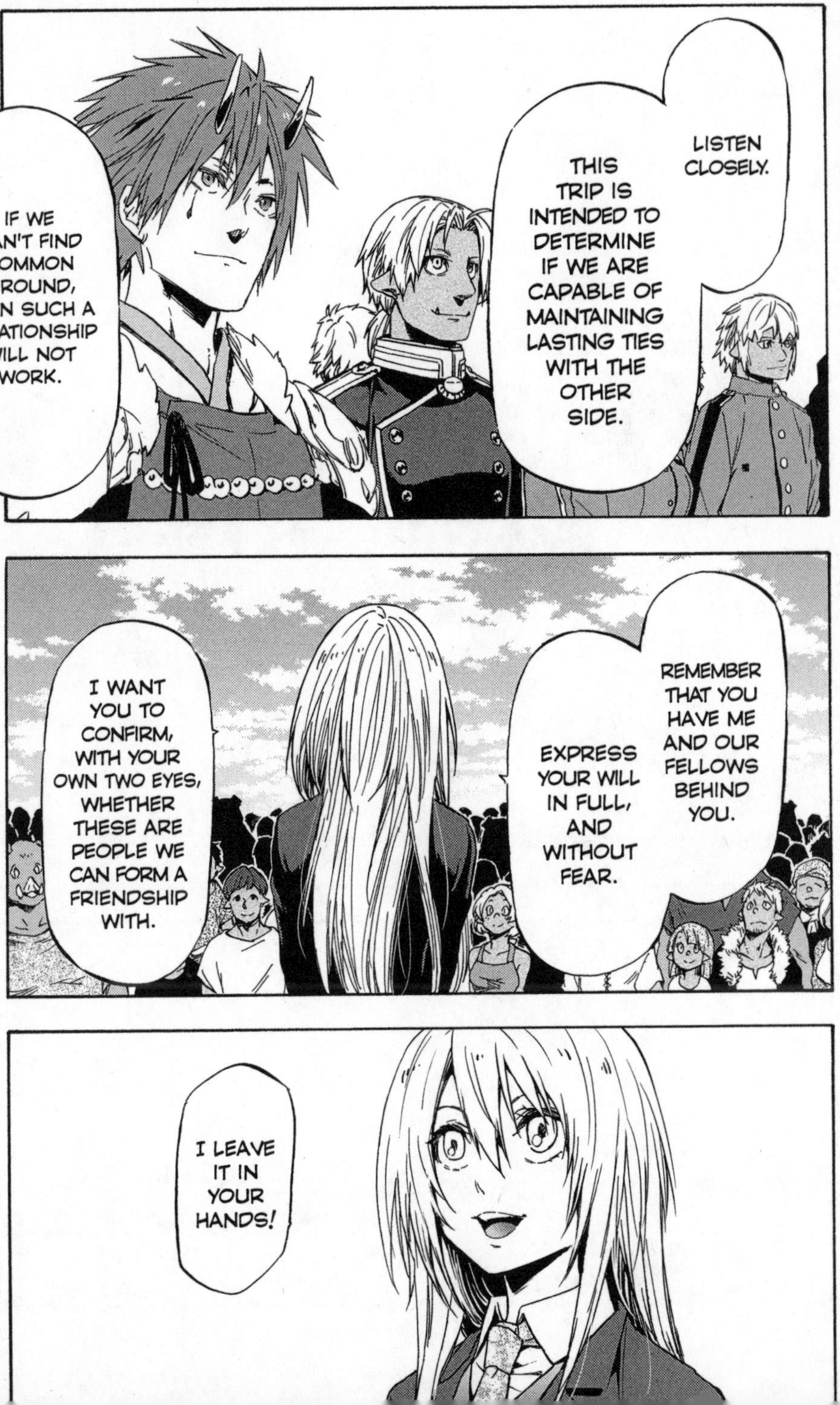
LISTEN CLOSELY.
THIS TRIP IS INTENDED TO DETERMINE IF WE ARE CAPABLE OF MAINTAINING LASTING TIES WITH THE OTHER SIDE.
IF WE CAN'T FIND COMMON GROUND, THEN SUCH A RELATIONSHIP WILL NOT WORK.
REMEMBER THAT YOU HAVE ME AND OUR FELLOWS BEHIND YOU.
EXPRESS YOUR WILL IN FULL, AND WITHOUT FEAR.
I WANT YOU TO CONFIRM, WITH YOUR OWN TWO EYES, WHETHER THESE ARE PEOPLE WE CAN FORM A FRIENDSHIP WITH.
I LEAVE IT IN YOUR HANDS!

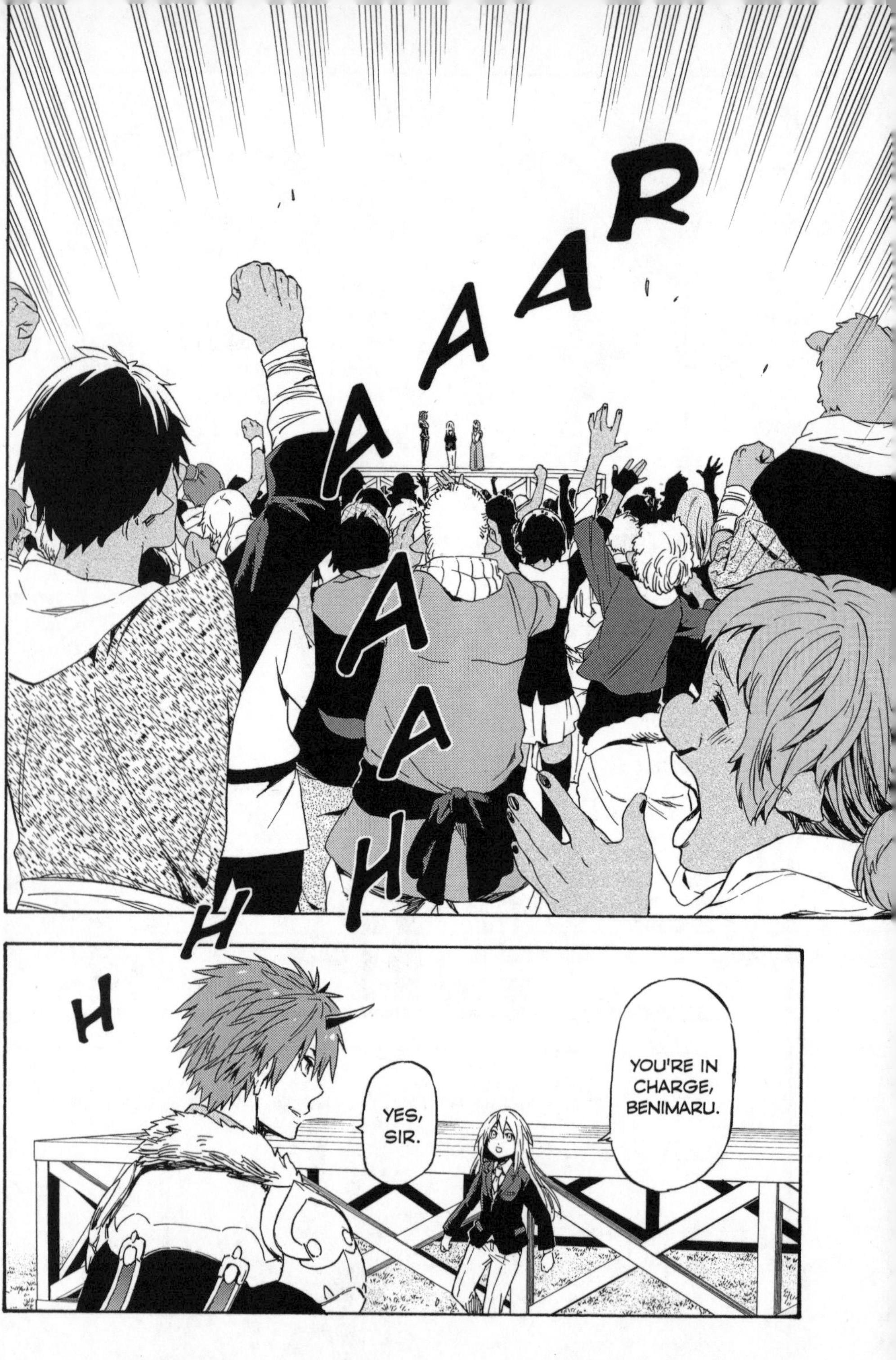
RAAAAAHHH
YOU'RE IN CHARGE, BENIMARU.
YES, SIR.

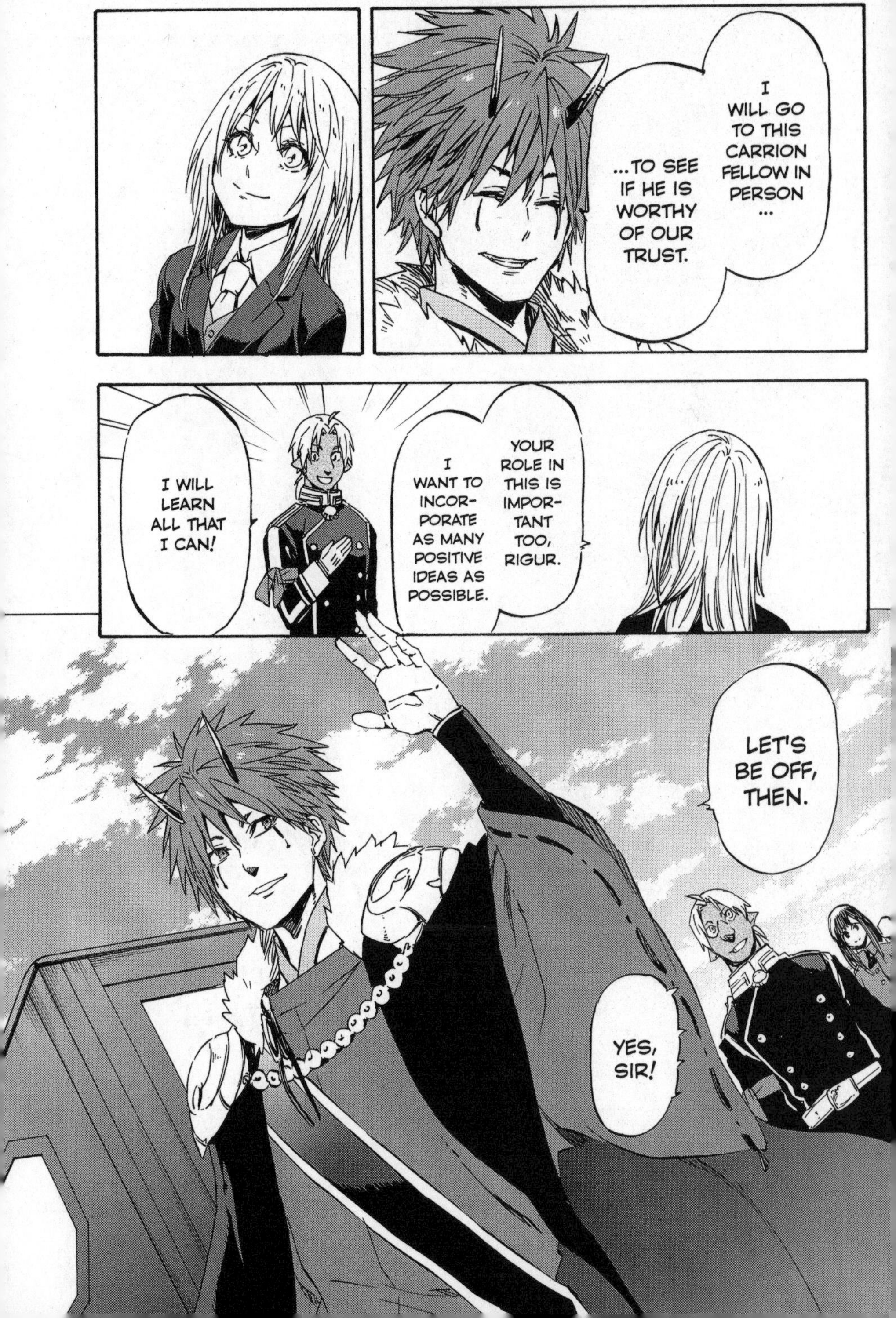
I WILL GO TO THIS CARRION FELLOW IN PERSON ...
...TO SEE IF HE IS WORTHY OF OUR TRUST.
YOUR ROLE IN THIS IS IMPORTANT TOO, RIGUR.
I WANT TO INCORPORATE AS MANY POSITIVE IDEAS AS POSSIBLE.
I WILL LEARN ALL THAT I CAN!
LET'S BE OFF, THEN.
YES, SIR!

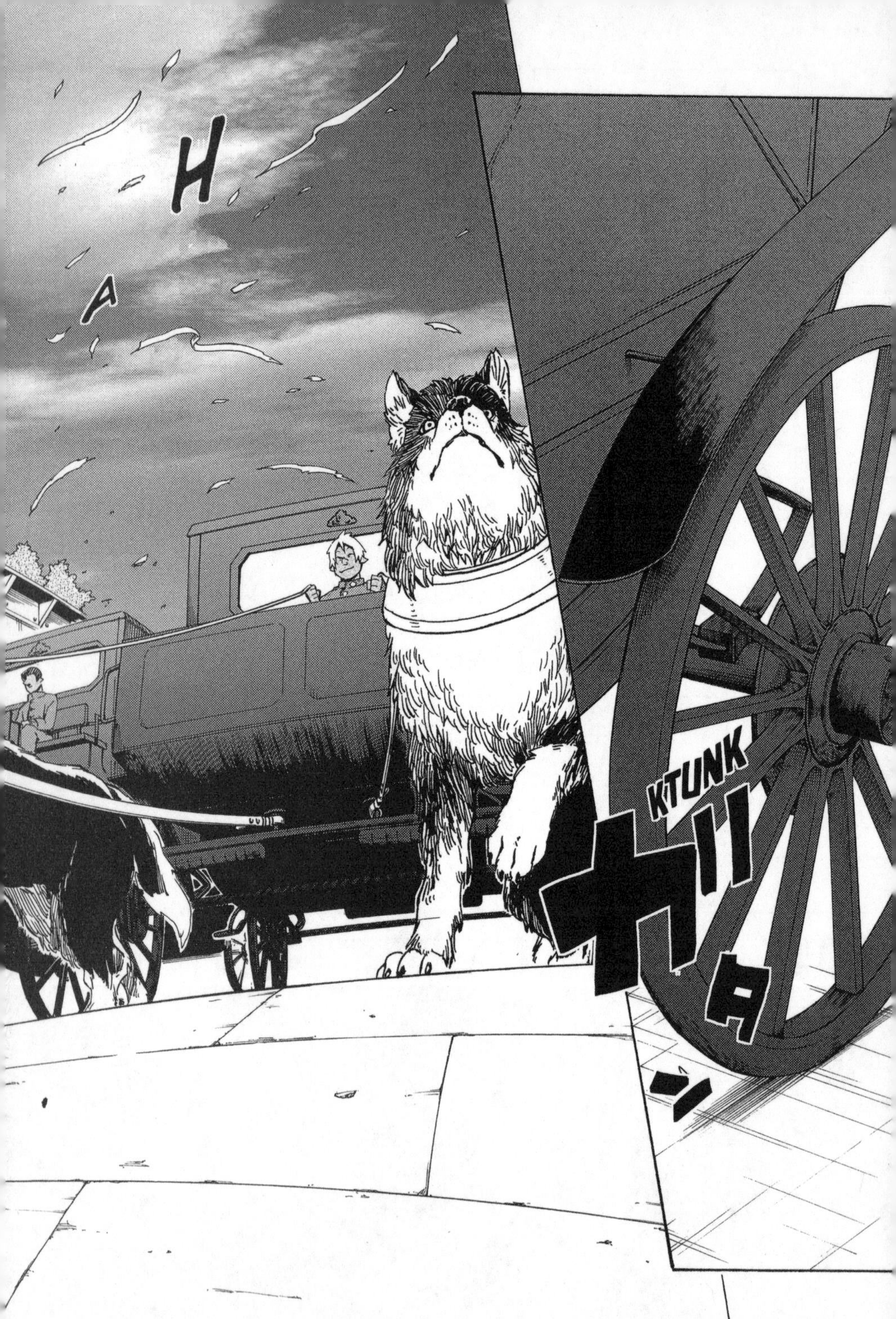
KTUNK
H
A

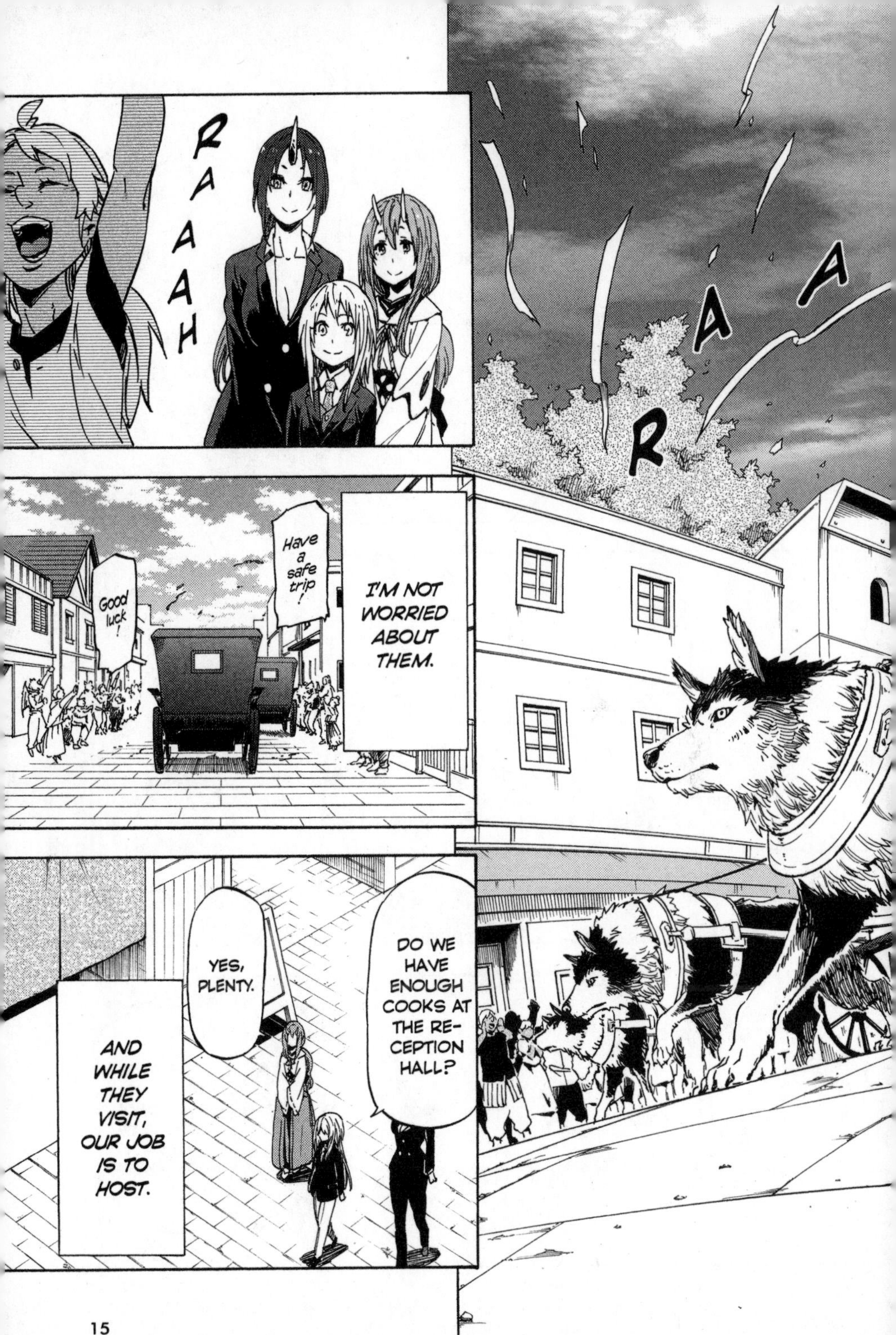
RAAA
RAAAH
I'M NOT WORRIED ABOUT THEM.
Have a safe trip!
Good luck!
DO WE HAVE ENOUGH COOKS AT THE RE-CEPTION HALL?
YES, PLENTY.
AND WHILE THEY VISIT, OUR JOB IS TO HOST.

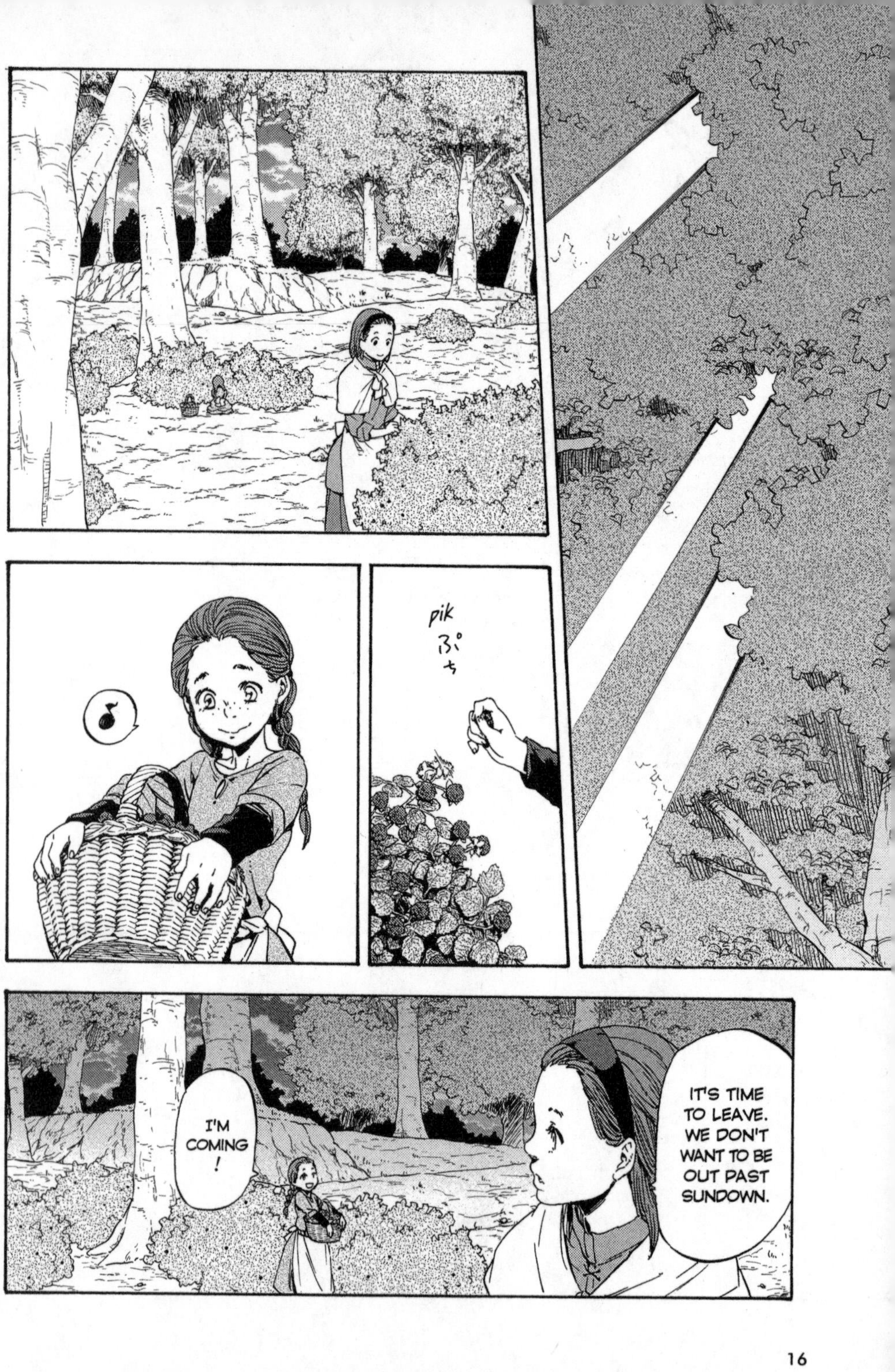
pik ぷち
IT'S TIME TO LEAVE. WE DON'T WANT TO BE OUT PAST SUNDOWN.
I'M COMING!

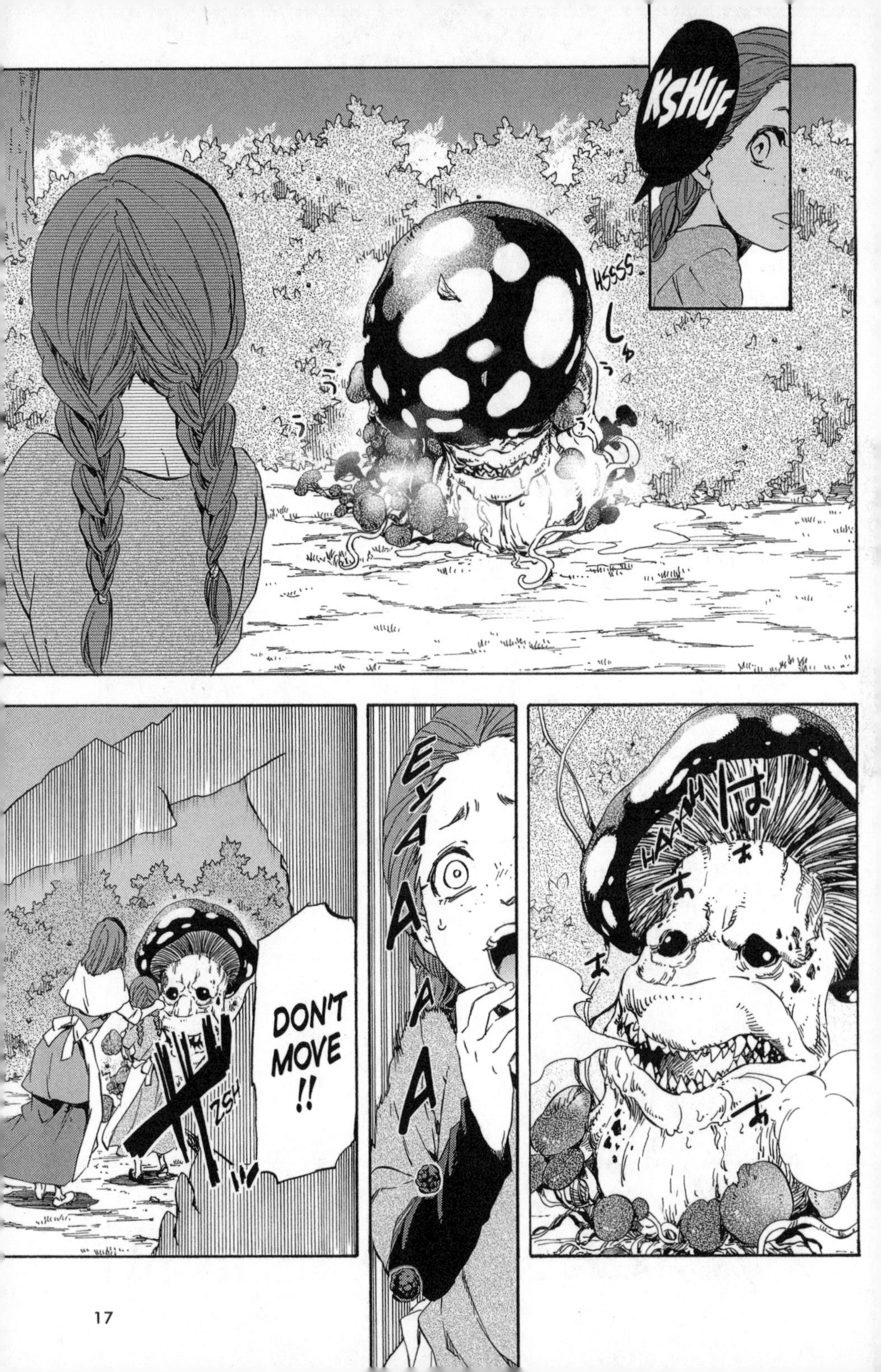
KSHUF
HSSSS
HAAAH
EYAAAAA
DON'T MOVE !!
ZSH

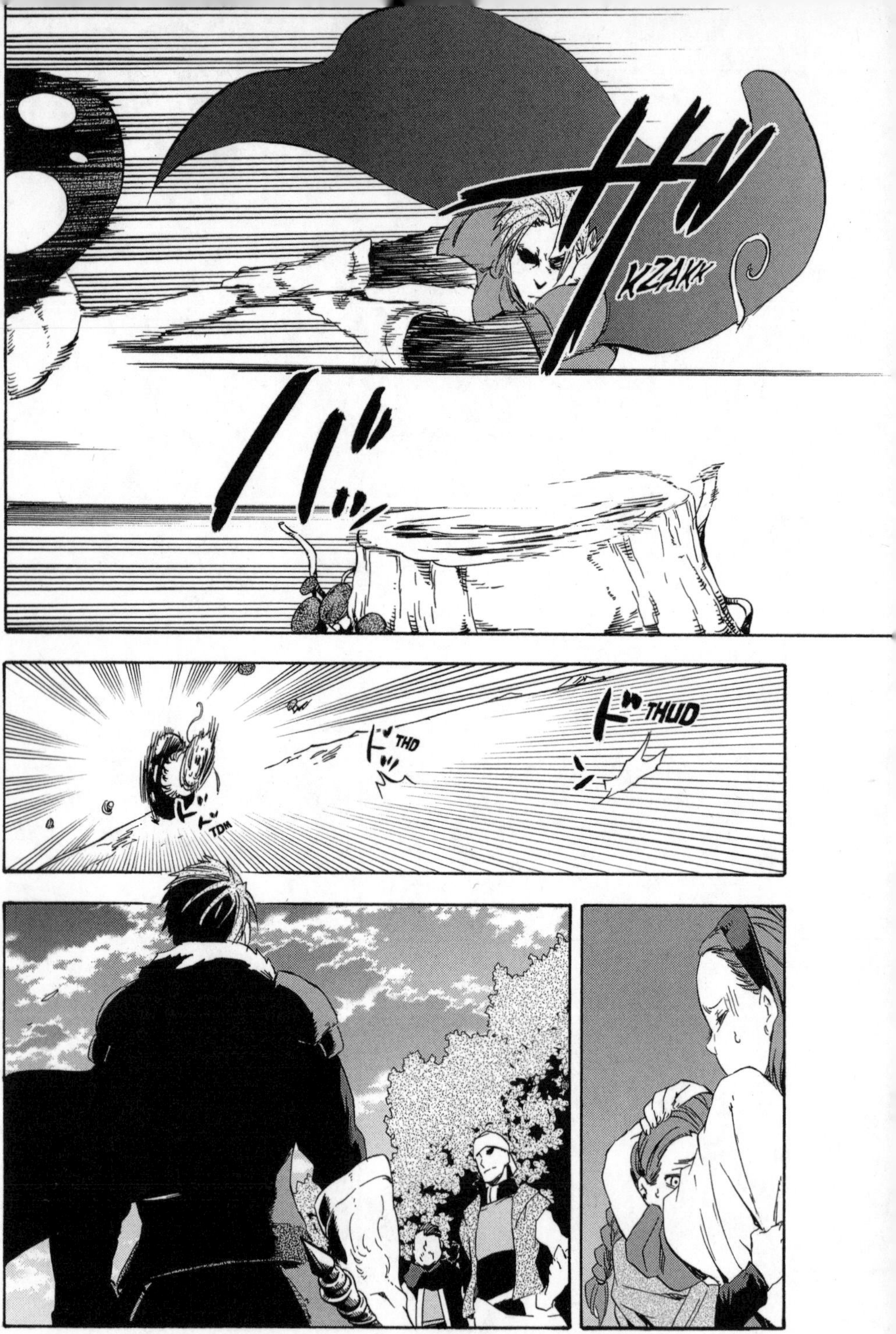
KZAKK
THUD
THD
TDM

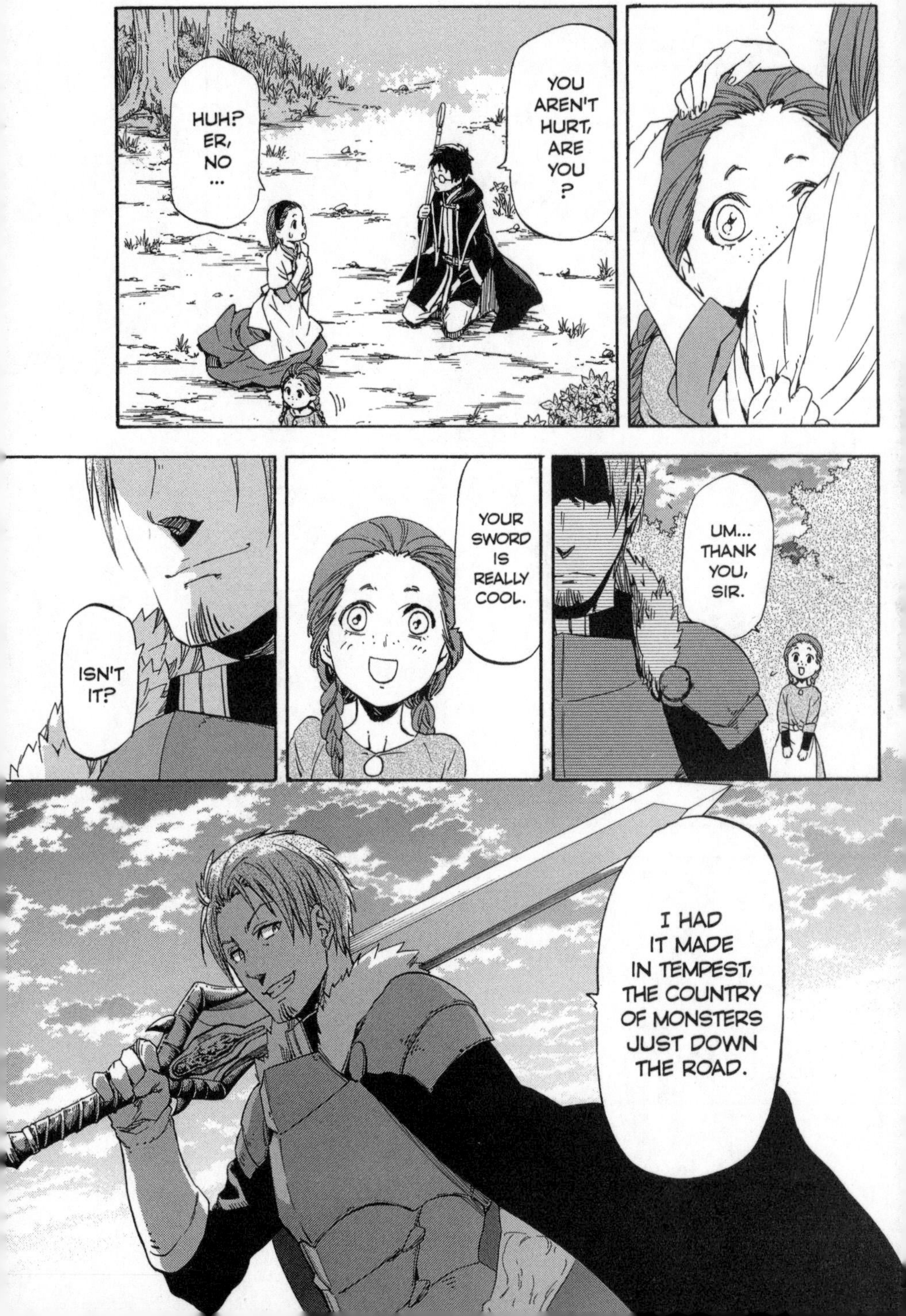
YOU AREN'T HURT, ARE YOU?
HUH? ER, NO ...
UM... THANK YOU, SIR.
YOUR SWORD IS REALLY COOL.
ISN'T IT?
I HAD IT MADE IN TEMPEST, THE COUNTRY OF MONSTERS JUST DOWN THE ROAD.

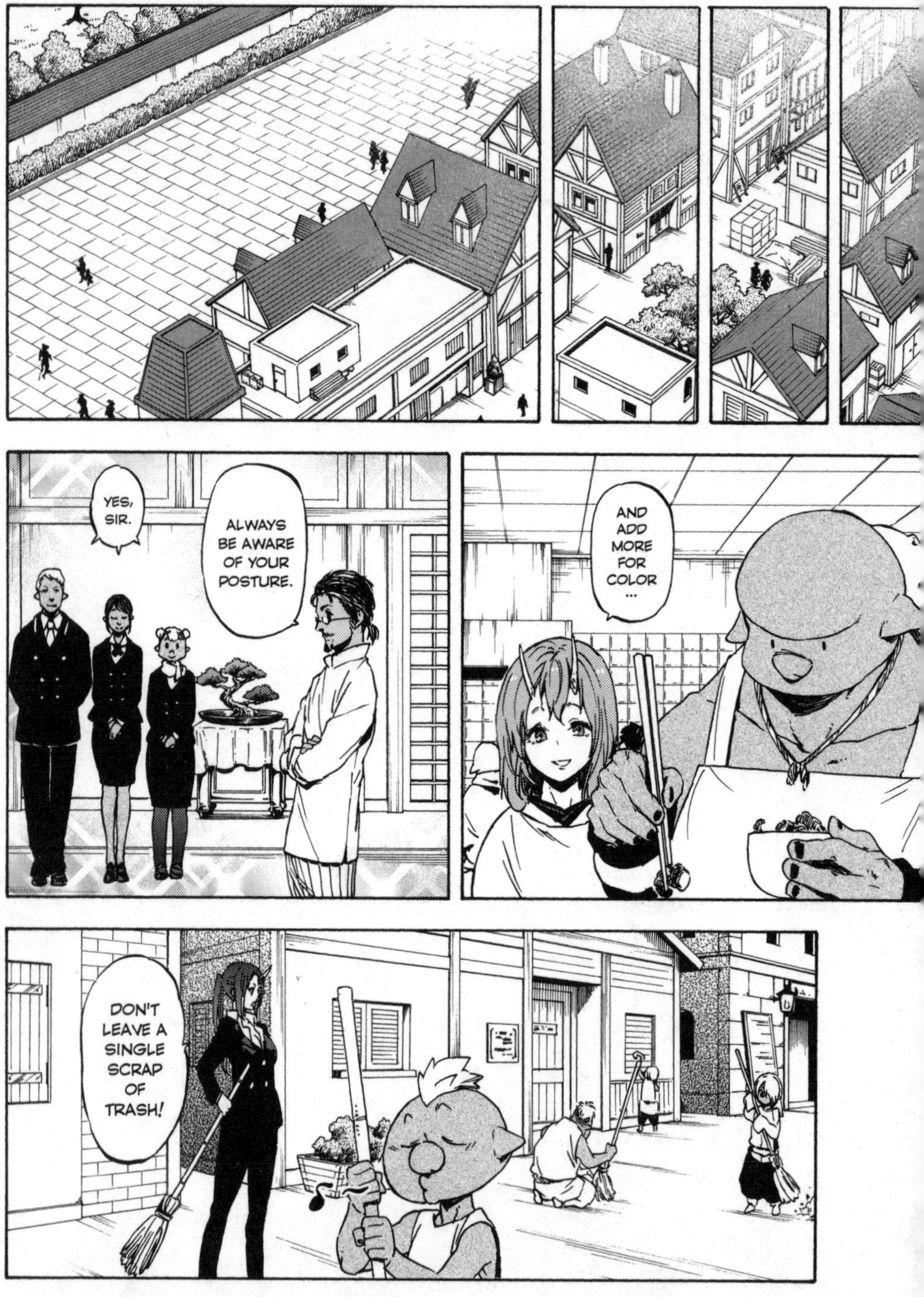
AND ADD MORE FOR COLOR ...
ALWAYS BE AWARE OF YOUR POSTURE.
YES, SIR.
DON'T LEAVE A SINGLE SCRAP OF TRASH!

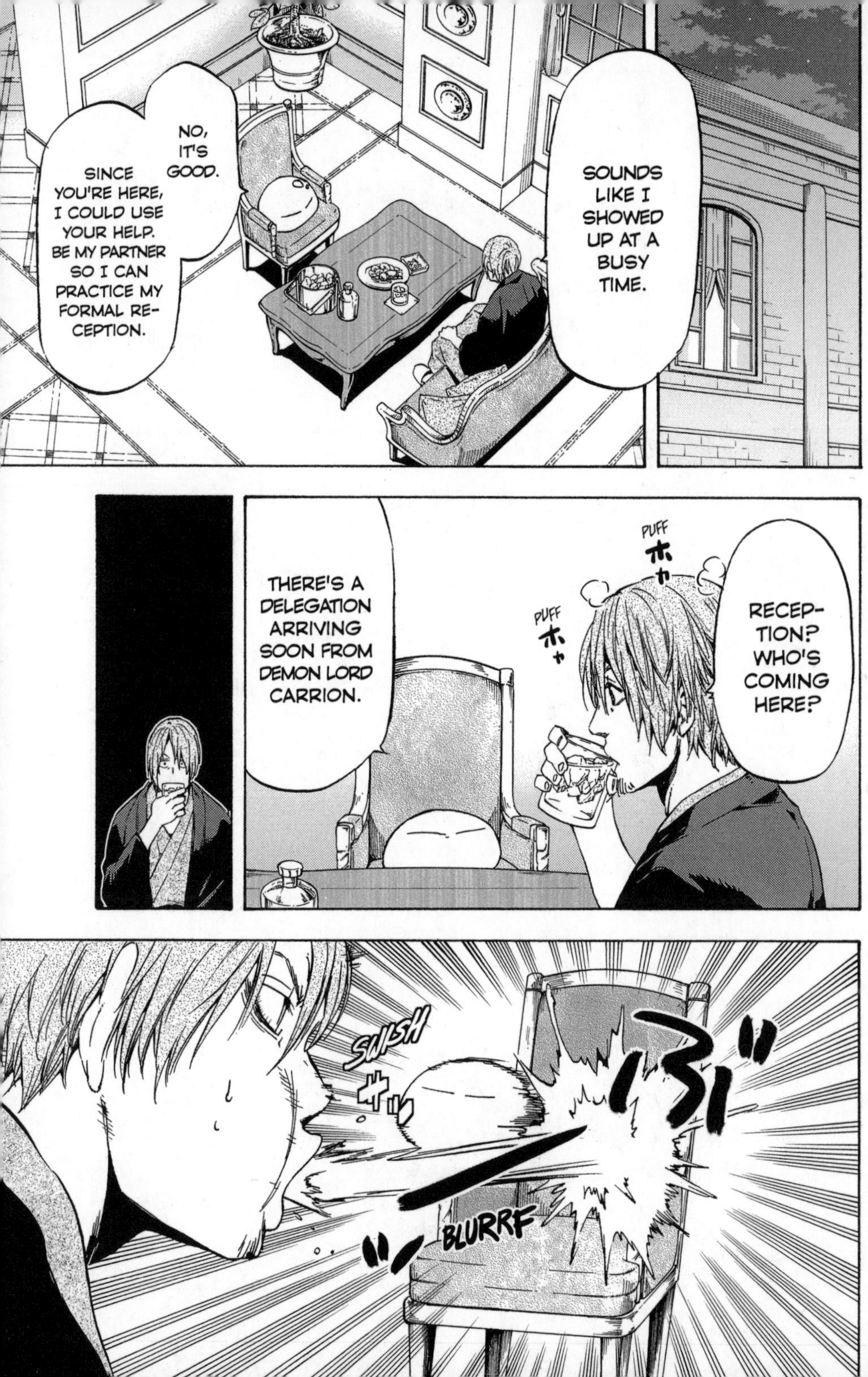
SOUNDS LIKE I SHOWED UP AT A BUSY TIME.
NO, IT'S GOOD.
SINCE YOU'RE HERE, I COULD USE YOUR HELP. BE MY PARTNER SO I CAN PRACTICE MY FORMAL RE-CEPTION.
PUFF
PUFF
RECEP-TION? WHO'S COMING HERE?
THERE'S A DELEGATION ARRIVING SOON FROM DEMON LORD CARRION.
SWISH
BLURRF

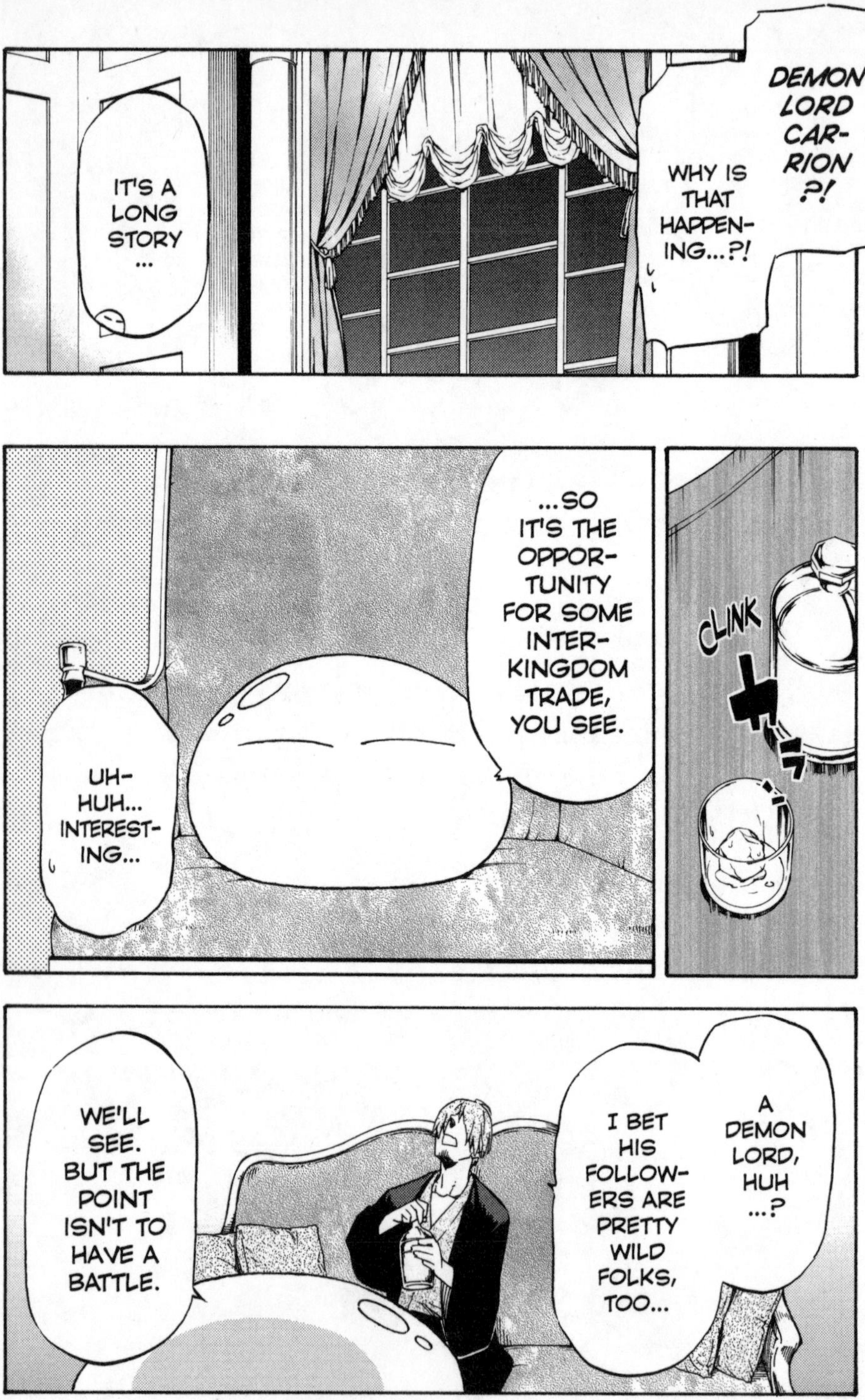
DEMON LORD CARRION?!
WHY IS THAT HAPPENING...?!
IT'S A LONG STORY...
CLINK
...SO IT'S THE OPPORTUNITY FOR SOME INTER-KINGDOM TRADE, YOU SEE.
UH-HUH... INTERESTING...
A DEMON LORD, HUH...?
I BET HIS FOLLOWERS ARE PRETTY WILD FOLKS, TOO...
WE'LL SEE. BUT THE POINT ISN'T TO HAVE A BATTLE.

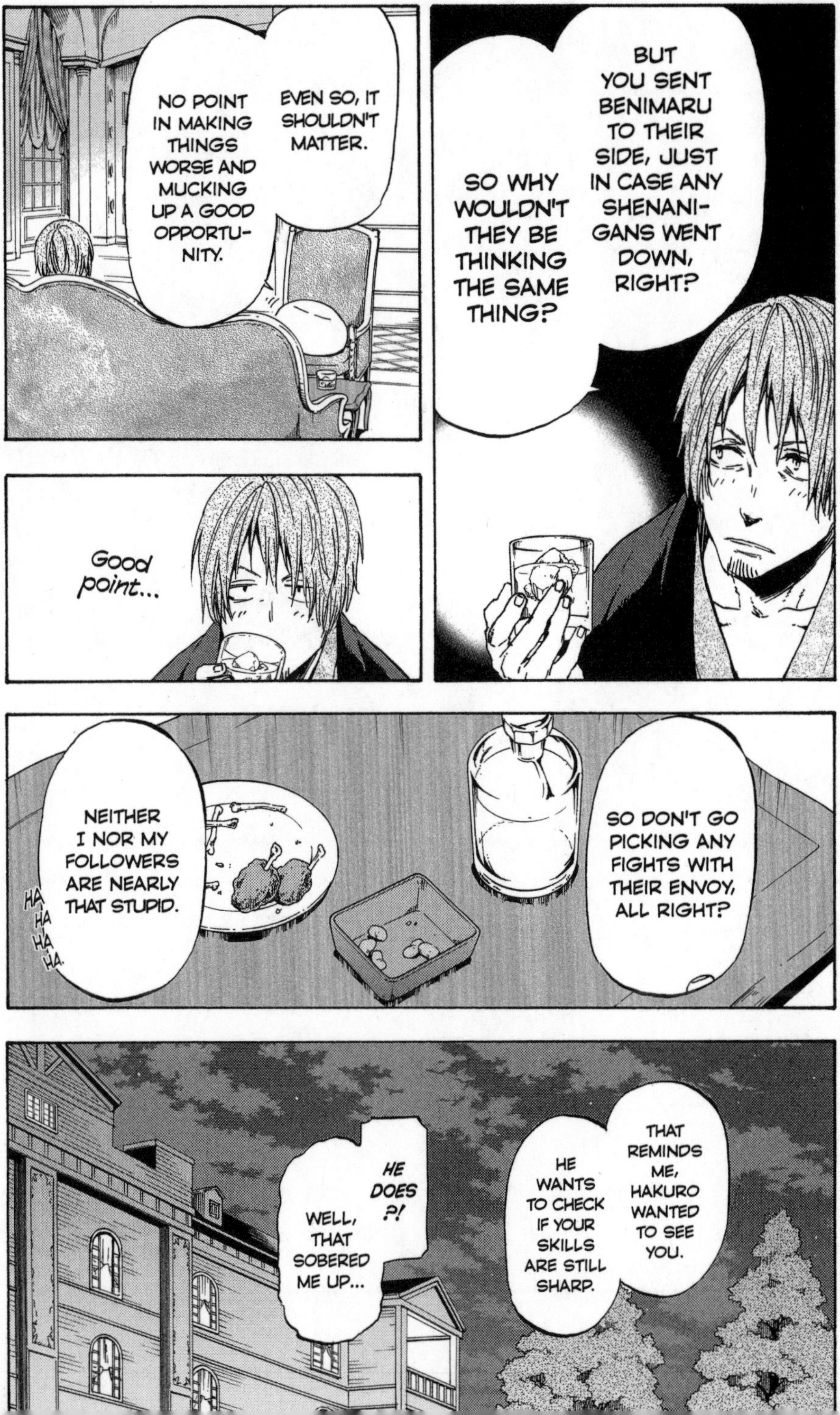
BUT YOU SENT BENIMARU TO THEIR SIDE, JUST IN CASE ANY SHENANIGANS WENT DOWN, RIGHT?
SO WHY WOULDN'T THEY BE THINKING THE SAME THING?
EVEN SO, IT SHOULDN'T MATTER.
NO POINT IN MAKING THINGS WORSE AND MUCKING UP A GOOD OPPORTUNITY.
Good point...
SO DON'T GO PICKING ANY FIGHTS WITH THEIR ENVOY, ALL RIGHT?
NEITHER I NOR MY FOLLOWERS ARE NEARLY THAT STUPID.
HA HA HA HA.
THAT REMINDS ME, HAKURO WANTED TO SEE YOU.
HE WANTS TO CHECK IF YOUR SKILLS ARE STILL SHARP.
HE DOES?!
WELL, THAT SOBERED ME UP...

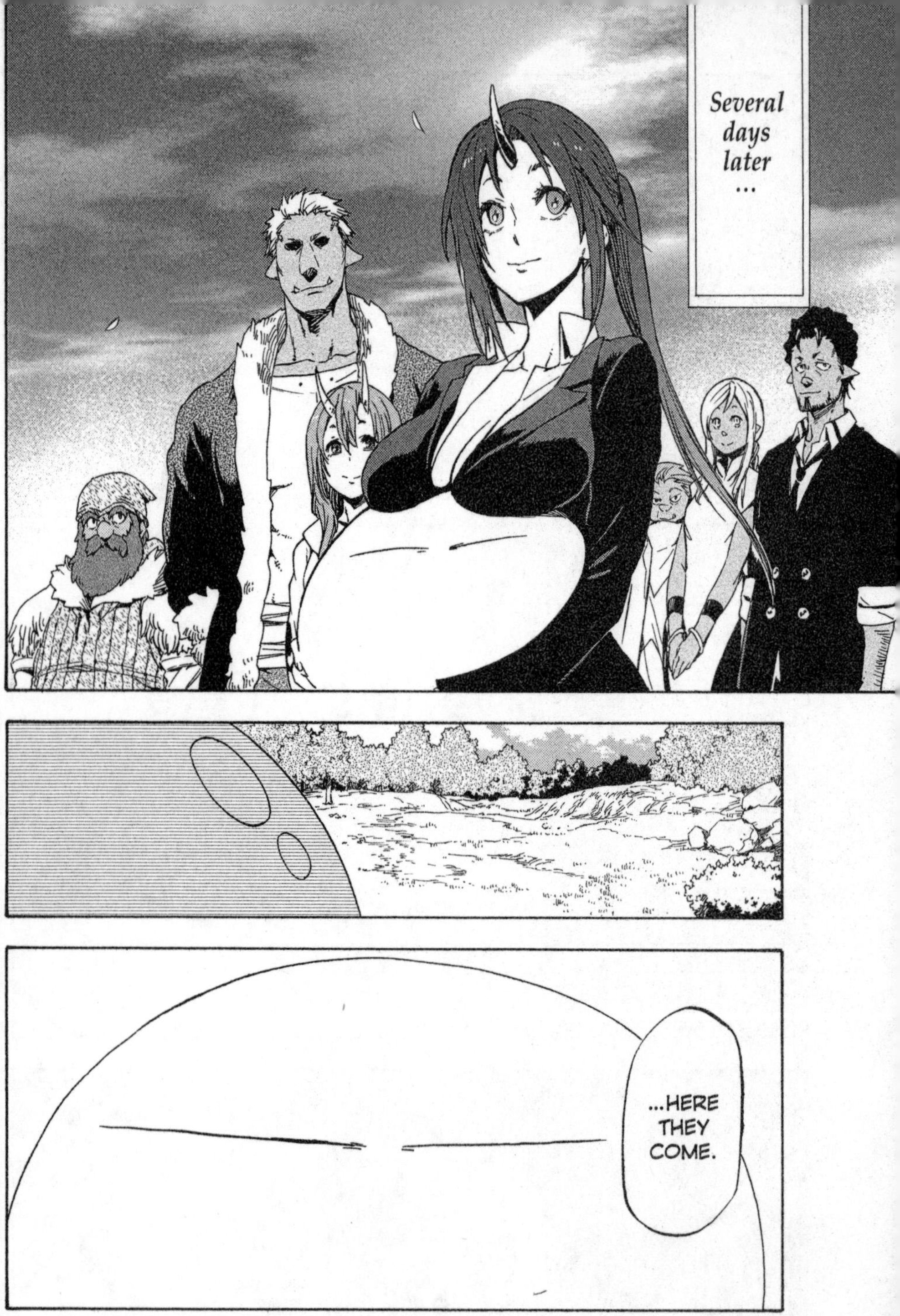
Several days later ...
...HERE THEY COME.

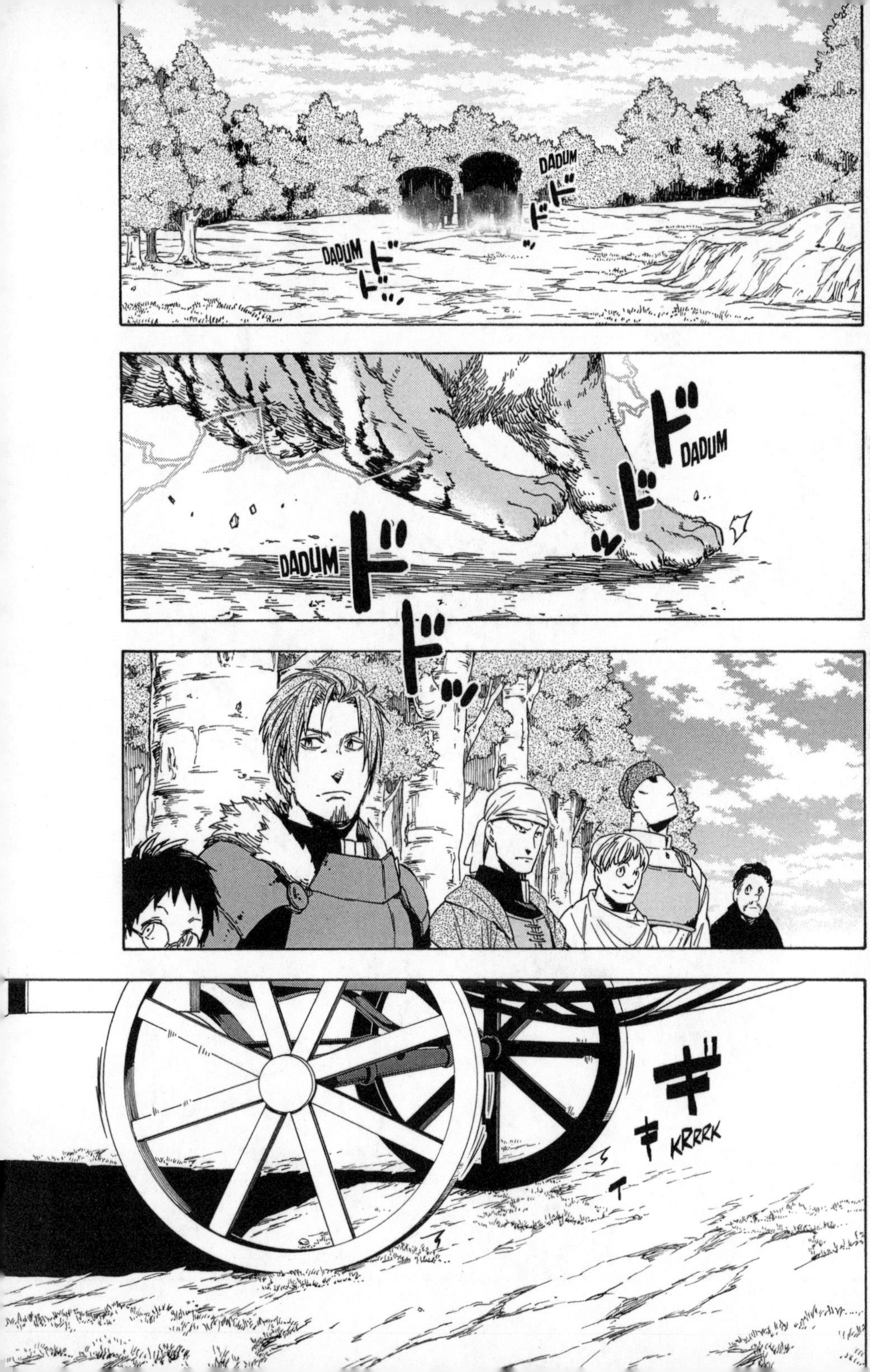
DADUM
ドドッ
DADUM
ドドッ
DADUM
ドドッ
DADUM
ドドッ
ギギッ
KRRRK

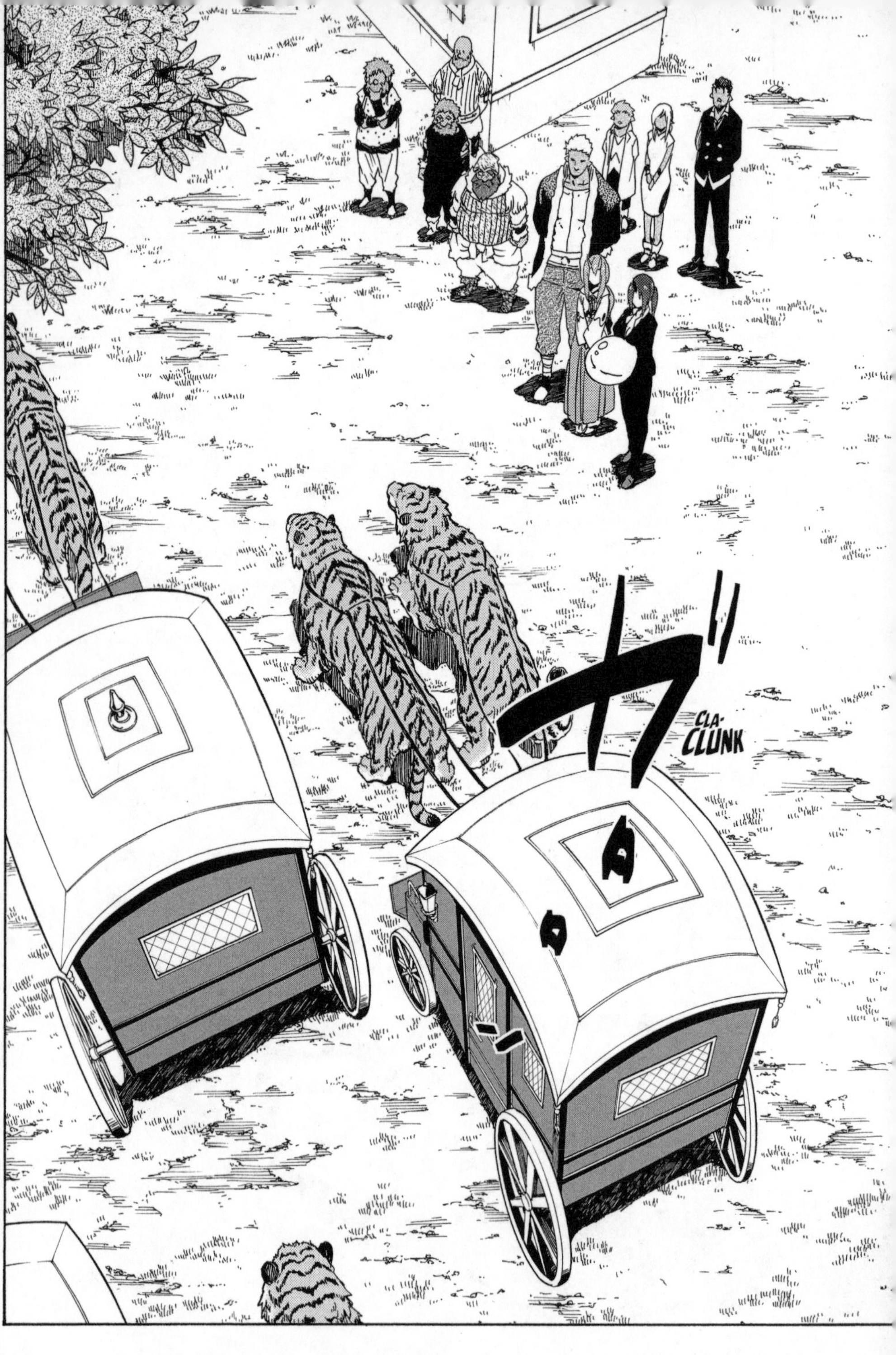
CLA-
CLUNK

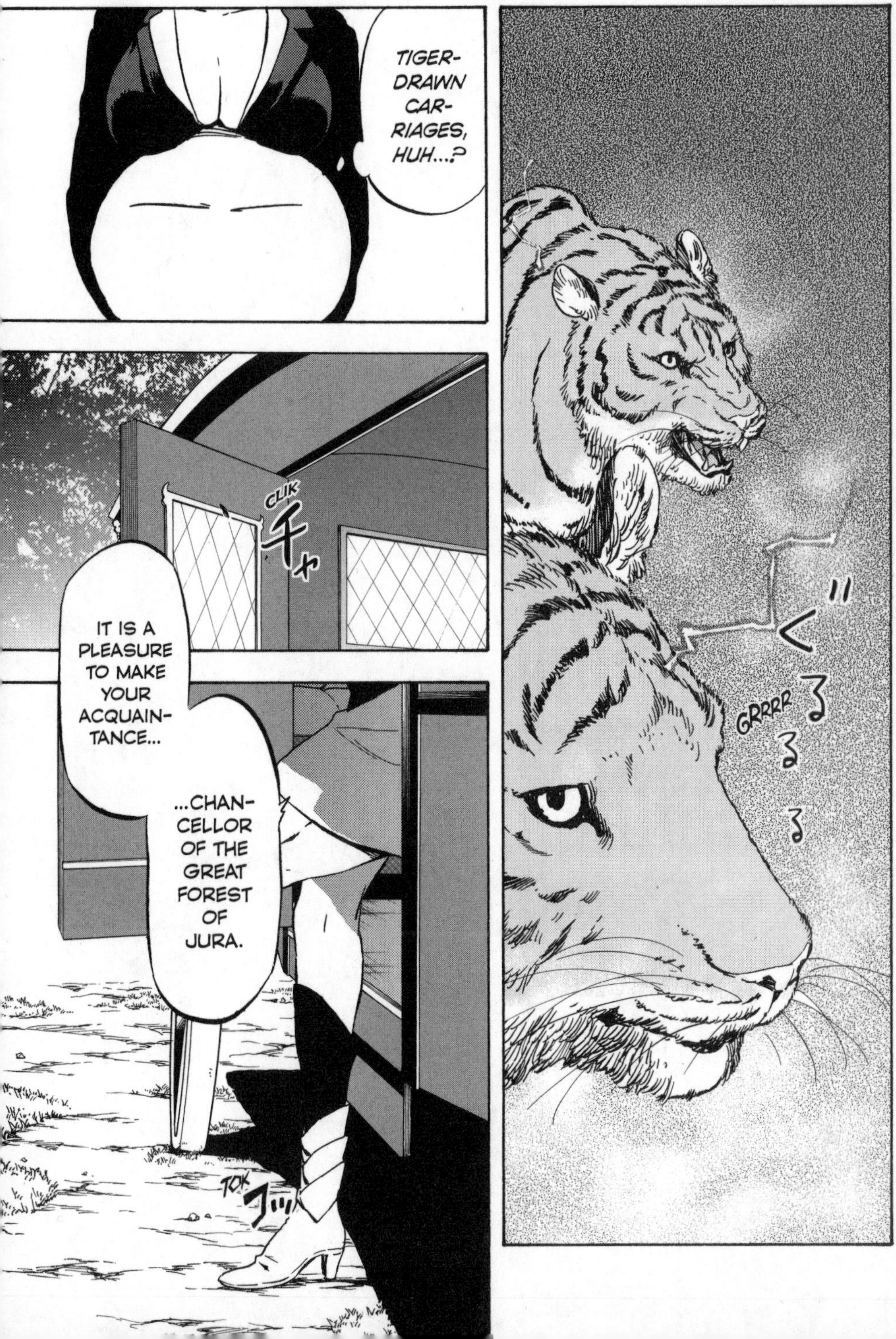
ぐるるる
GRRRR
TIGER-DRAWN CARRIAGES, HUH...?
チャ
CLIK
IT IS A PLEASURE TO MAKE YOUR ACQUAINTANCE...
...CHANCELLOR OF THE GREAT FOREST OF JURA.
TOK

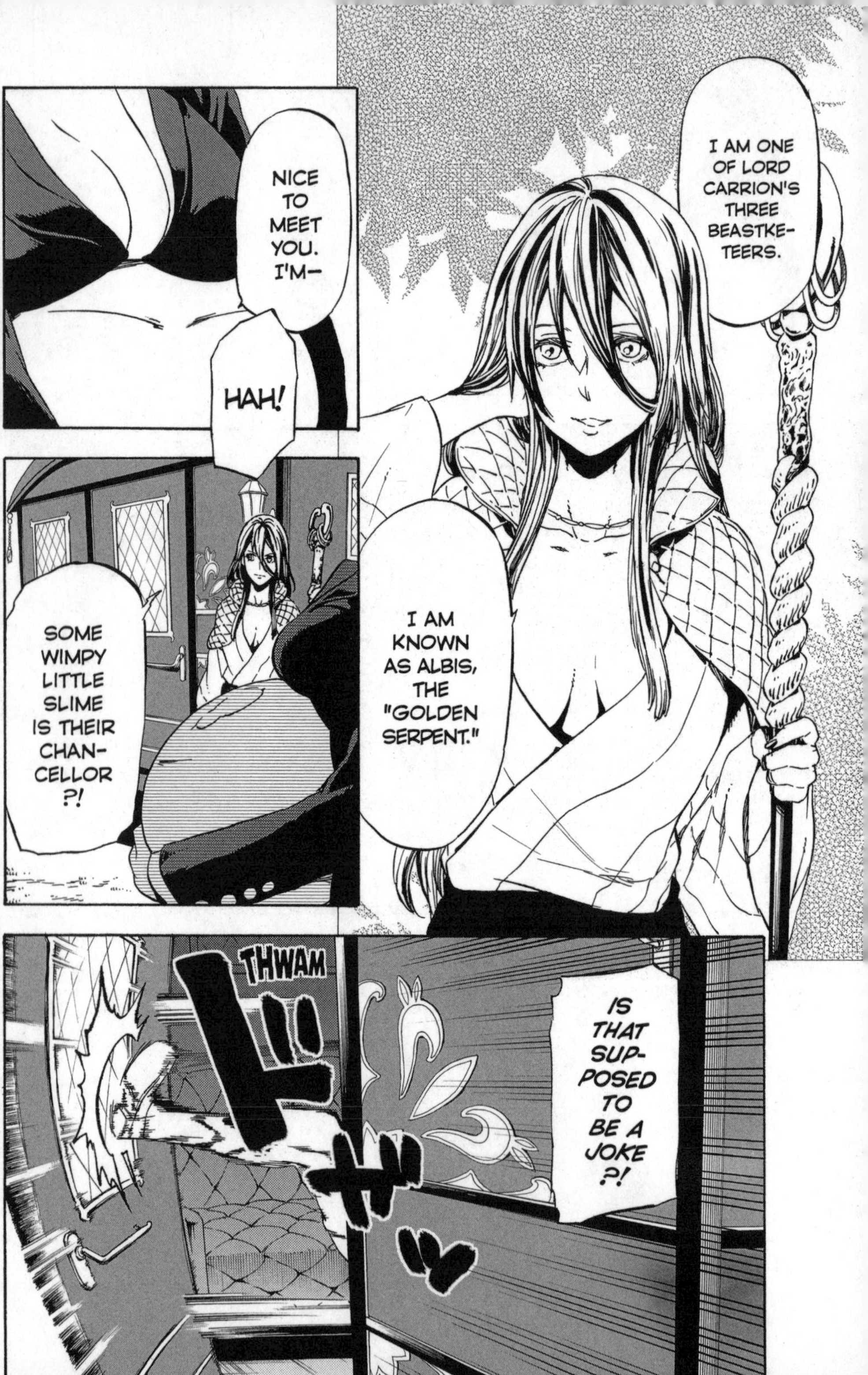
I AM ONE OF LORD CARRION'S THREE BEASTKE-TEERS.
I AM KNOWN AS ALBIS, THE "GOLDEN SERPENT."
NICE TO MEET YOU. I'M—
HAH!
SOME WIMPY LITTLE SLIME IS THEIR CHAN-CELLOR ?!
IS THAT SUP-POSED TO BE A JOKE ?!
THWAM

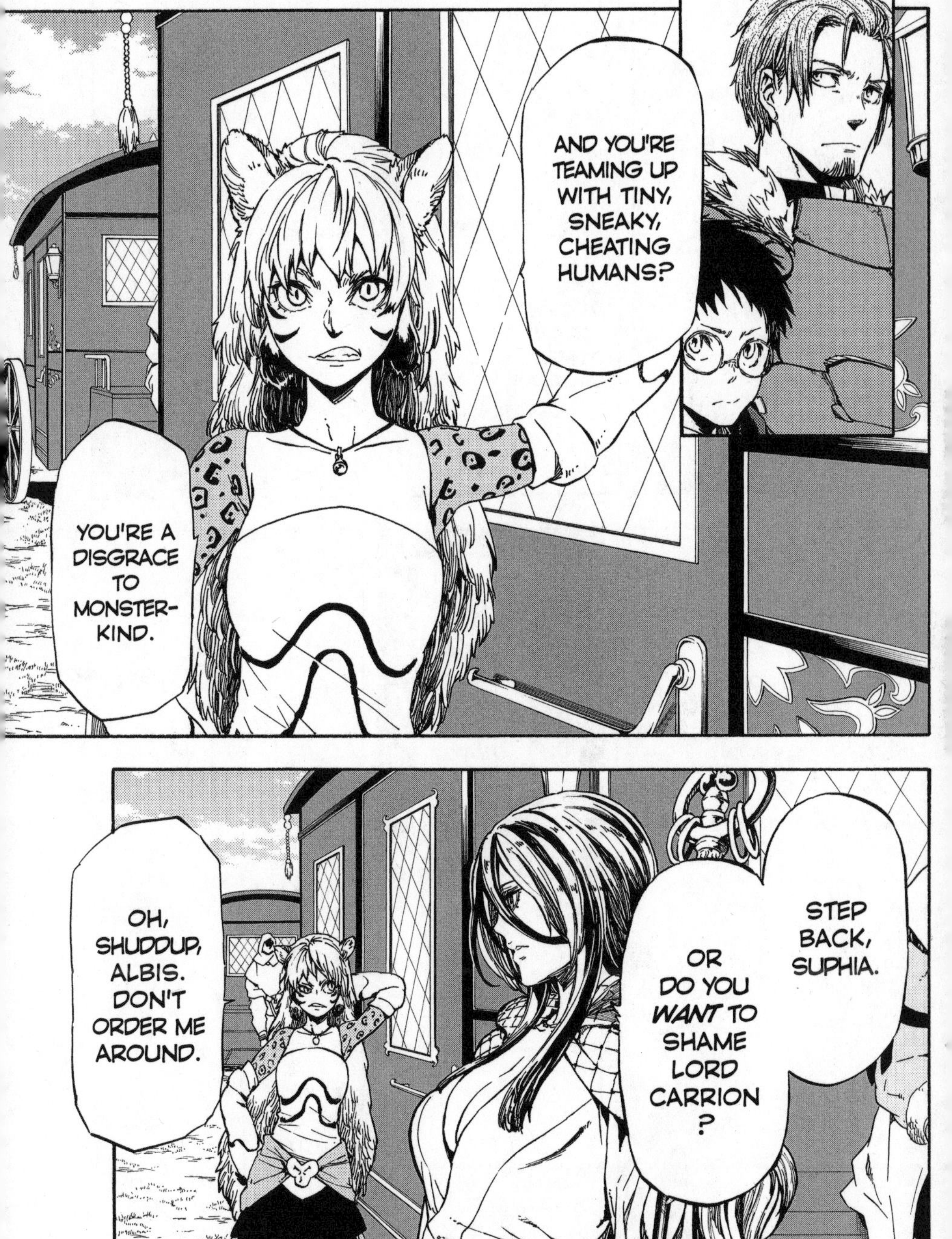
AND YOU'RE TEAMING UP WITH TINY, SNEAKY, CHEATING HUMANS?
YOU'RE A DISGRACE TO MONSTER-KIND.
STEP BACK, SUPHIA.
OR DO YOU *WANT* TO SHAME LORD CARRION?
OH, SHUDDUP, ALBIS. DON'T ORDER ME AROUND.

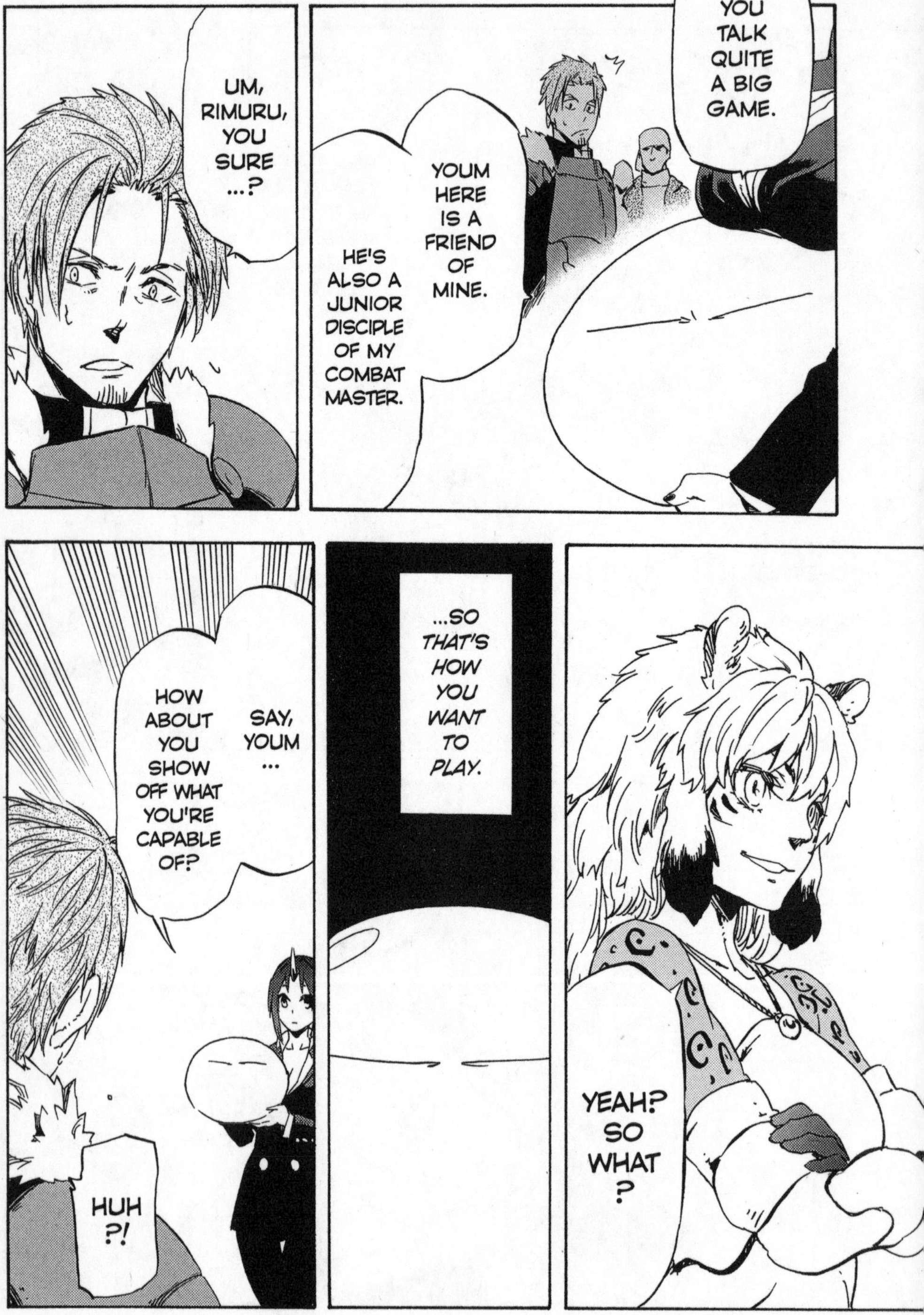
YOU TALK QUITE A BIG GAME.
YOUM HERE IS A FRIEND OF MINE.
HE'S ALSO A JUNIOR DISCIPLE OF MY COMBAT MASTER.
UM, RIMURU, YOU SURE ...?
YEAH? SO WHAT?
...SO *THAT'S HOW YOU WANT TO PLAY.*
SAY, YOUM ...
HOW ABOUT YOU SHOW OFF WHAT YOU'RE CAPABLE OF?
HUH?!

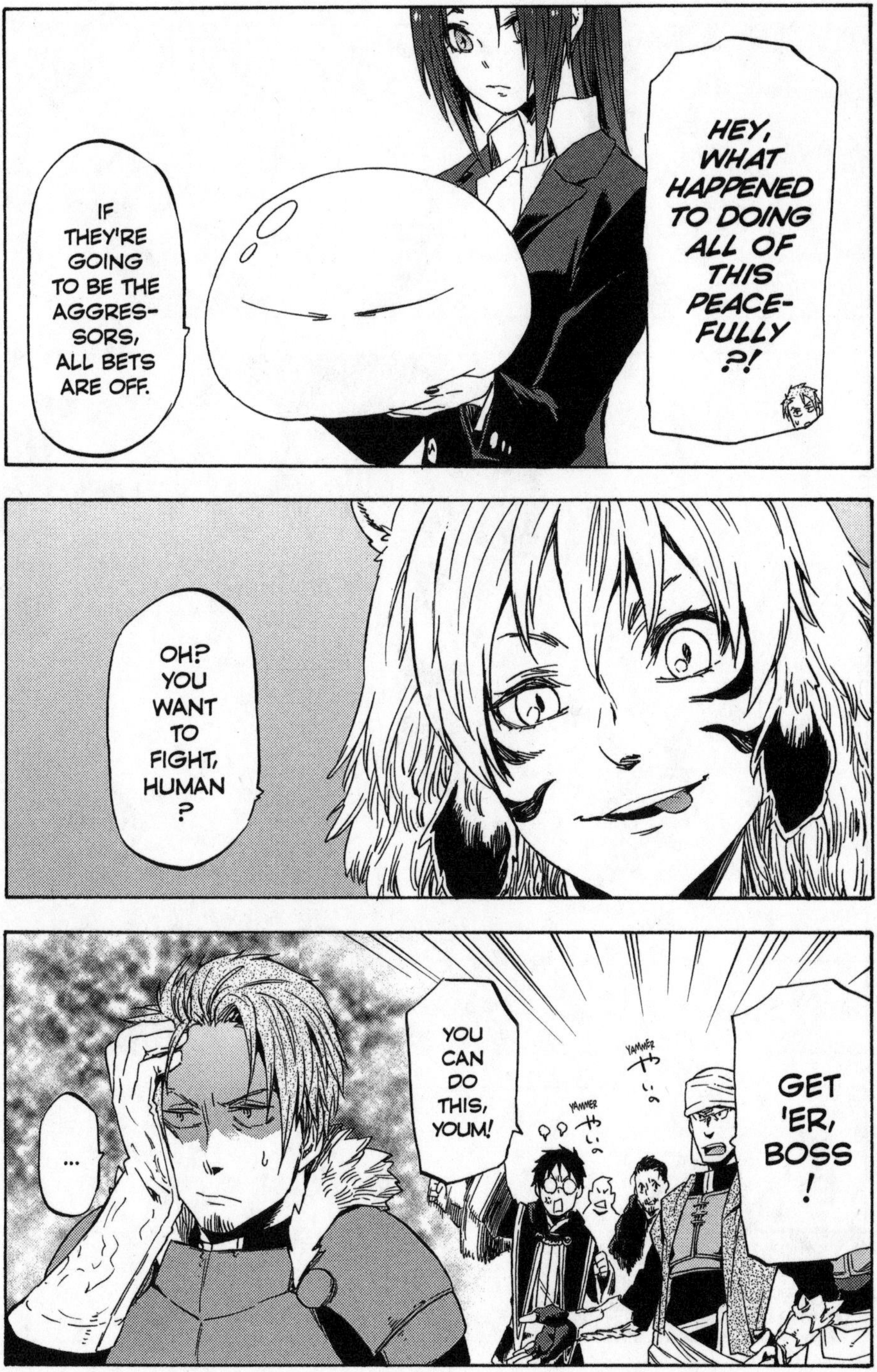
HEY, WHAT HAPPENED TO DOING ALL OF THIS PEACE-FULLY?!
IF THEY'RE GOING TO BE THE AGGRES-SORS, ALL BETS ARE OFF.
OH? YOU WANT TO FIGHT, HUMAN?
GET 'ER, BOSS!
YAMMER
やいの
YAMMER
やいの
YOU CAN DO THIS, YOUM!
...

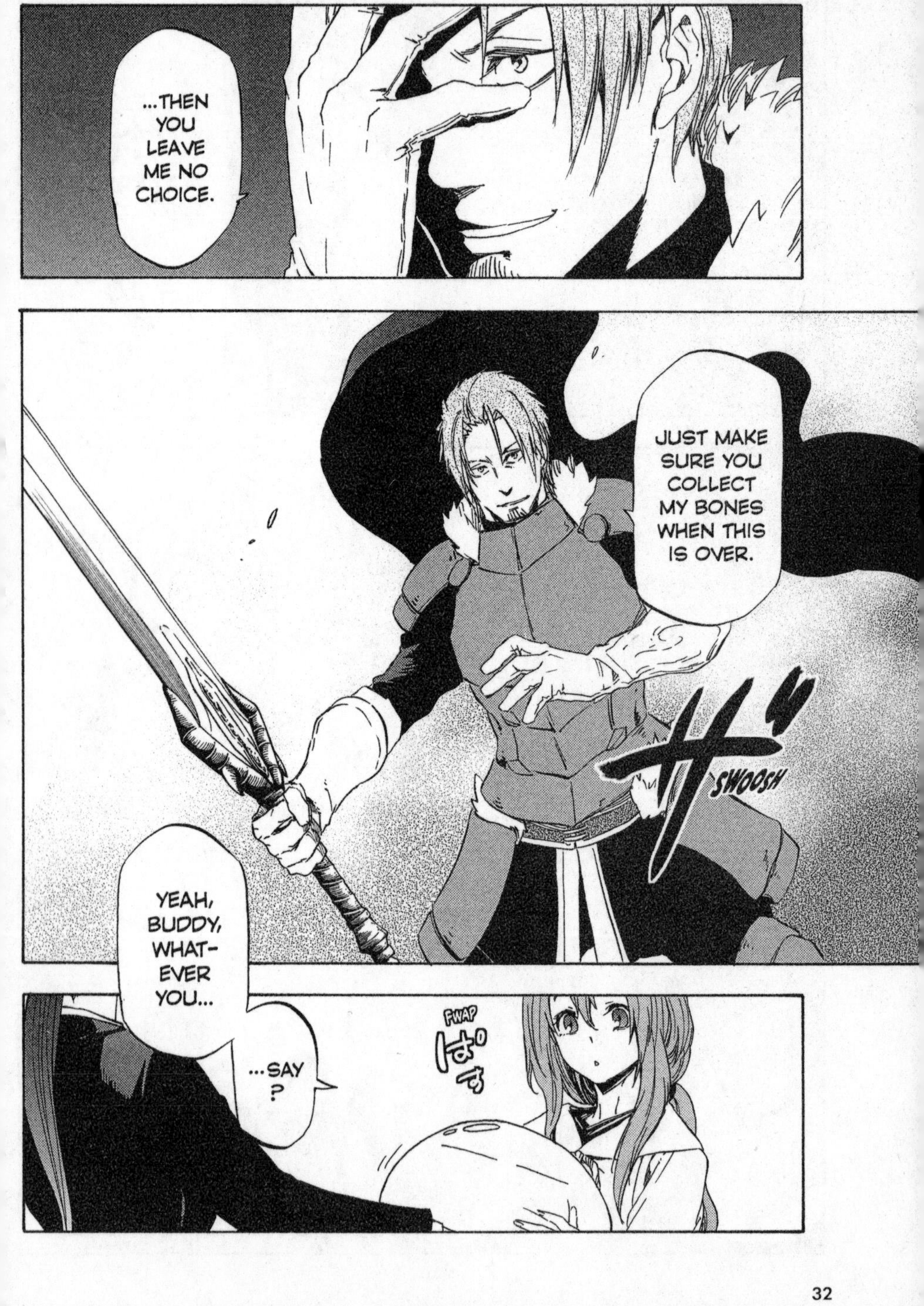
...THEN YOU LEAVE ME NO CHOICE.
JUST MAKE SURE YOU COLLECT MY BONES WHEN THIS IS OVER.
SWOOSH
YEAH, BUDDY, WHATEVER YOU...
FWAP
...SAY?

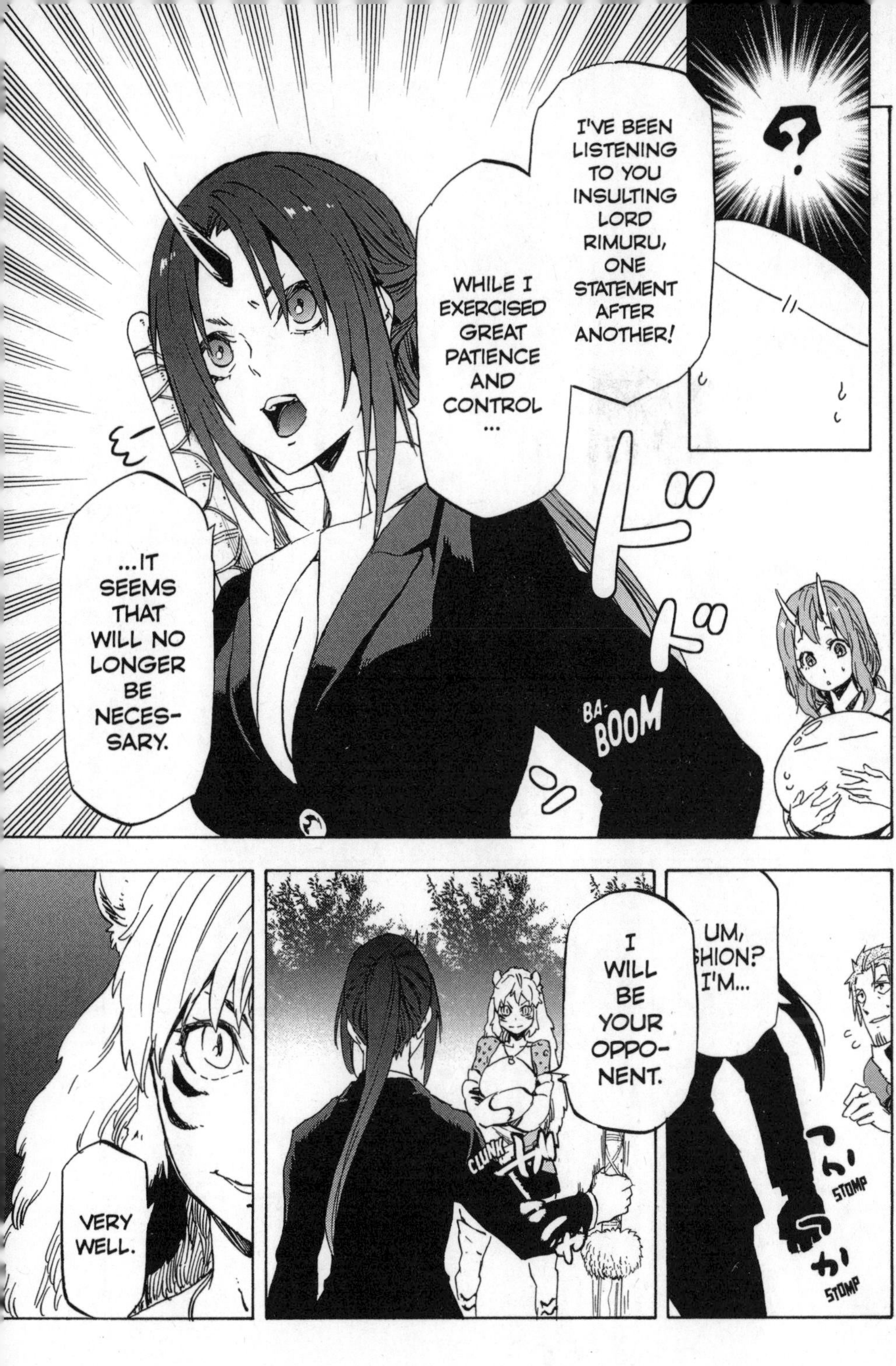
?
I'VE BEEN LISTENING TO YOU INSULTING LORD RIMURU, ONE STATEMENT AFTER ANOTHER!
WHILE I EXERCISED GREAT PATIENCE AND CONTROL...
...IT SEEMS THAT WILL NO LONGER BE NECES-SARY.
BA-BOOM
UM, SHION? I'M...
STOMP
STOMP
I WILL BE YOUR OPPO-NENT.
CLUNK
VERY WELL.

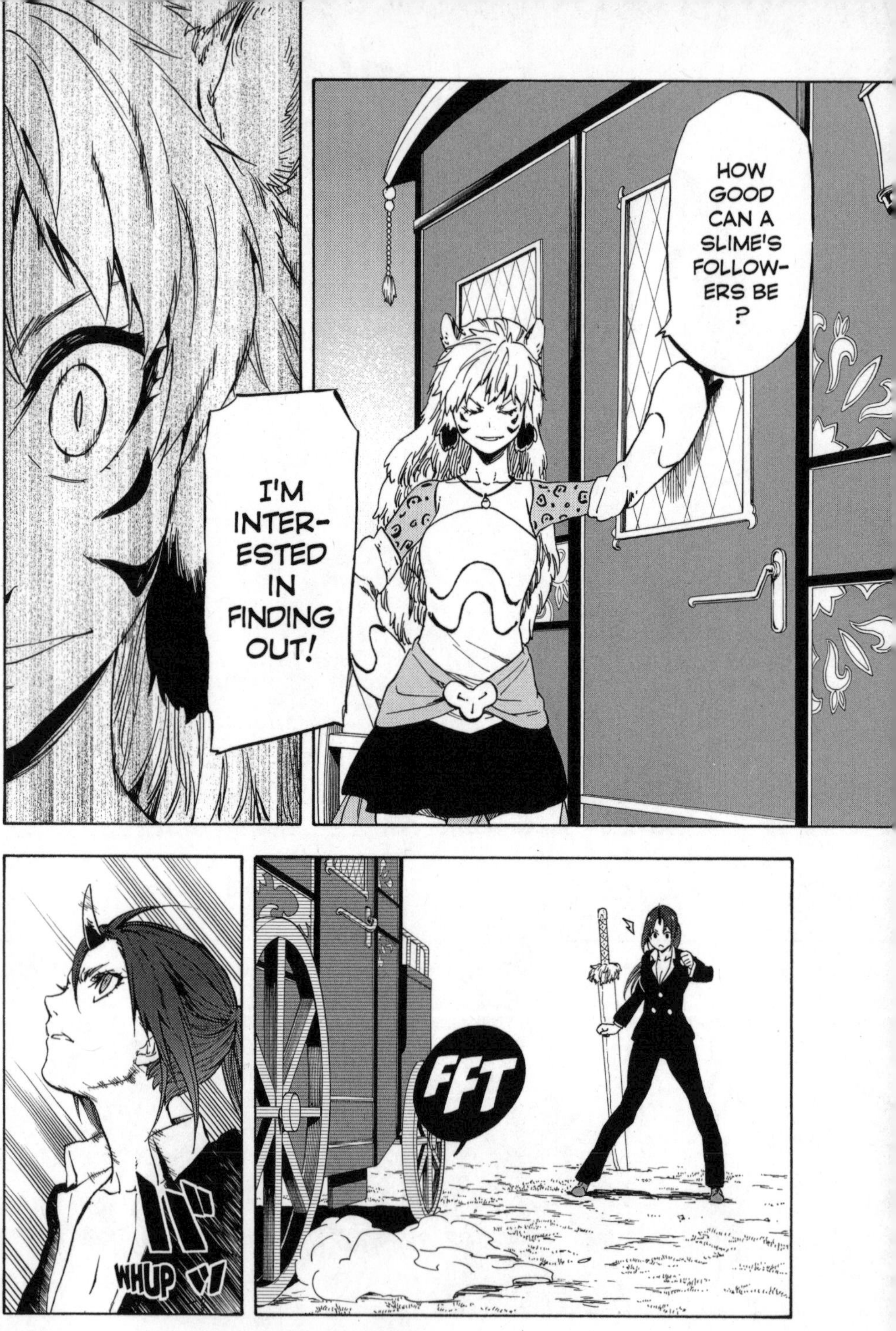
HOW GOOD CAN A SLIME'S FOLLOW-ERS BE ?
I'M INTER-ESTED IN FINDING OUT!
FFT
WHUP

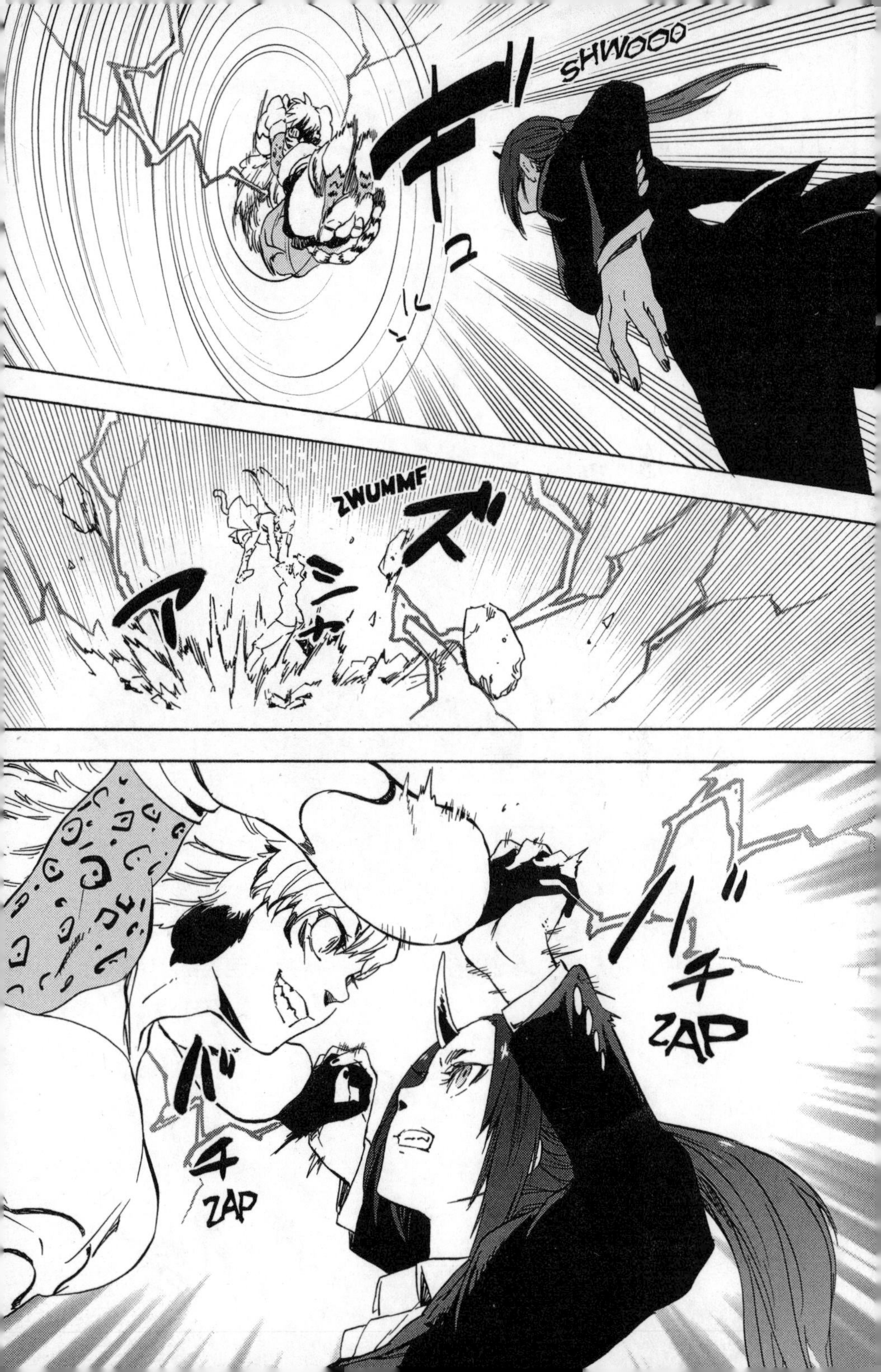
SHWOOO
ZWUMMF
ZAP
ZAP

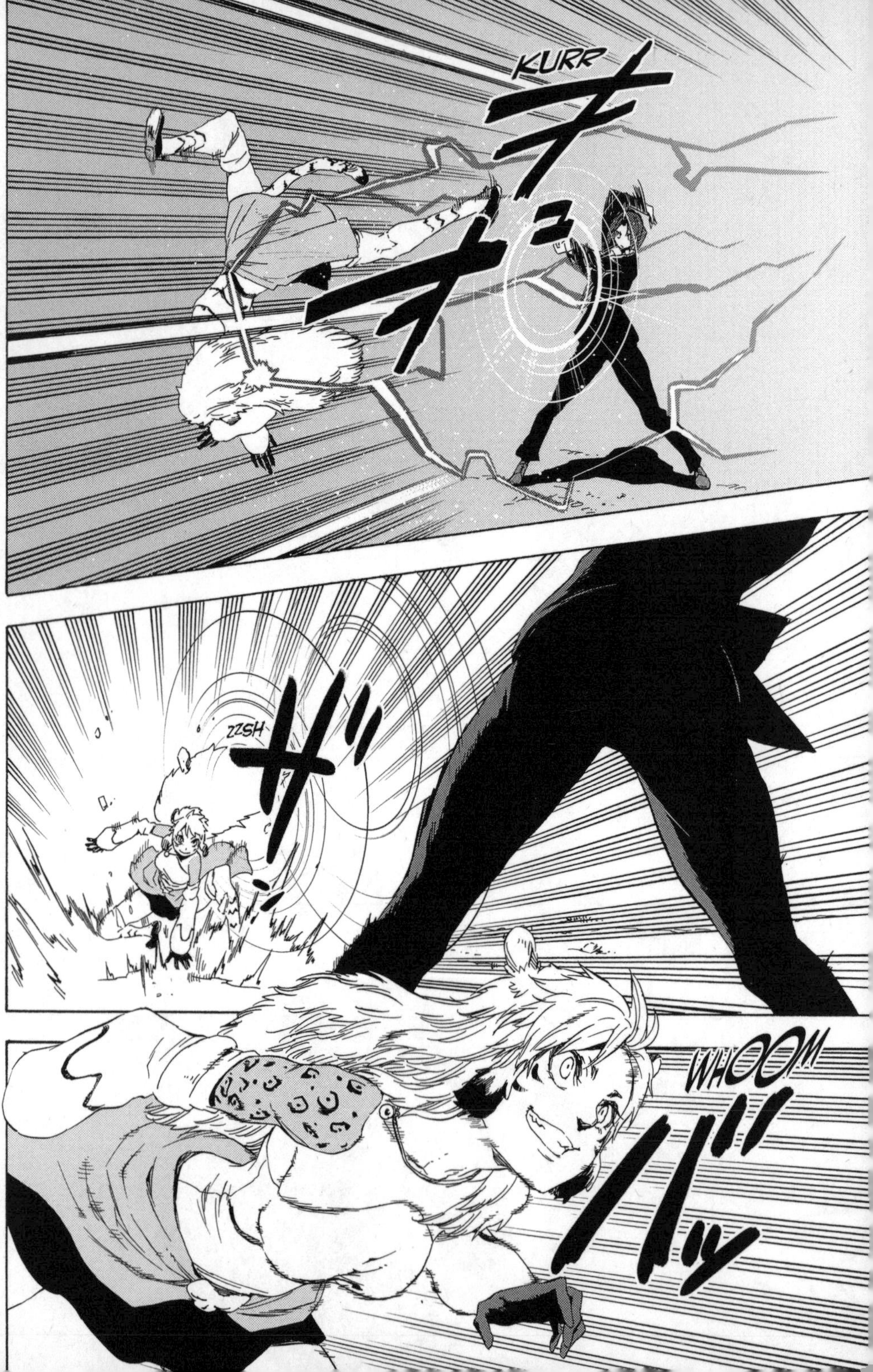
KURR
ZZSH
WHOOM

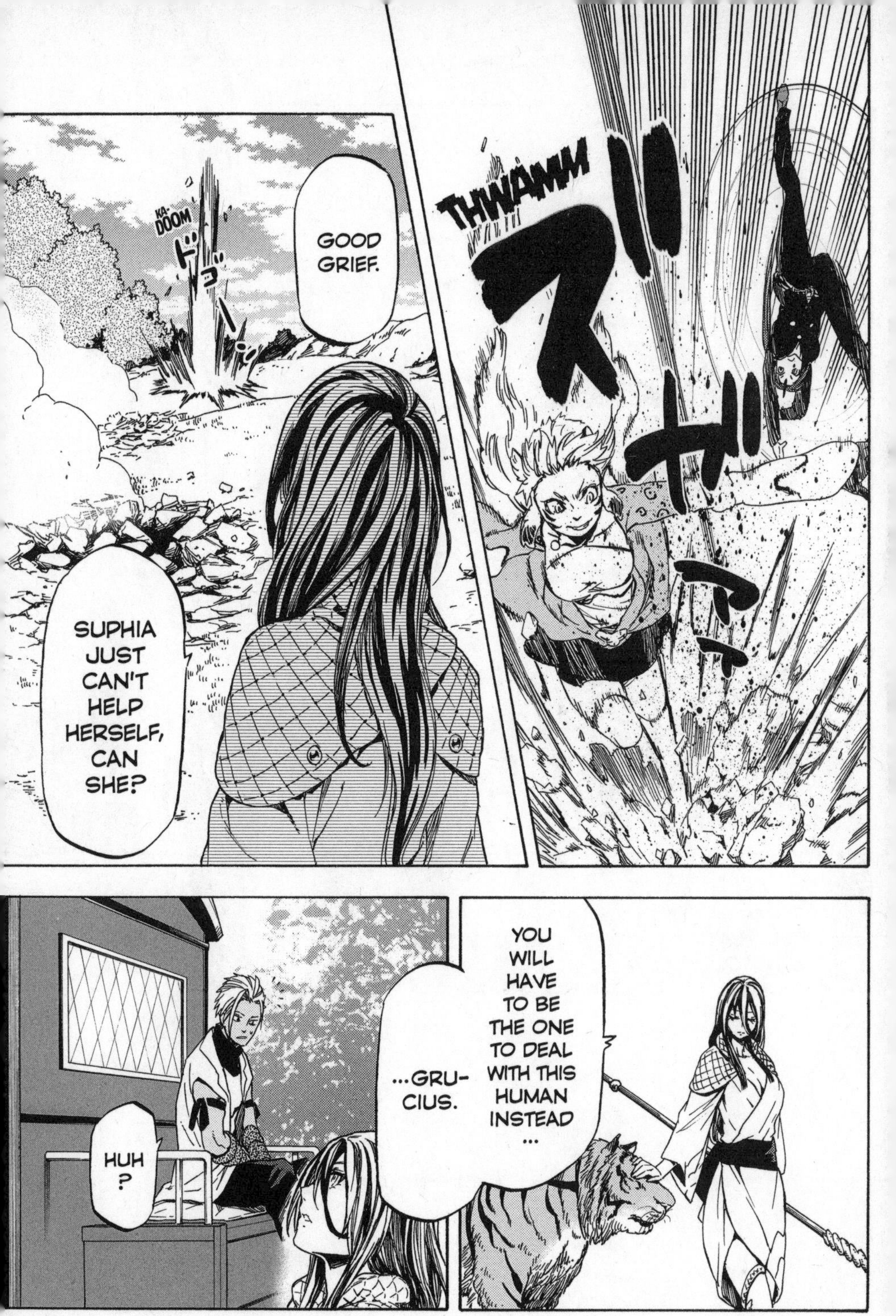
THWAMM
KA-DOOM
GOOD GRIEF.
SUPHIA JUST CAN'T HELP HERSELF, CAN SHE?
YOU WILL HAVE TO BE THE ONE TO DEAL WITH THIS HUMAN INSTEAD...
...GRU-CIUS.
HUH?

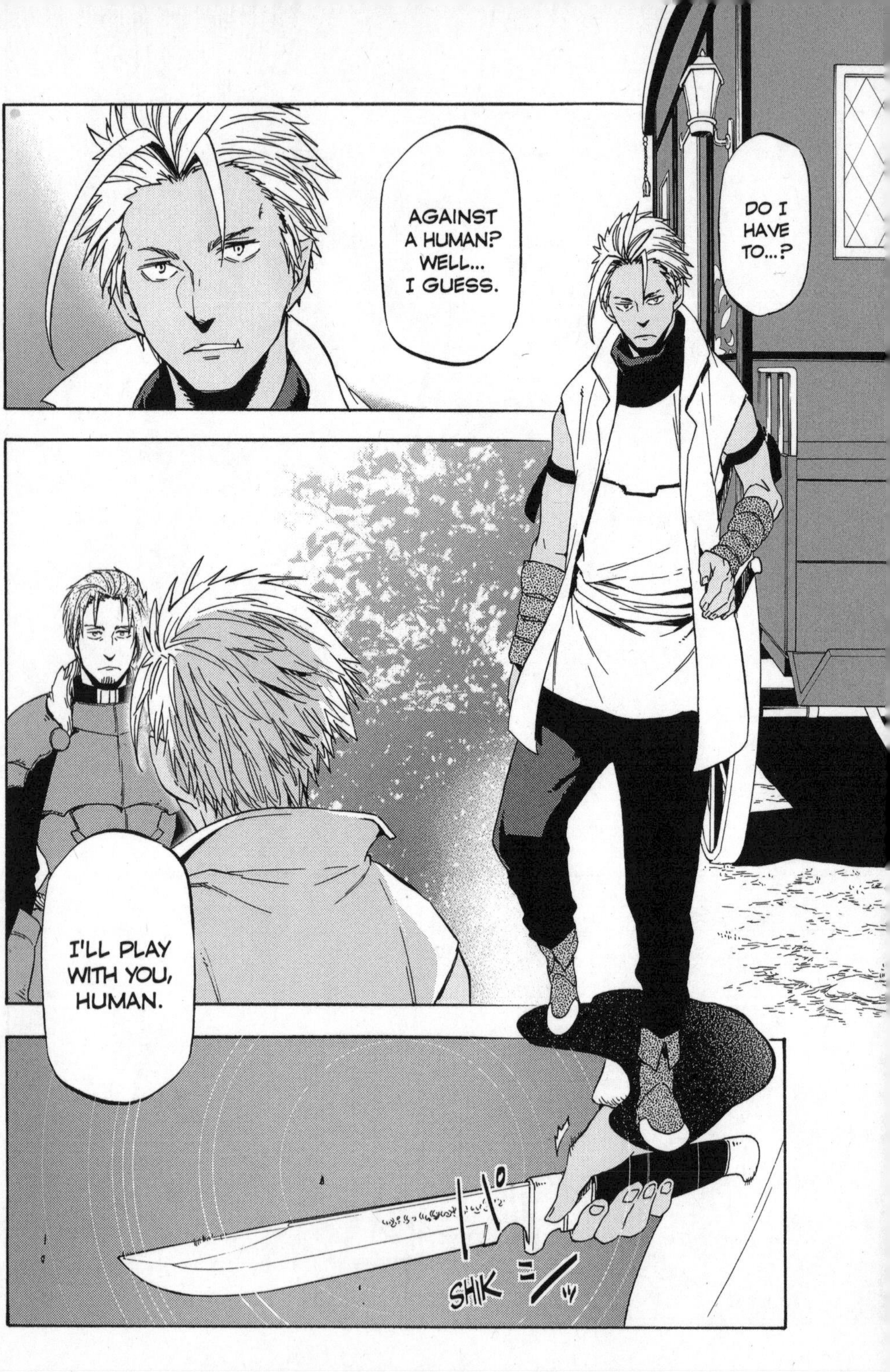
DO I HAVE TO...?
AGAINST A HUMAN? WELL... I GUESS.
I'LL PLAY WITH YOU, HUMAN.
SHIK

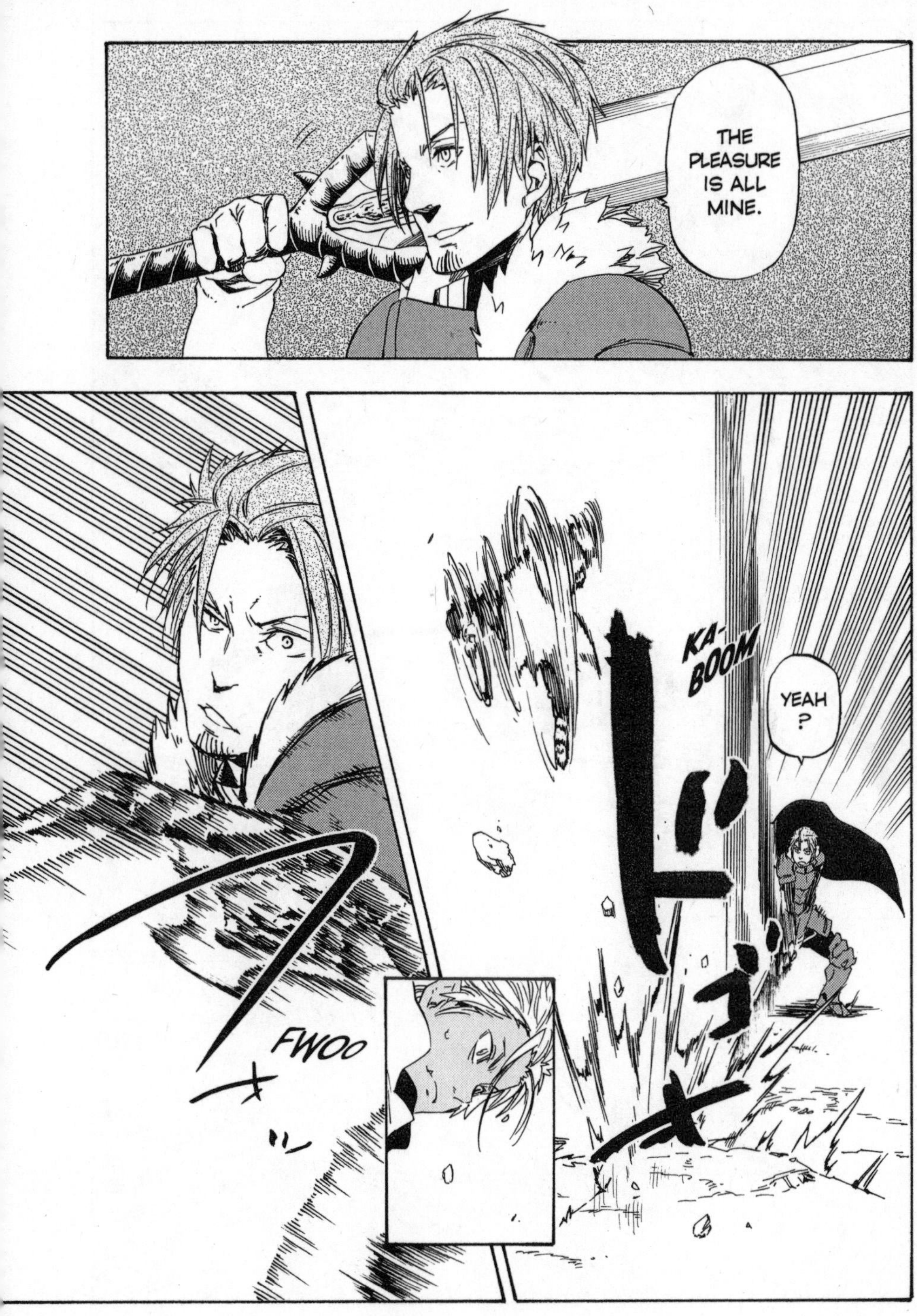
THE PLEASURE IS ALL MINE.
KA-BOOM
YEAH?
FWOO

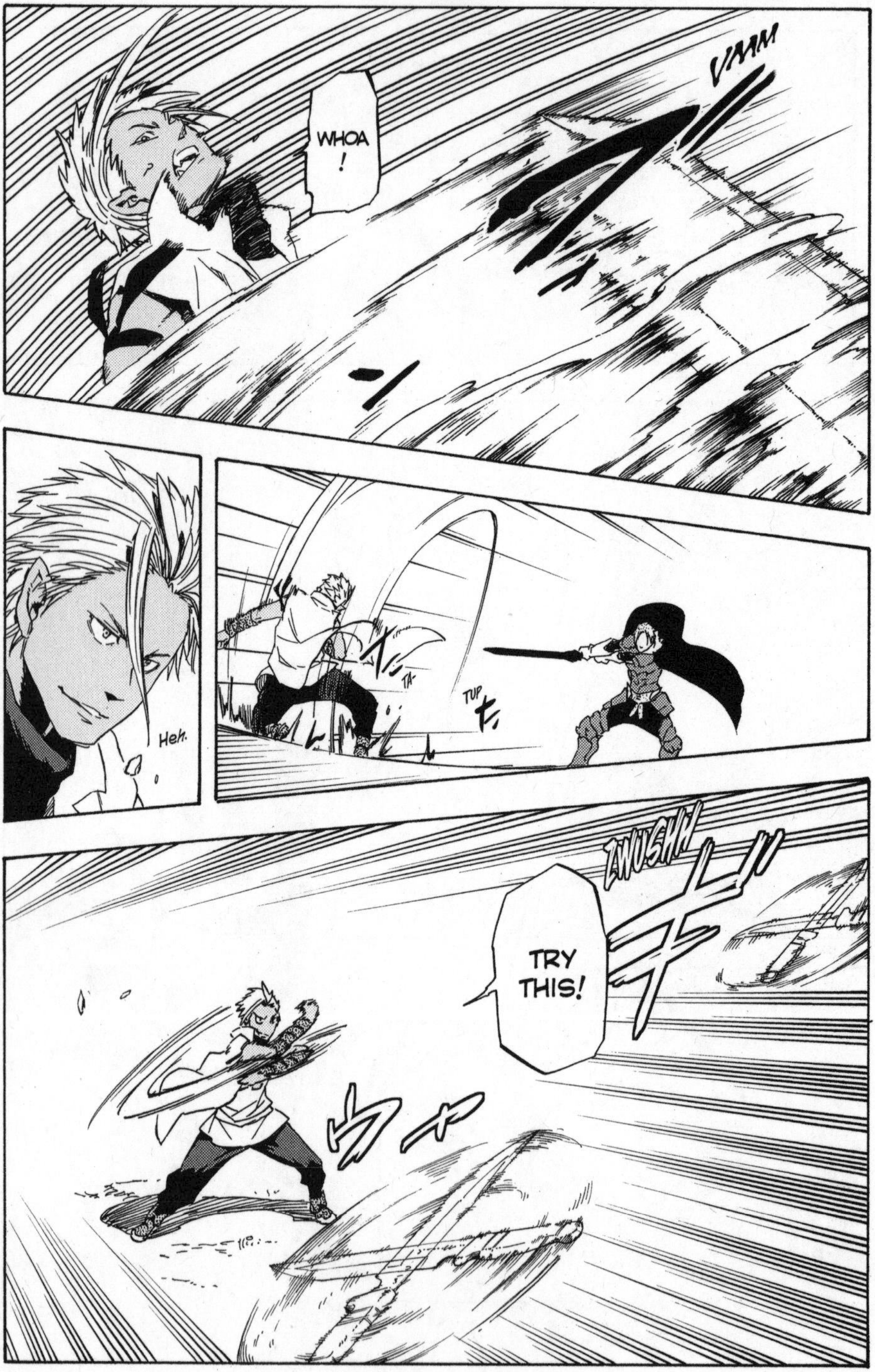
VMMM
WHOA!
TA
TUP
Heh.
ZWUSHH
TRY THIS!

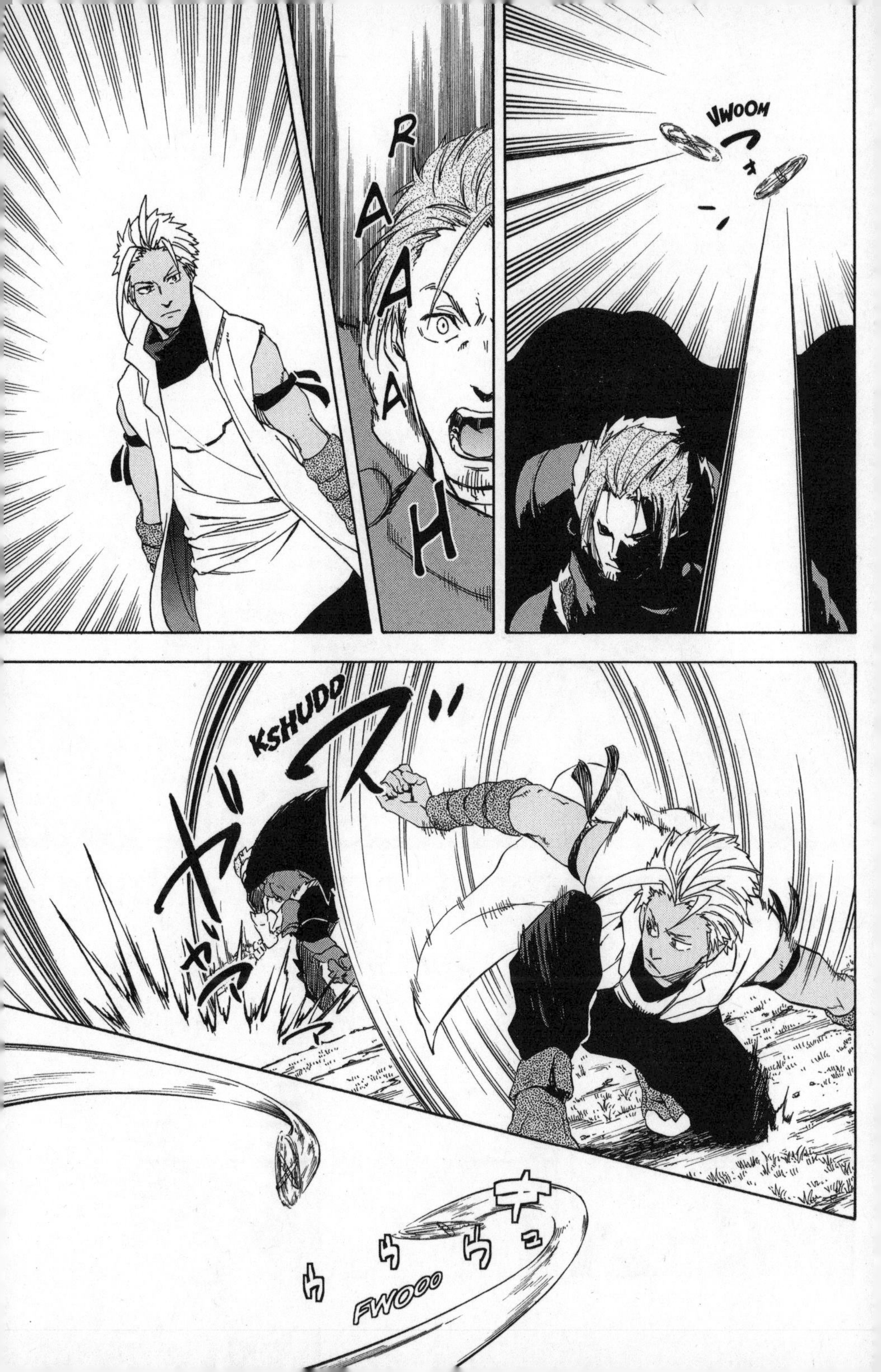
VWOOM
RAAAAH
KSHUDD
FWOOO

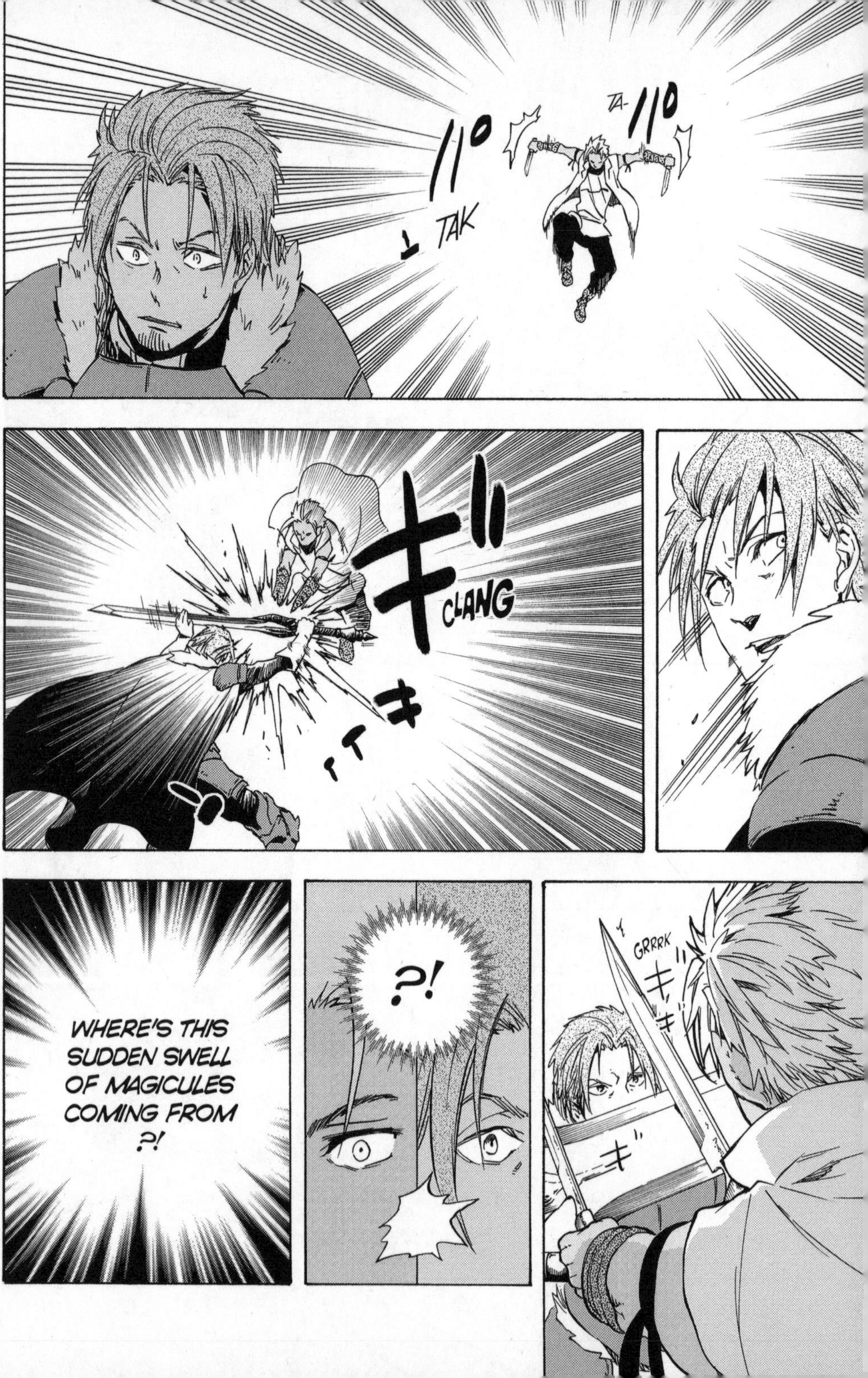
TA-
TAK
CLANG
GRRRK
?!
WHERE'S THIS SUDDEN SWELL OF MAGICULES COMING FROM ?!

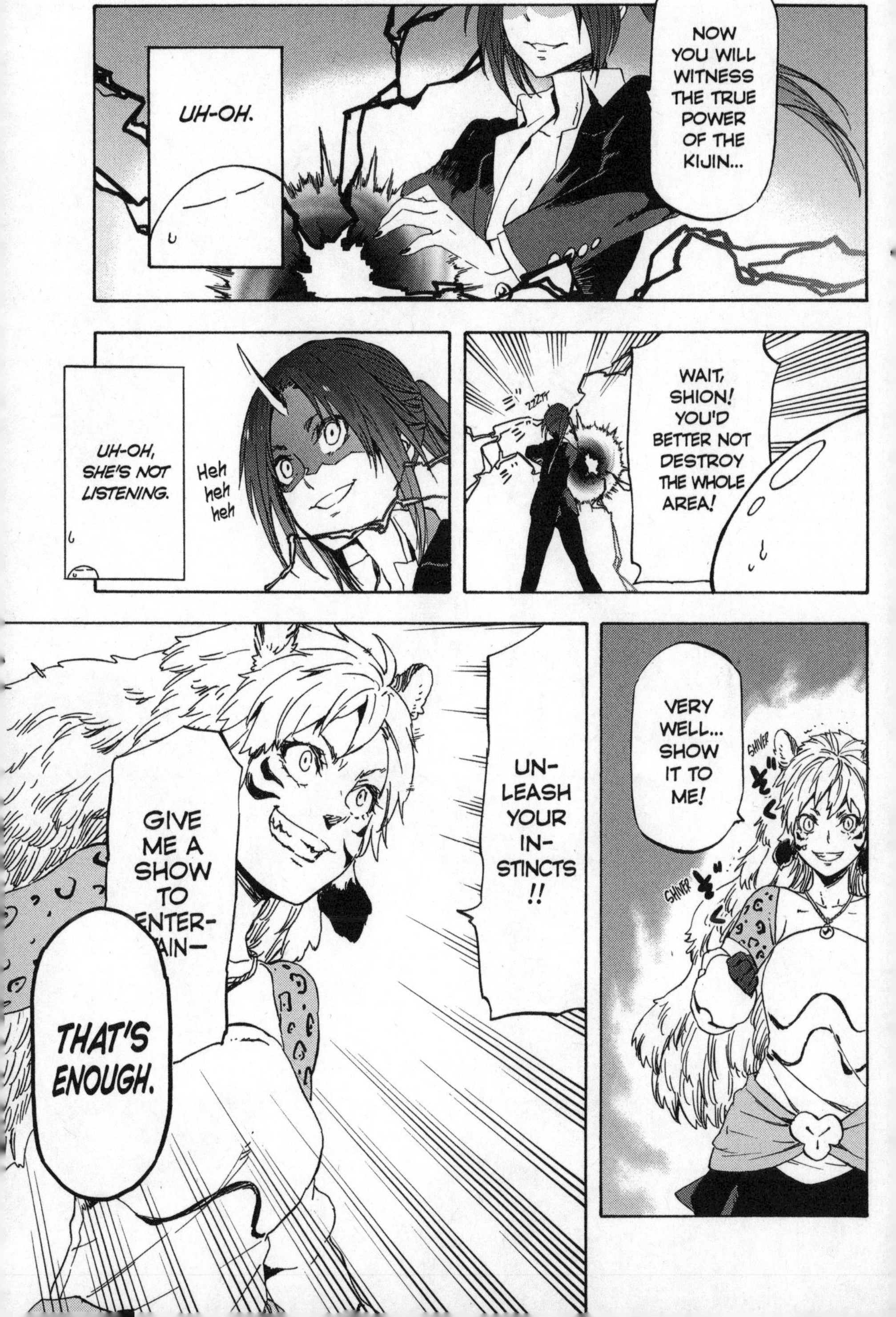
NOW YOU WILL WITNESS THE TRUE POWER OF THE KIJIN...
UH-OH.
ZZZTT
WAIT, SHION! YOU'D BETTER NOT DESTROY THE WHOLE AREA!
Heh heh heh
UH-OH, SHE'S NOT LISTENING.
VERY WELL... SHOW IT TO ME!
SHIVER
SHIVER
UN-LEASH YOUR IN-STINCTS!!
GIVE ME A SHOW TO ENTER-TAIN—
THAT'S ENOUGH.

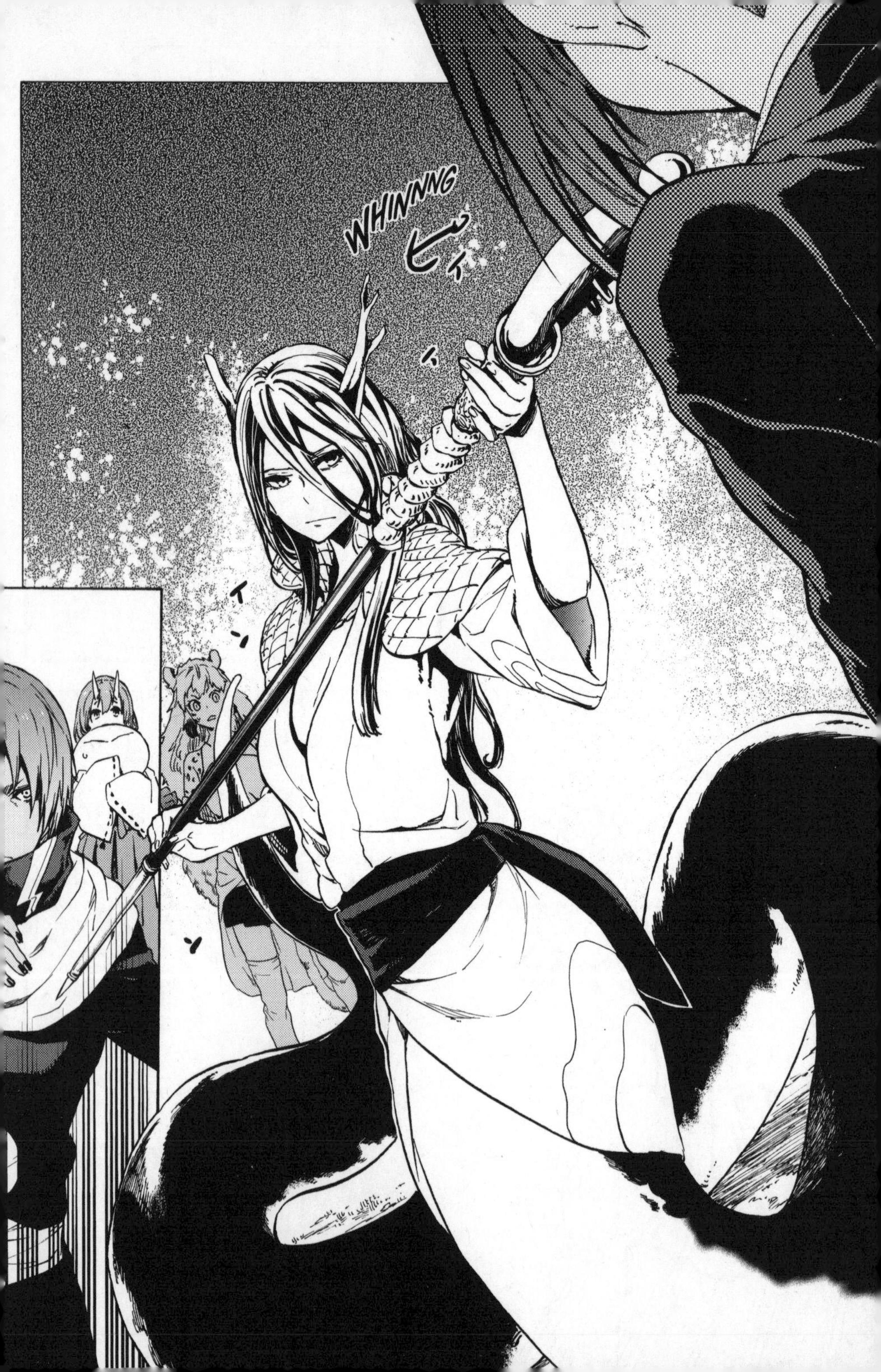
WHINNNG

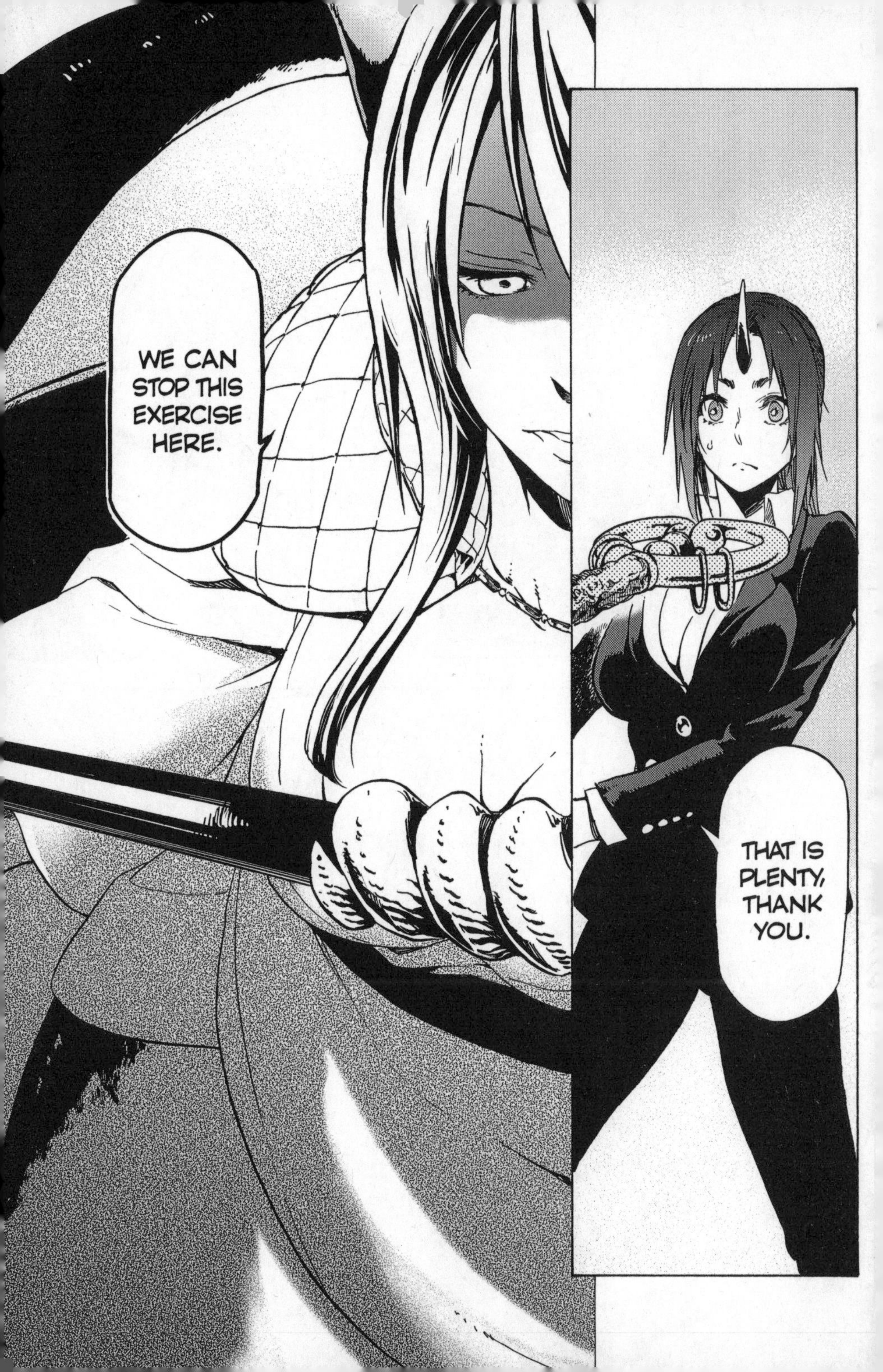
THAT IS PLENTY, THANK YOU.
WE CAN STOP THIS EXERCISE HERE.

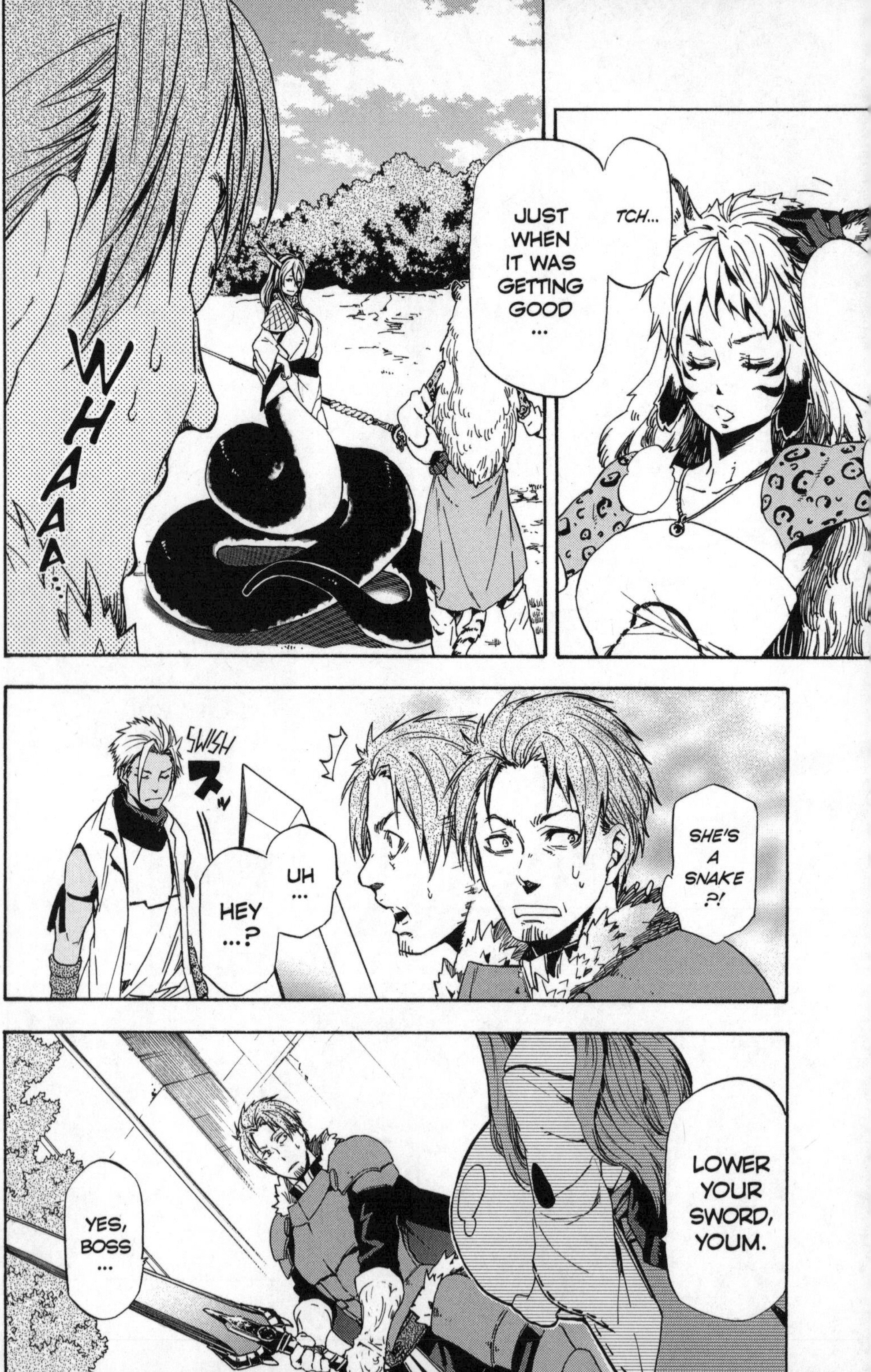
TCH...
JUST WHEN IT WAS GETTING GOOD ...
WHAAAA...
SHE'S A SNAKE ?!
UH ...
HEY ...?
SWISH
LOWER YOUR SWORD, YOUM.
YES, BOSS ...

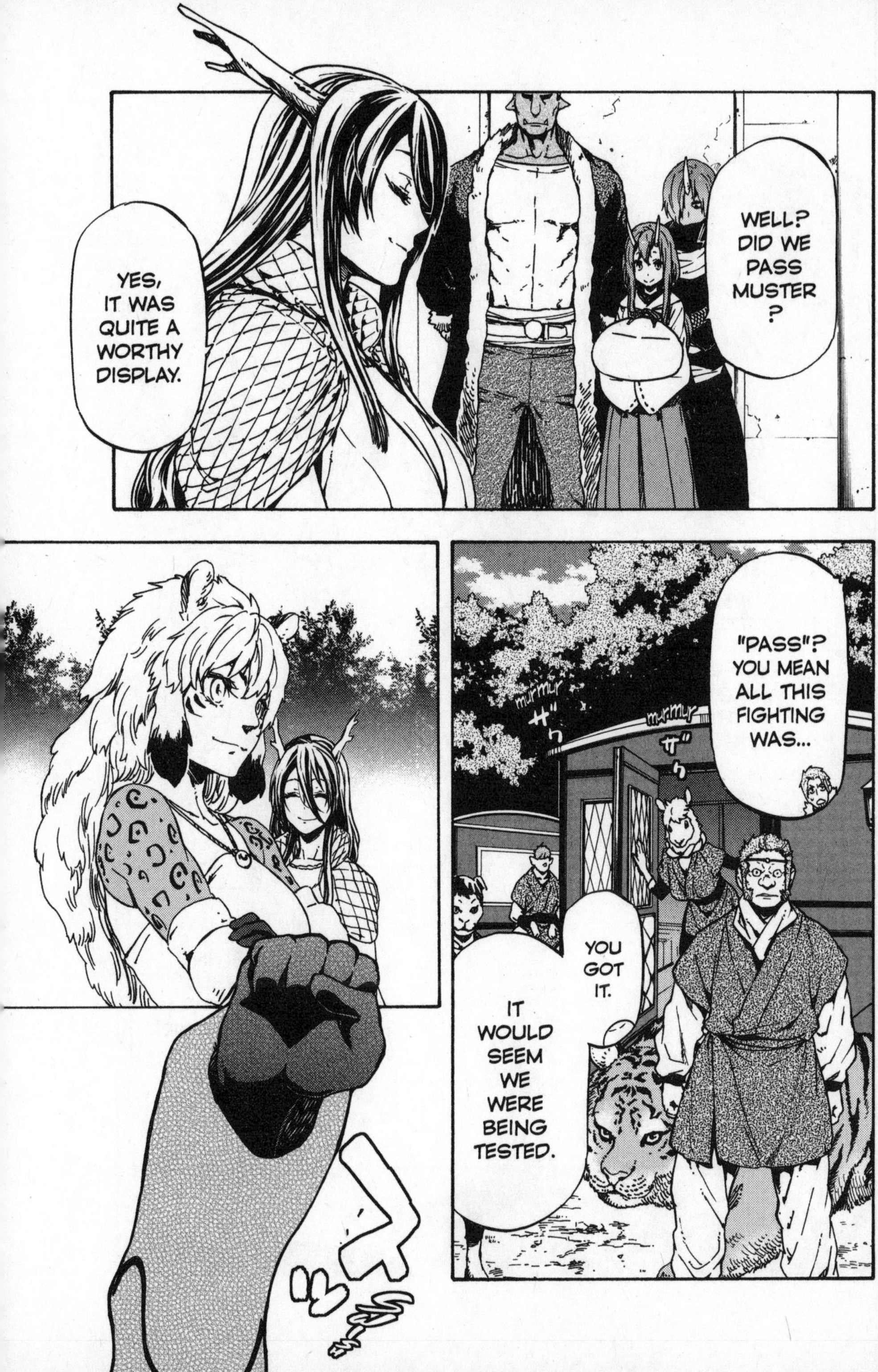
WELL? DID WE PASS MUSTER?
YES, IT WAS QUITE A WORTHY DISPLAY.
"PASS"? YOU MEAN ALL THIS FIGHTING WAS...
murmur
murmur
YOU GOT IT.
IT WOULD SEEM WE WERE BEING TESTED.

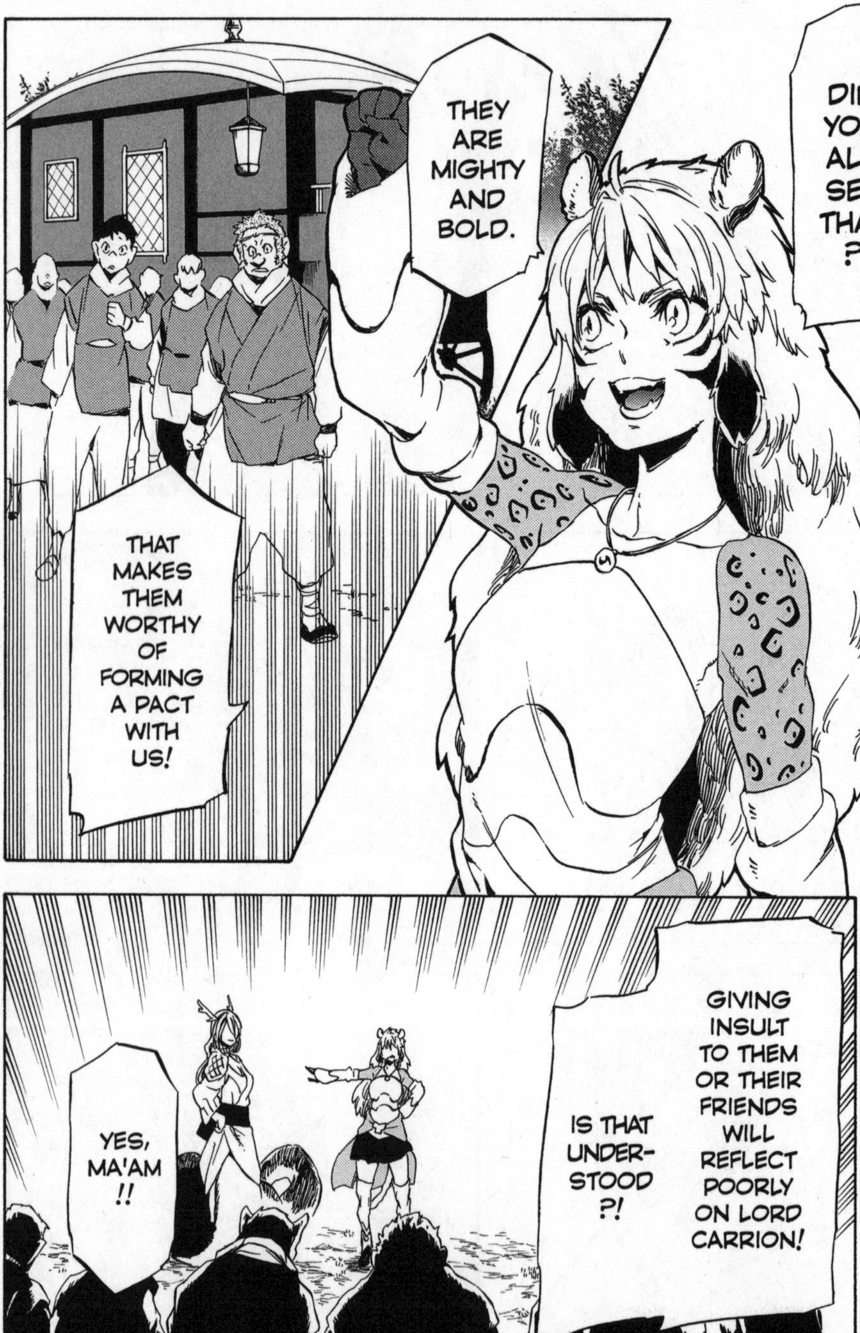
DID YOU ALL SEE THAT?
THEY ARE MIGHTY AND BOLD.
THAT MAKES THEM WORTHY OF FORMING A PACT WITH US!
GIVING INSULT TO THEM OR THEIR FRIENDS WILL REFLECT POORLY ON LORD CARRION!
IS THAT UNDER-STOOD?!
YES, MA'AM!!

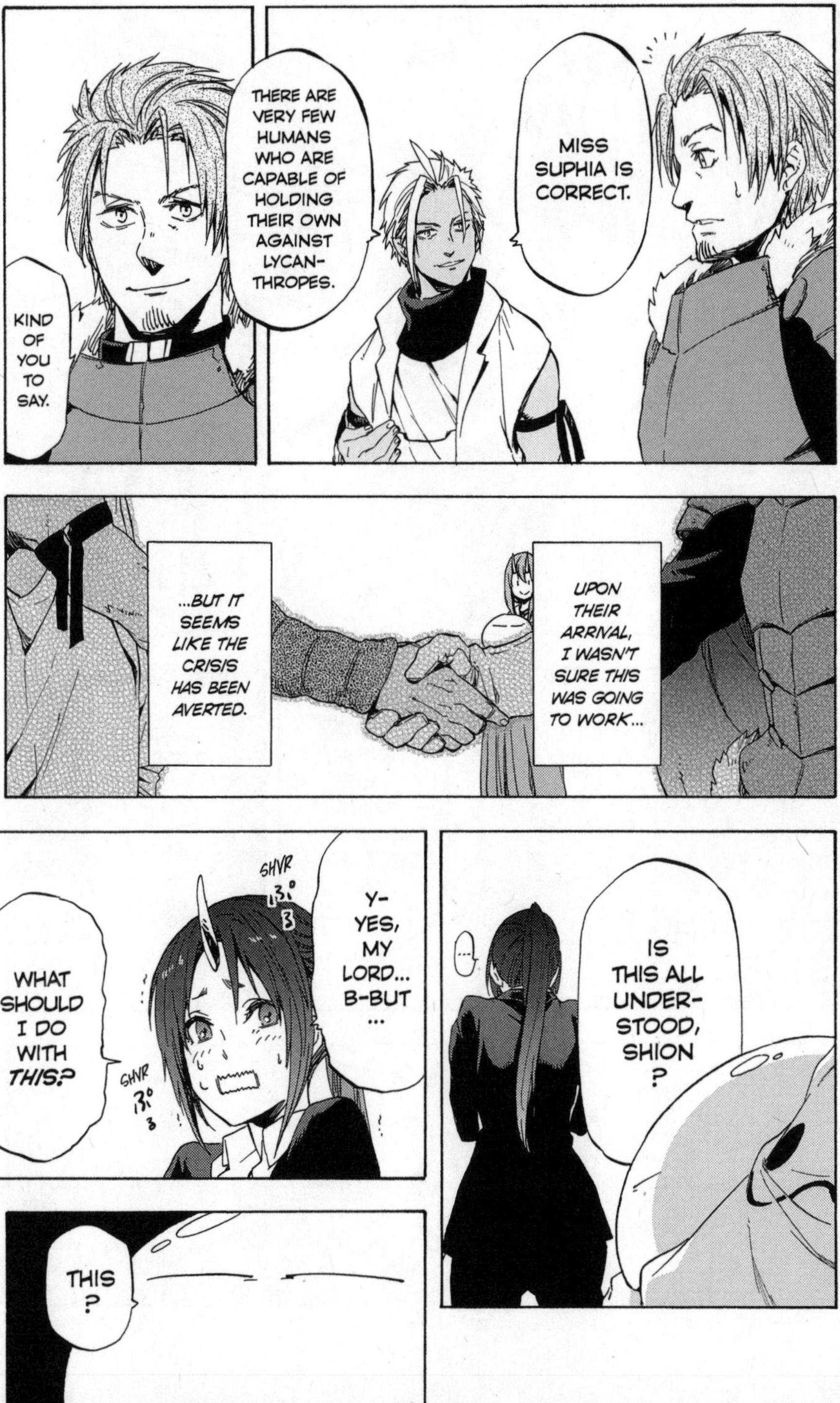
MISS SUPHIA IS CORRECT.
THERE ARE VERY FEW HUMANS WHO ARE CAPABLE OF HOLDING THEIR OWN AGAINST LYCANTHROPES.
KIND OF YOU TO SAY.
UPON THEIR ARRIVAL, I WASN'T SURE THIS WAS GOING TO WORK...
...BUT IT SEEMS LIKE THE CRISIS HAS BEEN AVERTED.
IS THIS ALL UNDERSTOOD, SHION?
...
Y-YES, MY LORD... B-BUT...
SHVR
WHAT SHOULD I DO WITH ***THIS?***
SHVR
THIS?

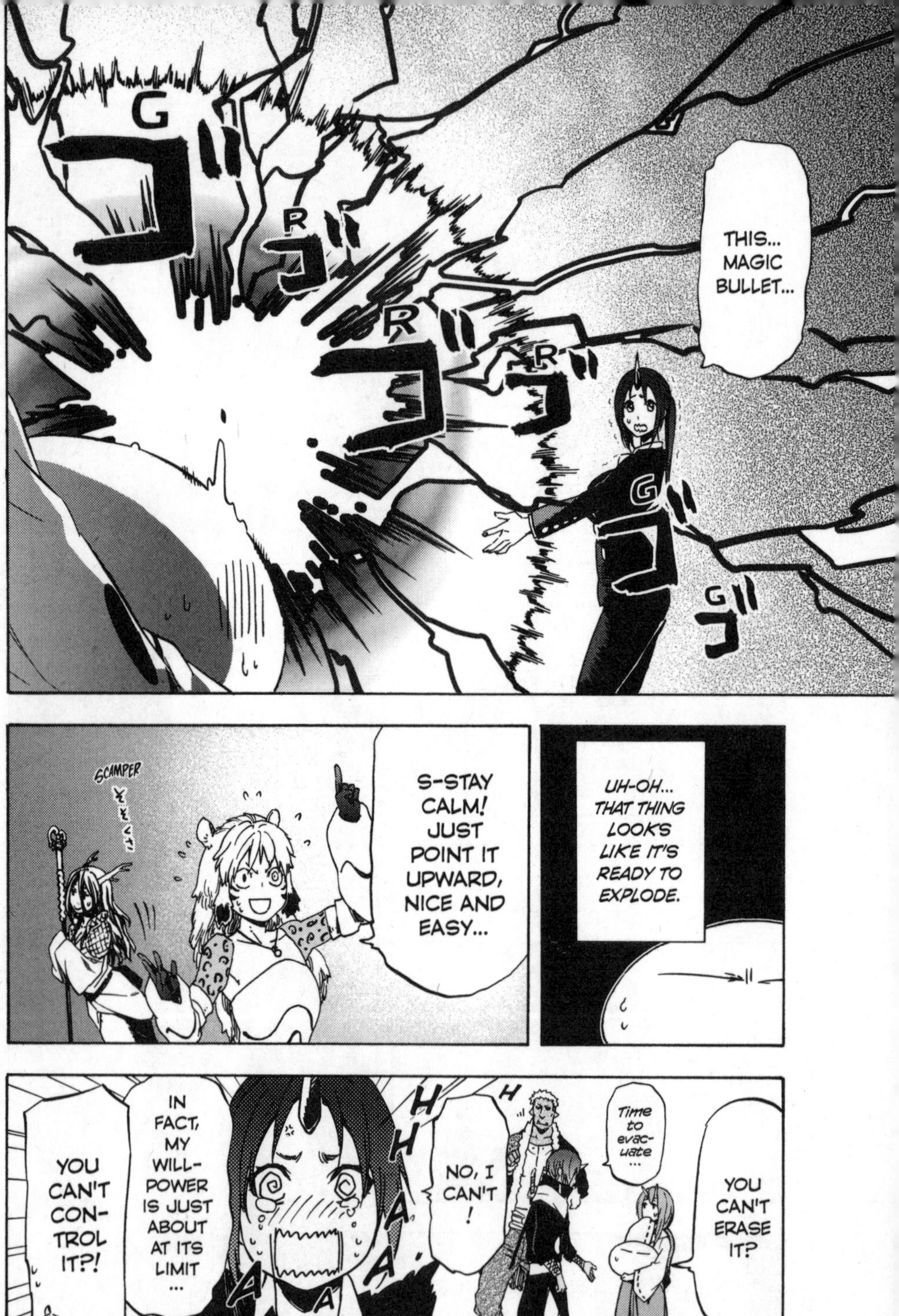

THIS... MAGIC BULLET...
G
R
R
R
G
UH-OH... THAT THING LOOKS LIKE IT'S READY TO EXPLODE.
S-STAY CALM! JUST POINT IT UPWARD, NICE AND EASY...
SCAMPER
YOU CAN'T ERASE IT?
Time to evacuate...
NO, I CAN'T!
H
IN FACT, MY WILL-POWER IS JUST ABOUT AT ITS LIMIT...
YOU CAN'T CON-TROL IT?!

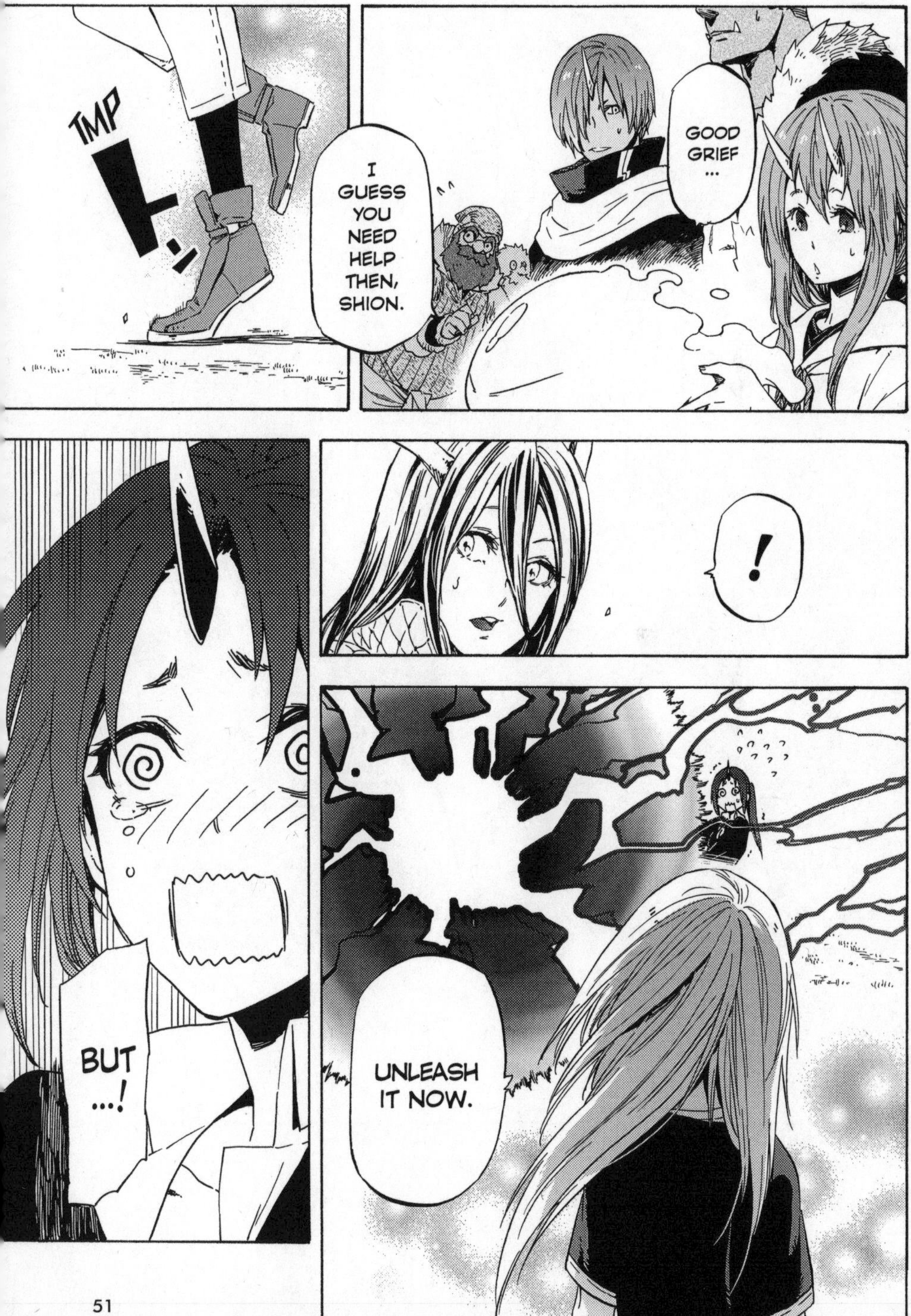
GOOD GRIEF ...
I GUESS YOU NEED HELP THEN, SHION.
TMP
!
UNLEASH IT NOW.
BUT ...!

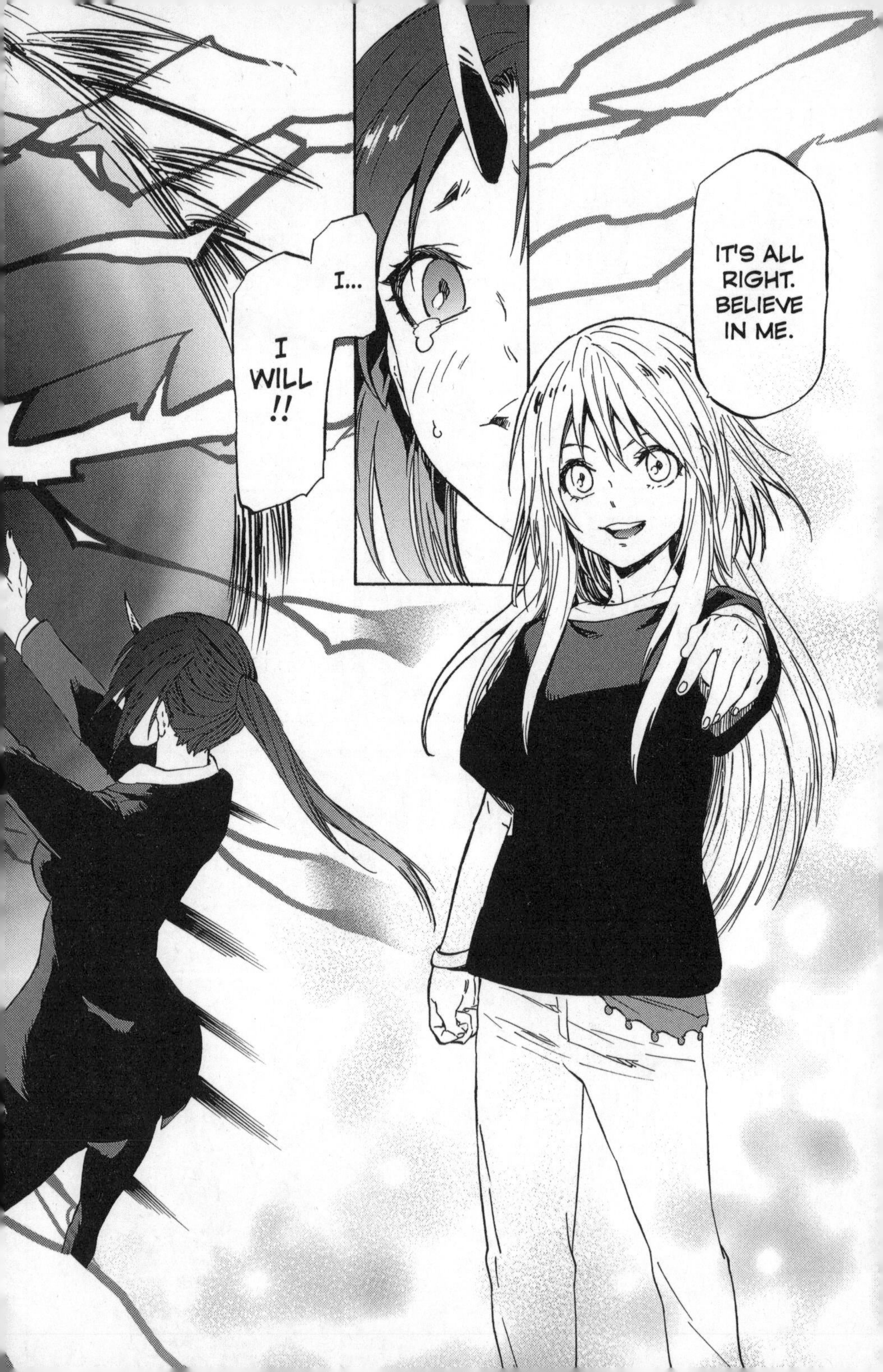
IT'S ALL RIGHT. BELIEVE IN ME.
I...
I WILL!!

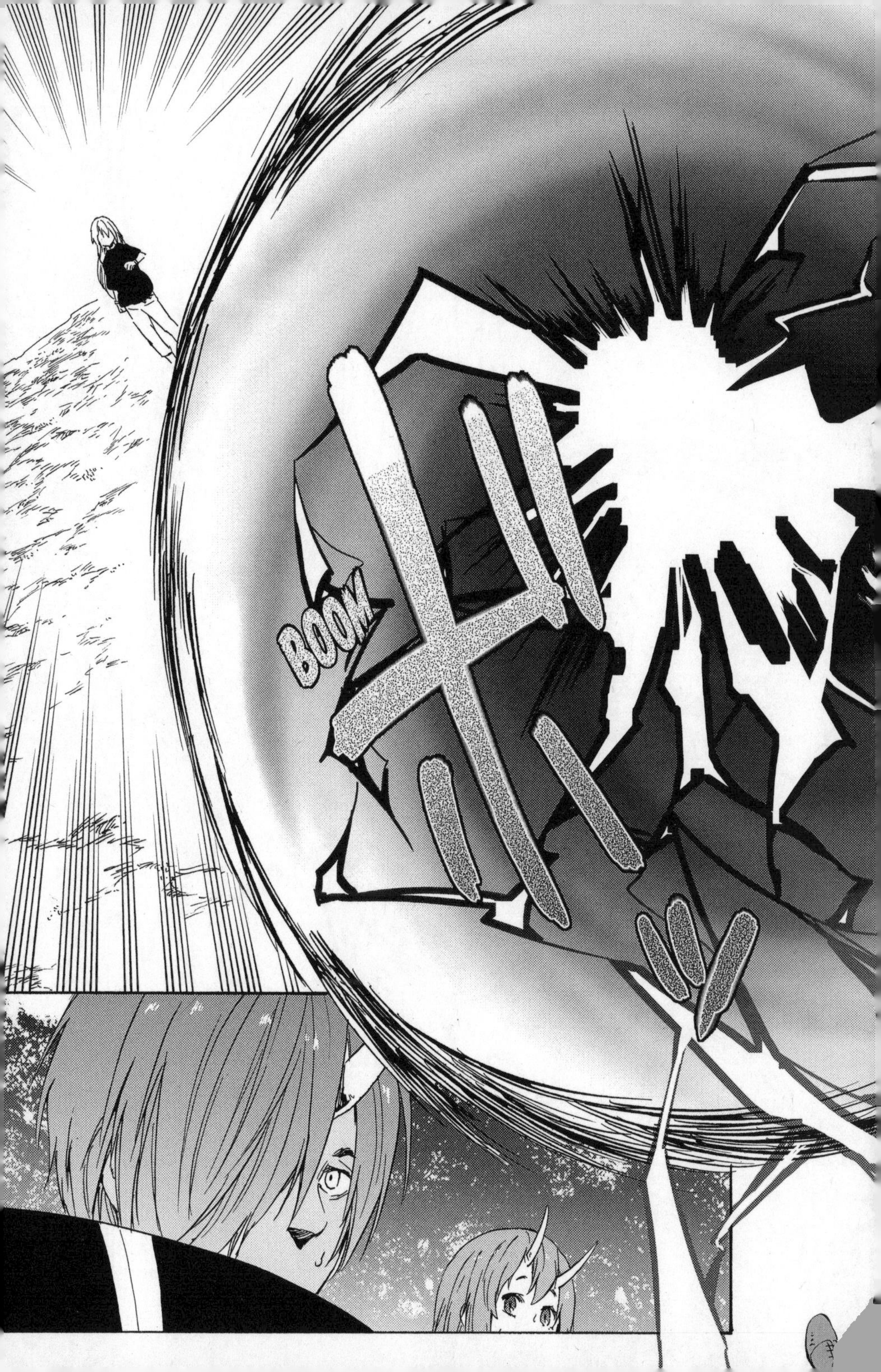
BOOM

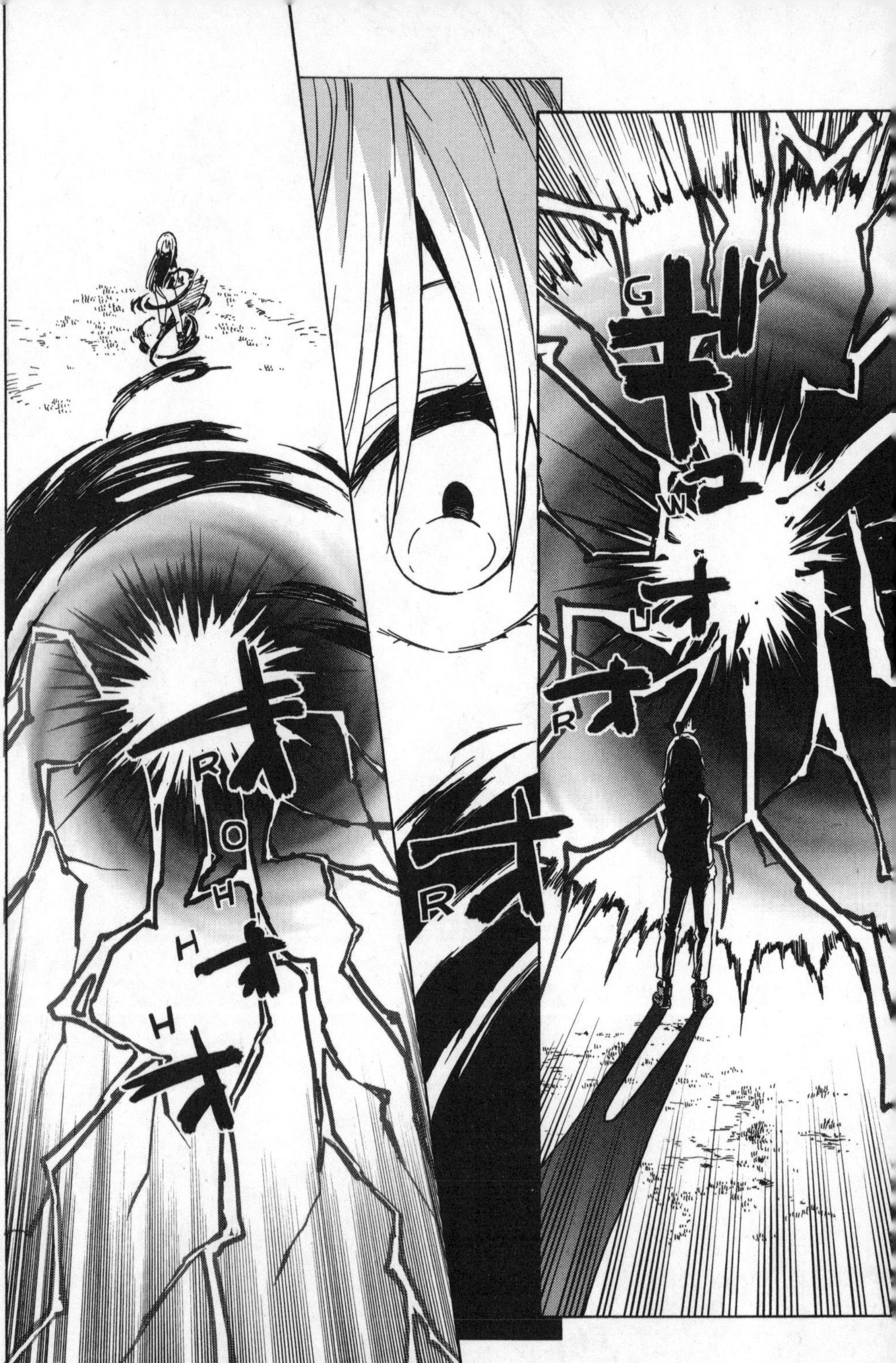
ギュオオ
GWUR
オ
R
オオオ
ROHHH

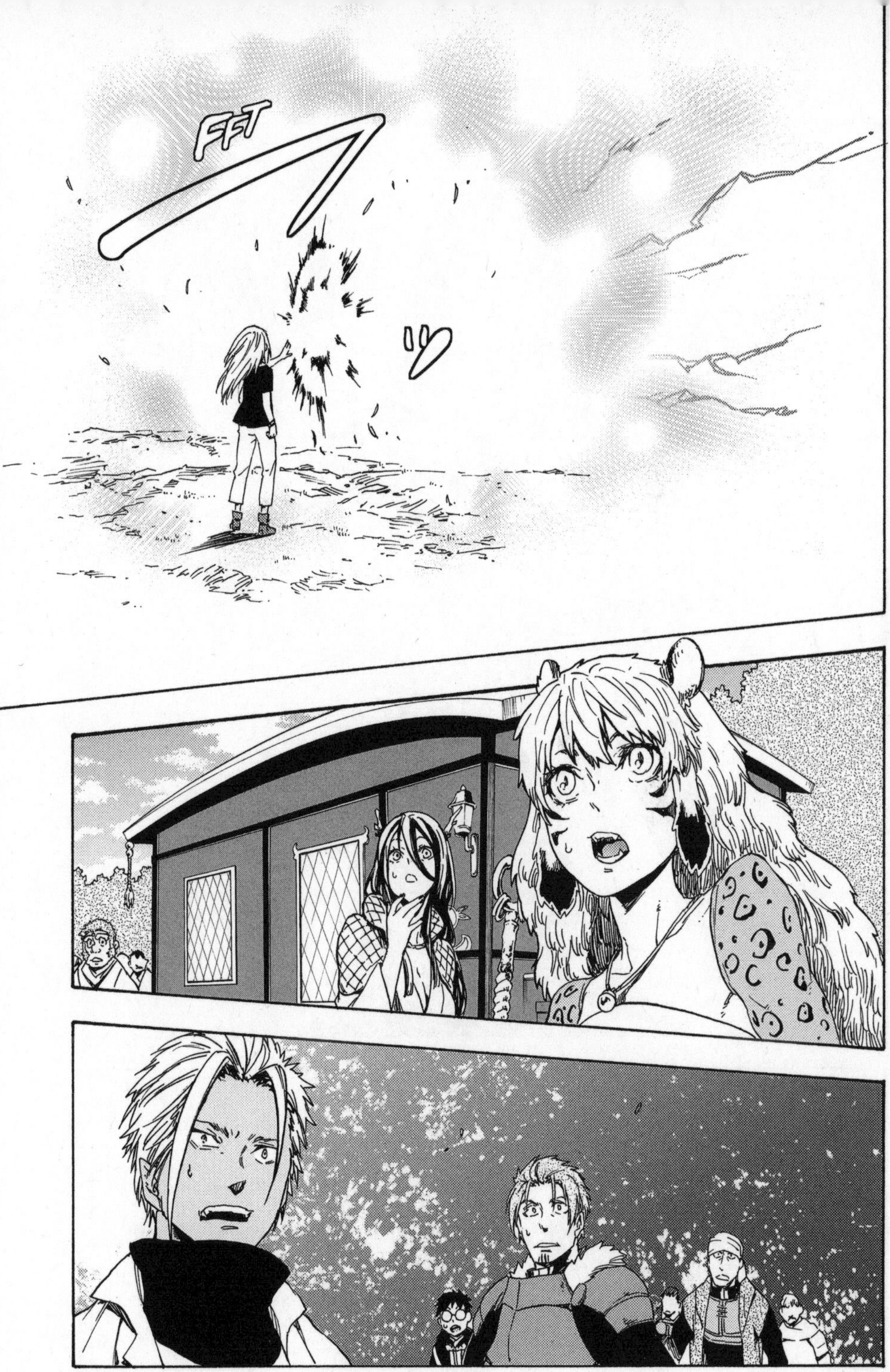
FFT

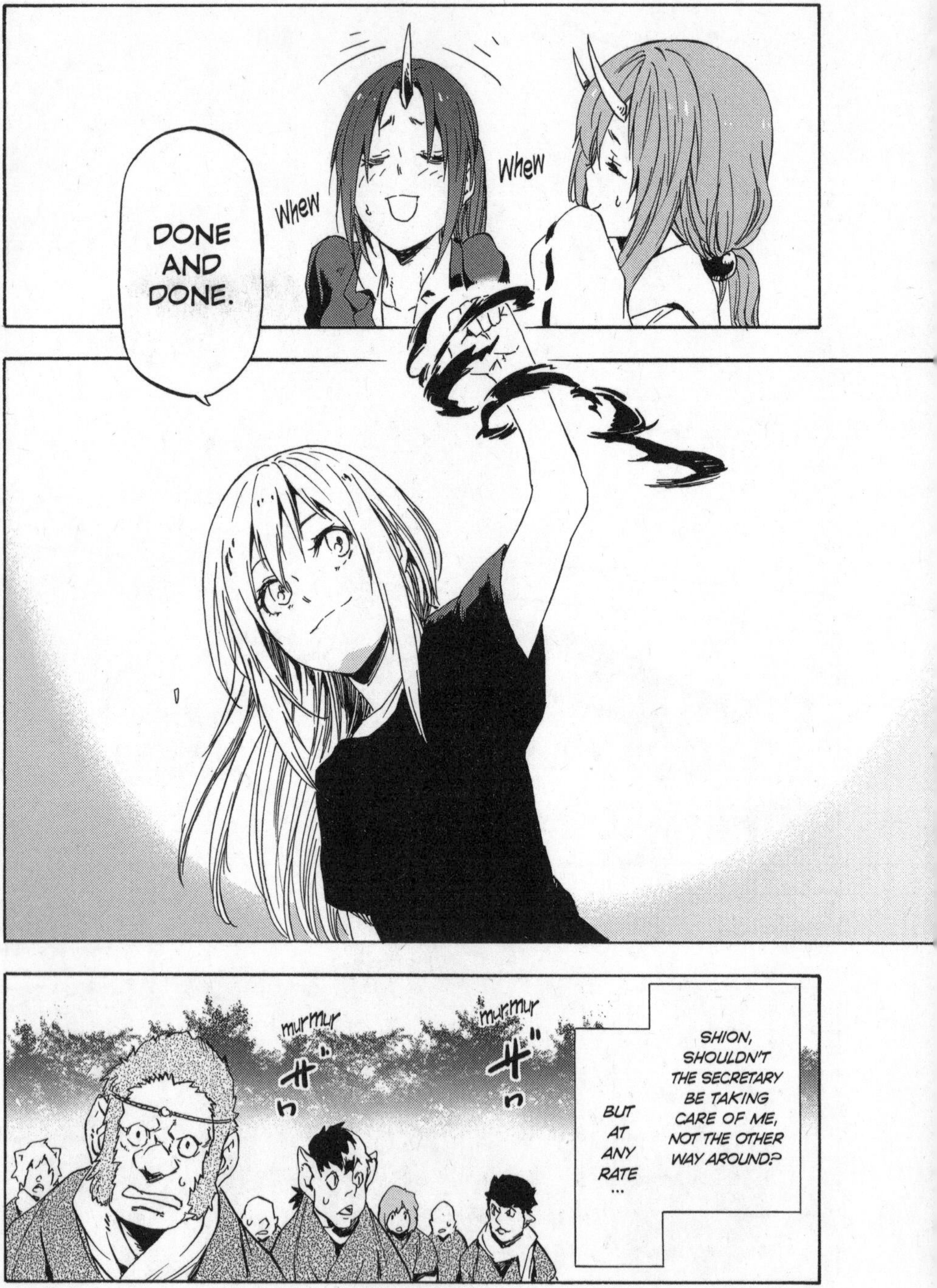
Whew
Whew
DONE AND DONE.
SHION, SHOULDN'T THE SECRETARY BE TAKING CARE OF ME, NOT THE OTHER WAY AROUND?
BUT AT ANY RATE ...
murmur
murmur

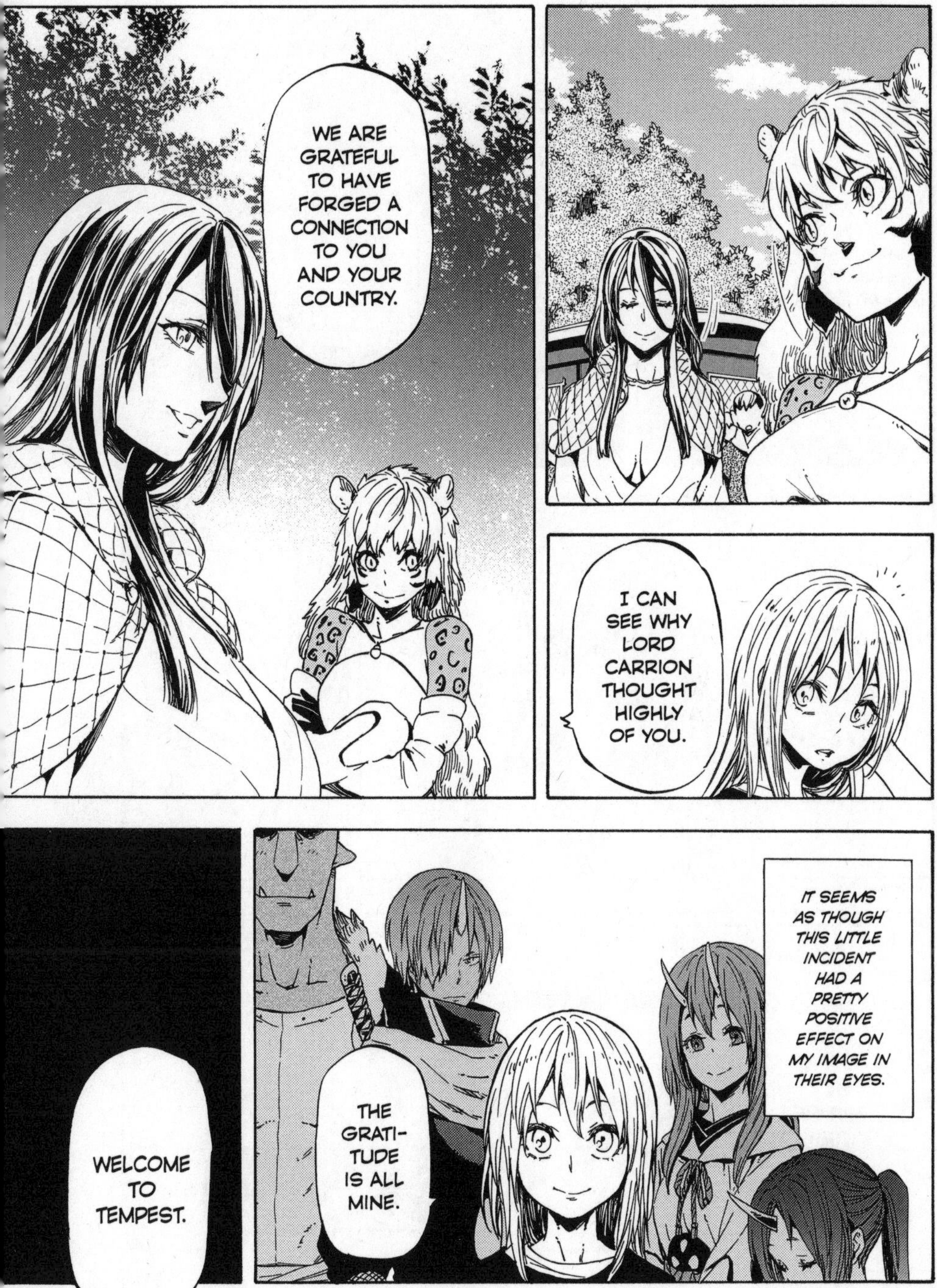
I CAN SEE WHY LORD CARRION THOUGHT HIGHLY OF YOU.
WE ARE GRATEFUL TO HAVE FORGED A CONNECTION TO YOU AND YOUR COUNTRY.
IT SEEMS AS THOUGH THIS LITTLE INCIDENT HAD A PRETTY POSITIVE EFFECT ON MY IMAGE IN THEIR EYES.
THE GRATI-TUDE IS ALL MINE.
WELCOME TO TEMPEST.

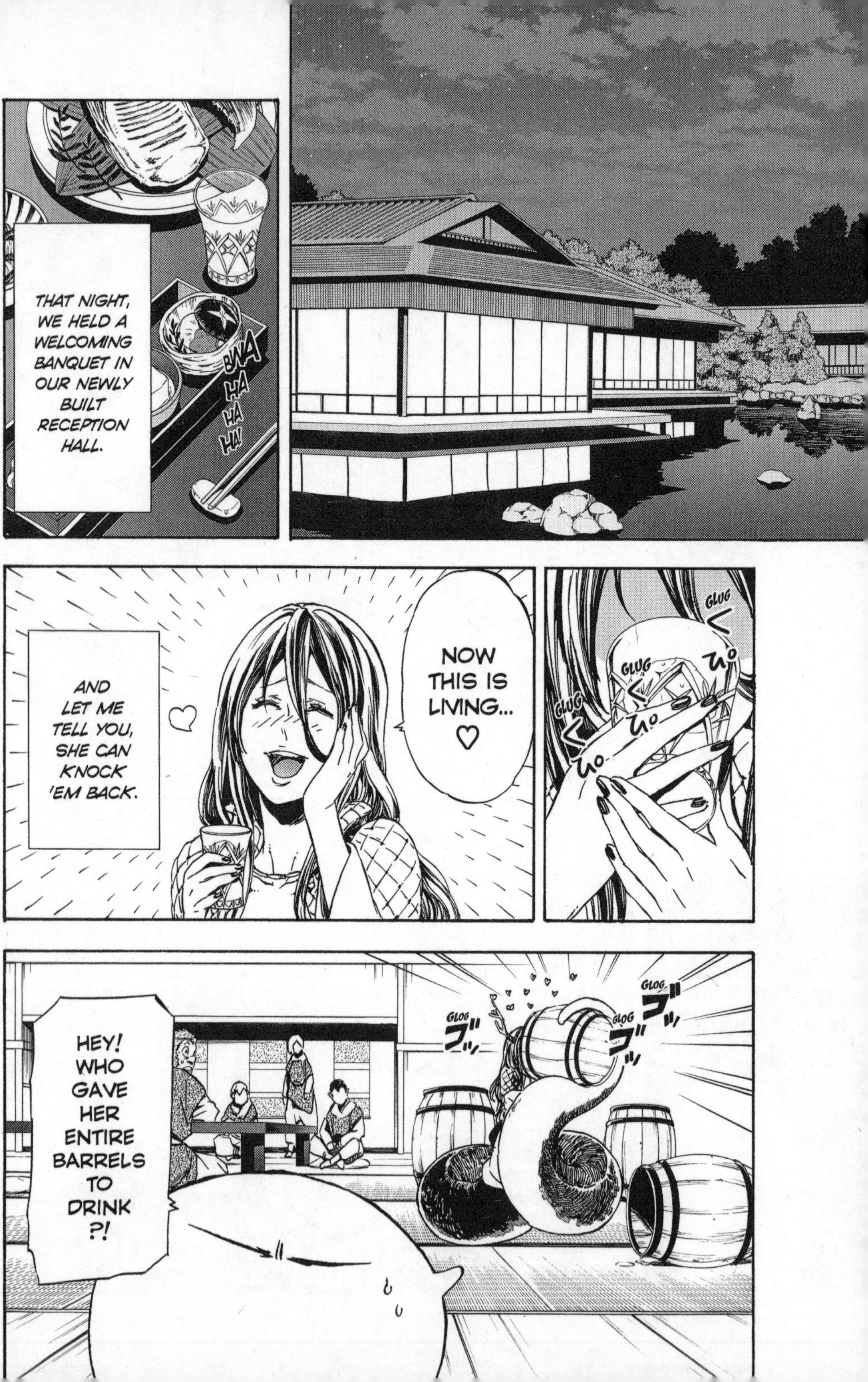
THAT NIGHT, WE HELD A WELCOMING BANQUET IN OUR NEWLY BUILT RECEPTION HALL.
BWA HA HA HA!
GLUG
GLUG
GLUG
NOW THIS IS LIVING... ♡
AND LET ME TELL YOU, SHE CAN KNOCK 'EM BACK.
GLOG
GLOG
GLOG
HEY! WHO GAVE HER ENTIRE BARRELS TO DRINK?!

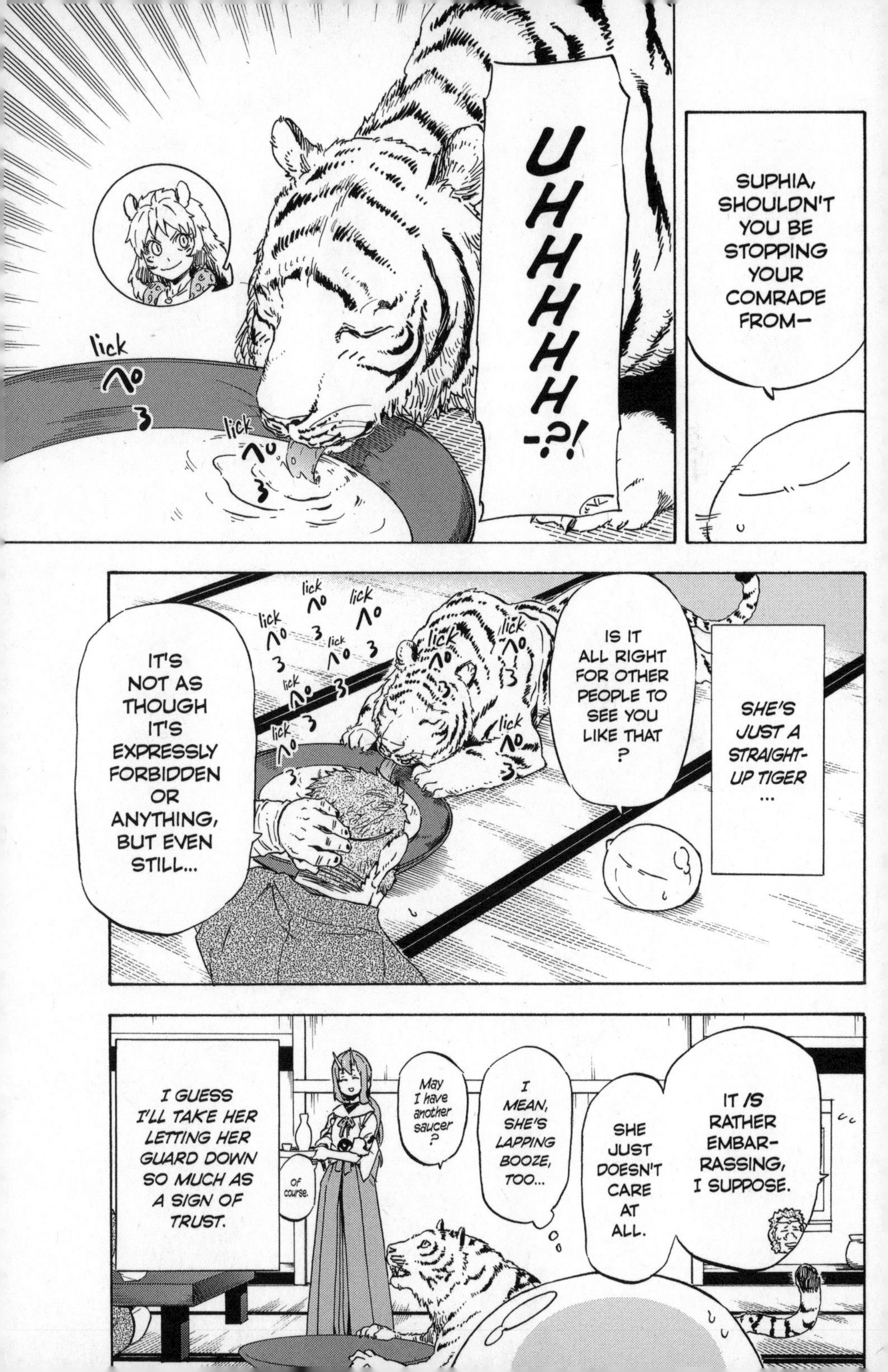
SUPHIA, SHOULDN'T YOU BE STOPPING YOUR COMRADE FROM—
UHHHHHH-?!
lick
lick
SHE'S JUST A STRAIGHT-UP TIGER...
IS IT ALL RIGHT FOR OTHER PEOPLE TO SEE YOU LIKE THAT?
lick
lick
lick
lick
lick
lick
lick
lick
IT'S NOT AS THOUGH IT'S EXPRESSLY FORBIDDEN OR ANYTHING, BUT EVEN STILL...
IT IS RATHER EMBARRASSING, I SUPPOSE.
SHE JUST DOESN'T CARE AT ALL.
I MEAN, SHE'S LAPPING BOOZE, TOO...
May I have another saucer?
Of course.
I GUESS I'LL TAKE HER LETTING HER GUARD DOWN SO MUCH AS A SIGN OF TRUST.

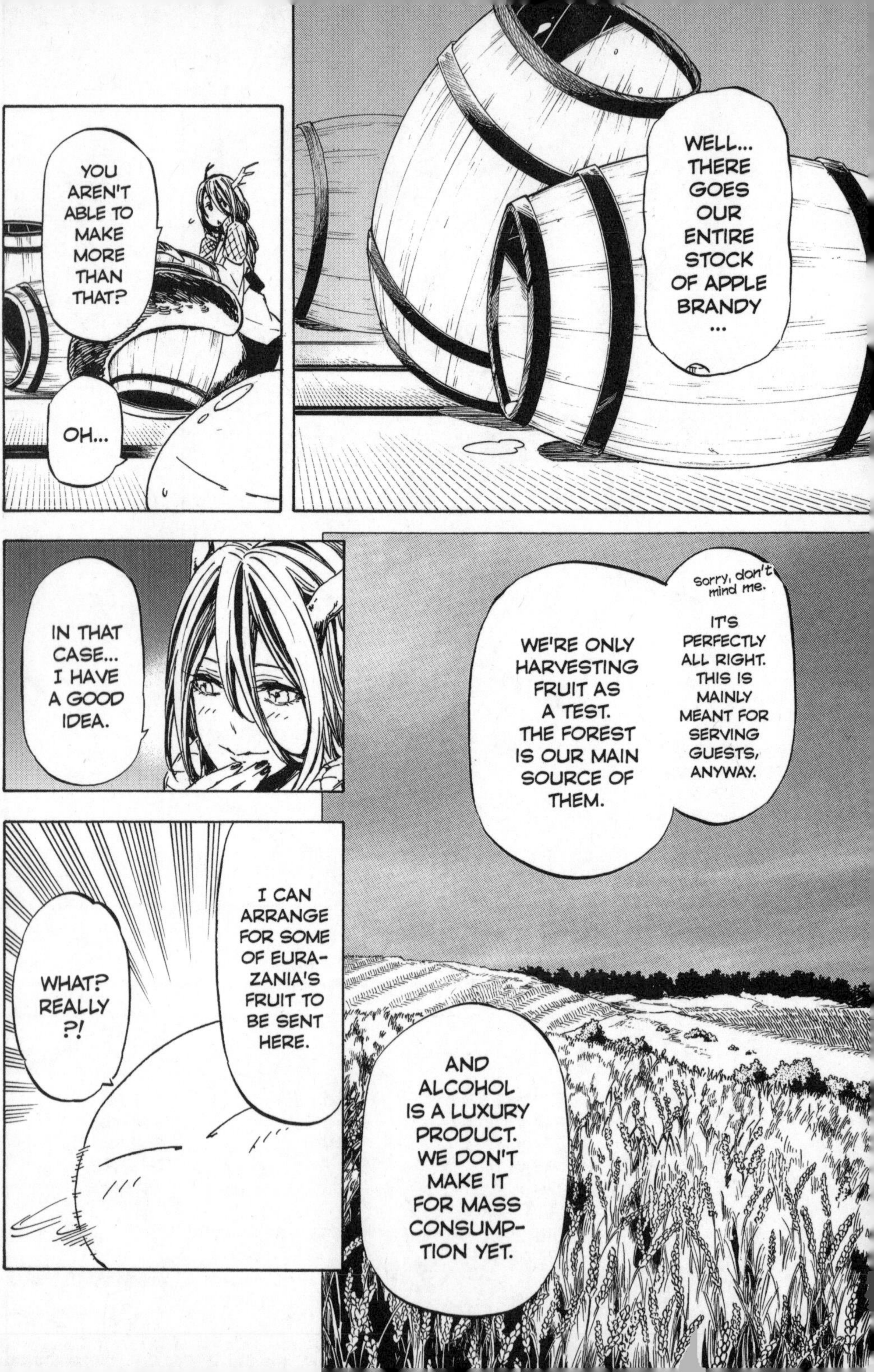
WELL... THERE GOES OUR ENTIRE STOCK OF APPLE BRANDY ...
YOU AREN'T ABLE TO MAKE MORE THAN THAT?
OH...
Sorry, don't mind me.
IT'S PERFECTLY ALL RIGHT. THIS IS MAINLY MEANT FOR SERVING GUESTS, ANYWAY.
WE'RE ONLY HARVESTING FRUIT AS A TEST. THE FOREST IS OUR MAIN SOURCE OF THEM.
AND ALCOHOL IS A LUXURY PRODUCT. WE DON'T MAKE IT FOR MASS CONSUMPTION YET.
IN THAT CASE... I HAVE A GOOD IDEA.
I CAN ARRANGE FOR SOME OF EURAZANIA'S FRUIT TO BE SENT HERE.
WHAT? REALLY ?!

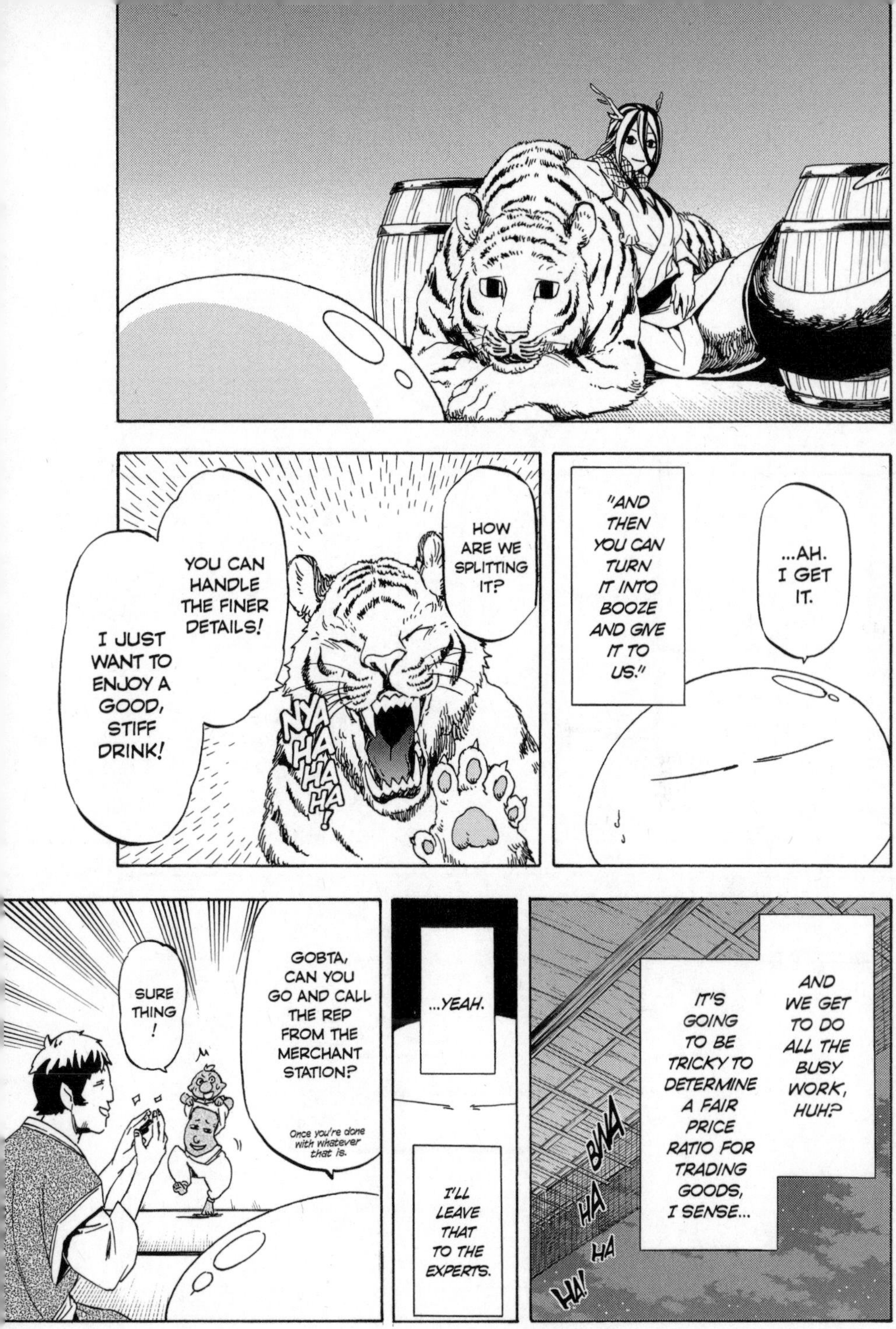
...AH. I GET IT.
"AND THEN YOU CAN TURN IT INTO BOOZE AND GIVE IT TO US."
HOW ARE WE SPLITTING IT?
YOU CAN HANDLE THE FINER DETAILS!
I JUST WANT TO ENJOY A GOOD, STIFF DRINK!
NYAHAHAHAHA!
AND WE GET TO DO ALL THE BUSY WORK, HUH?
IT'S GOING TO BE TRICKY TO DETERMINE A FAIR PRICE RATIO FOR TRADING GOODS, I SENSE...
BWAHAHAHA!
...YEAH.
I'LL LEAVE THAT TO THE EXPERTS.
GOBTA, CAN YOU GO AND CALL THE REP FROM THE MERCHANT STATION?
Once you're done with whatever that is.
SURE THING!

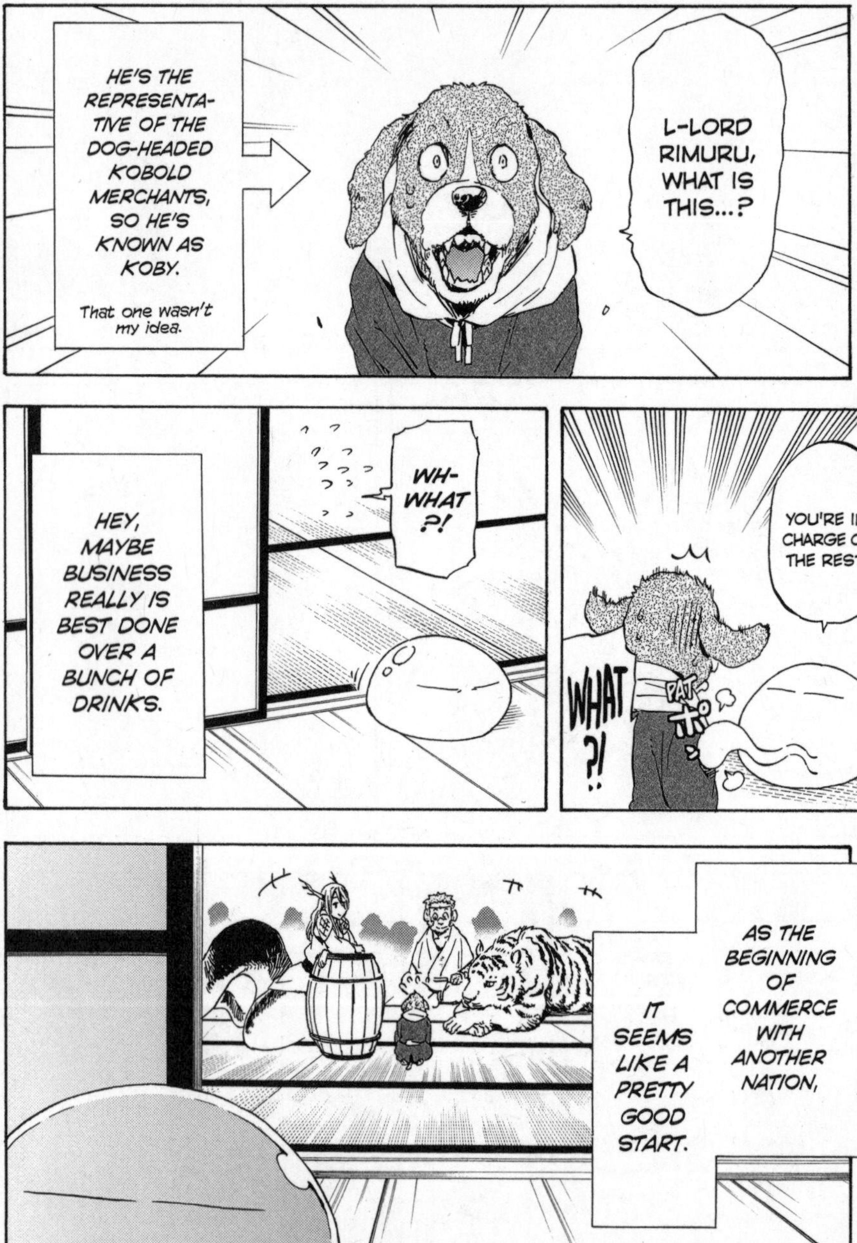
L-LORD RIMURU, WHAT IS THIS...?
HE'S THE REPRESENTATIVE OF THE DOG-HEADED KOBOLD MERCHANTS, SO HE'S KNOWN AS KOBY.
That one wasn't my idea.
YOU'RE IN CHARGE OF THE REST.
PAT
WHAT?!
WH-WHAT?!
HEY, MAYBE BUSINESS REALLY IS BEST DONE OVER A BUNCH OF DRINKS.
AS THE BEGINNING OF COMMERCE WITH ANOTHER NATION,
IT SEEMS LIKE A PRETTY GOOD START.

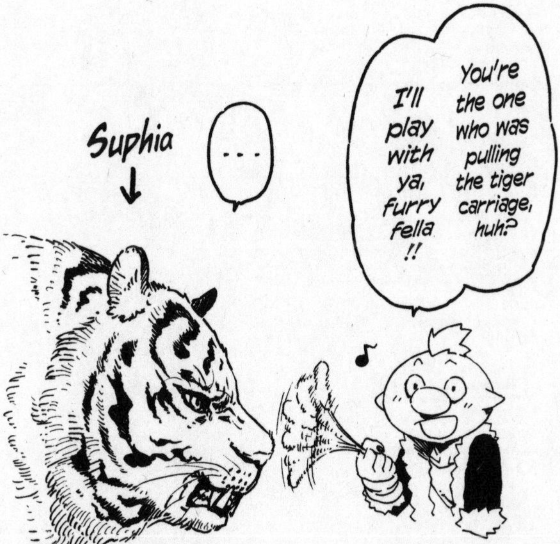
You're the one who was pulling the tiger carriage, huh?
I'll play with ya, furry fella!!
...
Suphia

CHAPTER 41 King Gazel's Invitation (Part One)

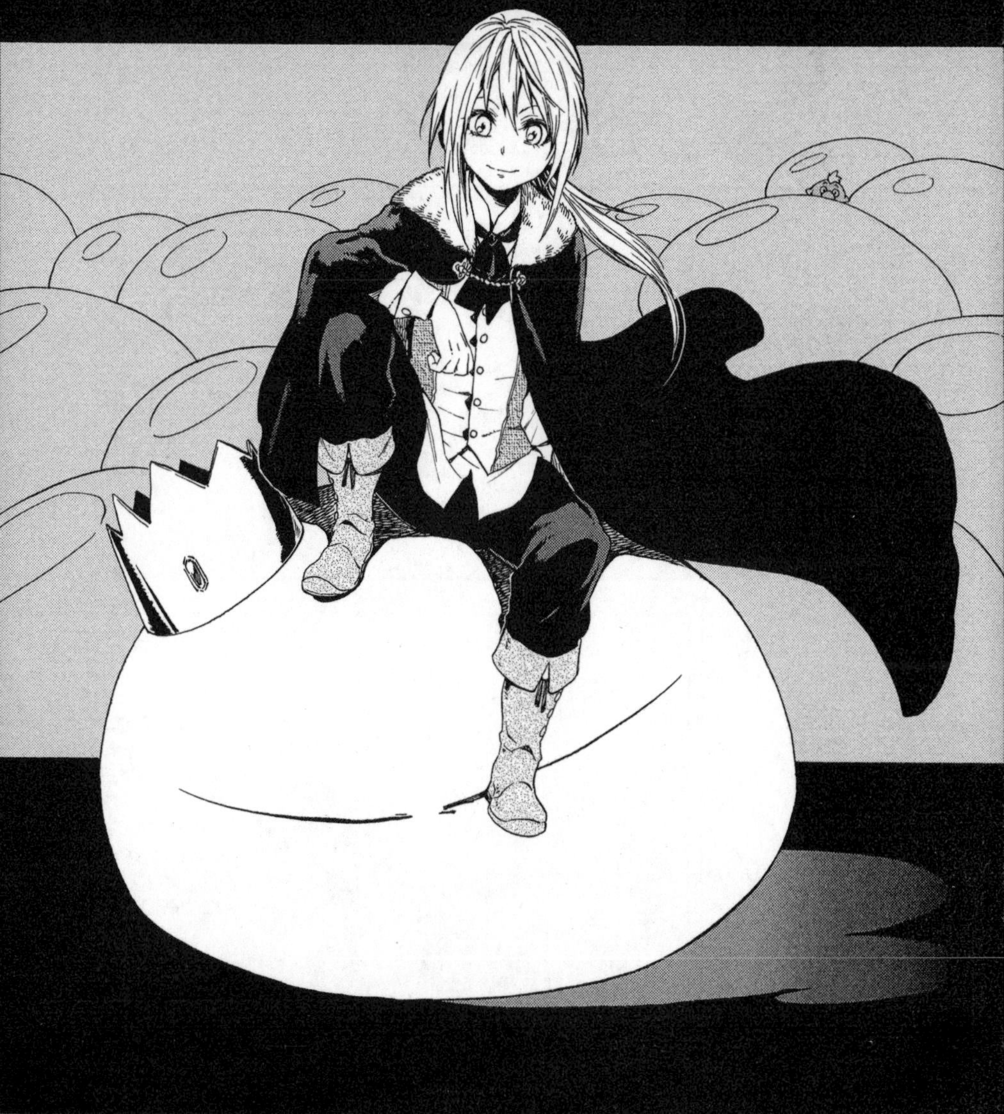

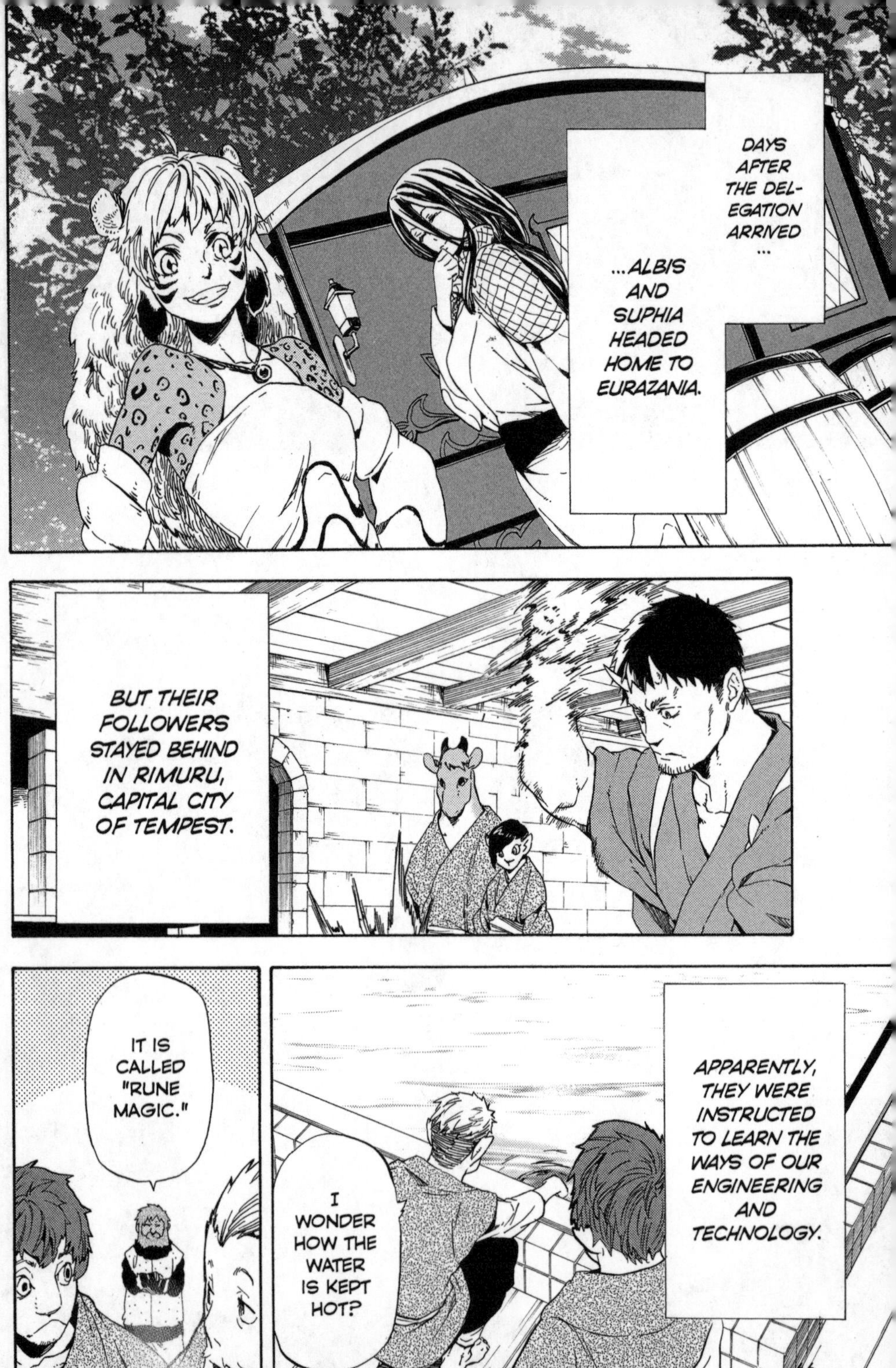
DAYS AFTER THE DEL-EGATION ARRIVED ...
...ALBIS AND SUPHIA HEADED HOME TO EURAZANIA.
BUT THEIR FOLLOWERS STAYED BEHIND IN RIMURU, CAPITAL CITY OF TEMPEST.
APPARENTLY, THEY WERE INSTRUCTED TO LEARN THE WAYS OF OUR ENGINEERING AND TECHNOLOGY.
I WONDER HOW THE WATER IS KEPT HOT?
IT IS CALLED "RUNE MAGIC."

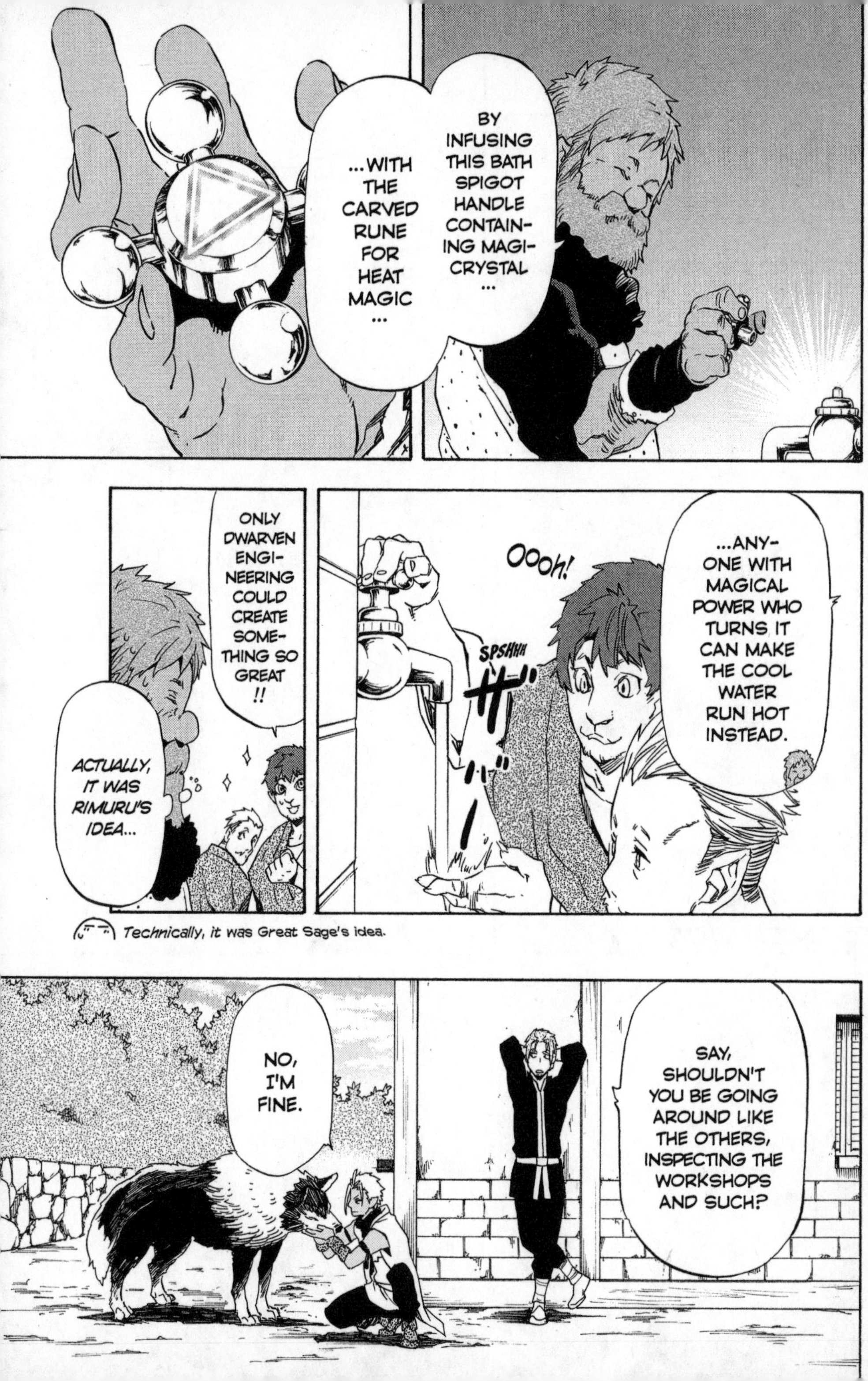
BY INFUSING THIS BATH SPIGOT HANDLE CONTAINING MAGI-CRYSTAL...
...WITH THE CARVED RUNE FOR HEAT MAGIC...
...ANY-ONE WITH MAGICAL POWER WHO TURNS IT CAN MAKE THE COOL WATER RUN HOT INSTEAD.
Oooh!
SPSHHH
ONLY DWARVEN ENGI-NEERING COULD CREATE SOME-THING SO GREAT!!
ACTUALLY, IT WAS RIMURU'S IDEA...
Technically, it was Great Sage's idea.
SAY, SHOULDN'T YOU BE GOING AROUND LIKE THE OTHERS, INSPECTING THE WORKSHOPS AND SUCH?
NO, I'M FINE.

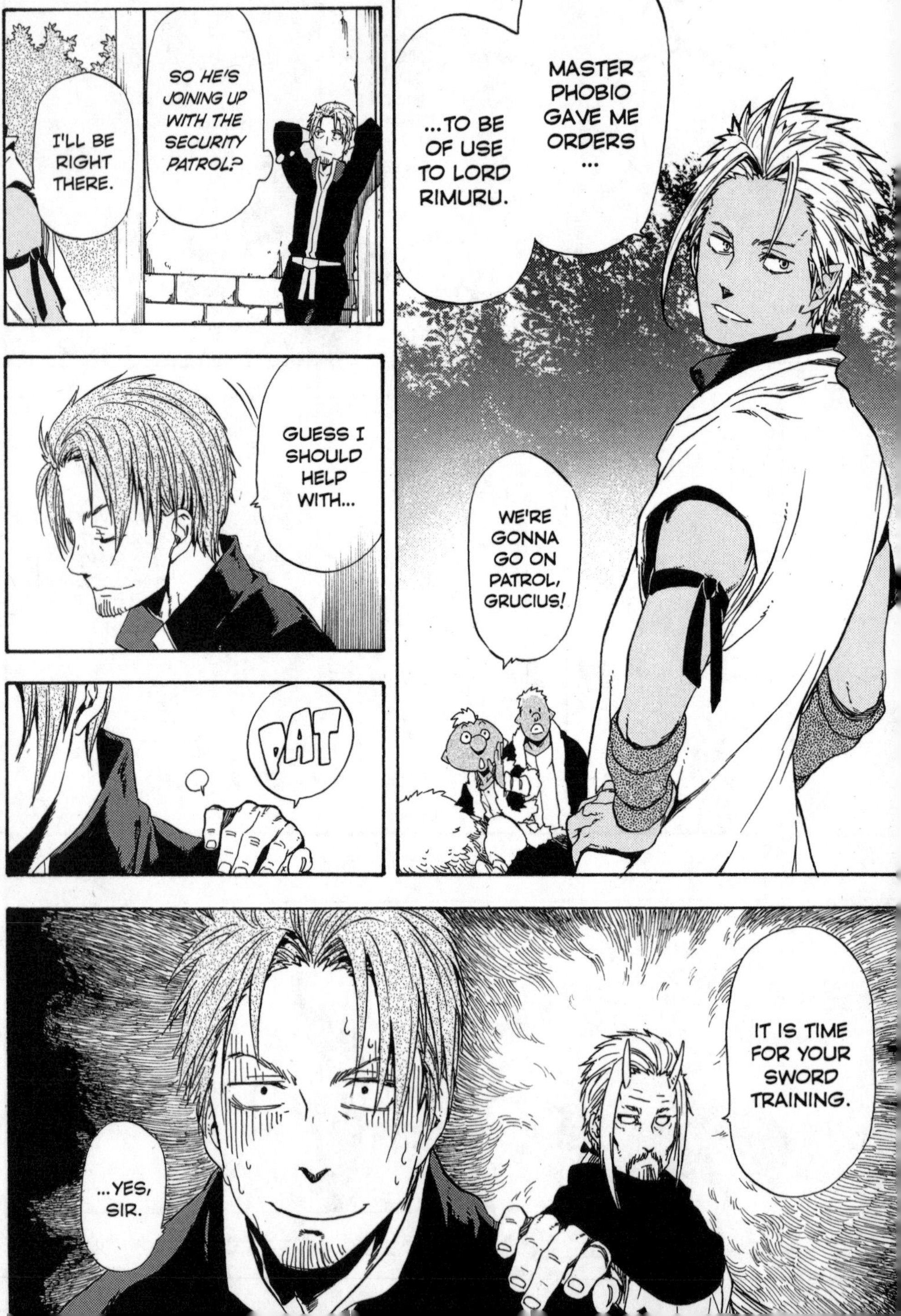
MASTER PHOBIO GAVE ME ORDERS ...
...TO BE OF USE TO LORD RIMURU.
WE'RE GONNA GO ON PATROL, GRUCIUS!
SO HE'S JOINING UP WITH THE SECURITY PATROL?
I'LL BE RIGHT THERE.
GUESS I SHOULD HELP WITH...
PAT
IT IS TIME FOR YOUR SWORD TRAINING.
...YES, SIR.

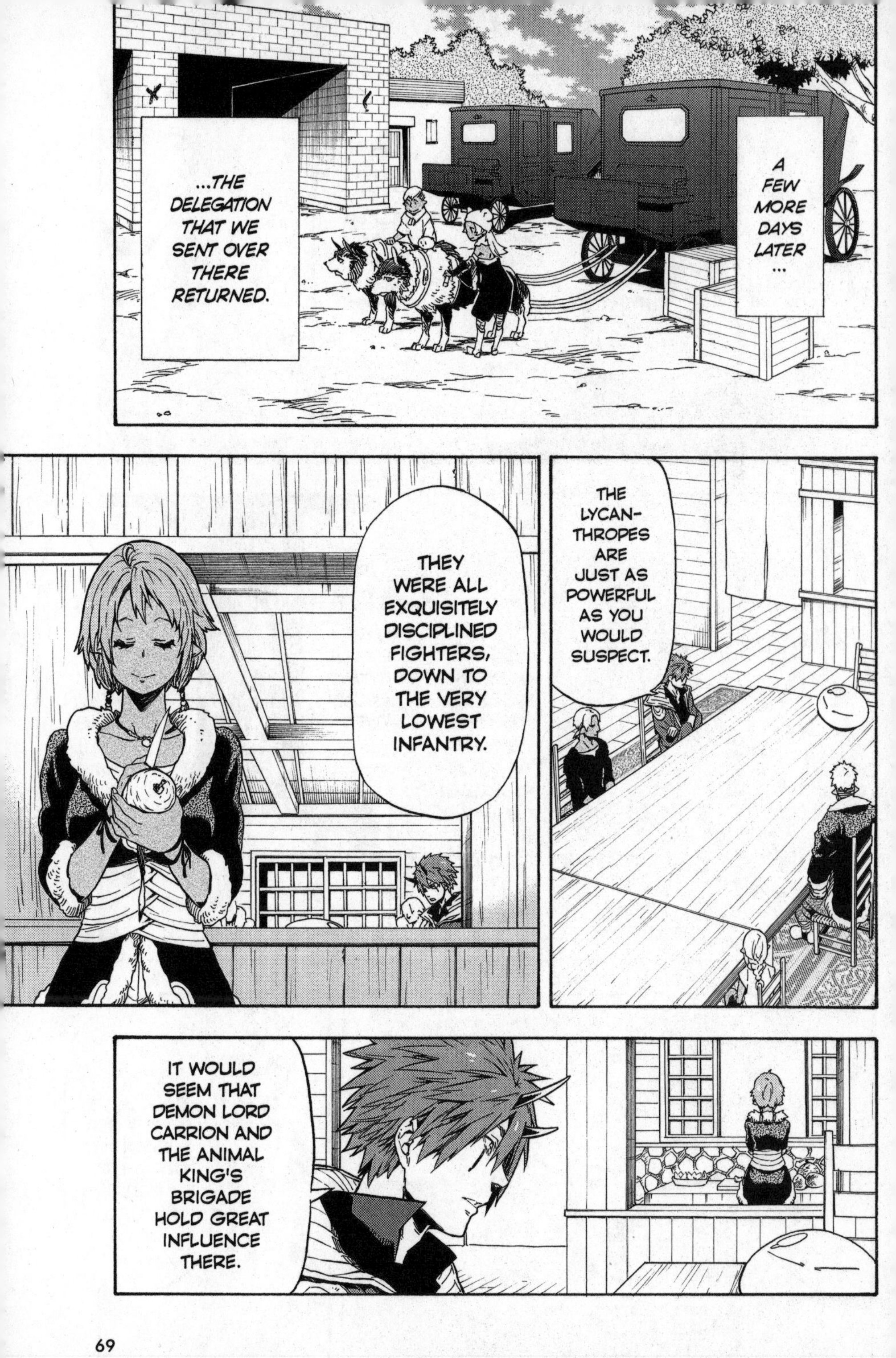
A FEW MORE DAYS LATER ...
...THE DELEGATION THAT WE SENT OVER THERE RETURNED.
THE LYCAN-THROPES ARE JUST AS POWERFUL AS YOU WOULD SUSPECT.
THEY WERE ALL EXQUISITELY DISCIPLINED FIGHTERS, DOWN TO THE VERY LOWEST INFANTRY.
IT WOULD SEEM THAT DEMON LORD CARRION AND THE ANIMAL KING'S BRIGADE HOLD GREAT INFLUENCE THERE.

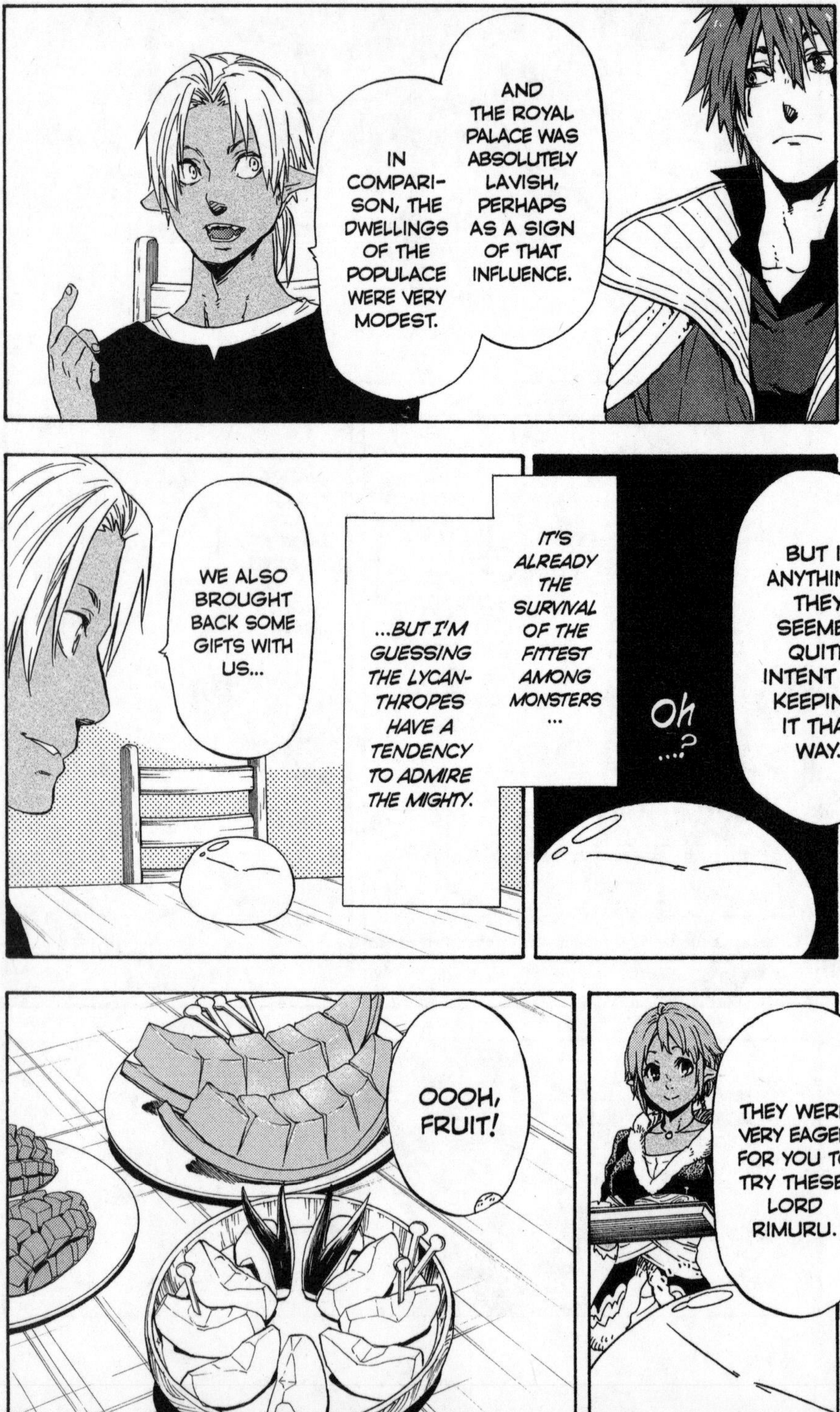
AND THE ROYAL PALACE WAS ABSOLUTELY LAVISH, PERHAPS AS A SIGN OF THAT INFLUENCE.
IN COMPARISON, THE DWELLINGS OF THE POPULACE WERE VERY MODEST.
BUT IF ANYTHING, THEY SEEMED QUITE INTENT ON KEEPING IT THAT WAY.
Oh ...?
IT'S ALREADY THE SURVIVAL OF THE FITTEST AMONG MONSTERS ...
...BUT I'M GUESSING THE LYCANTHROPES HAVE A TENDENCY TO ADMIRE THE MIGHTY.
WE ALSO BROUGHT BACK SOME GIFTS WITH US...
THEY WERE VERY EAGER FOR YOU TO TRY THESE, LORD RIMURU.
OOOH, FRUIT!

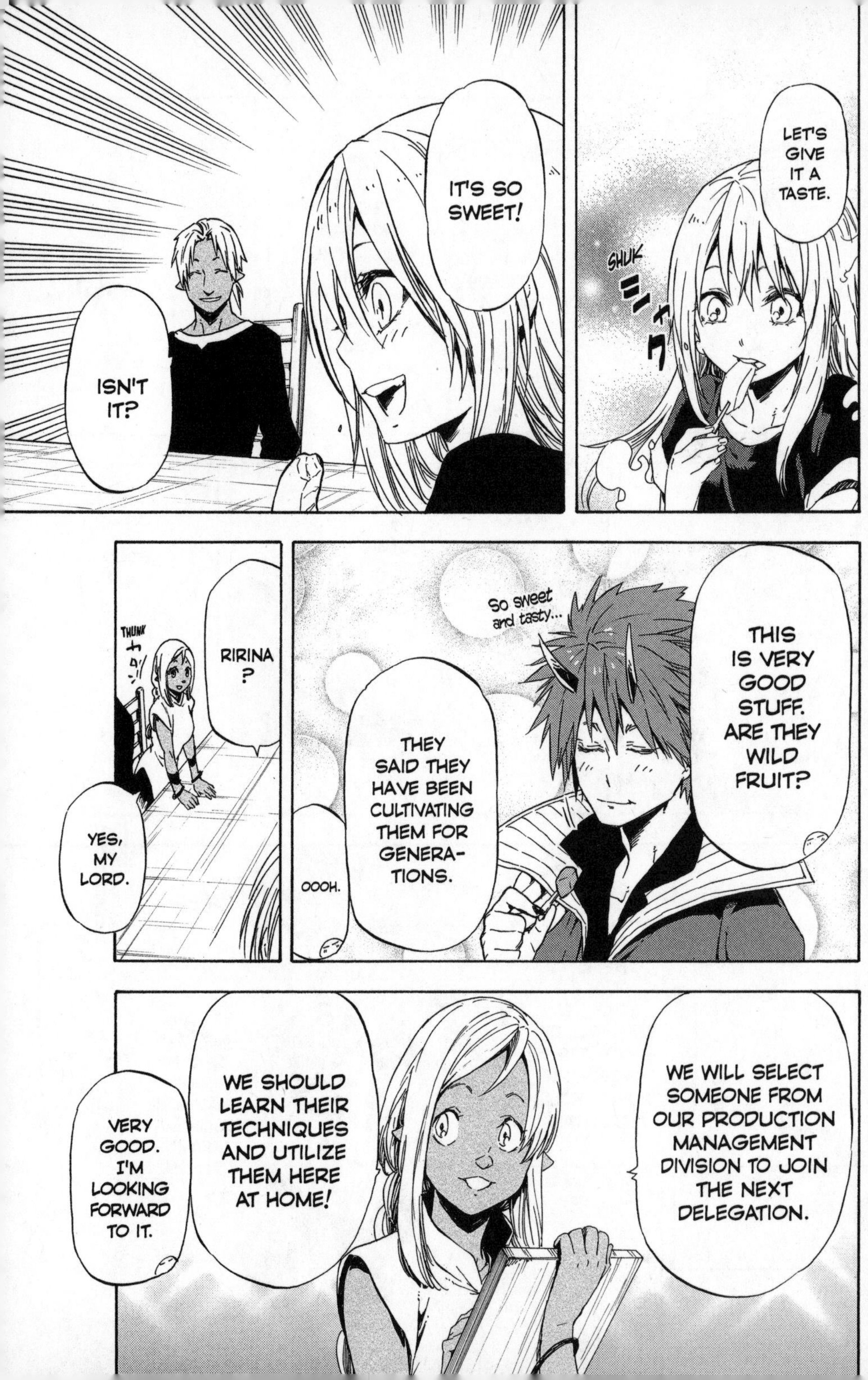
LET'S GIVE IT A TASTE.
SHUK
IT'S SO SWEET!
ISN'T IT?
THIS IS VERY GOOD STUFF. ARE THEY WILD FRUIT?
So sweet and tasty...
THEY SAID THEY HAVE BEEN CULTIVATING THEM FOR GENERA-TIONS.
OOOH.
RIRINA?
THUNK
YES, MY LORD.
WE WILL SELECT SOMEONE FROM OUR PRODUCTION MANAGEMENT DIVISION TO JOIN THE NEXT DELEGATION.
WE SHOULD LEARN THEIR TECHNIQUES AND UTILIZE THEM HERE AT HOME!
VERY GOOD. I'M LOOKING FORWARD TO IT.

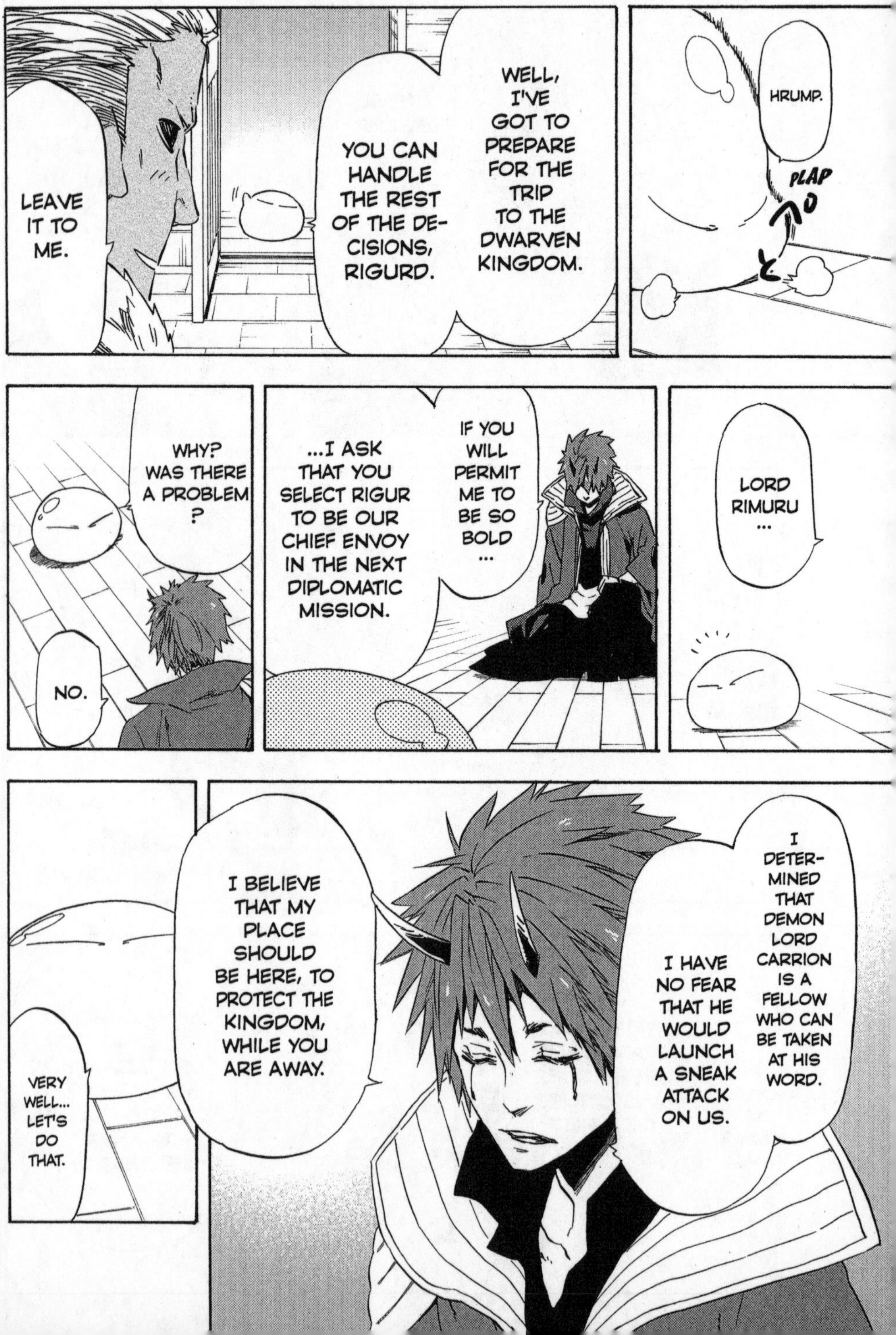
HRUMP.
PLAP
WELL, I'VE GOT TO PREPARE FOR THE TRIP TO THE DWARVEN KINGDOM.
YOU CAN HANDLE THE REST OF THE DE-CISIONS, RIGURD.
LEAVE IT TO ME.
LORD RIMURU...
IF YOU WILL PERMIT ME TO BE SO BOLD...
...I ASK THAT YOU SELECT RIGUR TO BE OUR CHIEF ENVOY IN THE NEXT DIPLOMATIC MISSION.
WHY? WAS THERE A PROBLEM?
NO.
I DETER-MINED THAT DEMON LORD CARRION IS A FELLOW WHO CAN BE TAKEN AT HIS WORD.
I HAVE NO FEAR THAT HE WOULD LAUNCH A SNEAK ATTACK ON US.
I BELIEVE THAT MY PLACE SHOULD BE HERE, TO PROTECT THE KINGDOM, WHILE YOU ARE AWAY.
VERY WELL... LET'S DO THAT.

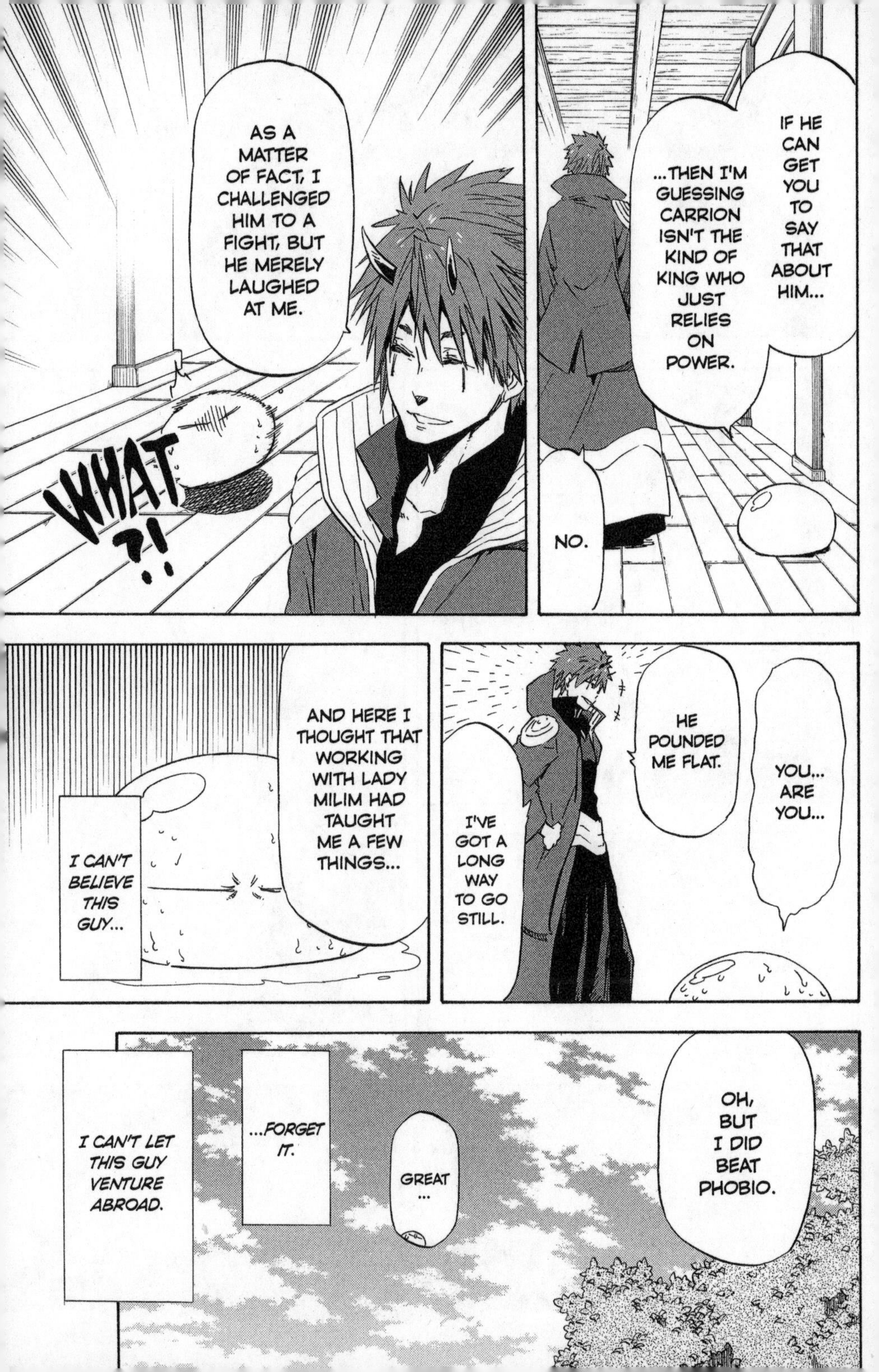
IF HE CAN GET YOU TO SAY THAT ABOUT HIM...
...THEN I'M GUESSING CARRION ISN'T THE KIND OF KING WHO JUST RELIES ON POWER.
NO.
AS A MATTER OF FACT, I CHALLENGED HIM TO A FIGHT, BUT HE MERELY LAUGHED AT ME.
WHAT ?!
YOU... ARE YOU...
HE POUNDED ME FLAT.
I'VE GOT A LONG WAY TO GO STILL.
AND HERE I THOUGHT THAT WORKING WITH LADY MILIM HAD TAUGHT ME A FEW THINGS...
I CAN'T BELIEVE THIS GUY...
OH, BUT I DID BEAT PHOBIO.
GREAT ...
...FORGET IT.
I CAN'T LET THIS GUY VENTURE ABROAD.

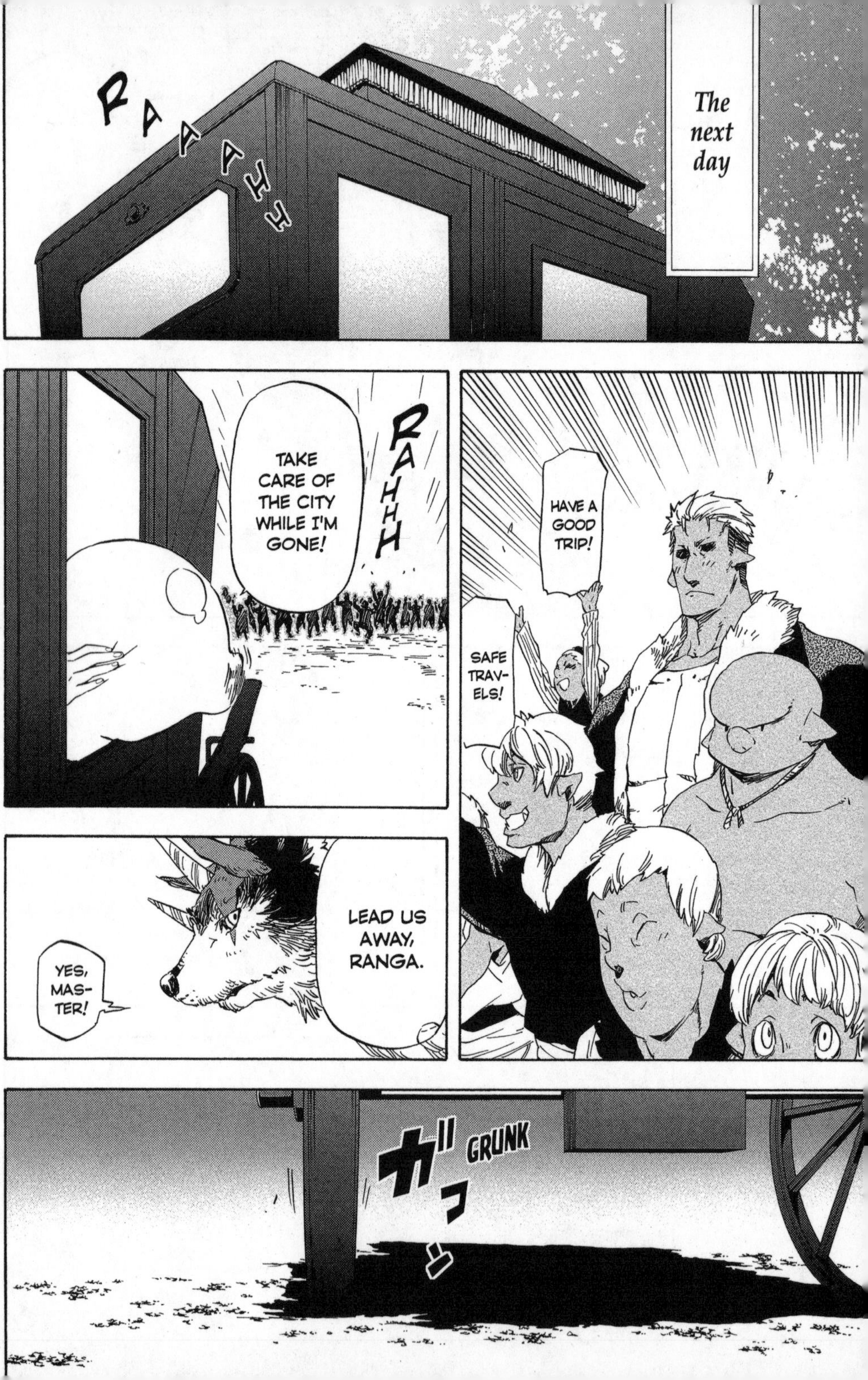
The next day
RAAAHH
HAVE A GOOD TRIP!
SAFE TRAVELS!
TAKE CARE OF THE CITY WHILE I'M GONE!
RAHHH
LEAD US AWAY, RANGA.
YES, MASTER!
ガッ
GRUNK

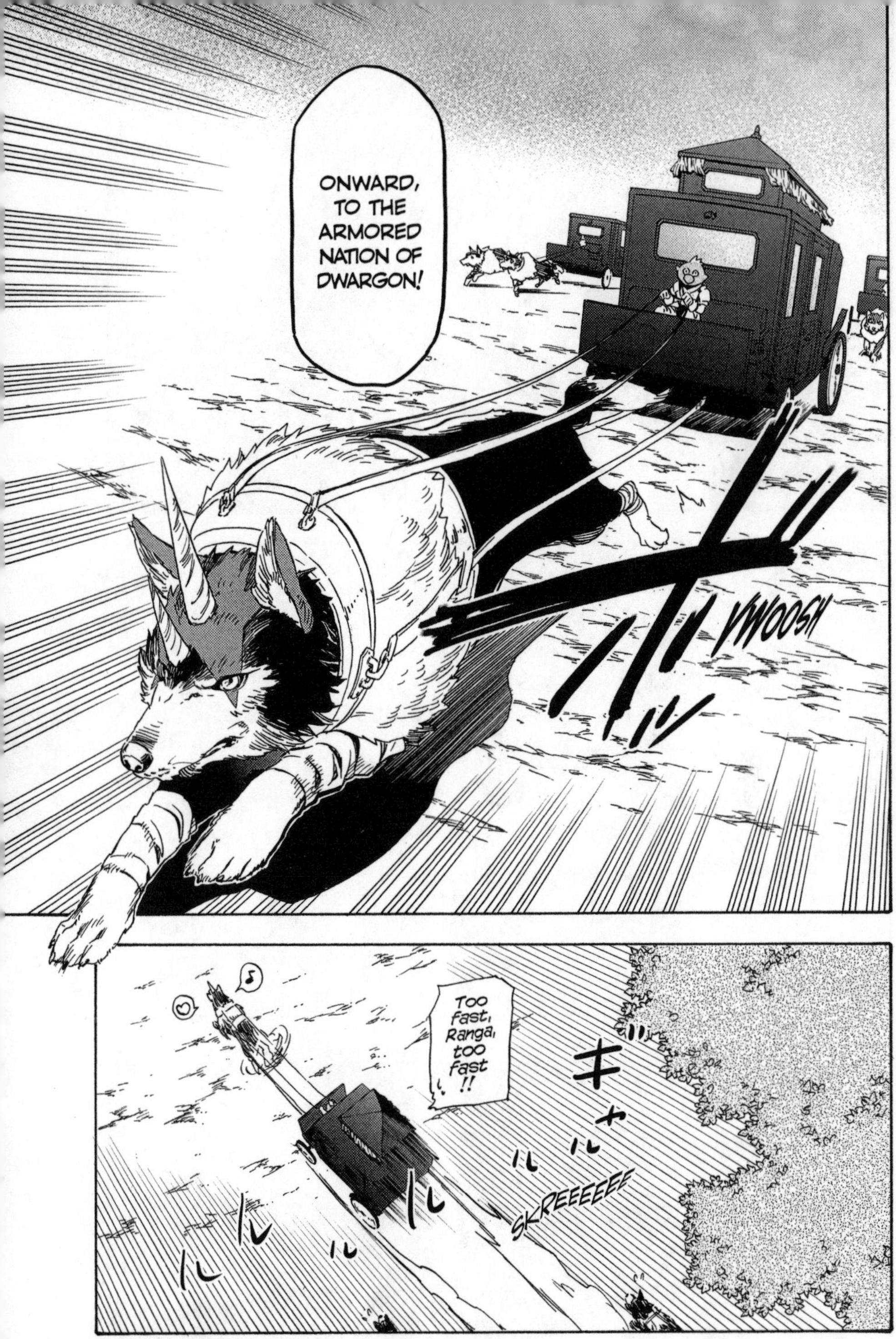
ONWARD, TO THE ARMORED NATION OF DWARGON!
VWOOSH
Too fast, Ranga, too fast!!
SKREEEEEEE

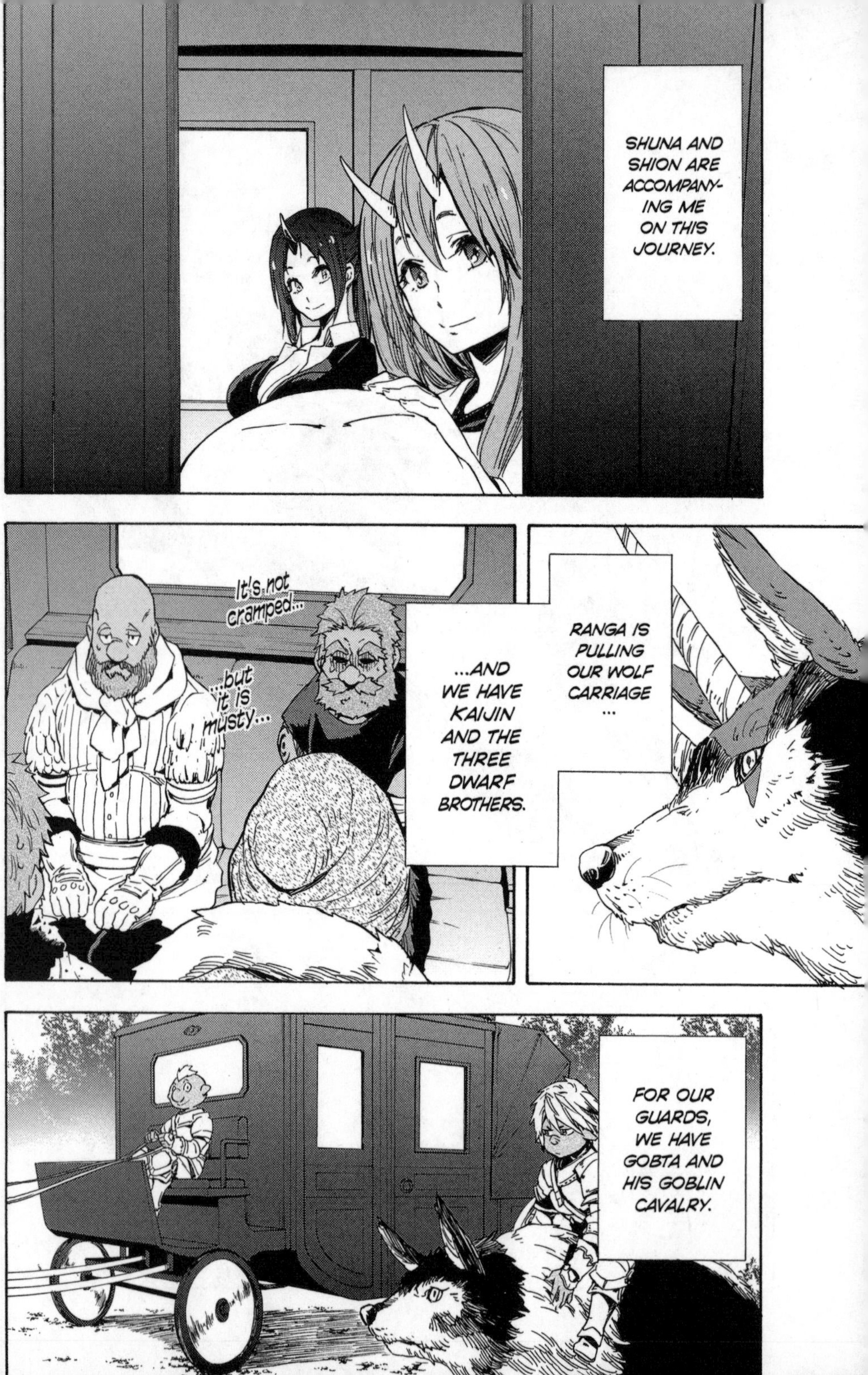
SHUNA AND SHION ARE ACCOMPANYING ME ON THIS JOURNEY.
RANGA IS PULLING OUR WOLF CARRIAGE ...
...AND WE HAVE KAIJIN AND THE THREE DWARF BROTHERS.
It's not cramped...
...but it is musty...
FOR OUR GUARDS, WE HAVE GOBTA AND HIS GOBLIN CAVALRY.

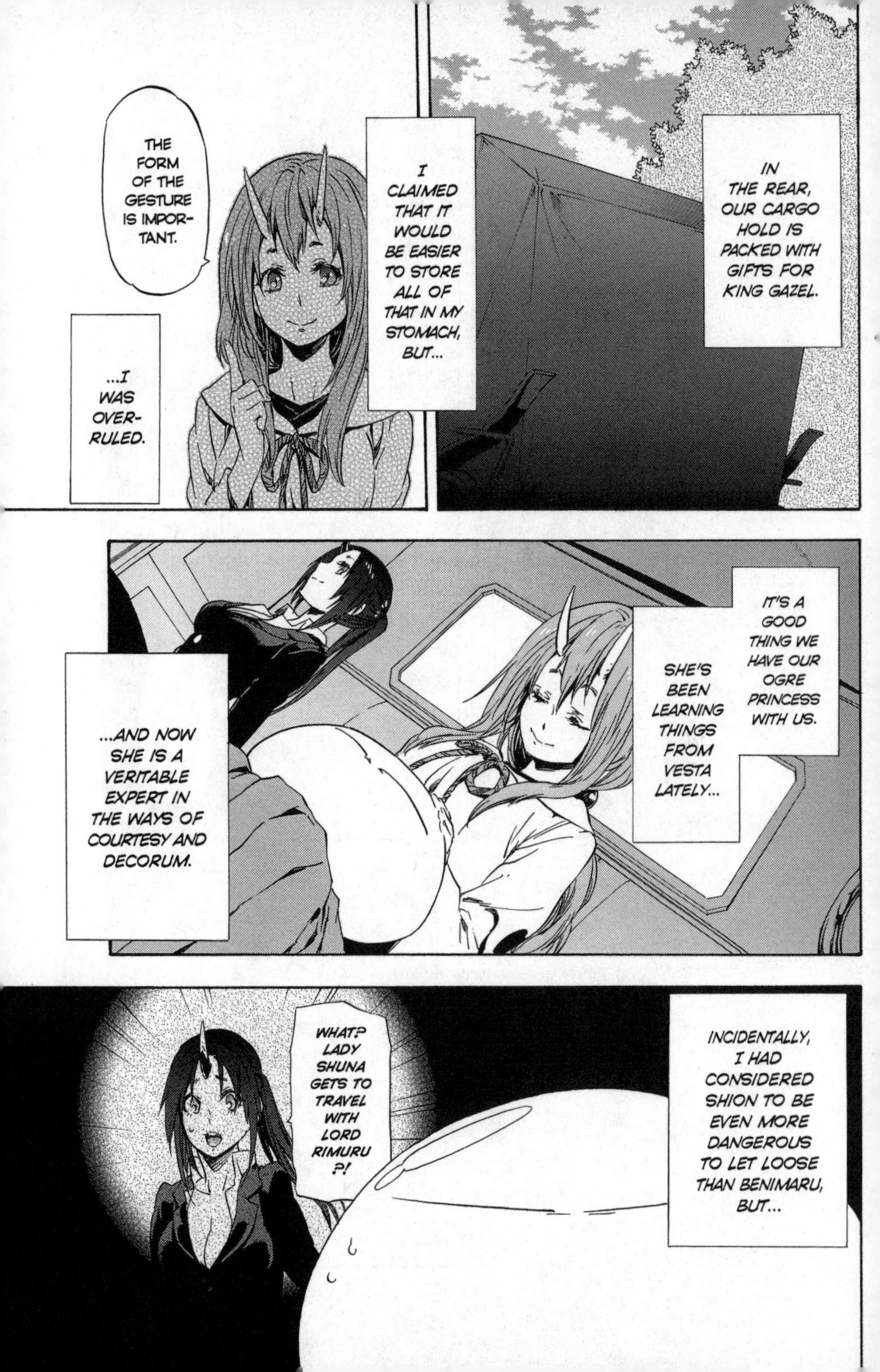
IN THE REAR, OUR CARGO HOLD IS PACKED WITH GIFTS FOR KING GAZEL.
I CLAIMED THAT IT WOULD BE EASIER TO STORE ALL OF THAT IN MY STOMACH, BUT...
THE FORM OF THE GESTURE IS IMPORTANT.
...I WAS OVERRULED.
IT'S A GOOD THING WE HAVE OUR OGRE PRINCESS WITH US.
SHE'S BEEN LEARNING THINGS FROM VESTA LATELY...
...AND NOW SHE IS A VERITABLE EXPERT IN THE WAYS OF COURTESY AND DECORUM.
INCIDENTALLY, I HAD CONSIDERED SHION TO BE EVEN MORE DANGEROUS TO LET LOOSE THAN BENIMARU, BUT...
WHAT? LADY SHUNA GETS TO TRAVEL WITH LORD RIMURU?!

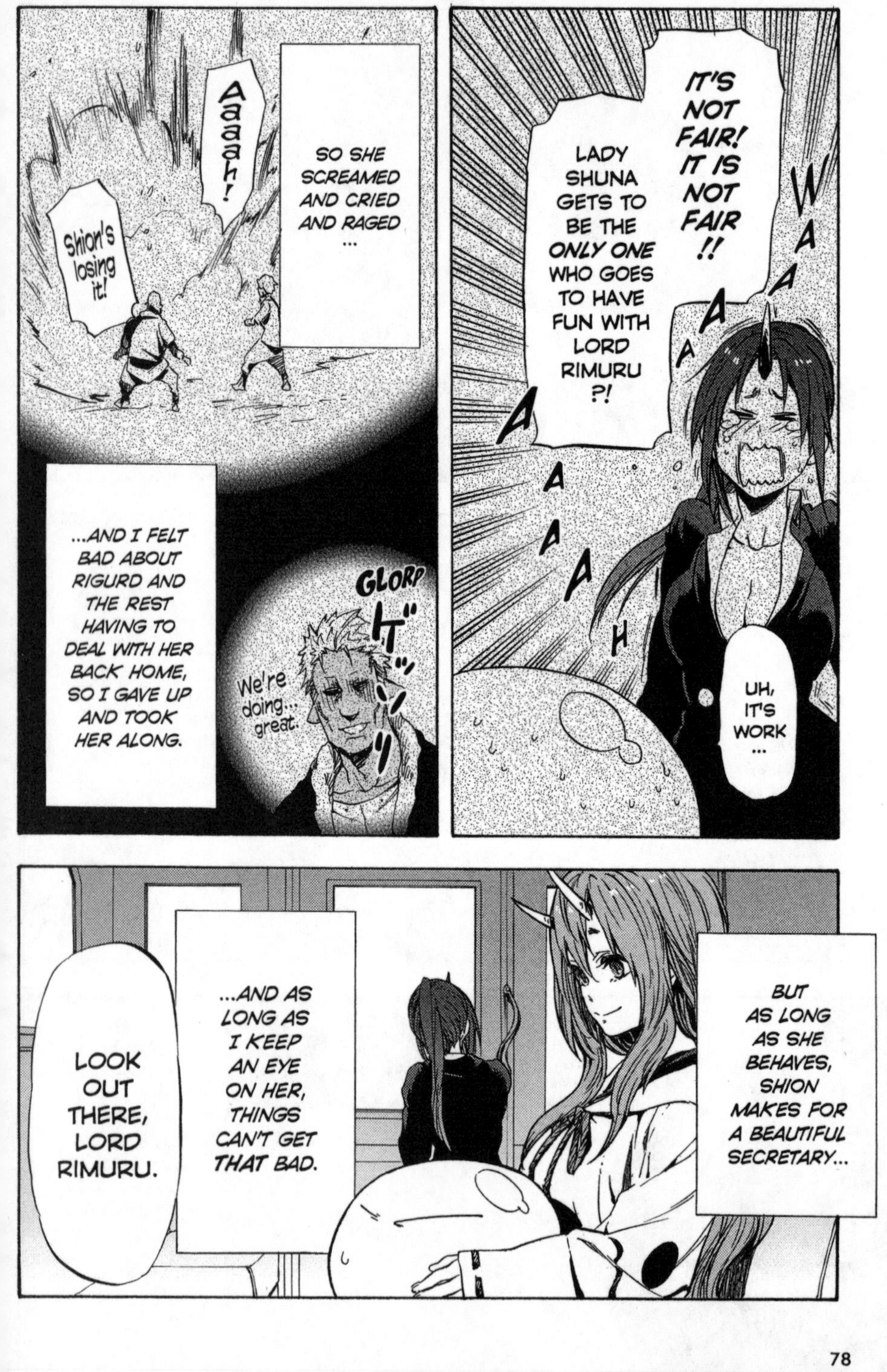
WAAAAAAAAH
IT'S NOT FAIR! IT IS NOT FAIR!!
LADY SHUNA GETS TO BE THE ONLY ONE WHO GOES TO HAVE FUN WITH LORD RIMURU ?!
UH, IT'S WORK ...
SO SHE SCREAMED AND CRIED AND RAGED ...
Aaaah!
Shion's losing it!
GLORP
We're doing... great.
...AND I FELT BAD ABOUT RIGURD AND THE REST HAVING TO DEAL WITH HER BACK HOME, SO I GAVE UP AND TOOK HER ALONG.
BUT AS LONG AS SHE BEHAVES, SHION MAKES FOR A BEAUTIFUL SECRETARY...
...AND AS LONG AS I KEEP AN EYE ON HER, THINGS CAN'T GET THAT BAD.
LOOK OUT THERE, LORD RIMURU.

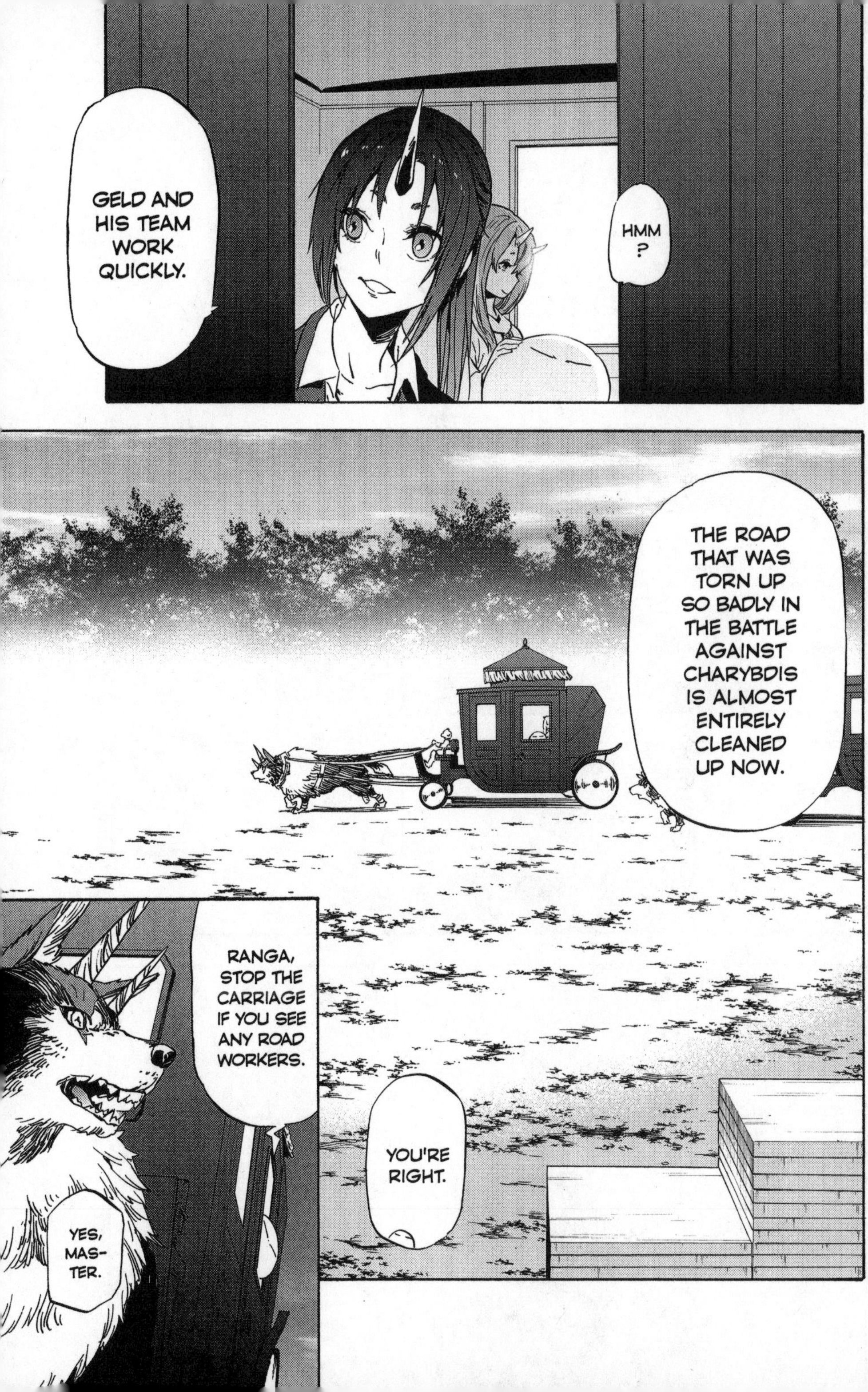
HMM ?
GELD AND HIS TEAM WORK QUICKLY.
THE ROAD THAT WAS TORN UP SO BADLY IN THE BATTLE AGAINST CHARYBDIS IS ALMOST ENTIRELY CLEANED UP NOW.
YOU'RE RIGHT.
RANGA, STOP THE CARRIAGE IF YOU SEE ANY ROAD WORKERS.
YES, MAS-TER.

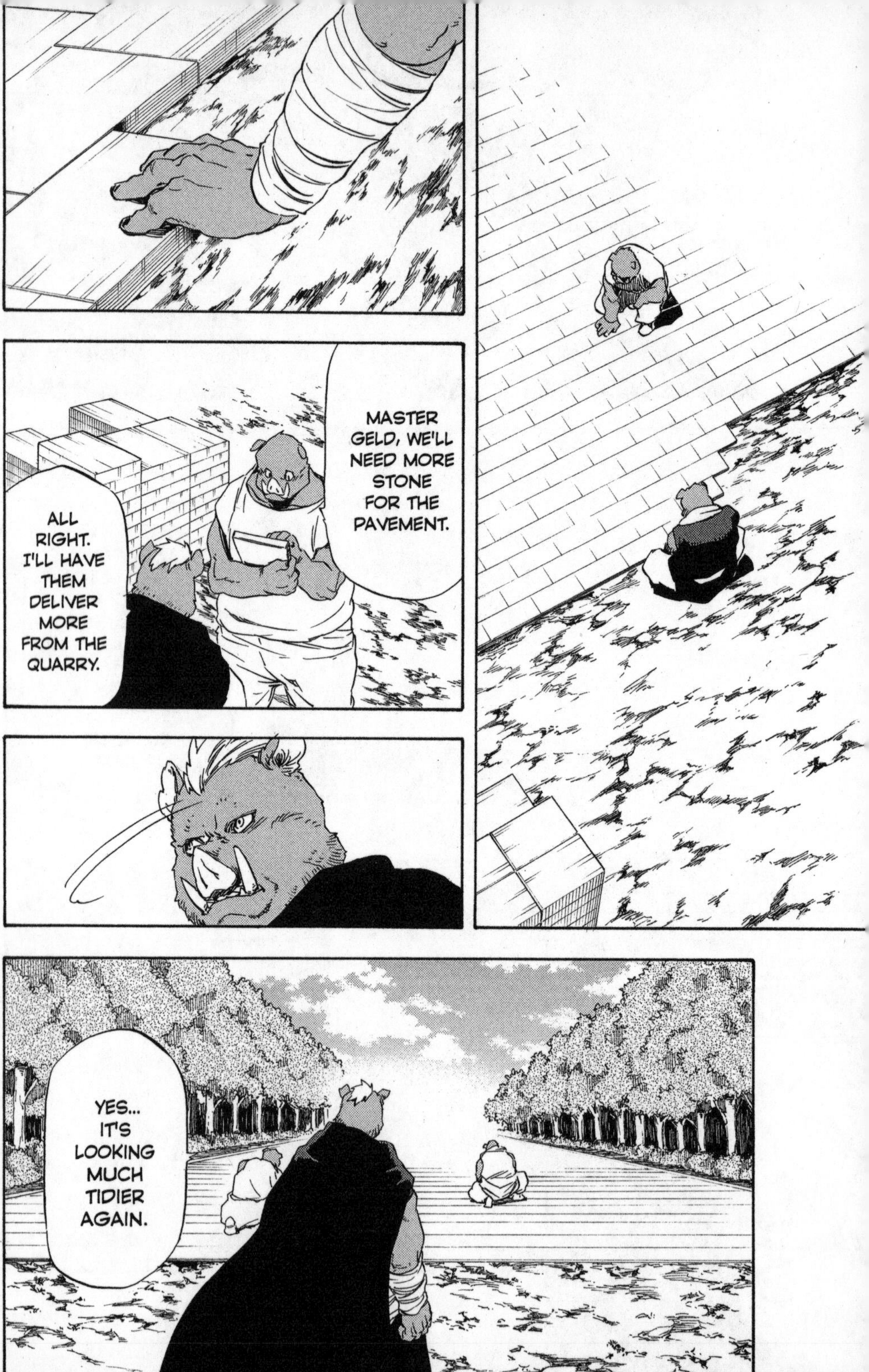
MASTER GELD, WE'LL NEED MORE STONE FOR THE PAVEMENT.
ALL RIGHT. I'LL HAVE THEM DELIVER MORE FROM THE QUARRY.
YES... IT'S LOOKING MUCH TIDIER AGAIN.

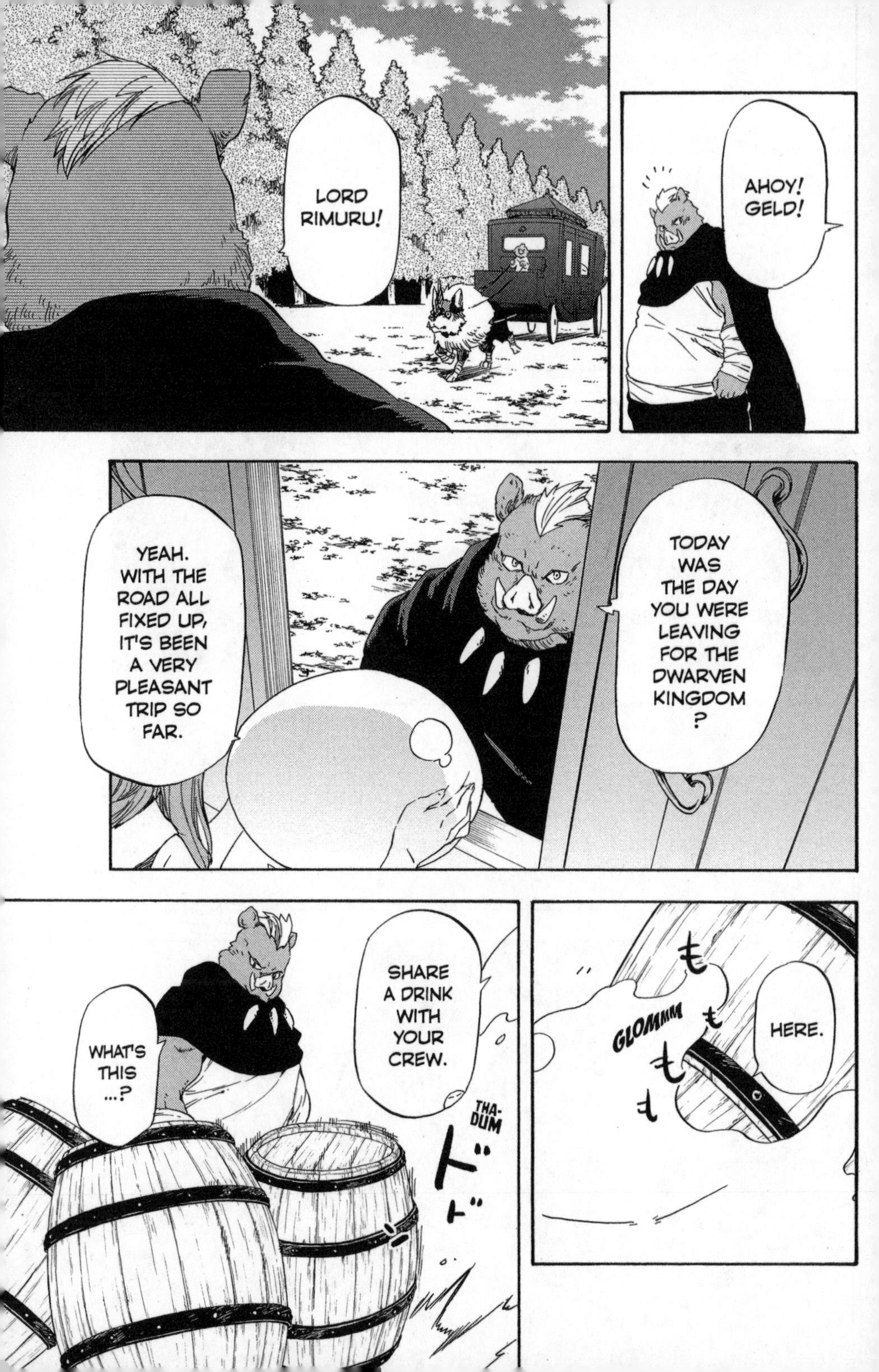
AHOY! GELD!
LORD RIMURU!
TODAY WAS THE DAY YOU WERE LEAVING FOR THE DWARVEN KINGDOM?
YEAH. WITH THE ROAD ALL FIXED UP, IT'S BEEN A VERY PLEASANT TRIP SO FAR.
HERE.
GLOMMM
SHARE A DRINK WITH YOUR CREW.
WHAT'S THIS ...?
THA-DUM

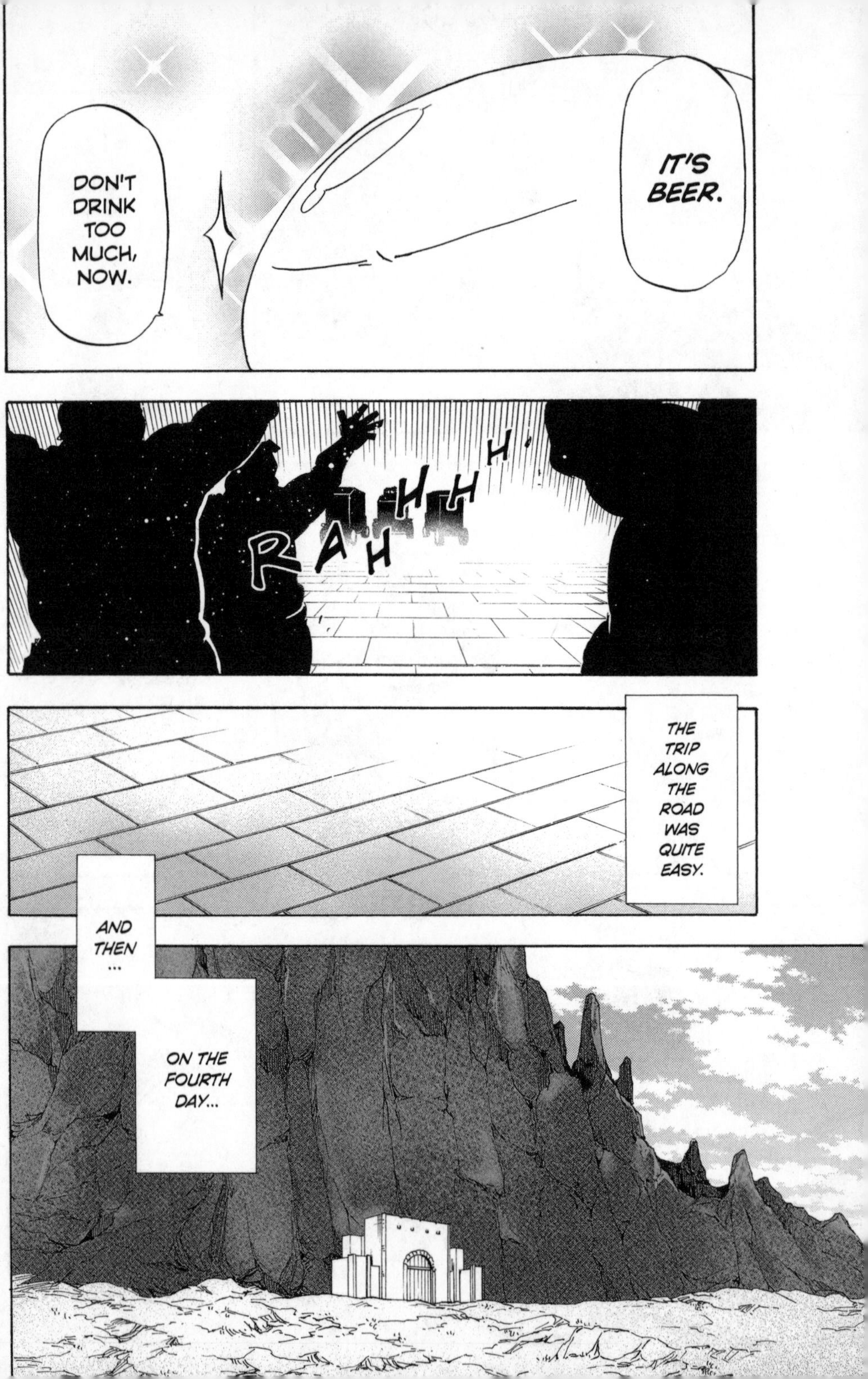
IT'S BEER.
DON'T DRINK TOO MUCH, NOW.
RAHHHHH
THE TRIP ALONG THE ROAD WAS QUITE EASY.
AND THEN...
ON THE FOURTH DAY...

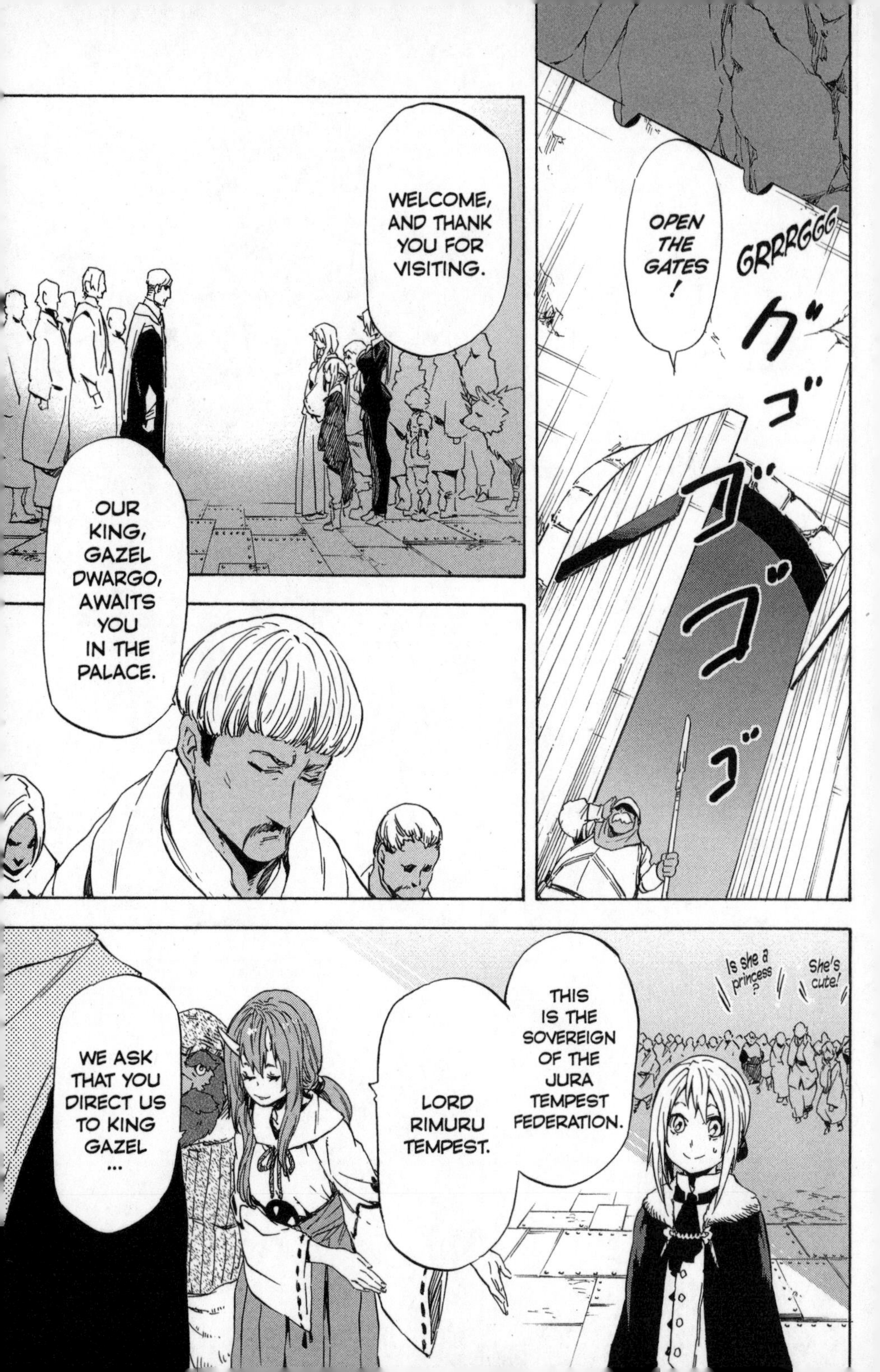
OPEN THE GATES!
GRRRGGG
WELCOME, AND THANK YOU FOR VISITING.
OUR KING, GAZEL DWARGO, AWAITS YOU IN THE PALACE.
Is she a princess?
She's cute!
THIS IS THE SOVEREIGN OF THE JURA TEMPEST FEDERATION.
LORD RIMURU TEMPEST.
WE ASK THAT YOU DIRECT US TO KING GAZEL...

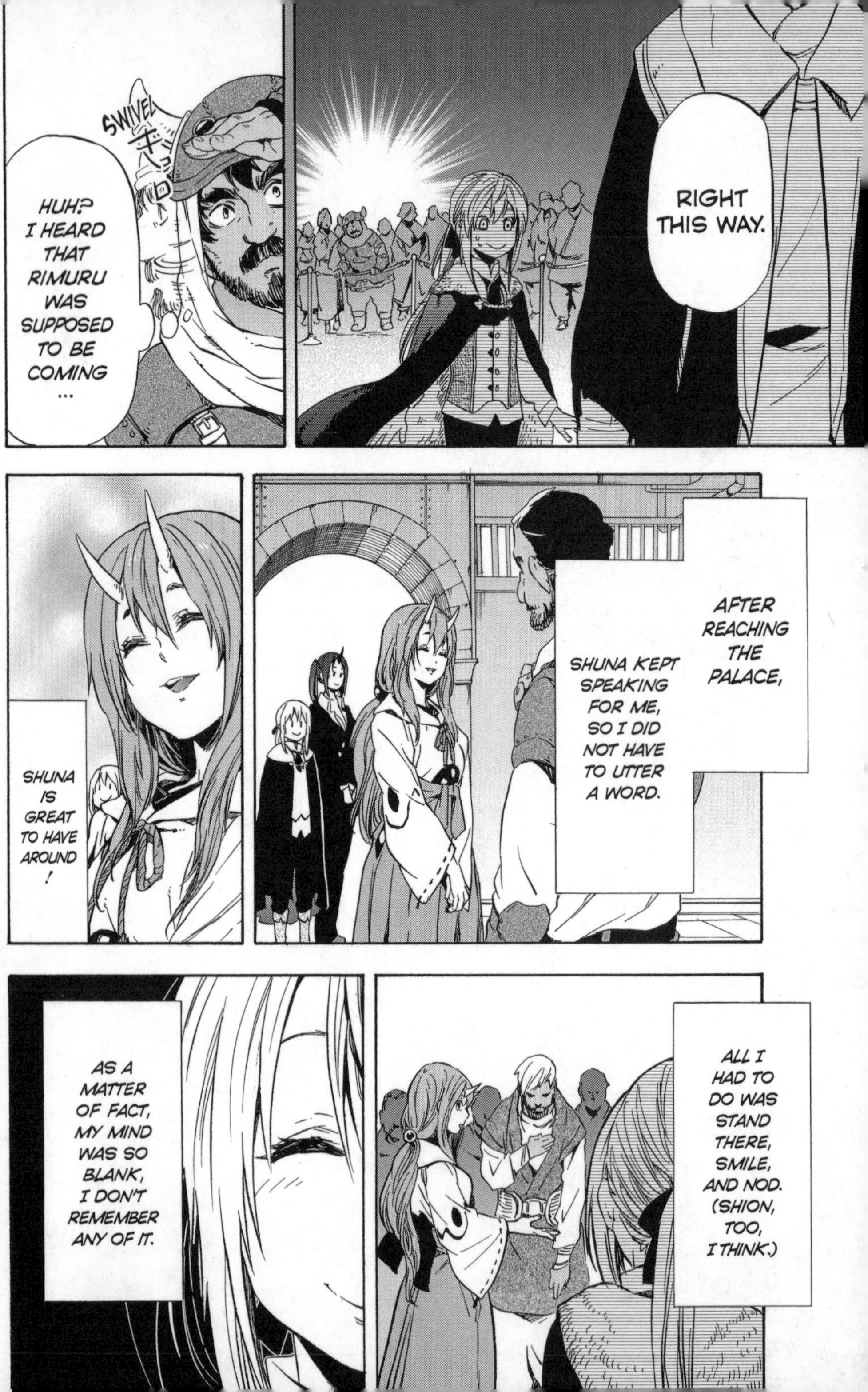
RIGHT THIS WAY.
SWIVEL
HUH? I HEARD THAT RIMURU WAS SUPPOSED TO BE COMING ...
AFTER REACHING THE PALACE,
SHUNA KEPT SPEAKING FOR ME, SO I DID NOT HAVE TO UTTER A WORD.
SHUNA IS GREAT TO HAVE AROUND!
ALL I HAD TO DO WAS STAND THERE, SMILE, AND NOD. (SHION, TOO, I THINK.)
AS A MATTER OF FACT, MY MIND WAS SO BLANK, I DON'T REMEMBER ANY OF IT.

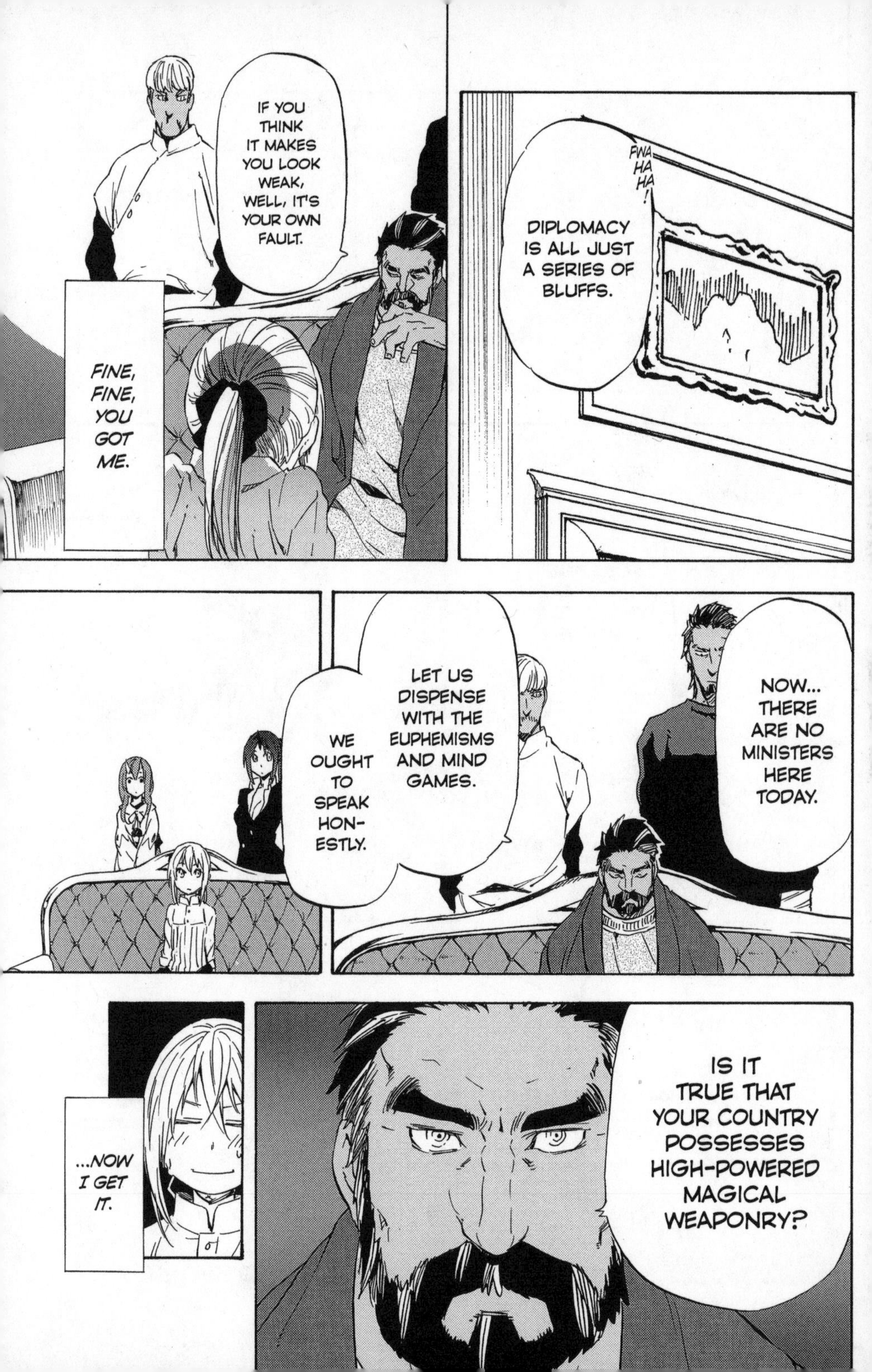
FWA HA HA!
DIPLOMACY IS ALL JUST A SERIES OF BLUFFS.
IF YOU THINK IT MAKES YOU LOOK WEAK, WELL, IT'S YOUR OWN FAULT.
FINE, FINE, YOU GOT ME.
NOW... THERE ARE NO MINISTERS HERE TODAY.
LET US DISPENSE WITH THE EUPHEMISMS AND MIND GAMES.
WE OUGHT TO SPEAK HON-ESTLY.
IS IT TRUE THAT YOUR COUNTRY POSSESSES HIGH-POWERED MAGICAL WEAPONRY?
...NOW I GET IT.

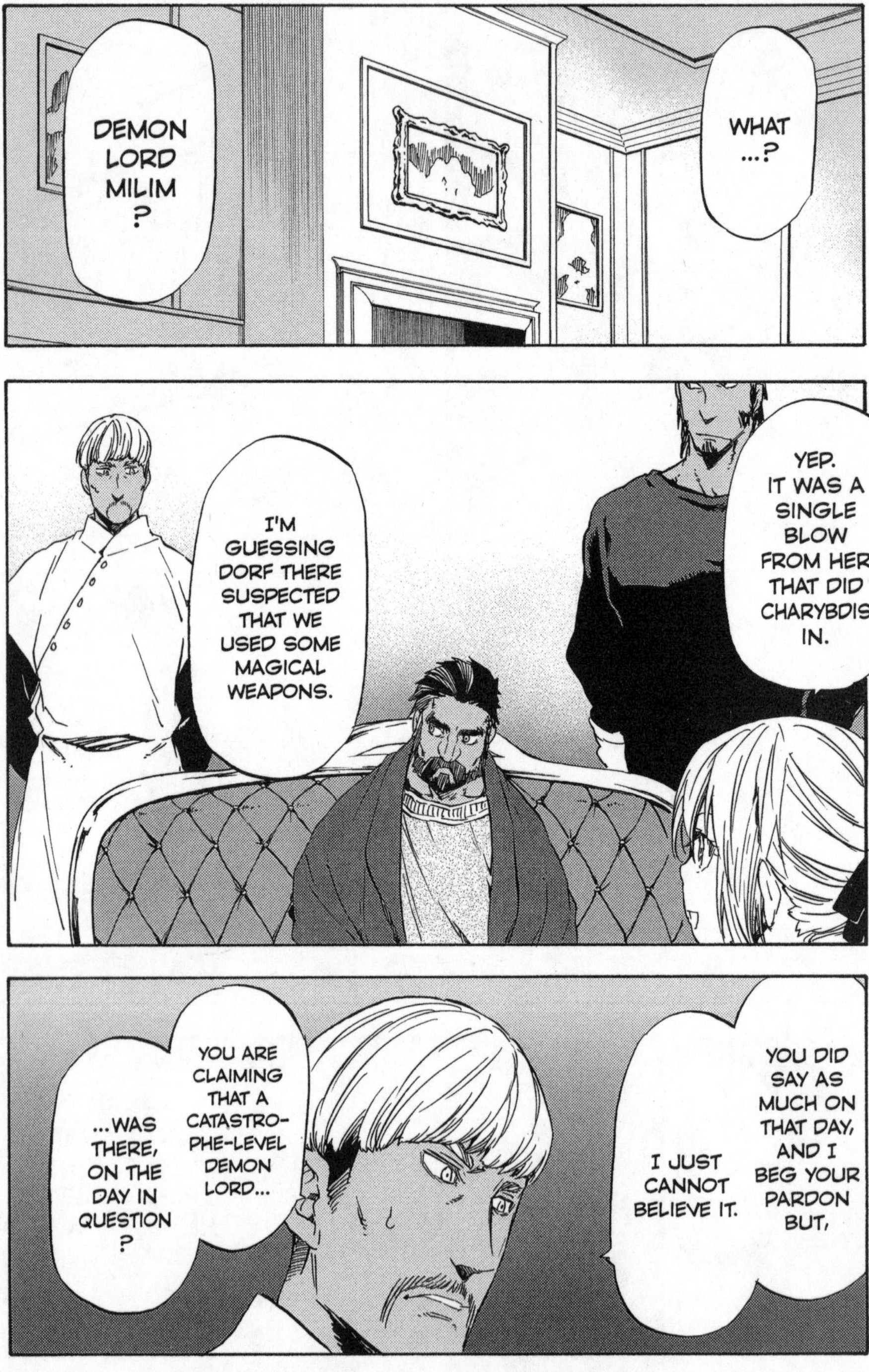
WHAT ...?
DEMON LORD MILIM ?
YEP. IT WAS A SINGLE BLOW FROM HER THAT DID CHARYBDIS IN.
I'M GUESSING DORF THERE SUSPECTED THAT WE USED SOME MAGICAL WEAPONS.
YOU DID SAY AS MUCH ON THAT DAY, AND I BEG YOUR PARDON BUT,
I JUST CANNOT BELIEVE IT.
YOU ARE CLAIMING THAT A CATASTRO-PHE-LEVEL DEMON LORD...
...WAS THERE, ON THE DAY IN QUESTION ?

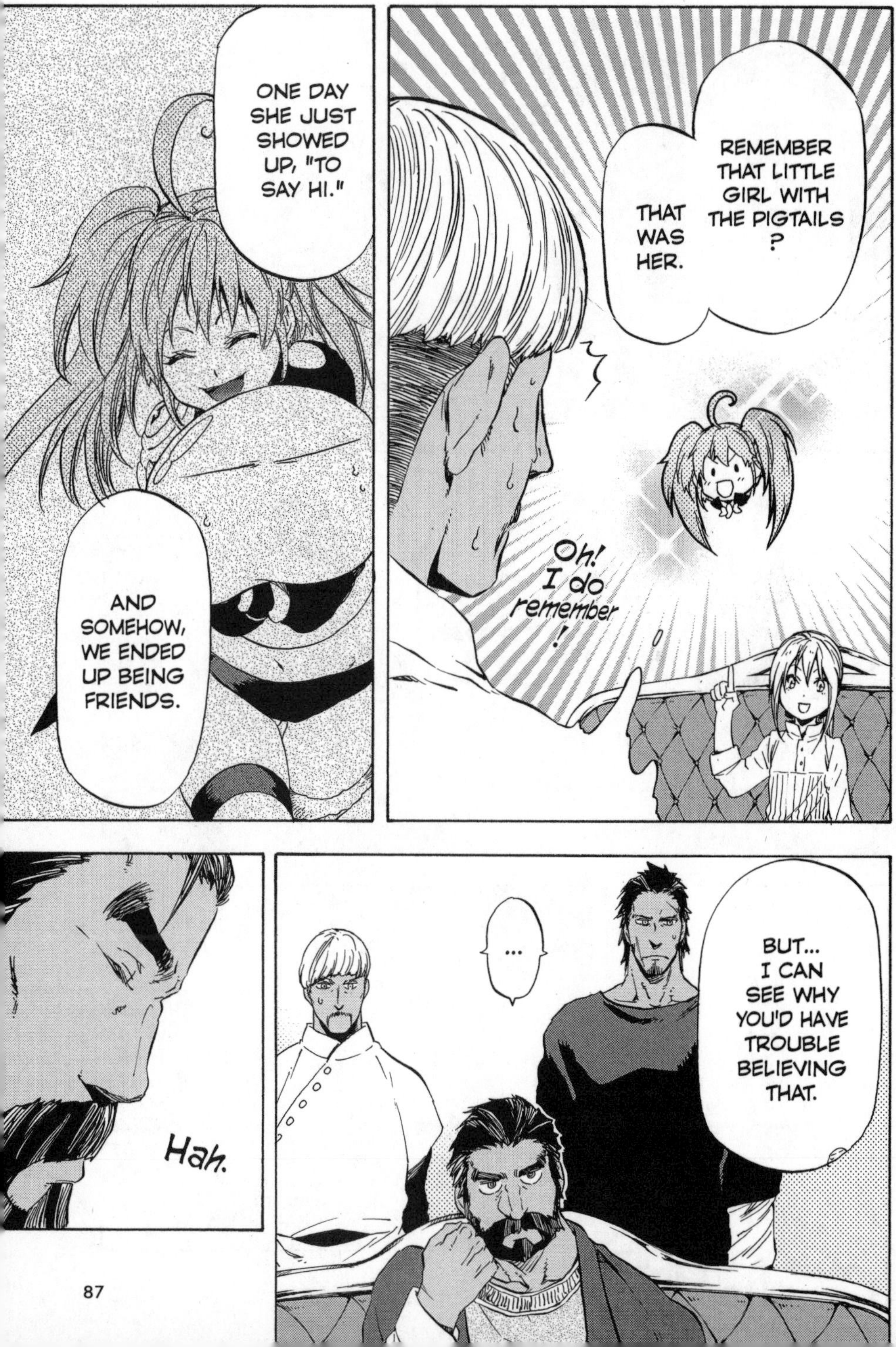
REMEMBER THAT LITTLE GIRL WITH THE PIGTAILS?
THAT WAS HER.
Oh! I do remember!
ONE DAY SHE JUST SHOWED UP, "TO SAY HI."
AND SOMEHOW, WE ENDED UP BEING FRIENDS.
BUT... I CAN SEE WHY YOU'D HAVE TROUBLE BELIEVING THAT.
...
Hah.

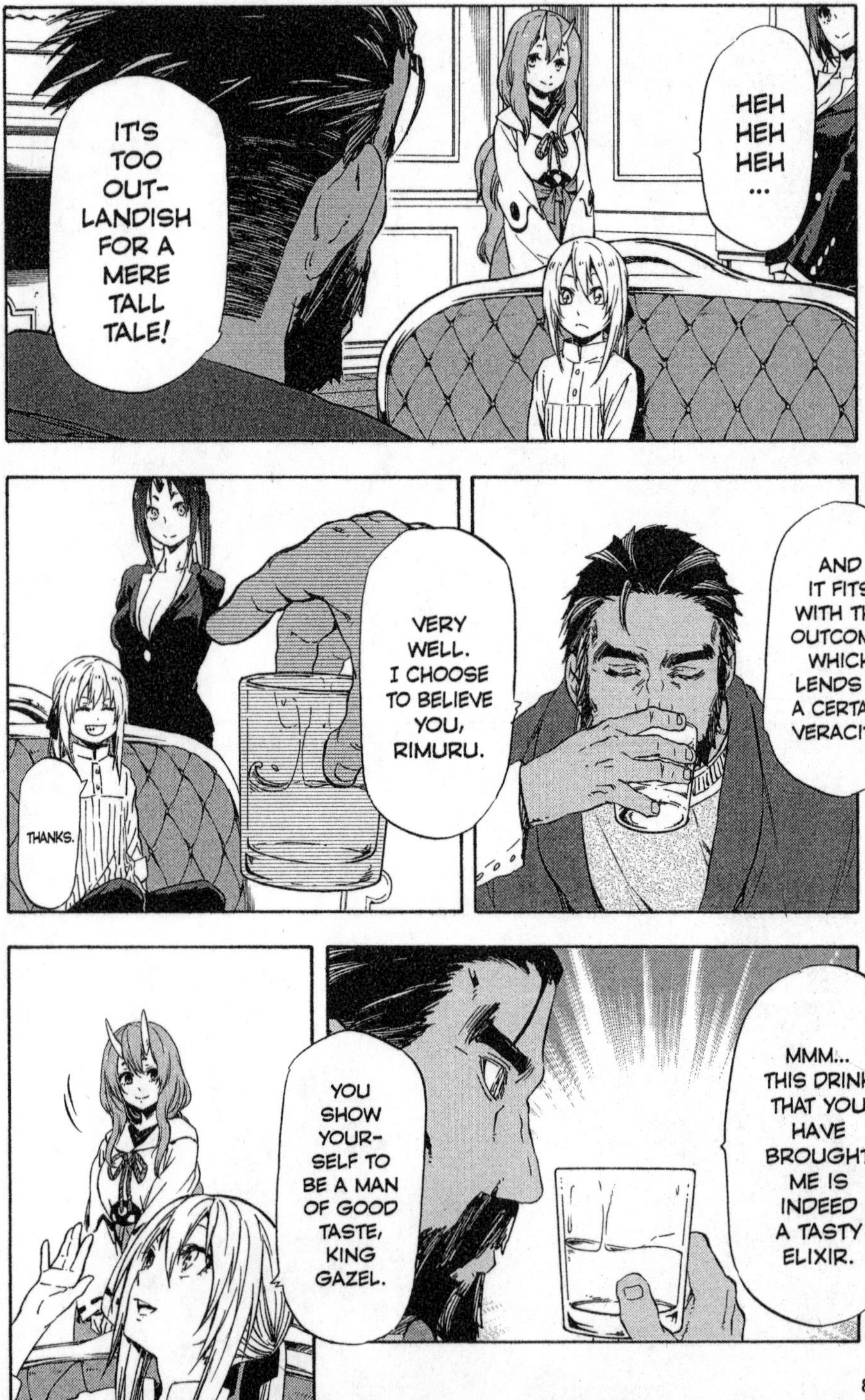
HEH HEH HEH ...
IT'S TOO OUT-LANDISH FOR A MERE TALL TALE!
AND IT FITS WITH THE OUTCOME, WHICH LENDS IT A CERTAIN VERACITY.
VERY WELL. I CHOOSE TO BELIEVE YOU, RIMURU.
THANKS.
MMM... THIS DRINK THAT YOU HAVE BROUGHT ME IS INDEED A TASTY ELIXIR.
YOU SHOW YOUR-SELF TO BE A MAN OF GOOD TASTE, KING GAZEL.

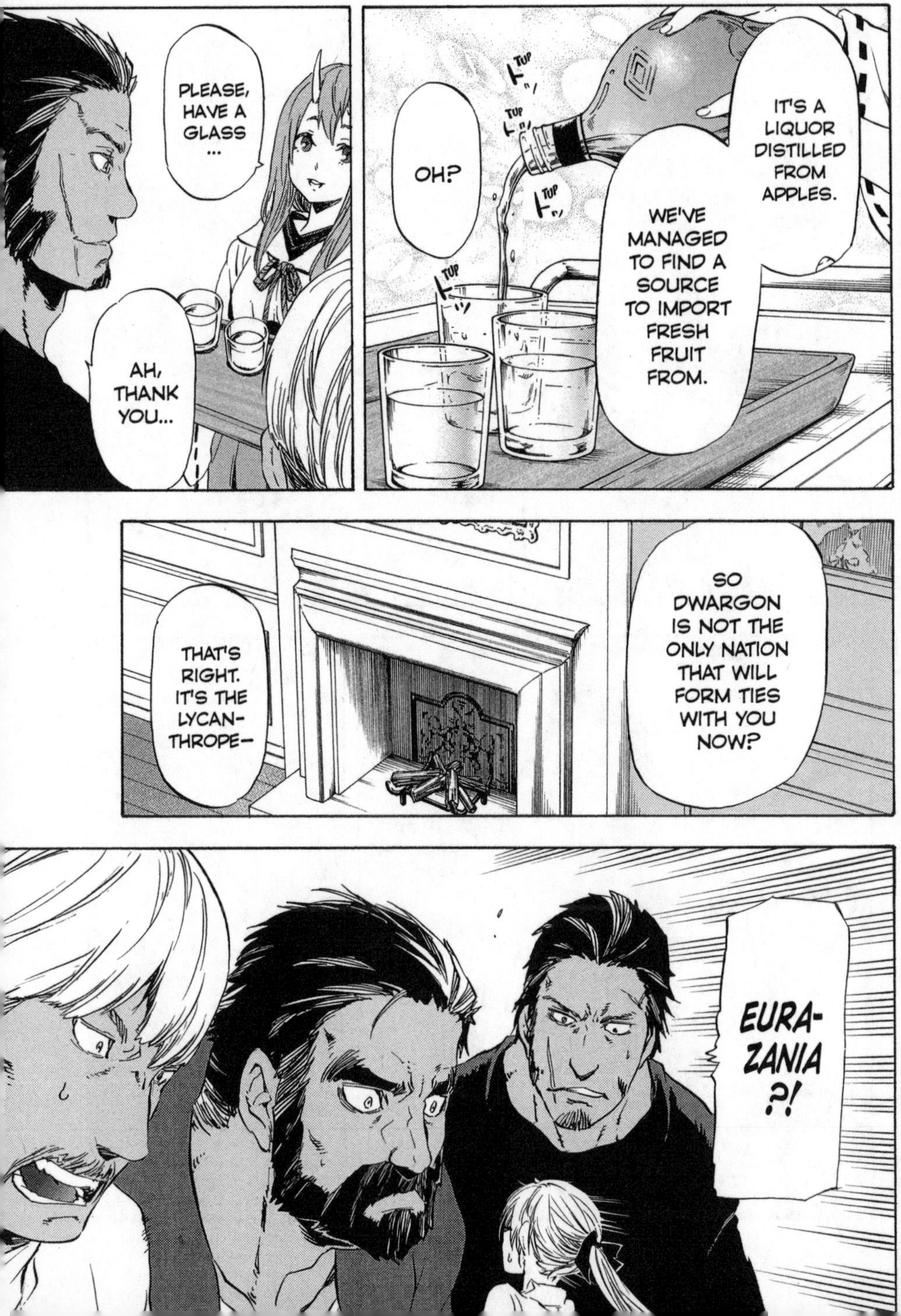
IT'S A LIQUOR DISTILLED FROM APPLES.
WE'VE MANAGED TO FIND A SOURCE TO IMPORT FRESH FRUIT FROM.
TUP
TUP
TUP
OH?
TUP
PLEASE, HAVE A GLASS ...
AH, THANK YOU...
SO DWARGON IS NOT THE ONLY NATION THAT WILL FORM TIES WITH YOU NOW?
THAT'S RIGHT. IT'S THE LYCAN-THROPE-
EURA-ZANIA ?!

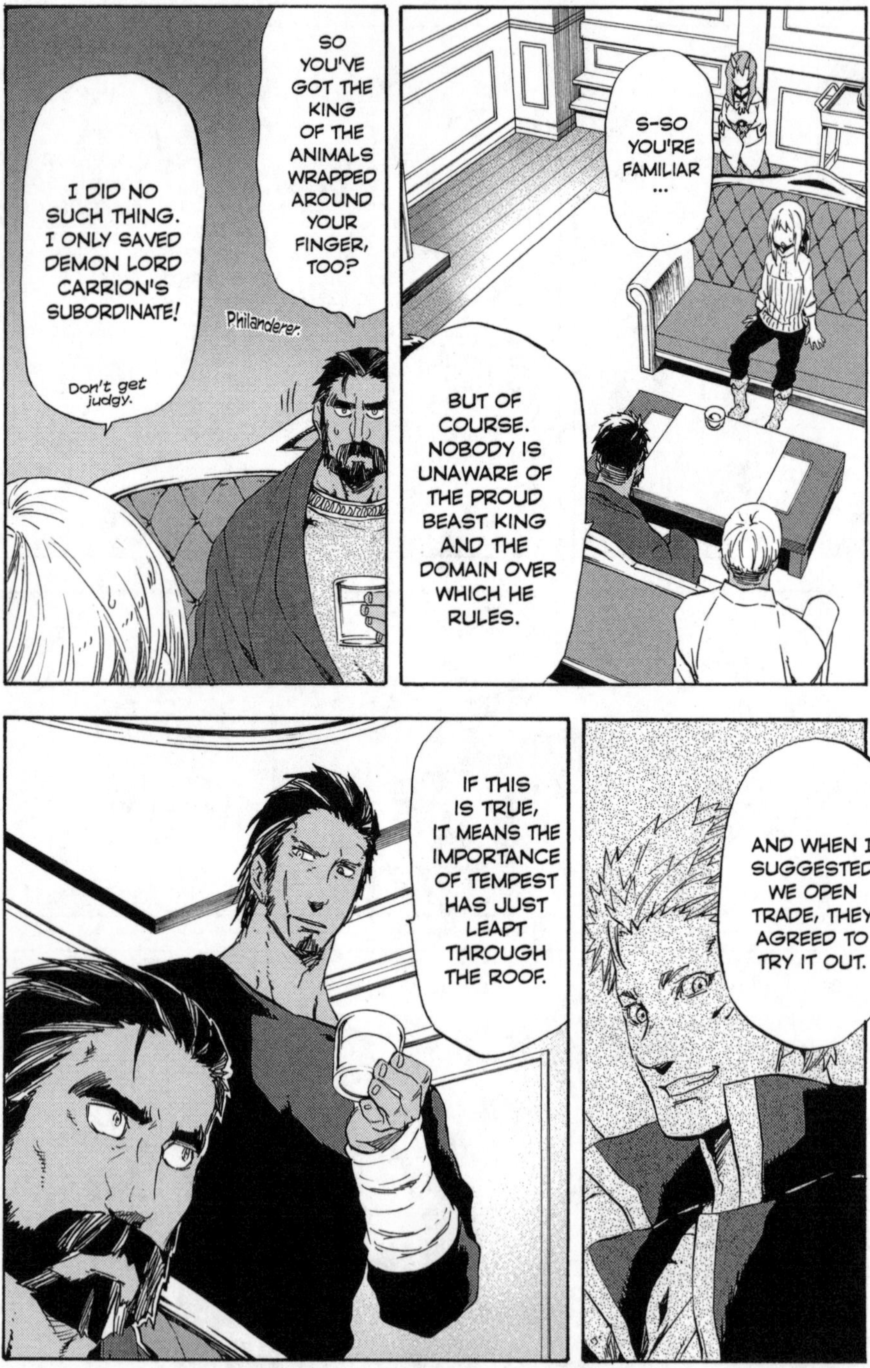
S-SO YOU'RE FAMILIAR ...
BUT OF COURSE. NOBODY IS UNAWARE OF THE PROUD BEAST KING AND THE DOMAIN OVER WHICH HE RULES.
SO YOU'VE GOT THE KING OF THE ANIMALS WRAPPED AROUND YOUR FINGER, TOO?
Philanderer.
I DID NO SUCH THING. I ONLY SAVED DEMON LORD CARRION'S SUBORDINATE!
Don't get judgy.
AND WHEN I SUGGESTED WE OPEN TRADE, THEY AGREED TO TRY IT OUT.
IF THIS IS TRUE, IT MEANS THE IMPORTANCE OF TEMPEST HAS JUST LEAPT THROUGH THE ROOF.

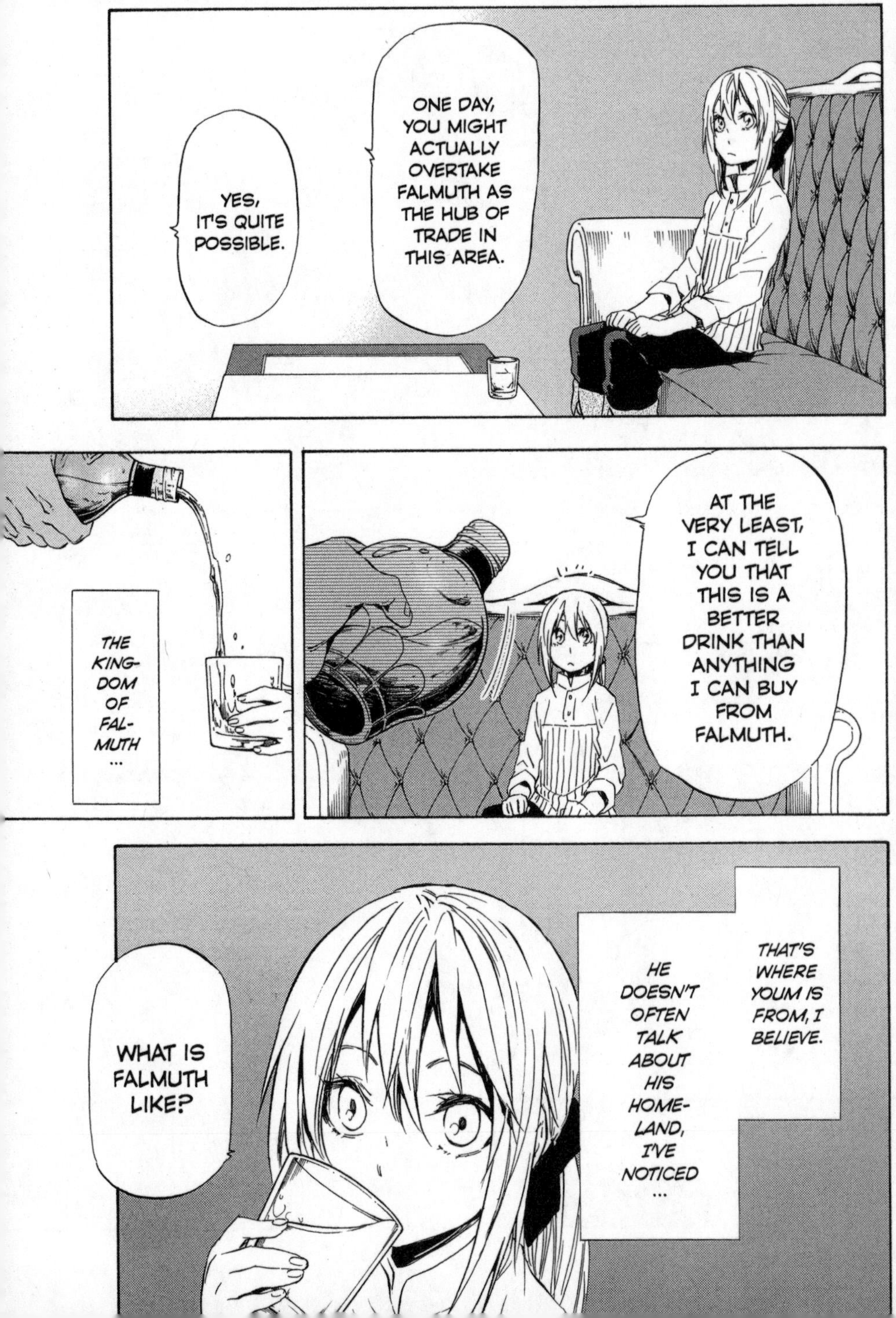
ONE DAY, YOU MIGHT ACTUALLY OVERTAKE FALMUTH AS THE HUB OF TRADE IN THIS AREA.
YES, IT'S QUITE POSSIBLE.
AT THE VERY LEAST, I CAN TELL YOU THAT THIS IS A BETTER DRINK THAN ANYTHING I CAN BUY FROM FALMUTH.
THE KING-DOM OF FAL-MUTH ...
THAT'S WHERE YOUM IS FROM, I BELIEVE.
HE DOESN'T OFTEN TALK ABOUT HIS HOME-LAND, I'VE NOTICED ...
WHAT IS FALMUTH LIKE?

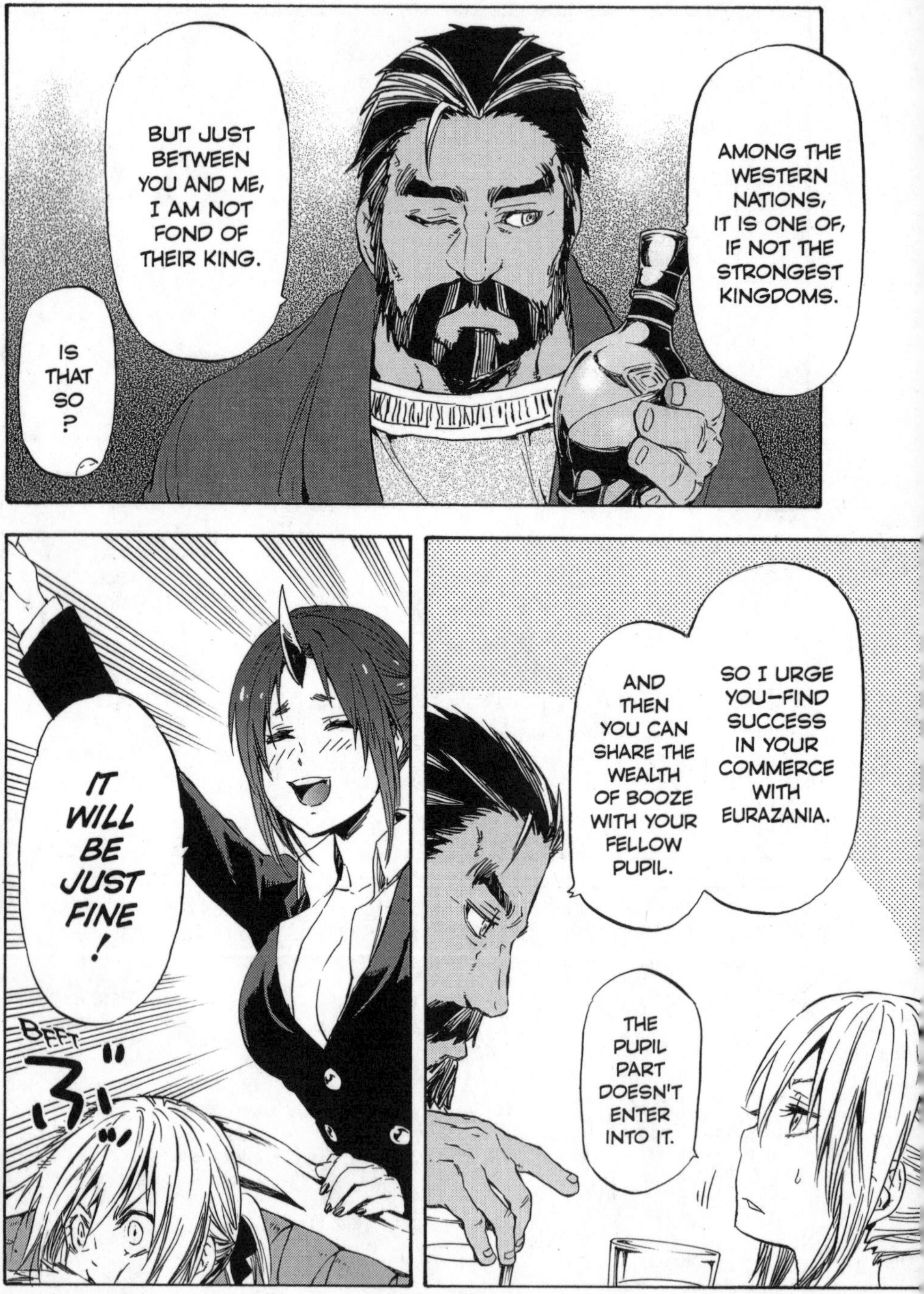
AMONG THE WESTERN NATIONS, IT IS ONE OF, IF NOT THE STRONGEST KINGDOMS.
BUT JUST BETWEEN YOU AND ME, I AM NOT FOND OF THEIR KING.
IS THAT SO?
SO I URGE YOU—FIND SUCCESS IN YOUR COMMERCE WITH EURAZANIA.
AND THEN YOU CAN SHARE THE WEALTH OF BOOZE WITH YOUR FELLOW PUPIL.
THE PUPIL PART DOESN'T ENTER INTO IT.
IT WILL BE JUST FINE!
BFFT
ぶ"

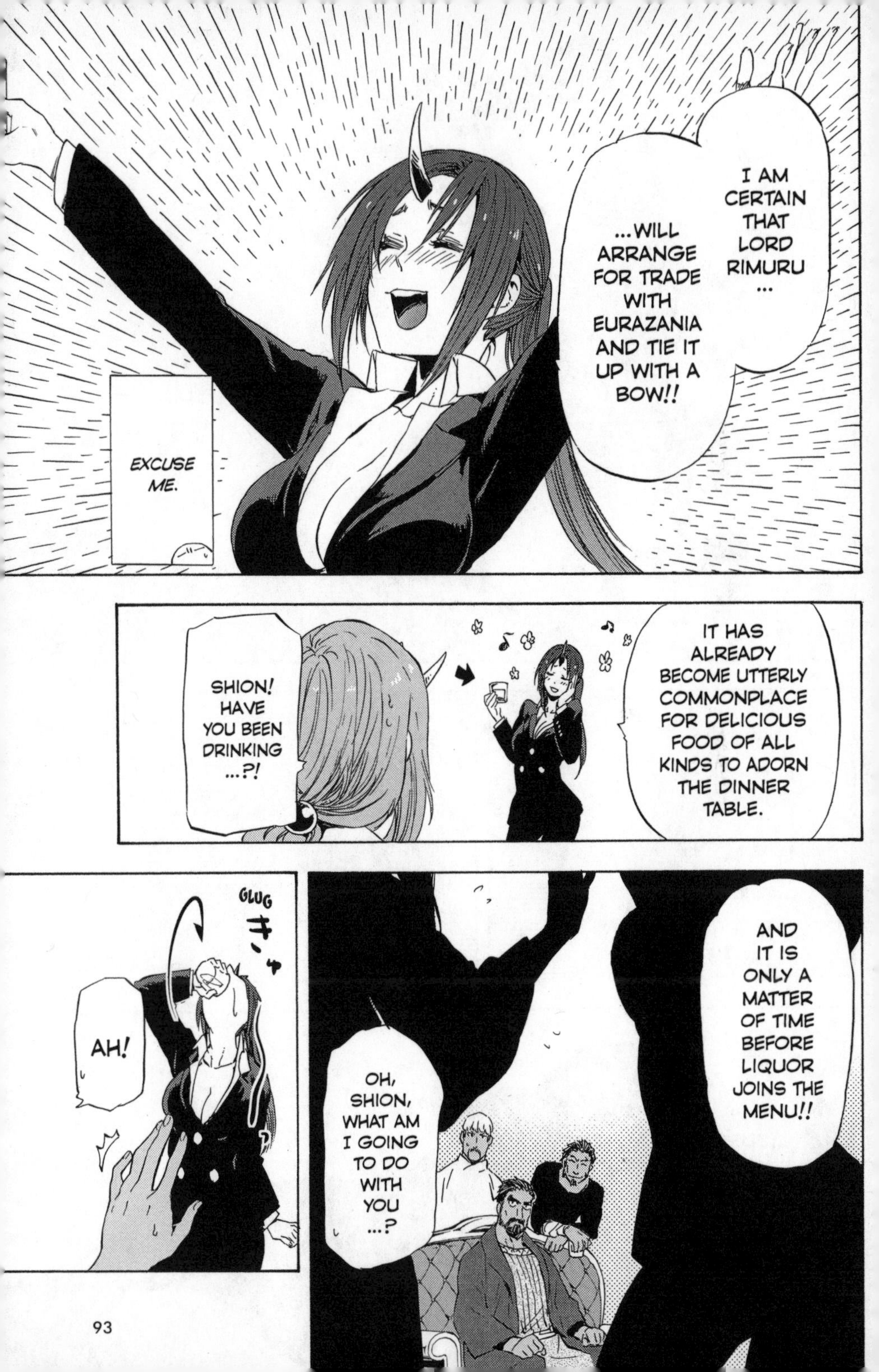
I AM CERTAIN THAT LORD RIMURU ...
...WILL ARRANGE FOR TRADE WITH EURAZANIA AND TIE IT UP WITH A BOW!!
EXCUSE ME.
IT HAS ALREADY BECOME UTTERLY COMMONPLACE FOR DELICIOUS FOOD OF ALL KINDS TO ADORN THE DINNER TABLE.
SHION! HAVE YOU BEEN DRINKING ...?!
AND IT IS ONLY A MATTER OF TIME BEFORE LIQUOR JOINS THE MENU!!
OH, SHION, WHAT AM I GOING TO DO WITH YOU ...?
GLUG
きゅ
AH!

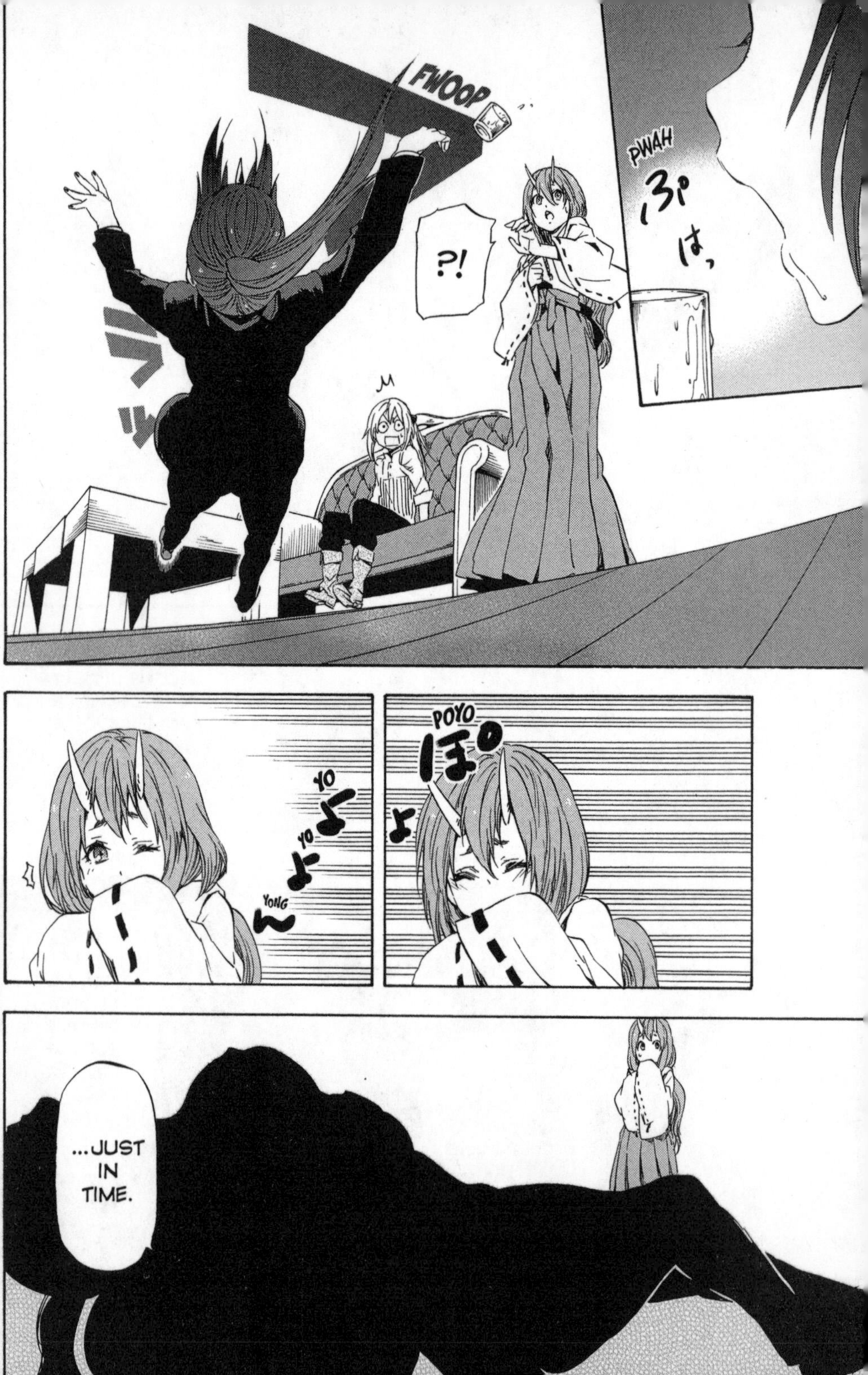
PWAH
ぷはっ
FWOOP
?!
ラッ
POYO
ぽよ
YO
よ
YO
よ
YONG
ん
...JUST IN TIME.

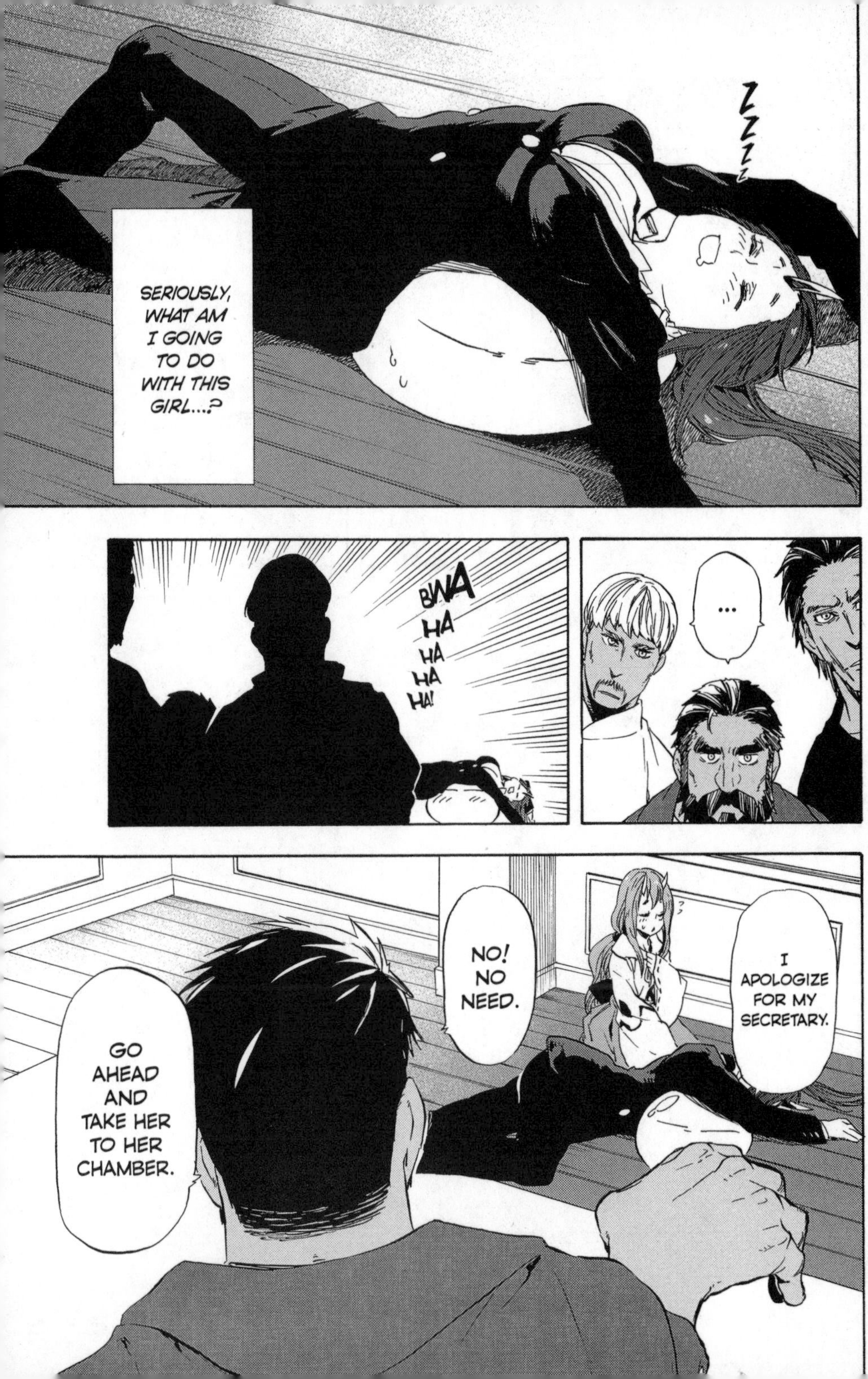
ZZZZ
SERIOUSLY, WHAT AM I GOING TO DO WITH THIS GIRL...?
...
BWA HA HA HA HA!
I APOLOGIZE FOR MY SECRETARY.
NO! NO NEED.
GO AHEAD AND TAKE HER TO HER CHAMBER.

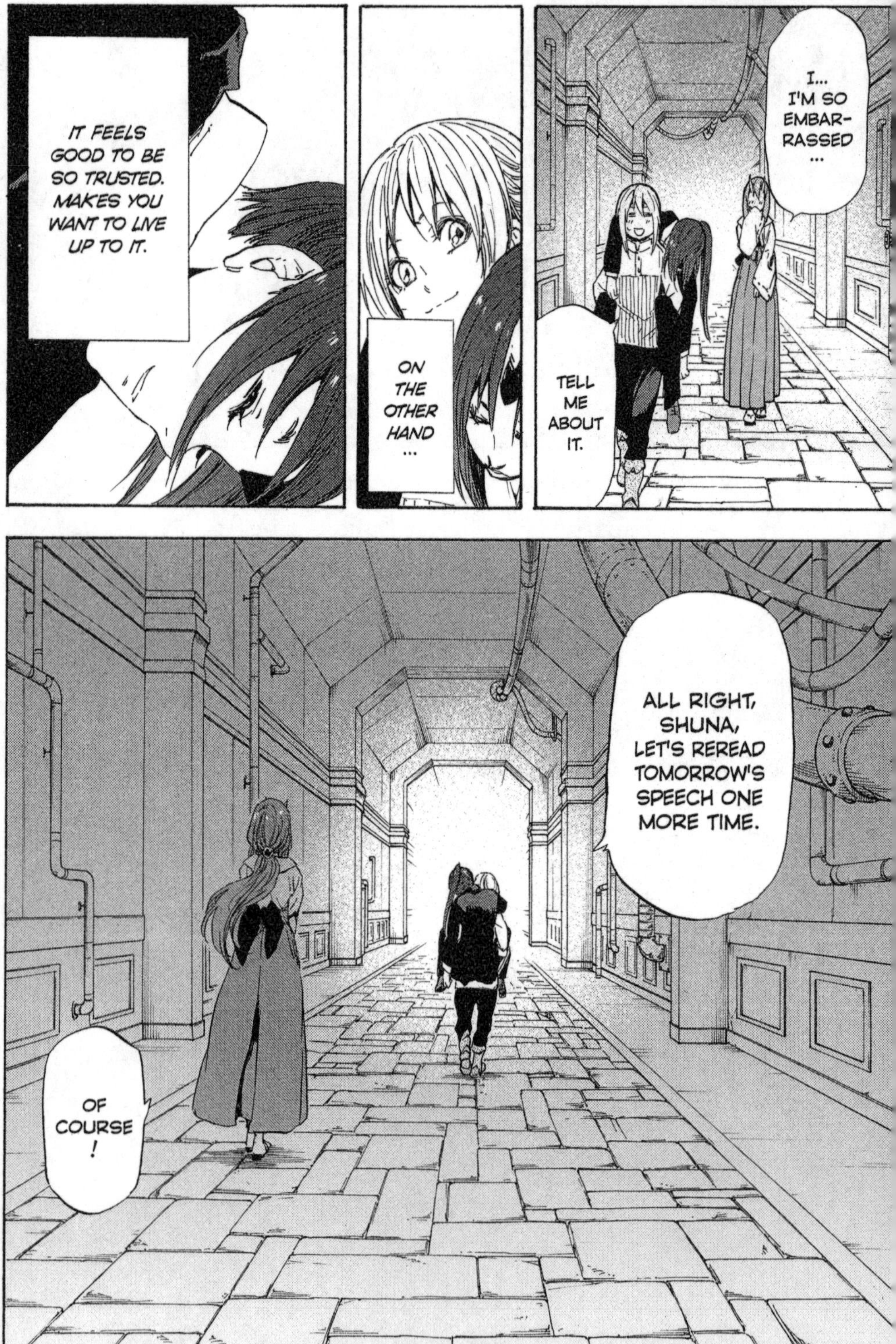
I... I'M SO EMBARRASSED...
TELL ME ABOUT IT.
ON THE OTHER HAND...
IT FEELS GOOD TO BE SO TRUSTED. MAKES YOU WANT TO LIVE UP TO IT.
ALL RIGHT, SHUNA, LET'S REREAD TOMORROW'S SPEECH ONE MORE TIME.
OF COURSE!

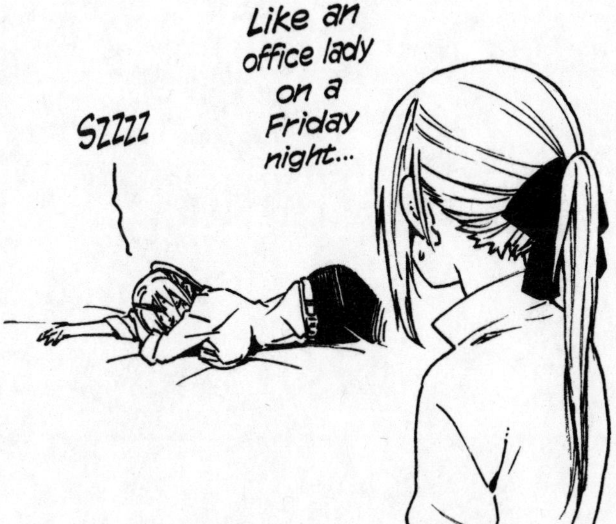
Like an office lady on a Friday night...
SZZZZ

CHAPTER 42 King Gazel's Invitation (Part Two)

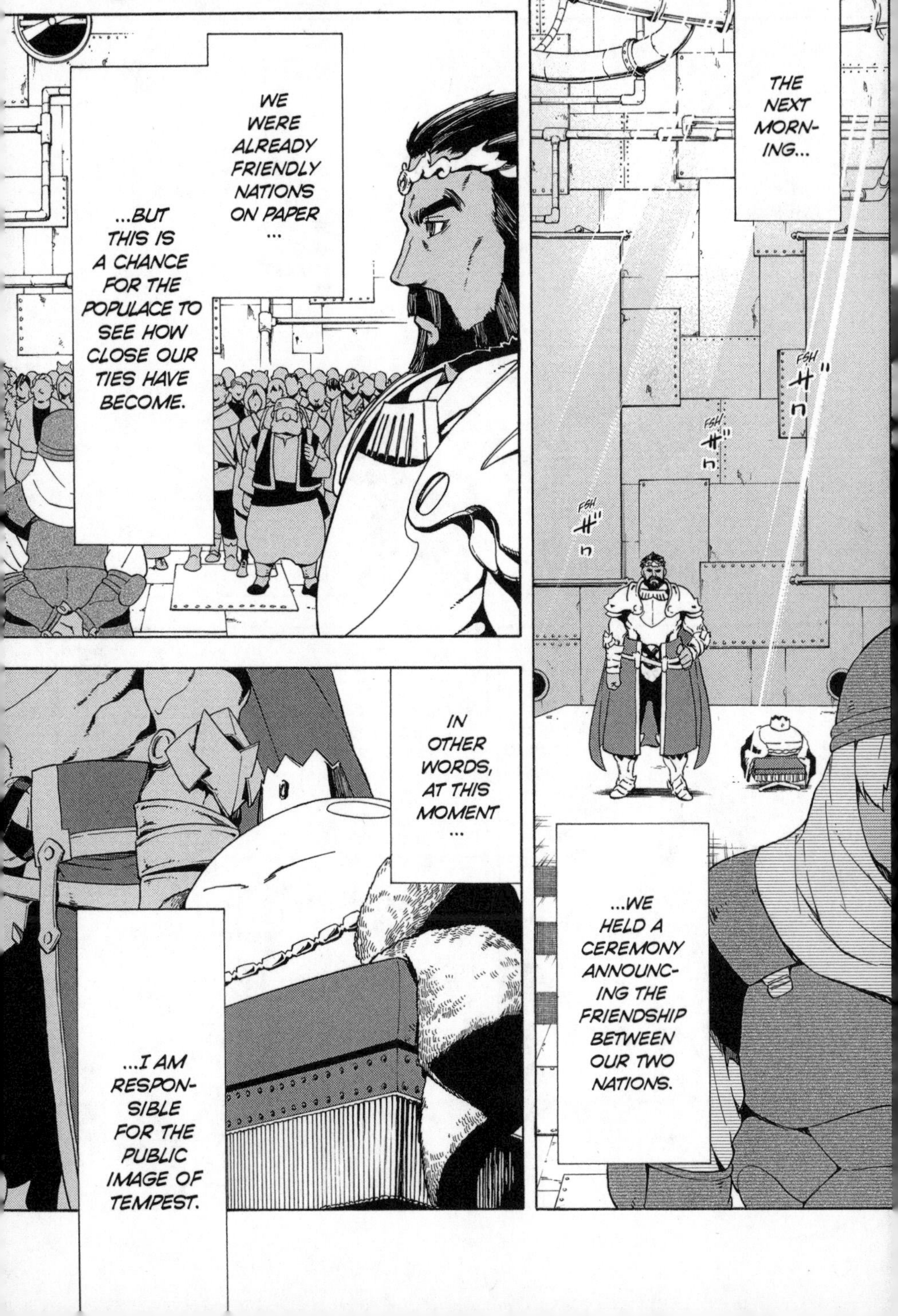
THE NEXT MORNING-ING...
FSH
FSH
FSH
...WE HELD A CEREMONY ANNOUNCING THE FRIENDSHIP BETWEEN OUR TWO NATIONS.
WE WERE ALREADY FRIENDLY NATIONS ON PAPER...
...BUT THIS IS A CHANCE FOR THE POPULACE TO SEE HOW CLOSE OUR TIES HAVE BECOME.
IN OTHER WORDS, AT THIS MOMENT...
...I AM RESPONSIBLE FOR THE PUBLIC IMAGE OF TEMPEST.

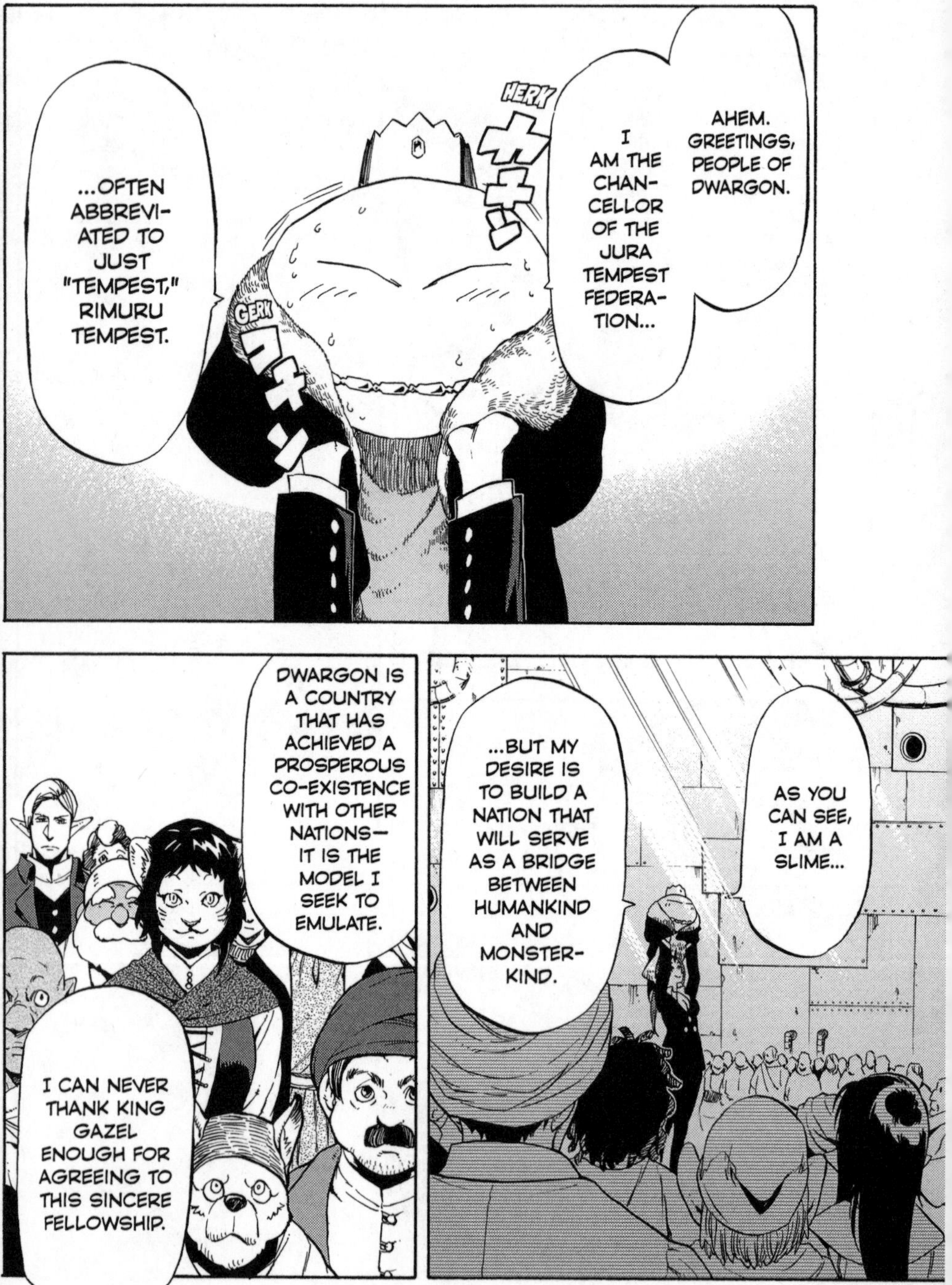
AHEM. GREETINGS, PEOPLE OF DWARGON.
I AM THE CHANCELLOR OF THE JURA TEMPEST FEDERATION...
HERK
GERK
...OFTEN ABBREVIATED TO JUST "TEMPEST," RIMURU TEMPEST.
AS YOU CAN SEE, I AM A SLIME...
...BUT MY DESIRE IS TO BUILD A NATION THAT WILL SERVE AS A BRIDGE BETWEEN HUMANKIND AND MONSTERKIND.
DWARGON IS A COUNTRY THAT HAS ACHIEVED A PROSPEROUS CO-EXISTENCE WITH OTHER NATIONS—IT IS THE MODEL I SEEK TO EMULATE.
I CAN NEVER THANK KING GAZEL ENOUGH FOR AGREEING TO THIS SINCERE FELLOWSHIP.

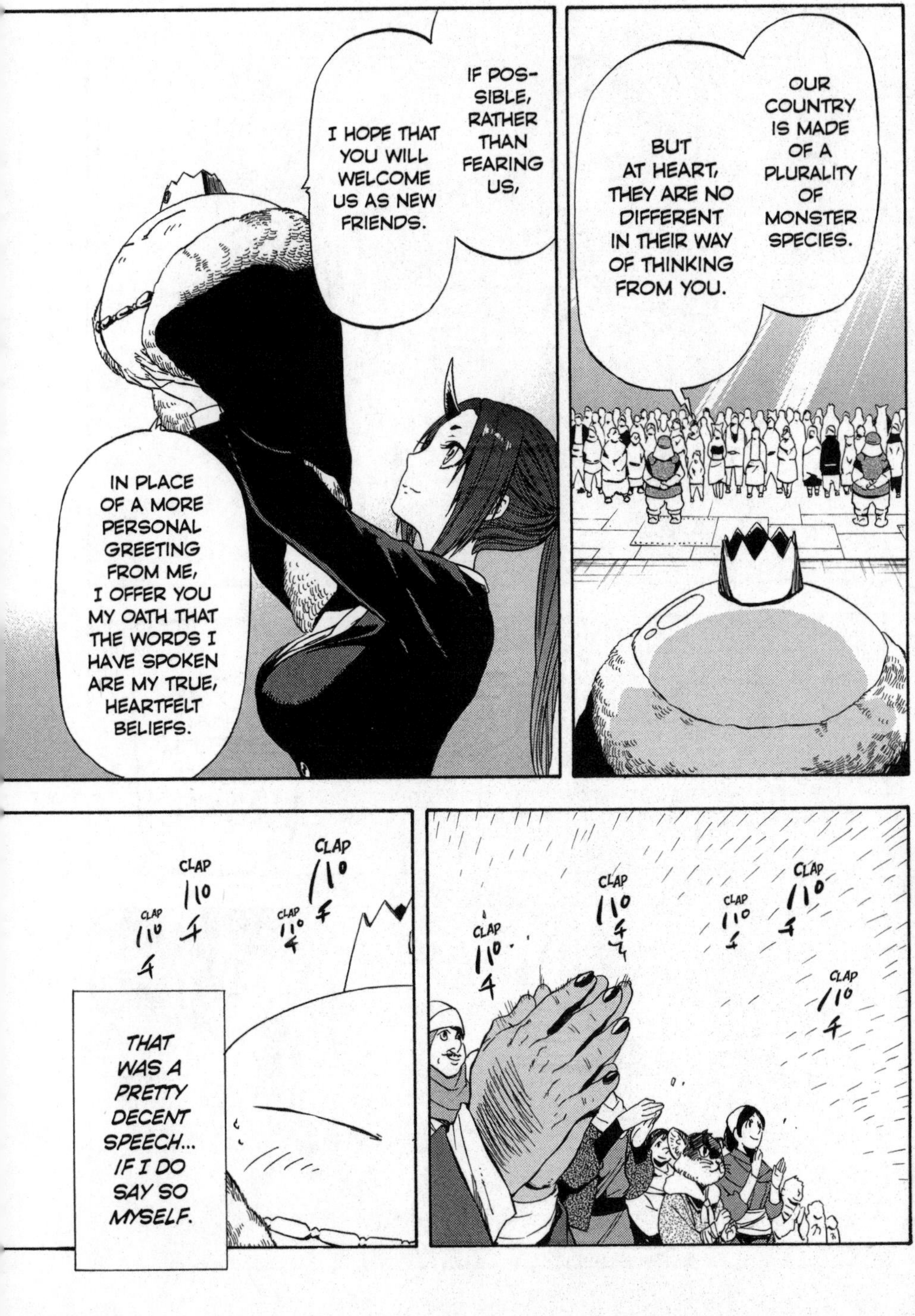
OUR COUNTRY IS MADE OF A PLURALITY OF MONSTER SPECIES.
BUT AT HEART, THEY ARE NO DIFFERENT IN THEIR WAY OF THINKING FROM YOU.
IF POS-SIBLE, RATHER THAN FEARING US,
I HOPE THAT YOU WILL WELCOME US AS NEW FRIENDS.
IN PLACE OF A MORE PERSONAL GREETING FROM ME, I OFFER YOU MY OATH THAT THE WORDS I HAVE SPOKEN ARE MY TRUE, HEARTFELT BELIEFS.
CLAP
CLAP
CLAP
CLAP
CLAP
CLAP
CLAP
CLAP
CLAP
CLAP
THAT WAS A PRETTY DECENT SPEECH... IF I DO SAY SO MYSELF.

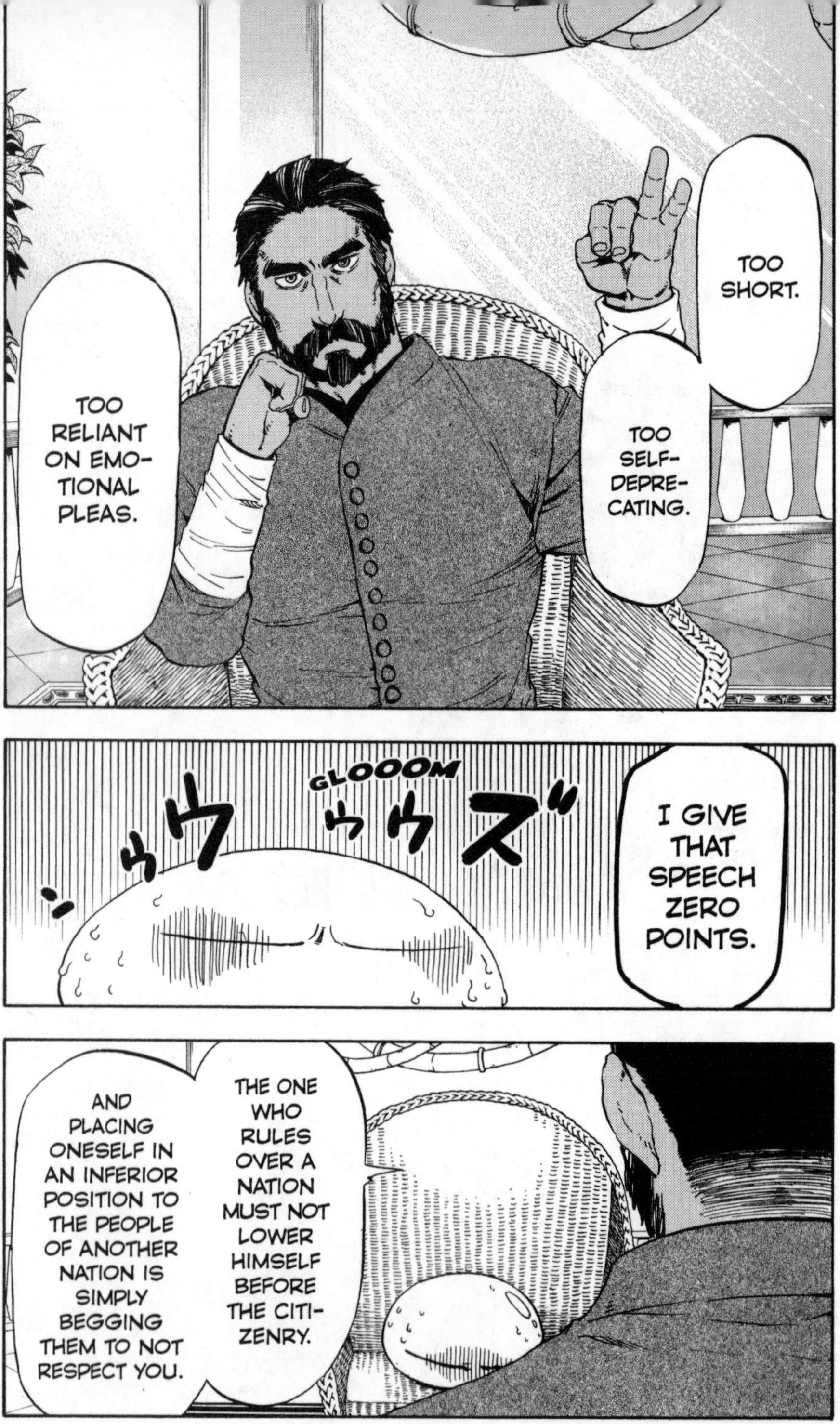
TOO SHORT.
TOO SELF-DEPRECATING.
TOO RELIANT ON EMOTIONAL PLEAS.
I GIVE THAT SPEECH ZERO POINTS.
GLOOOM
THE ONE WHO RULES OVER A NATION MUST NOT LOWER HIMSELF BEFORE THE CITIZENRY.
AND PLACING ONESELF IN AN INFERIOR POSITION TO THE PEOPLE OF ANOTHER NATION IS SIMPLY BEGGING THEM TO NOT RESPECT YOU.

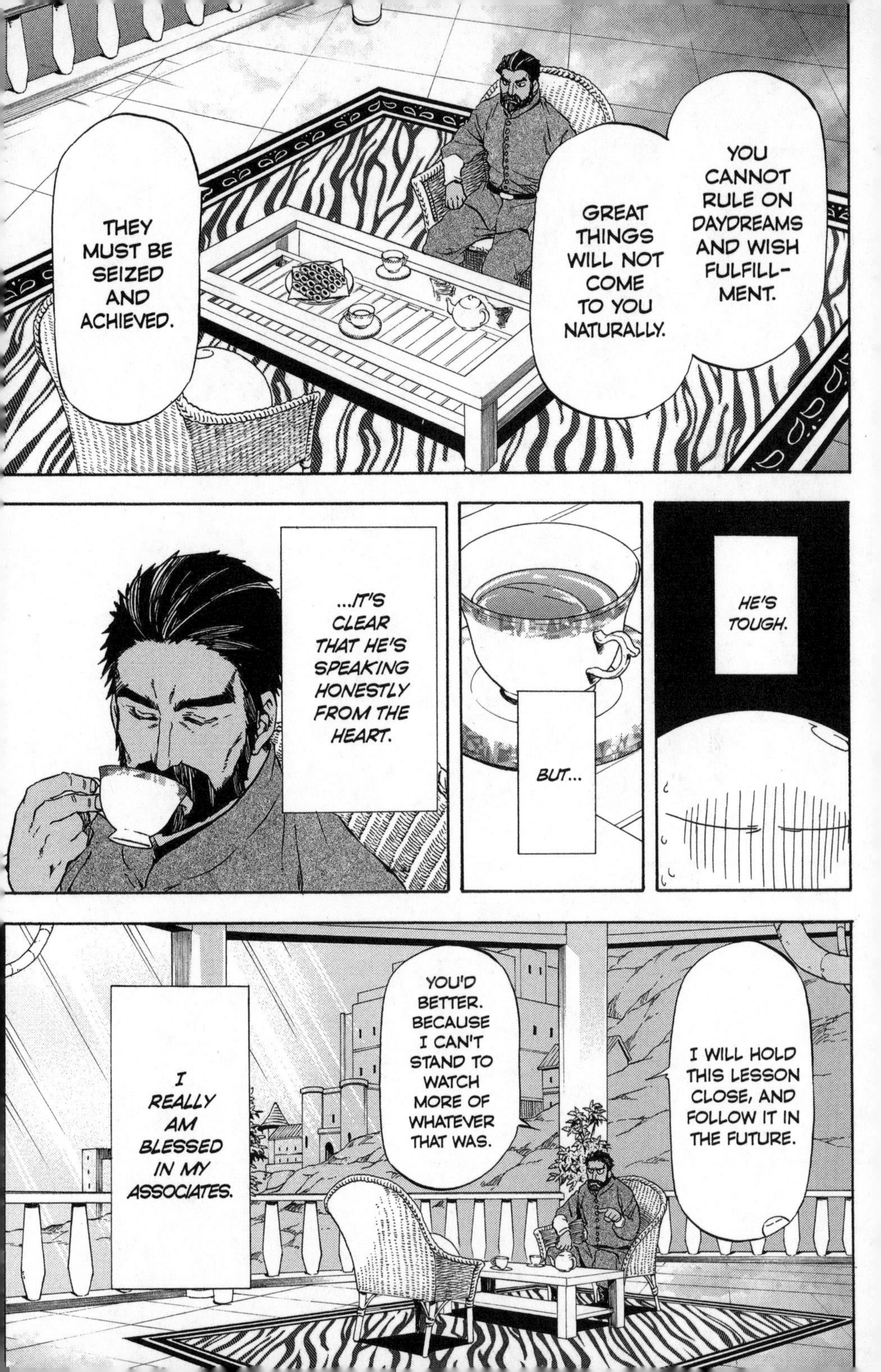
YOU CANNOT RULE ON DAYDREAMS AND WISH FULFILL-MENT.
GREAT THINGS WILL NOT COME TO YOU NATURALLY.
THEY MUST BE SEIZED AND ACHIEVED.
HE'S TOUGH.
BUT...
...IT'S CLEAR THAT HE'S SPEAKING HONESTLY FROM THE HEART.
I WILL HOLD THIS LESSON CLOSE, AND FOLLOW IT IN THE FUTURE.
YOU'D BETTER. BECAUSE I CAN'T STAND TO WATCH MORE OF WHATEVER THAT WAS.
I REALLY AM BLESSED IN MY ASSOCIATES.

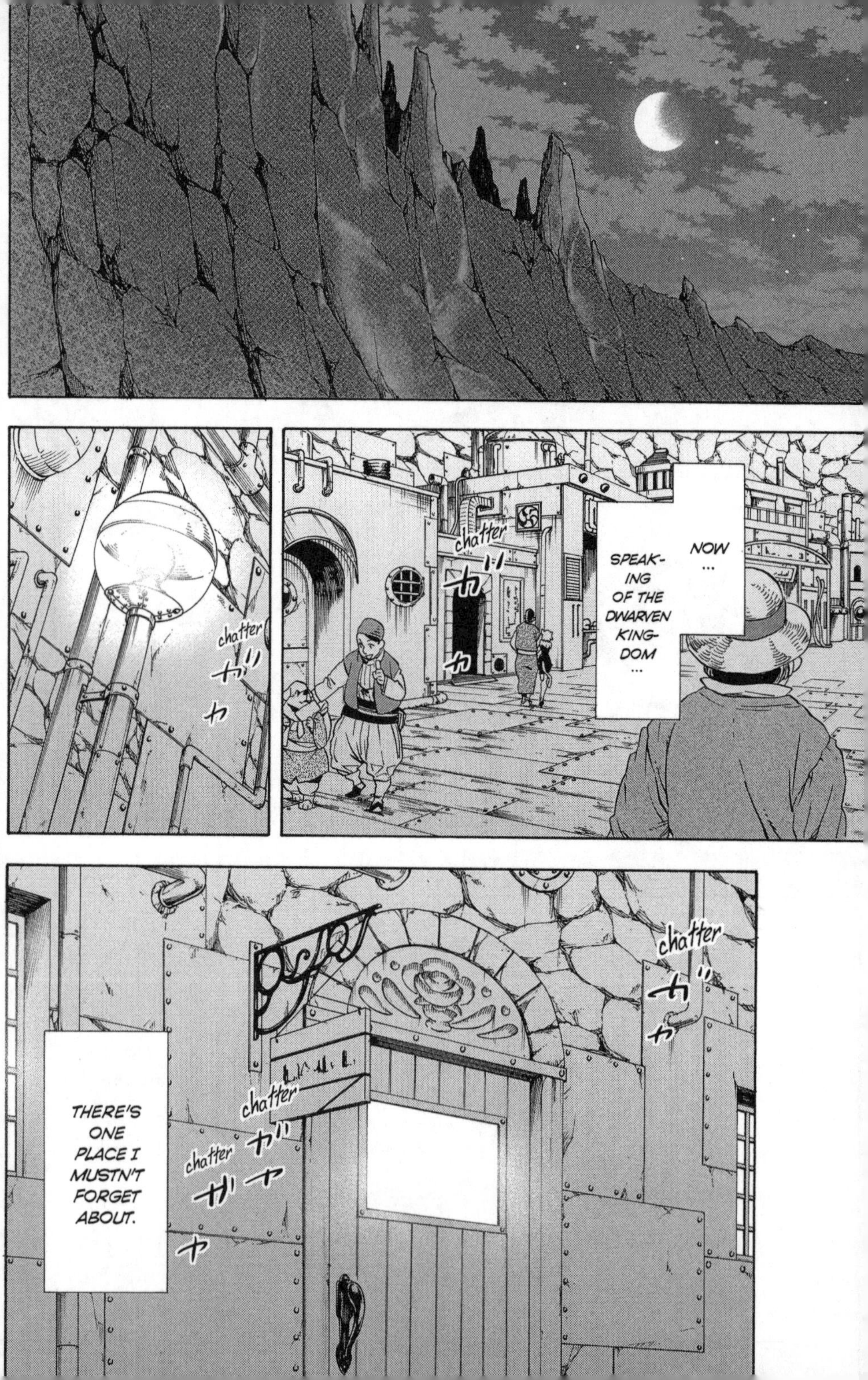
NOW ...
SPEAKING OF THE DWARVEN KINGDOM ...
chatter
chatter
chatter
chatter
chatter
THERE'S ONE PLACE I MUSTN'T FORGET ABOUT.

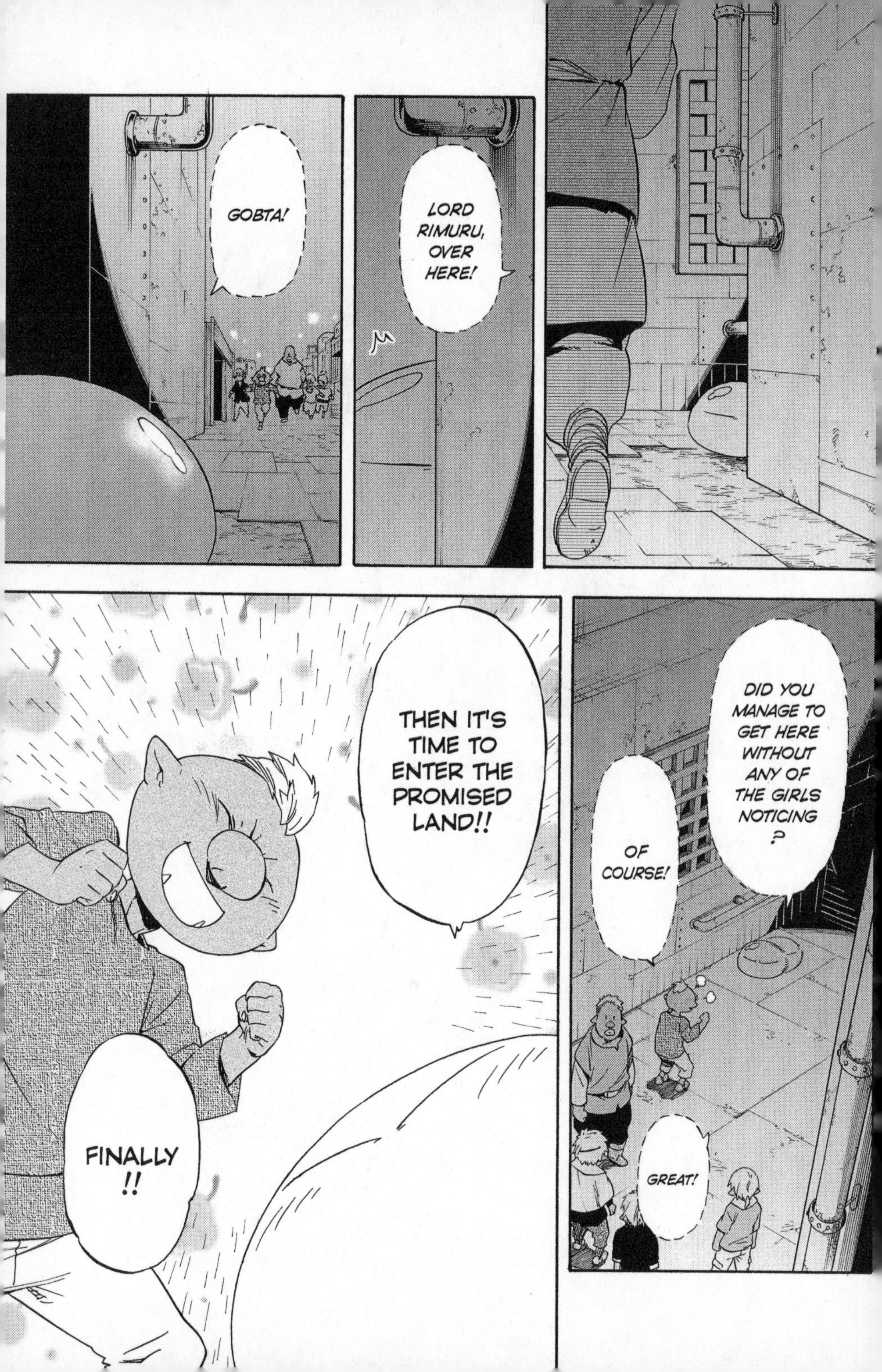
LORD RIMURU, OVER HERE!
GOBTA!
DID YOU MANAGE TO GET HERE WITHOUT ANY OF THE GIRLS NOTICING?
OF COURSE!
GREAT!
THEN IT'S TIME TO ENTER THE PROMISED LAND!!
FINALLY!!

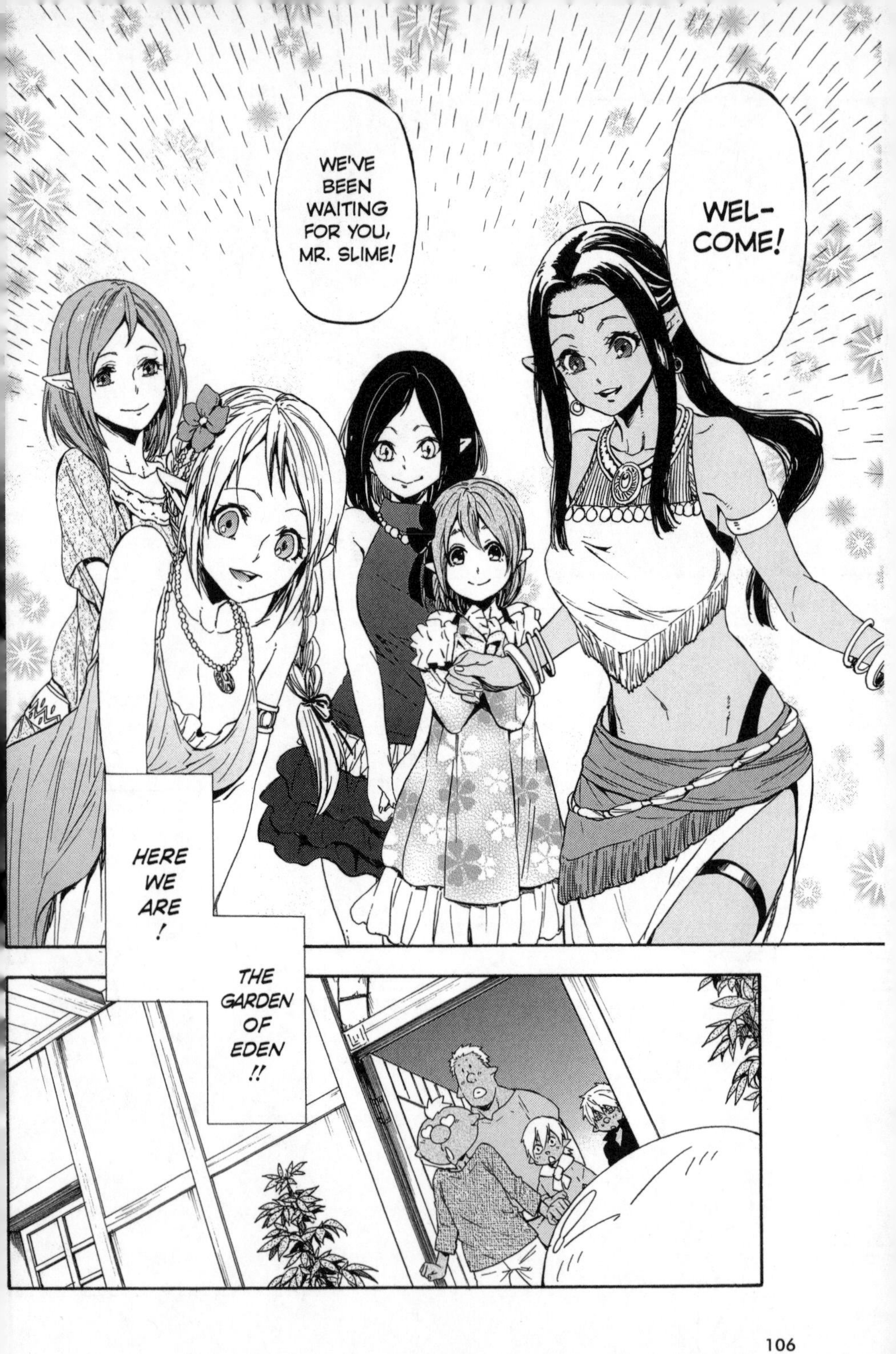
WEL-COME!
WE'VE BEEN WAITING FOR YOU, MR. SLIME!
HERE WE ARE!
THE GARDEN OF EDEN!!

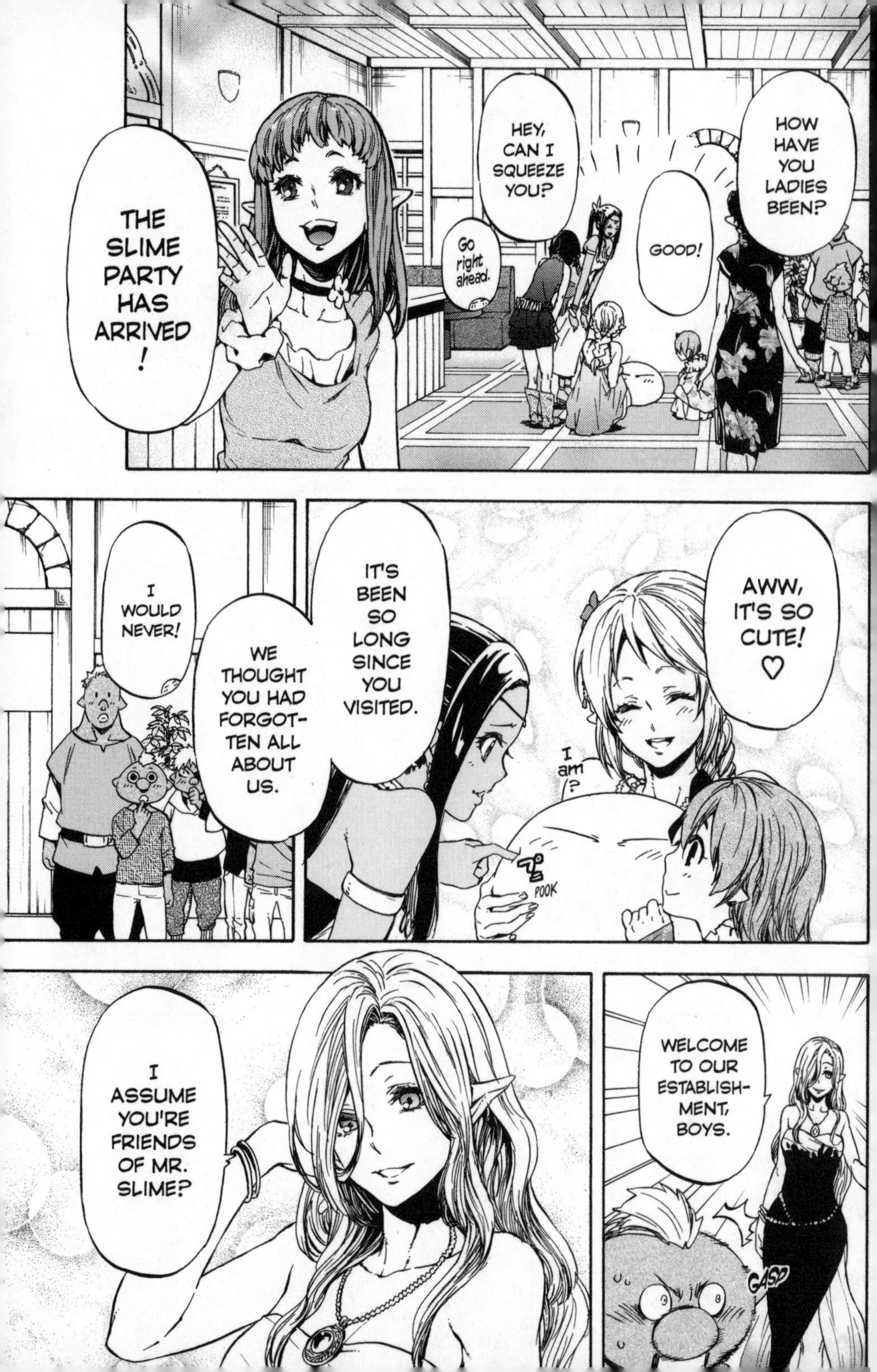
HOW HAVE YOU LADIES BEEN?
GOOD!
HEY, CAN I SQUEEZE YOU?
Go right ahead.
THE SLIME PARTY HAS ARRIVED!
AWW, IT'S SO CUTE! ♡
IT'S BEEN SO LONG SINCE YOU VISITED.
WE THOUGHT YOU HAD FORGOT-TEN ALL ABOUT US.
I am?
POOK
I WOULD NEVER!
WELCOME TO OUR ESTABLISH-MENT, BOYS.
GASP
I ASSUME YOU'RE FRIENDS OF MR. SLIME?

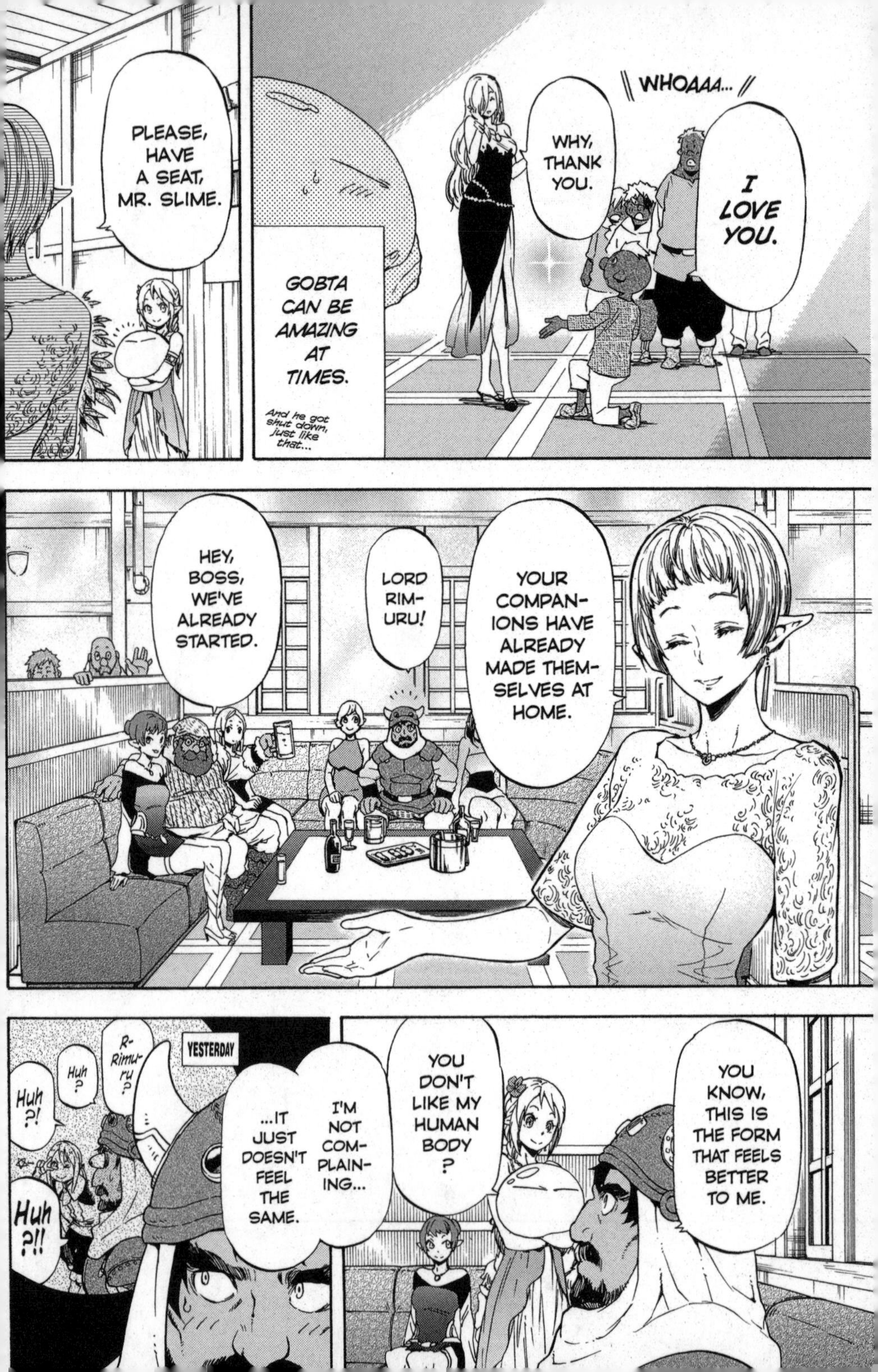

WHOAAA...
I LOVE YOU.
WHY, THANK YOU.
GOBTA CAN BE AMAZING AT TIMES.
And he got shut down, just like that...
PLEASE, HAVE A SEAT, MR. SLIME.
YOUR COMPANIONS HAVE ALREADY MADE THEMSELVES AT HOME.
LORD RIMURU!
HEY, BOSS, WE'VE ALREADY STARTED.
YOU KNOW, THIS IS THE FORM THAT FEELS BETTER TO ME.
YOU DON'T LIKE MY HUMAN BODY?
I'M NOT COMPLAINING...
...IT JUST DOESN'T FEEL THE SAME.
YESTERDAY
R-Rimuru?
Huh?
Huh?!
...
Huh?!!

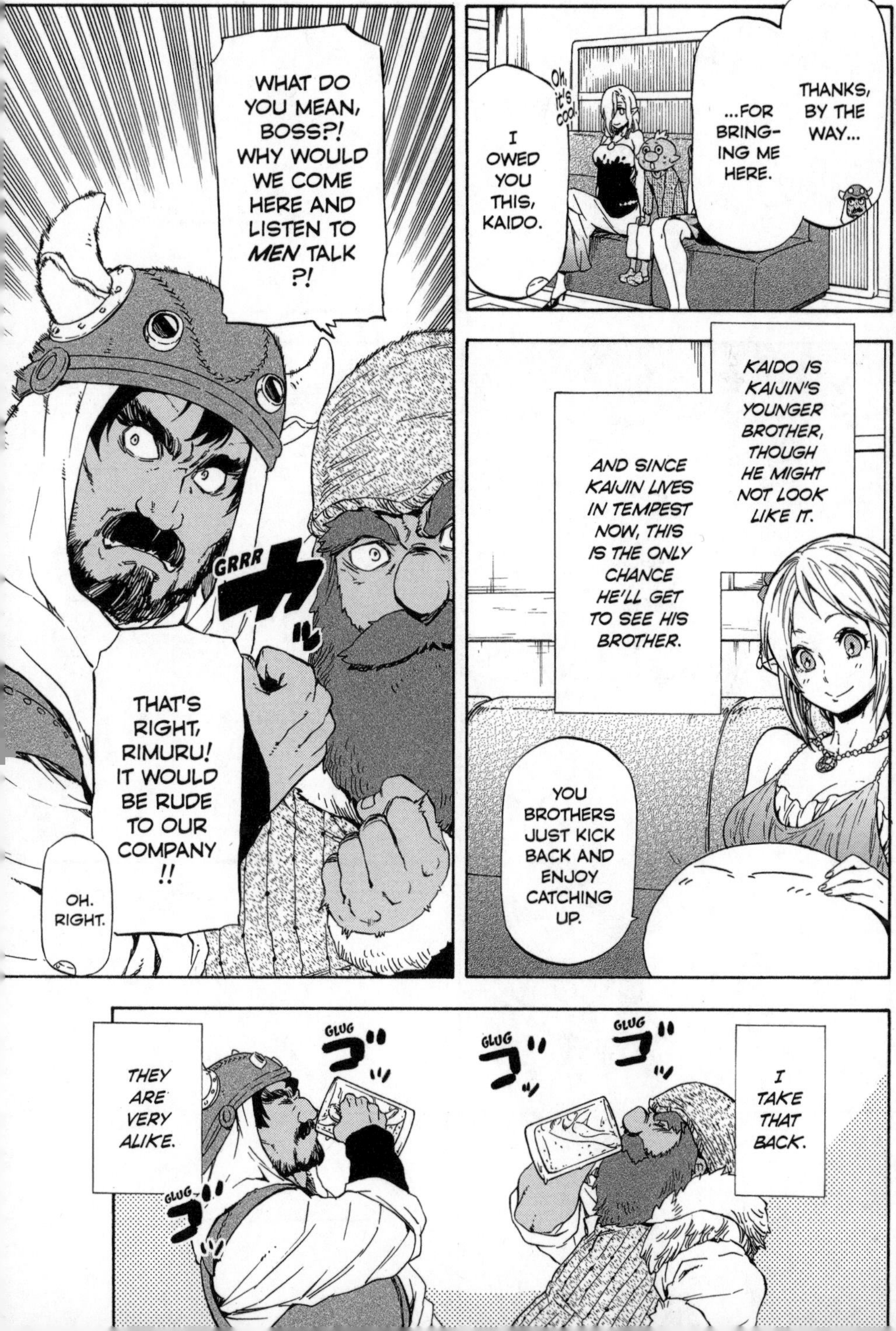
THANKS, BY THE WAY...
...FOR BRINGING ME HERE.
Oh, it's cool.
I OWED YOU THIS, KAIDO.
KAIDO IS KAIJIN'S YOUNGER BROTHER, THOUGH HE MIGHT NOT LOOK LIKE IT.
AND SINCE KAIJIN LIVES IN TEMPEST NOW, THIS IS THE ONLY CHANCE HE'LL GET TO SEE HIS BROTHER.
YOU BROTHERS JUST KICK BACK AND ENJOY CATCHING UP.
WHAT DO YOU MEAN, BOSS?! WHY WOULD WE COME HERE AND LISTEN TO *MEN* TALK?!
GRRR
THAT'S RIGHT, RIMURU! IT WOULD BE RUDE TO OUR COMPANY!!
OH. RIGHT.
I TAKE THAT BACK.
GLUG
GLUG
GLUG
GLUG
THEY ARE VERY ALIKE.

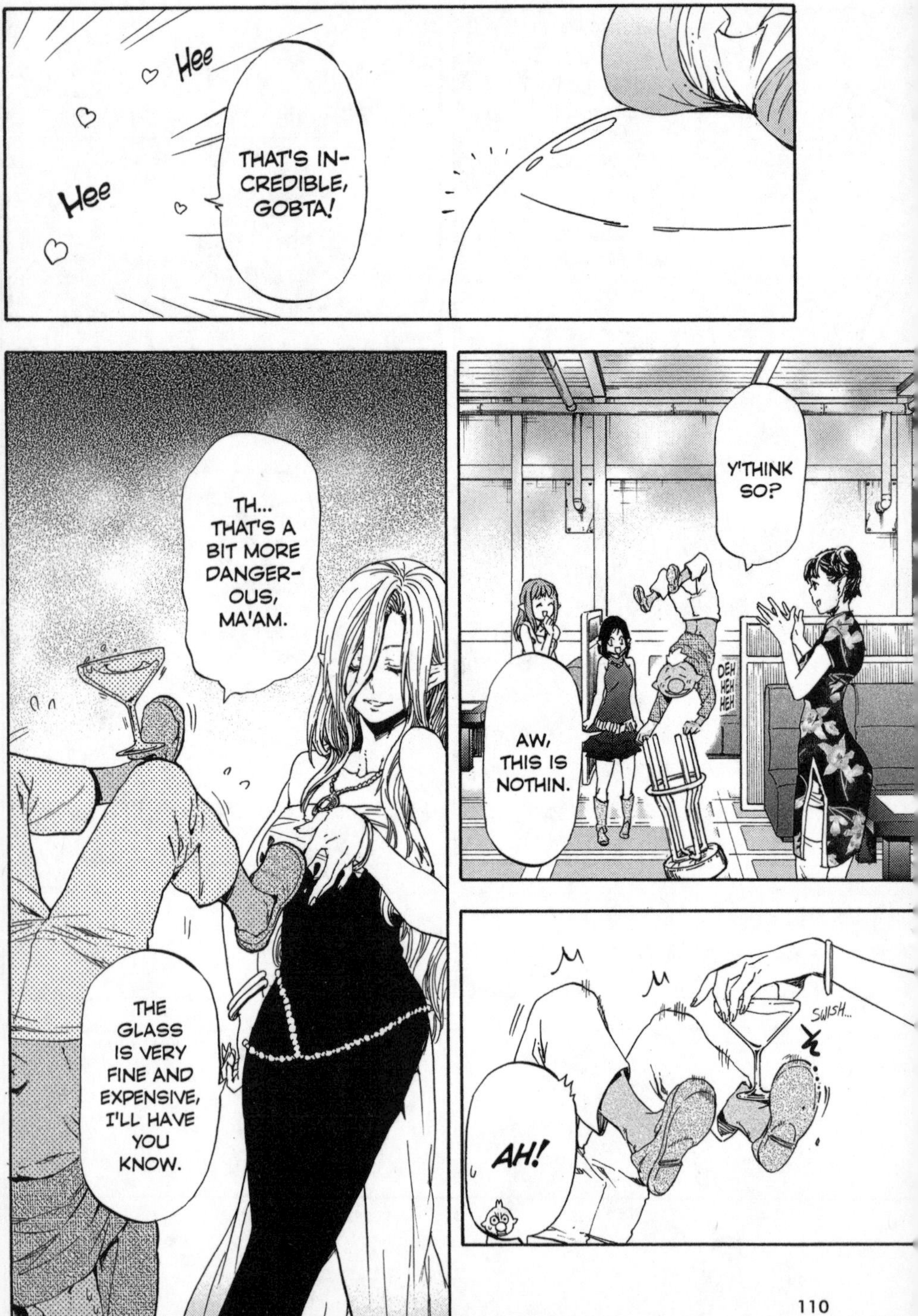
THAT'S IN-CREDIBLE, GOBTA!
Hee
Hee
Y'THINK SO?
DEH HEH HEH
AW, THIS IS NOTHIN.
SWISH...
AH!
TH... THAT'S A BIT MORE DANGER-OUS, MA'AM.
THE GLASS IS VERY FINE AND EXPENSIVE, I'LL HAVE YOU KNOW.

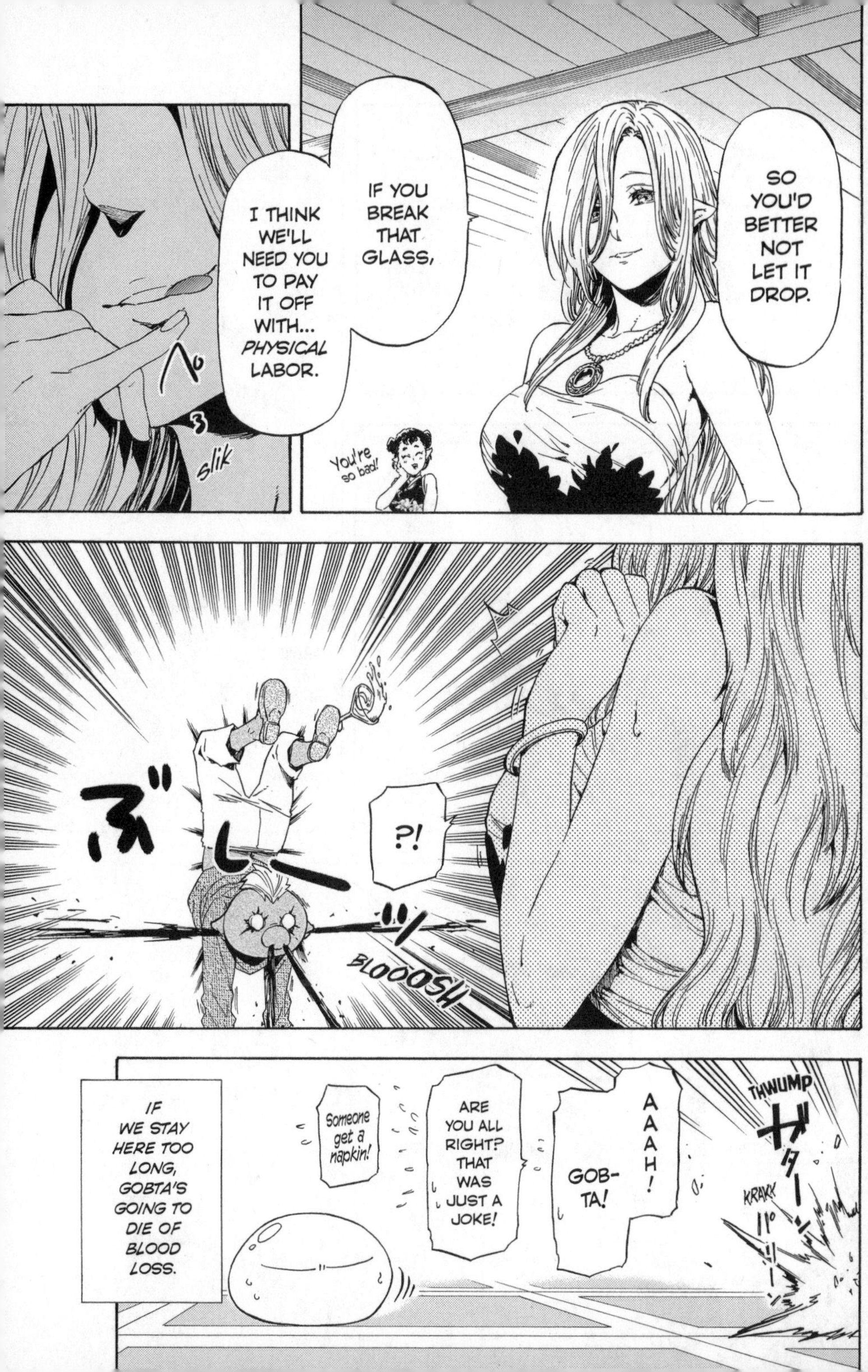

SO YOU'D BETTER NOT LET IT DROP.
IF YOU BREAK THAT GLASS,
I THINK WE'LL NEED YOU TO PAY IT OFF WITH... *PHYSICAL* LABOR.
You're so bad!
slik
?!
BLOOOSH
THWUMP
KRAKK
AAAH!
GOB-TA!
ARE YOU ALL RIGHT? THAT WAS JUST A JOKE!
Someone get a napkin!
IF WE STAY HERE TOO LONG, GOBTA'S GOING TO DIE OF BLOOD LOSS.

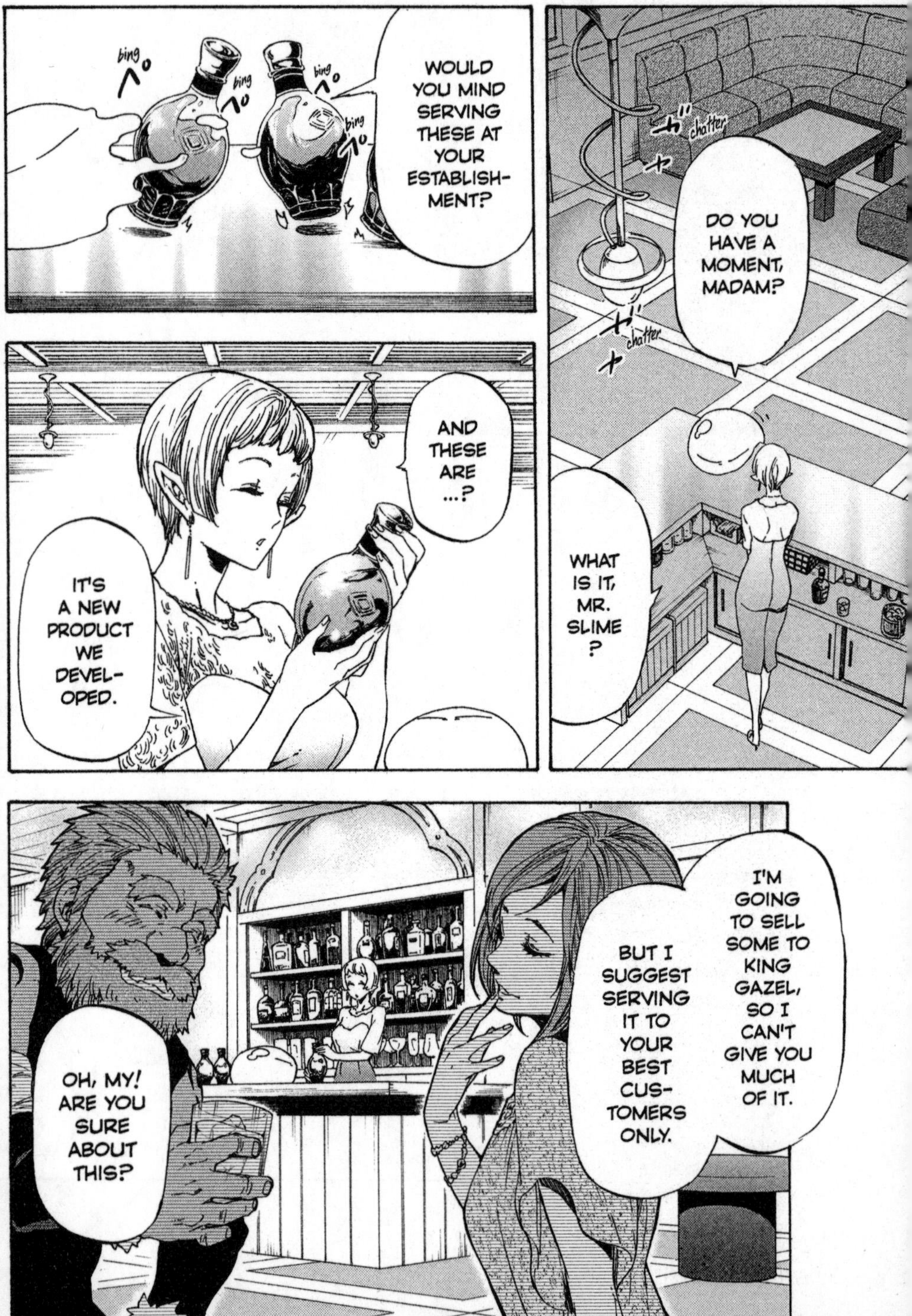
chatter
chatter
DO YOU HAVE A MOMENT, MADAM?
WHAT IS IT, MR. SLIME?
bing
bing
bing
bing
WOULD YOU MIND SERVING THESE AT YOUR ESTABLISHMENT?
AND THESE ARE ...?
IT'S A NEW PRODUCT WE DEVELOPED.
I'M GOING TO SELL SOME TO KING GAZEL, SO I CAN'T GIVE YOU MUCH OF IT.
BUT I SUGGEST SERVING IT TO YOUR BEST CUSTOMERS ONLY.
OH, MY! ARE YOU SURE ABOUT THIS?

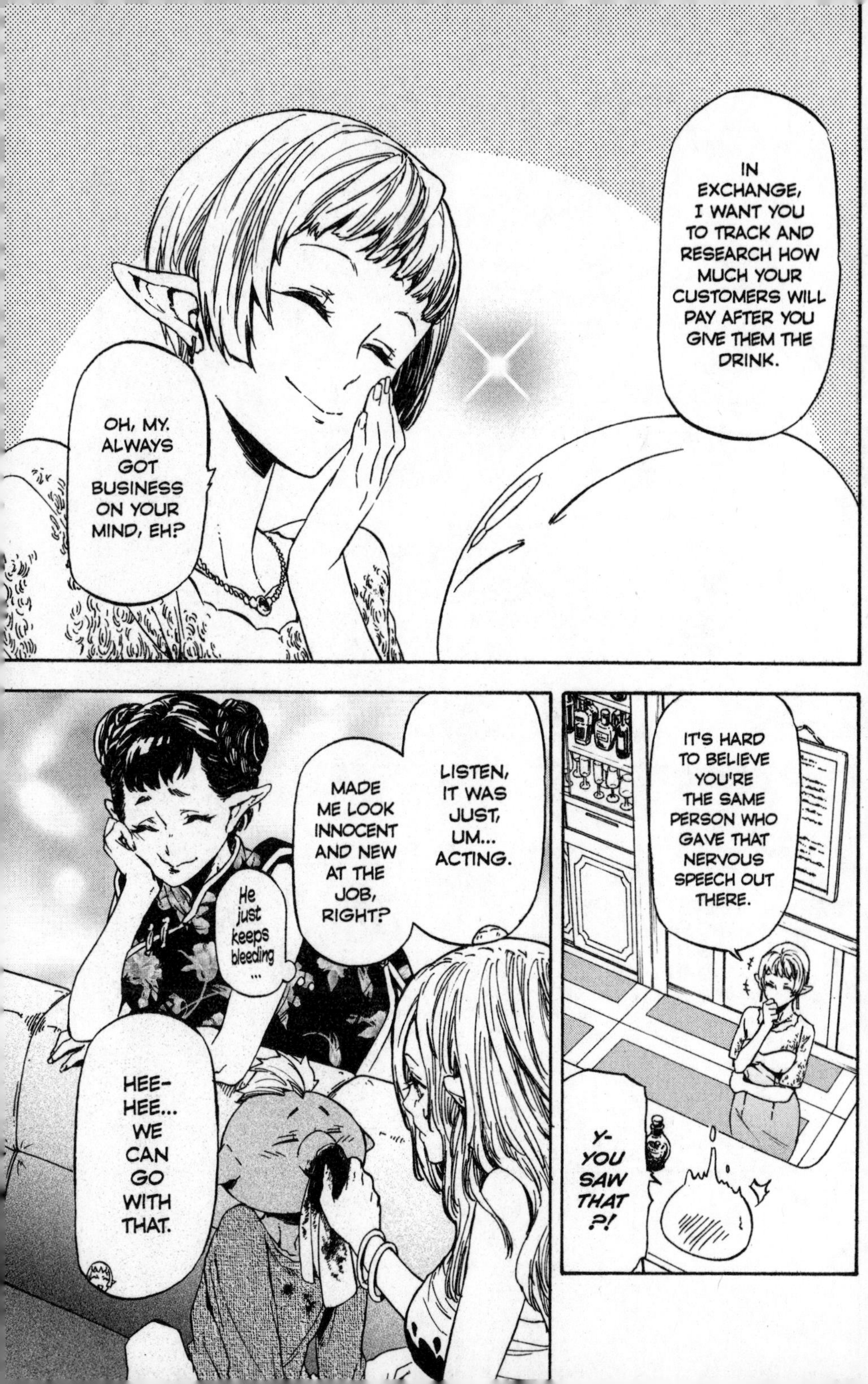
IN EXCHANGE, I WANT YOU TO TRACK AND RESEARCH HOW MUCH YOUR CUSTOMERS WILL PAY AFTER YOU GIVE THEM THE DRINK.
OH, MY. ALWAYS GOT BUSINESS ON YOUR MIND, EH?
IT'S HARD TO BELIEVE YOU'RE THE SAME PERSON WHO GAVE THAT NERVOUS SPEECH OUT THERE.
Y-YOU SAW THAT?!
LISTEN, IT WAS JUST, UM... ACTING.
MADE ME LOOK INNOCENT AND NEW AT THE JOB, RIGHT?
He just keeps bleeding...
HEE-HEE... WE CAN GO WITH THAT.

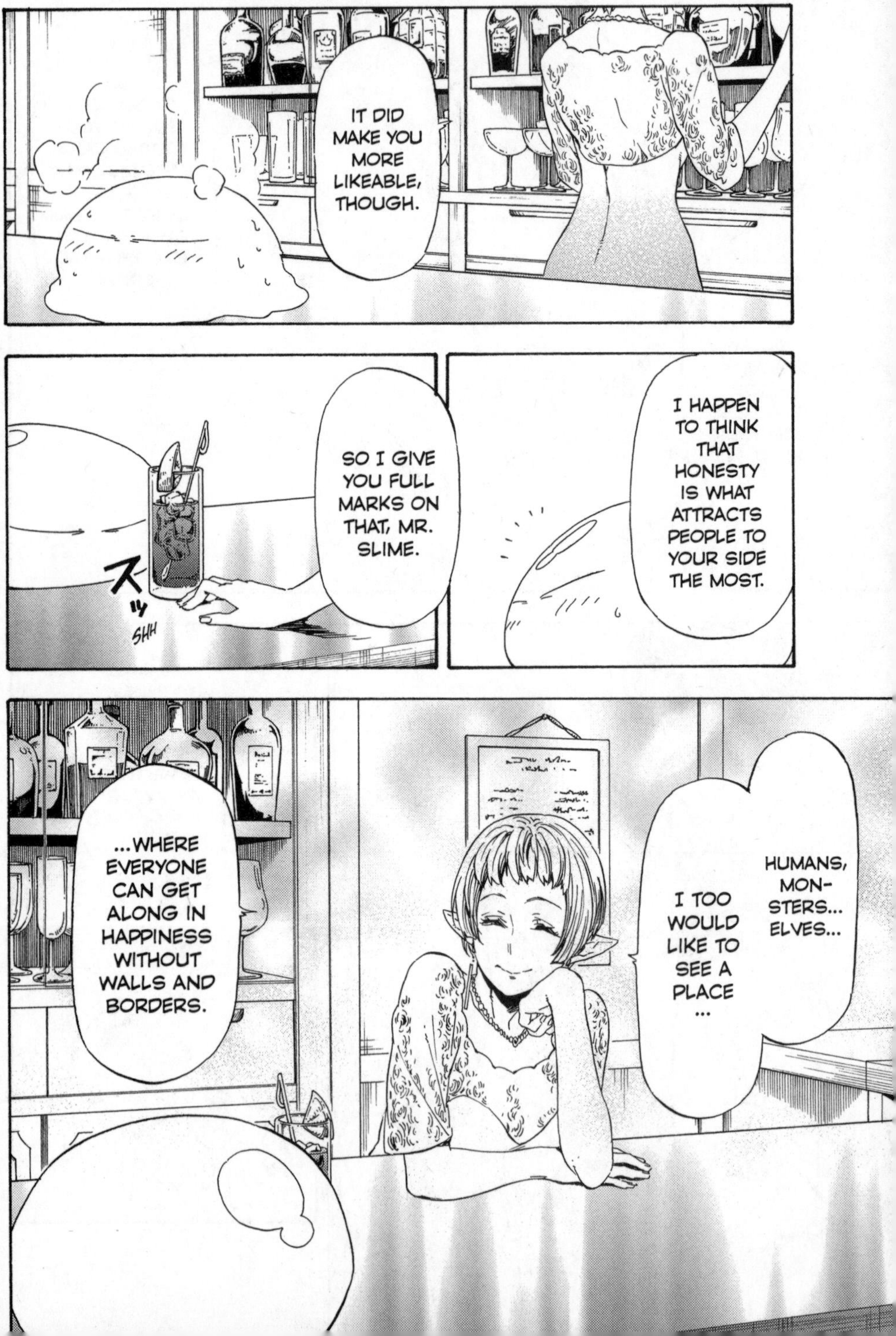
IT DID MAKE YOU MORE LIKEABLE, THOUGH.
I HAPPEN TO THINK THAT HONESTY IS WHAT ATTRACTS PEOPLE TO YOUR SIDE THE MOST.
SO I GIVE YOU FULL MARKS ON THAT, MR. SLIME.
スッ
SHH
HUMANS, MON-STERS... ELVES...
I TOO WOULD LIKE TO SEE A PLACE ...
...WHERE EVERYONE CAN GET ALONG IN HAPPINESS WITHOUT WALLS AND BORDERS.

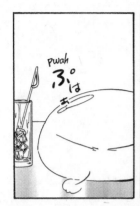

PWAH
ぷは

GLUG
GLUG
GLUG

...THANK YOU.

COME NOW, BROTHER... KEEP YOUR FOOTING STEADY.

WOBBL

WOBBL

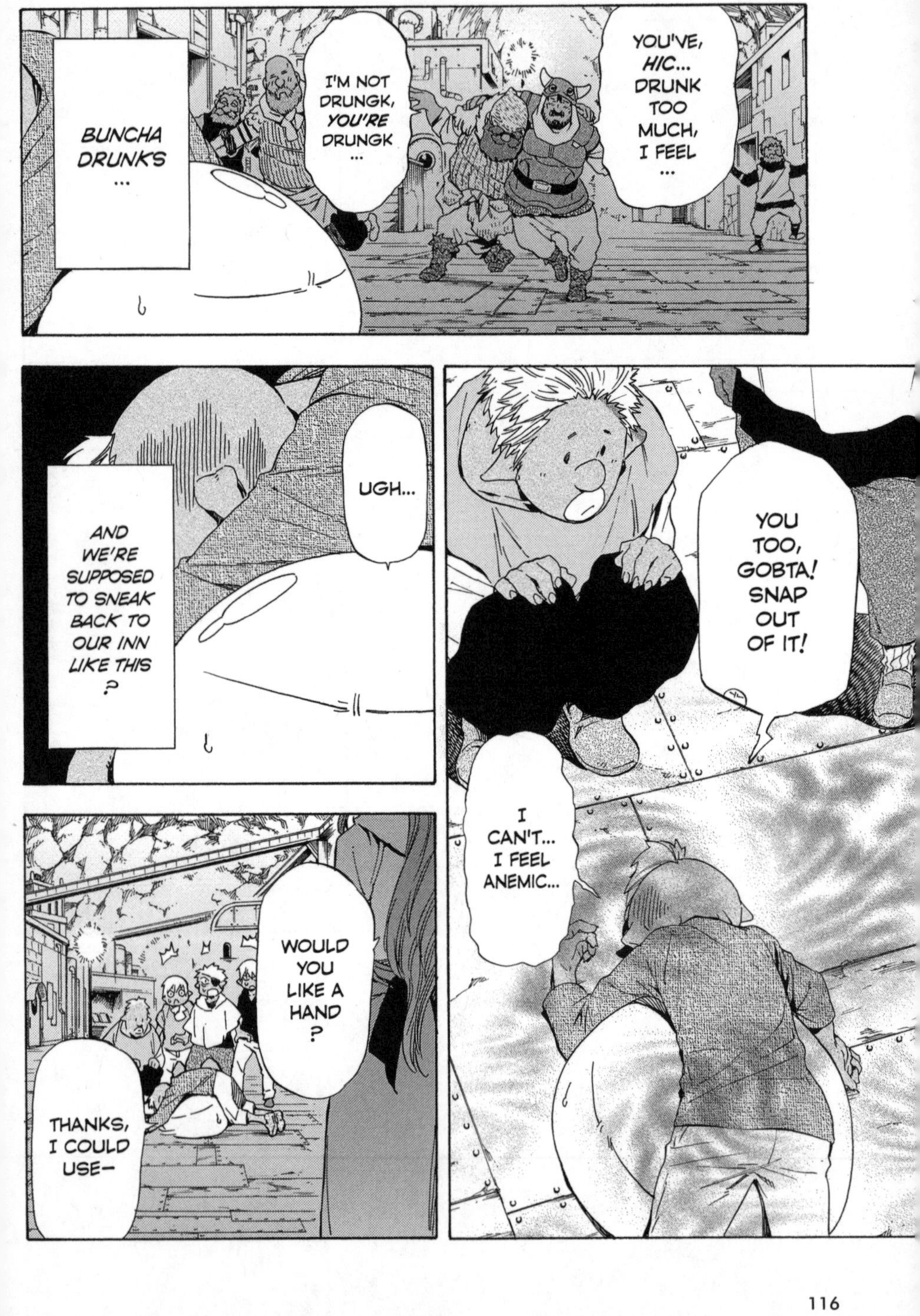
YOU'VE, *HIC*... DRUNK TOO MUCH, I FEEL...
I'M NOT DRUNGK, *YOU'RE* DRUNGK...
BUNCHA DRUNKS...
YOU TOO, GOBTA! SNAP OUT OF IT!
UGH...
AND WE'RE SUPPOSED TO SNEAK BACK TO OUR INN LIKE THIS?
I CAN'T... I FEEL ANEMIC...
WOULD YOU LIKE A HAND?
THANKS, I COULD USE—

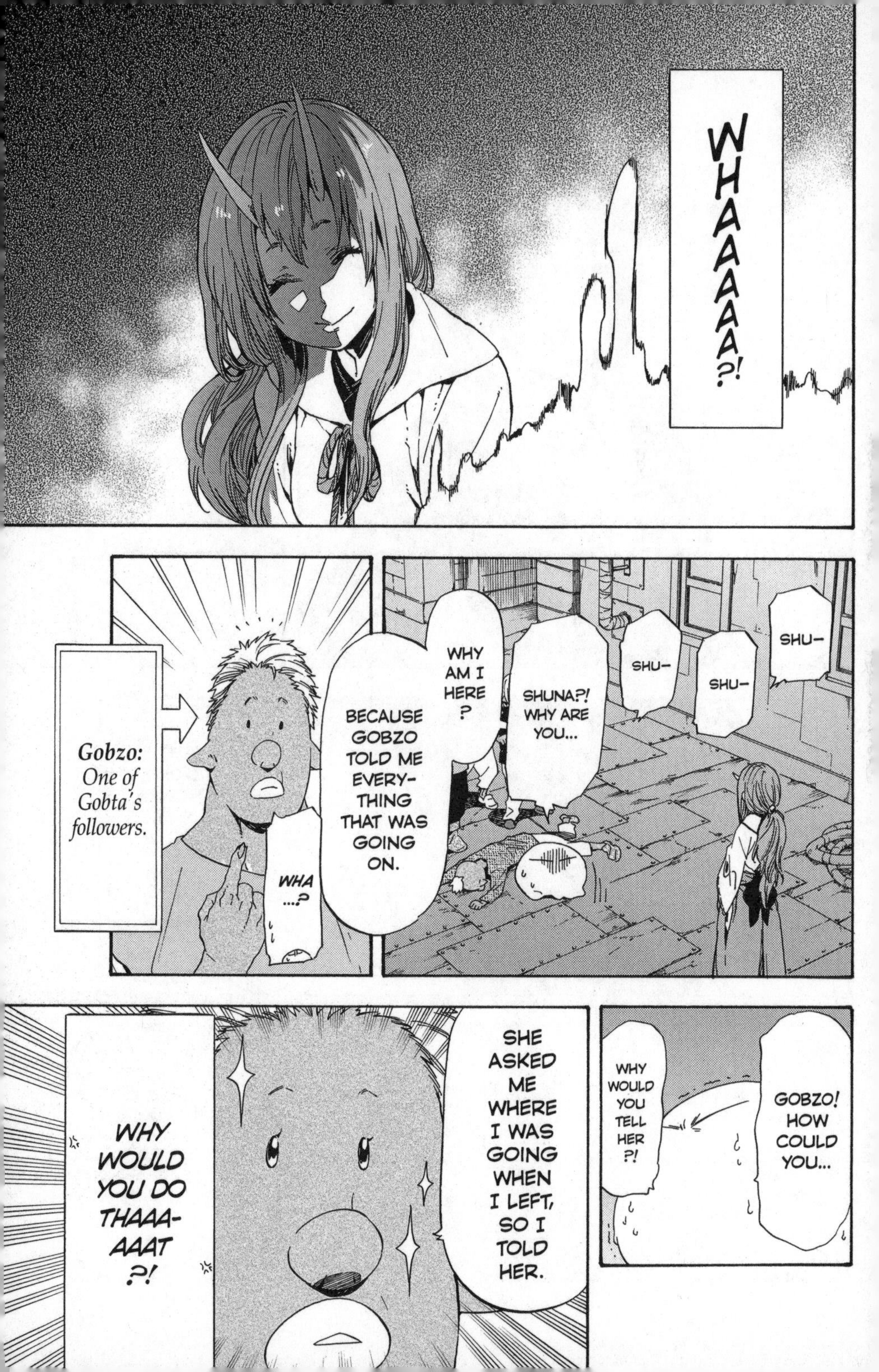
WHAAAAAA?!
SHU–
SHU–
SHU–
SHUNA?! WHY ARE YOU...
WHY AM I HERE?
BECAUSE GOBZO TOLD ME EVERY-THING THAT WAS GOING ON.
WHA...?
Gobzo: *One of Gobta's followers.*
GOBZO! HOW COULD YOU...
WHY WOULD YOU TELL HER?!
SHE ASKED ME WHERE I WAS GOING WHEN I LEFT, SO I TOLD HER.
WHY WOULD YOU DO THAAA-AAAT?!

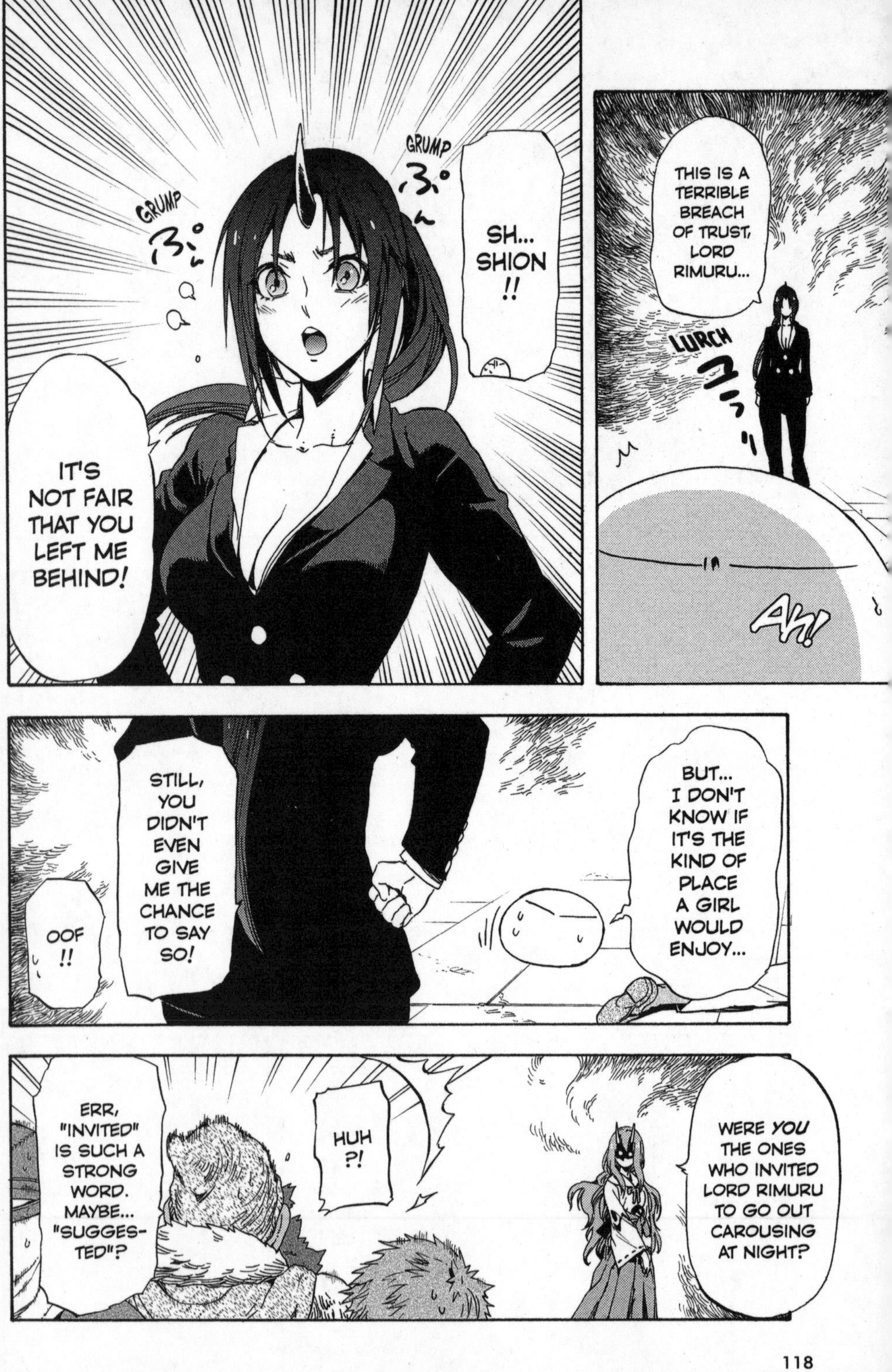

THIS IS A TERRIBLE BREACH OF TRUST, LORD RIMURU...
LURCH
AH!
GRUMP
SH... SHION!!
GRUMP
IT'S NOT FAIR THAT YOU LEFT ME BEHIND!
BUT... I DON'T KNOW IF IT'S THE KIND OF PLACE A GIRL WOULD ENJOY...
STILL, YOU DIDN'T EVEN GIVE ME THE CHANCE TO SAY SO!
OOF!!
WERE *YOU* THE ONES WHO INVITED LORD RIMURU TO GO OUT CAROUSING AT NIGHT?
HUH?!
ERR, "INVITED" IS SUCH A STRONG WORD. MAYBE... "SUGGESTED"?

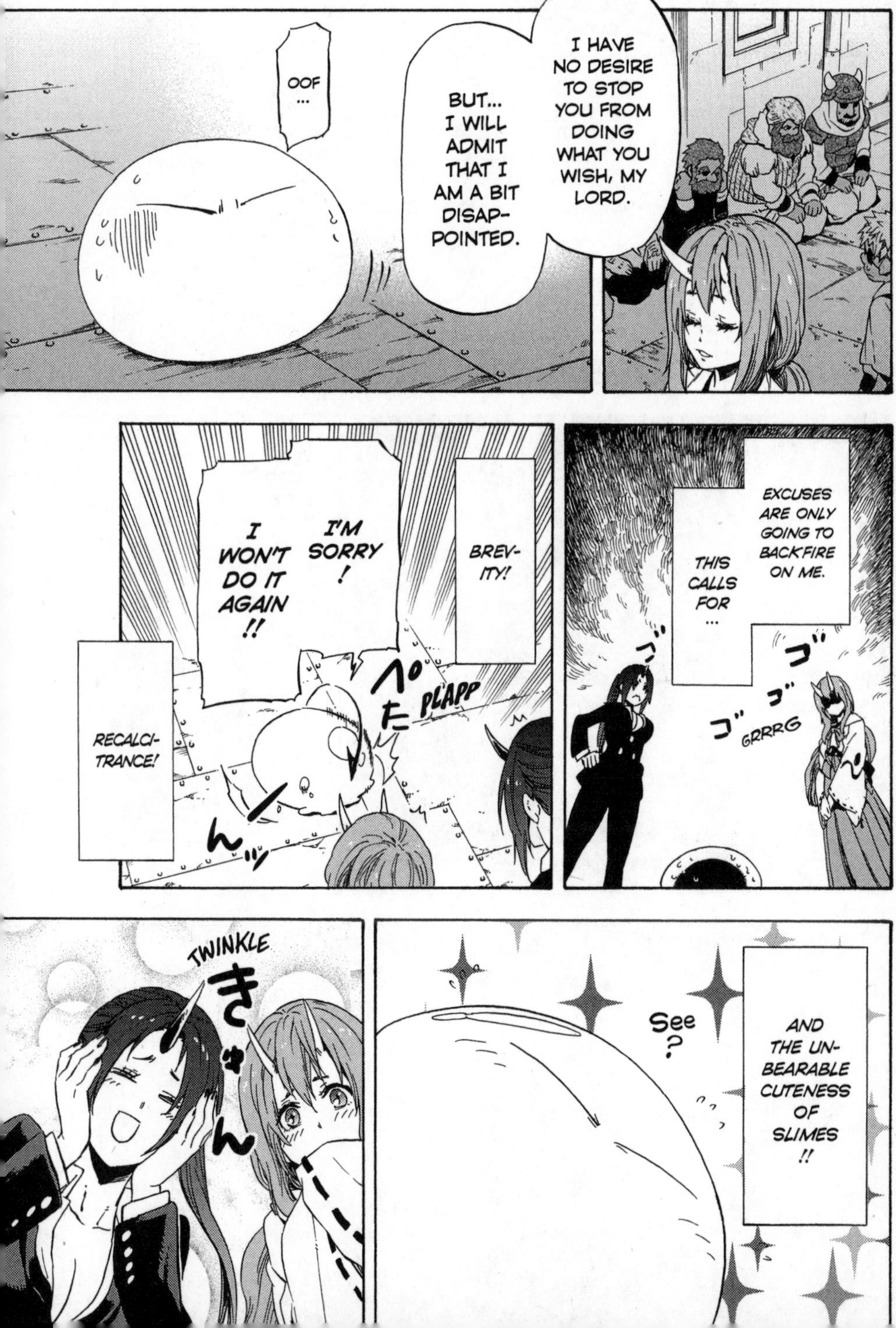
I HAVE NO DESIRE TO STOP YOU FROM DOING WHAT YOU WISH, MY LORD.
BUT... I WILL ADMIT THAT I AM A BIT DISAP-POINTED.
OOF ...
EXCUSES ARE ONLY GOING TO BACKFIRE ON ME.
THIS CALLS FOR ...
GRRRG
BREV-ITY!
I'M SORRY!
I WON'T DO IT AGAIN!!
RECALCI-TRANCE!
PLAPP
へた
AND THE UN-BEARABLE CUTENESS OF SLIMES!!
See?
TWINKLE
きゅん

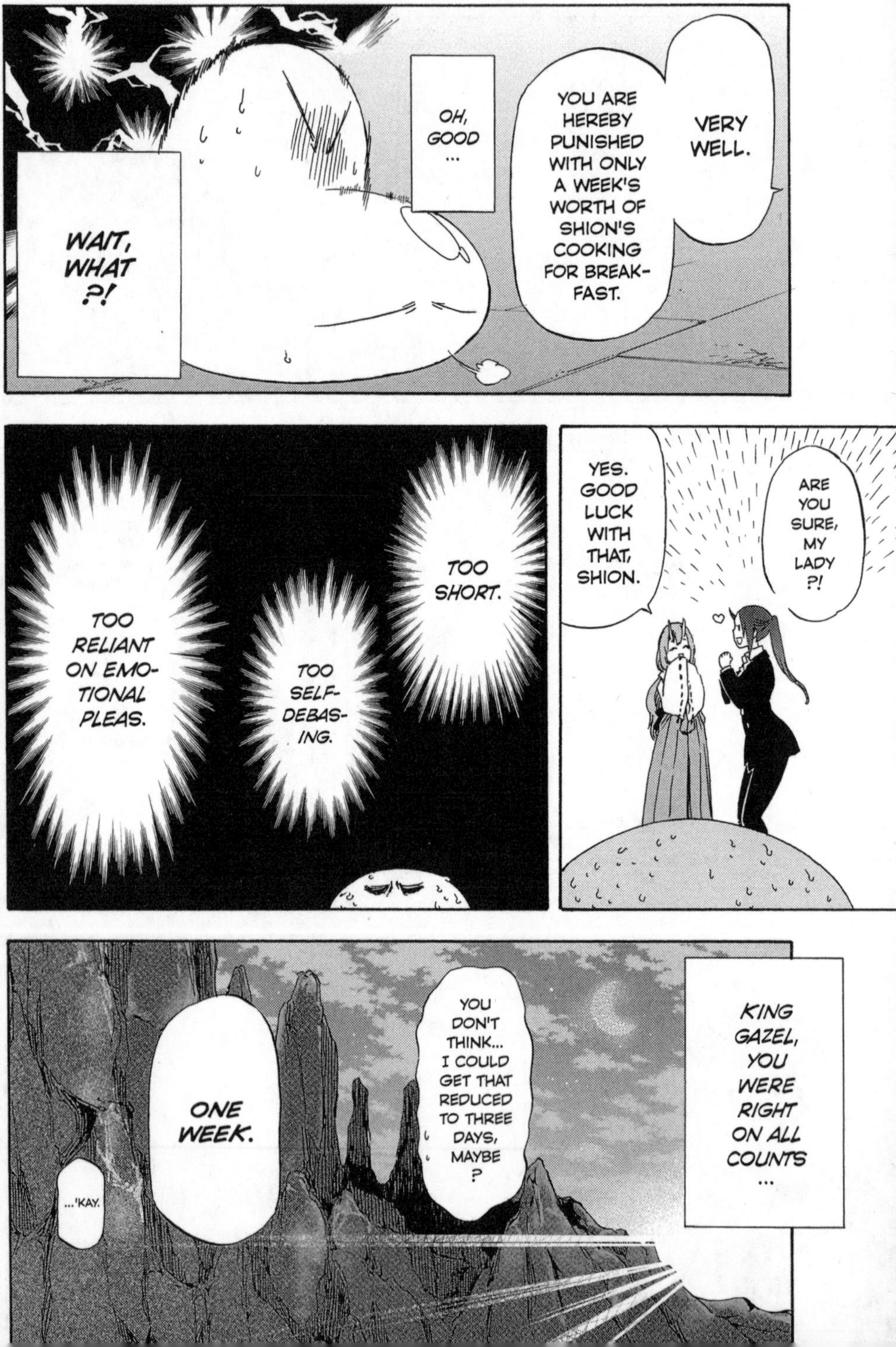
VERY WELL.
YOU ARE HEREBY PUNISHED WITH ONLY A WEEK'S WORTH OF SHION'S COOKING FOR BREAK-FAST.
OH, GOOD...
WAIT, WHAT?!
ARE YOU SURE, MY LADY?!
YES. GOOD LUCK WITH THAT, SHION.
TOO SHORT.
TOO SELF-DEBAS-ING.
TOO RELIANT ON EMO-TIONAL PLEAS.
KING GAZEL, YOU WERE RIGHT ON ALL COUNTS...
YOU DON'T THINK... I COULD GET THAT REDUCED TO THREE DAYS, MAYBE?
ONE WEEK.
...'KAY.

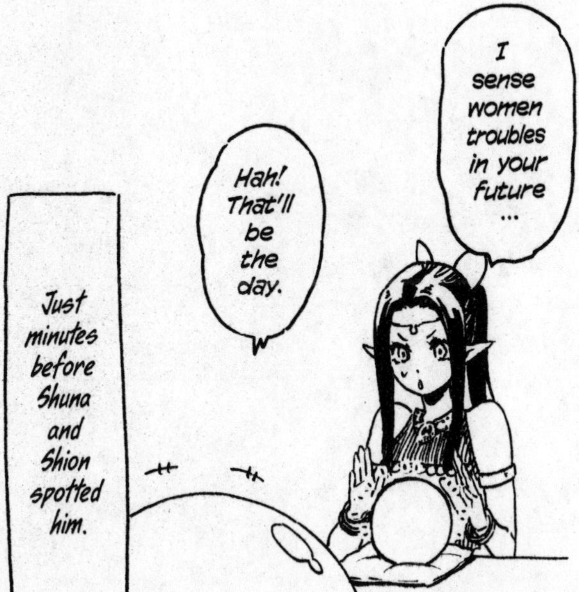
I sense women troubles in your future ...
Hah! That'll be the day.
Just minutes before Shuna and Shion spotted him.

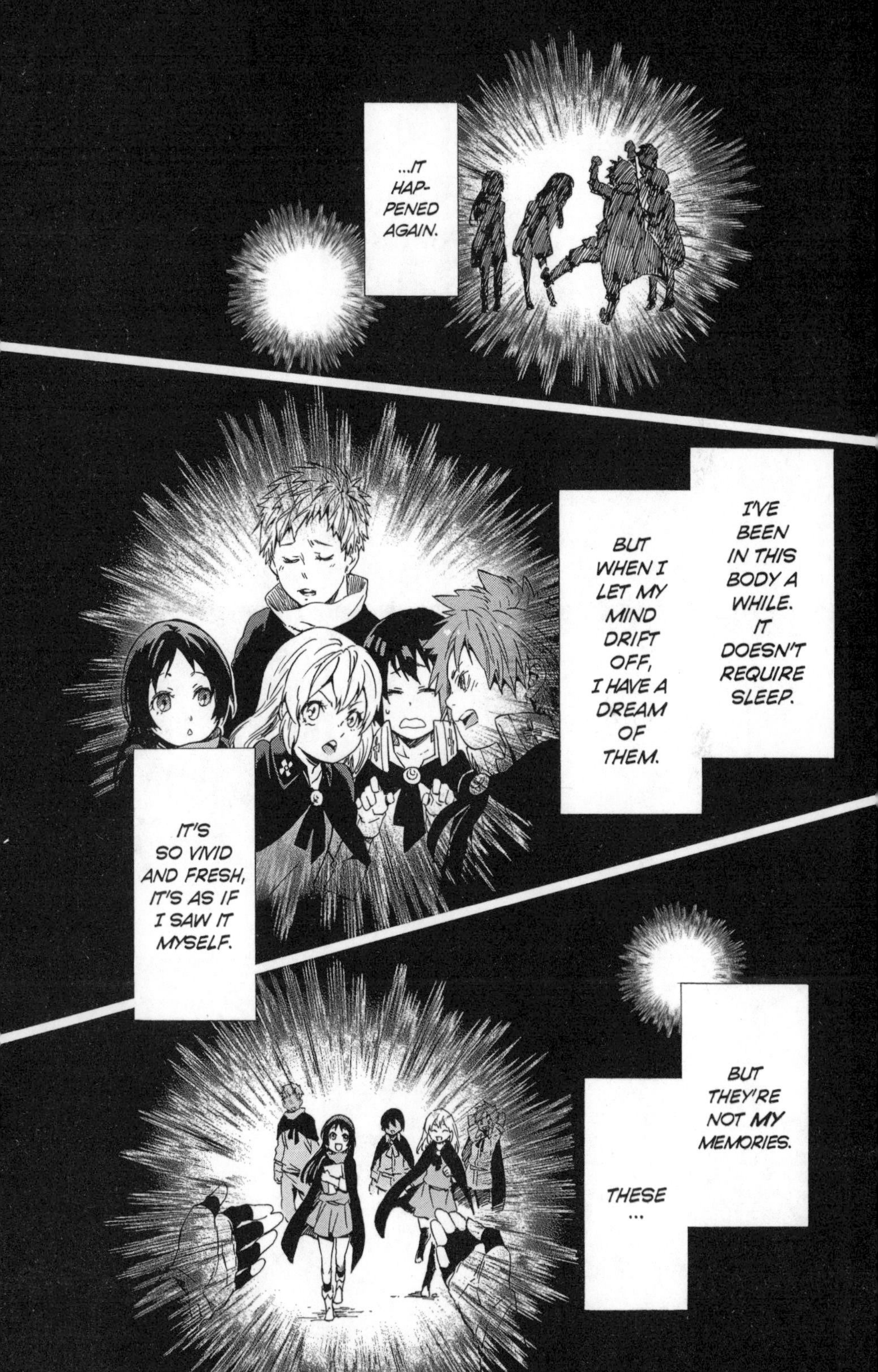
...IT HAP-PENED AGAIN.
I'VE BEEN IN THIS BODY A WHILE. IT DOESN'T REQUIRE SLEEP.
BUT WHEN I LET MY MIND DRIFT OFF, I HAVE A DREAM OF THEM.
IT'S SO VIVID AND FRESH, IT'S AS IF I SAW IT MYSELF.
BUT THEY'RE NOT MY MEMORIES.
THESE ...

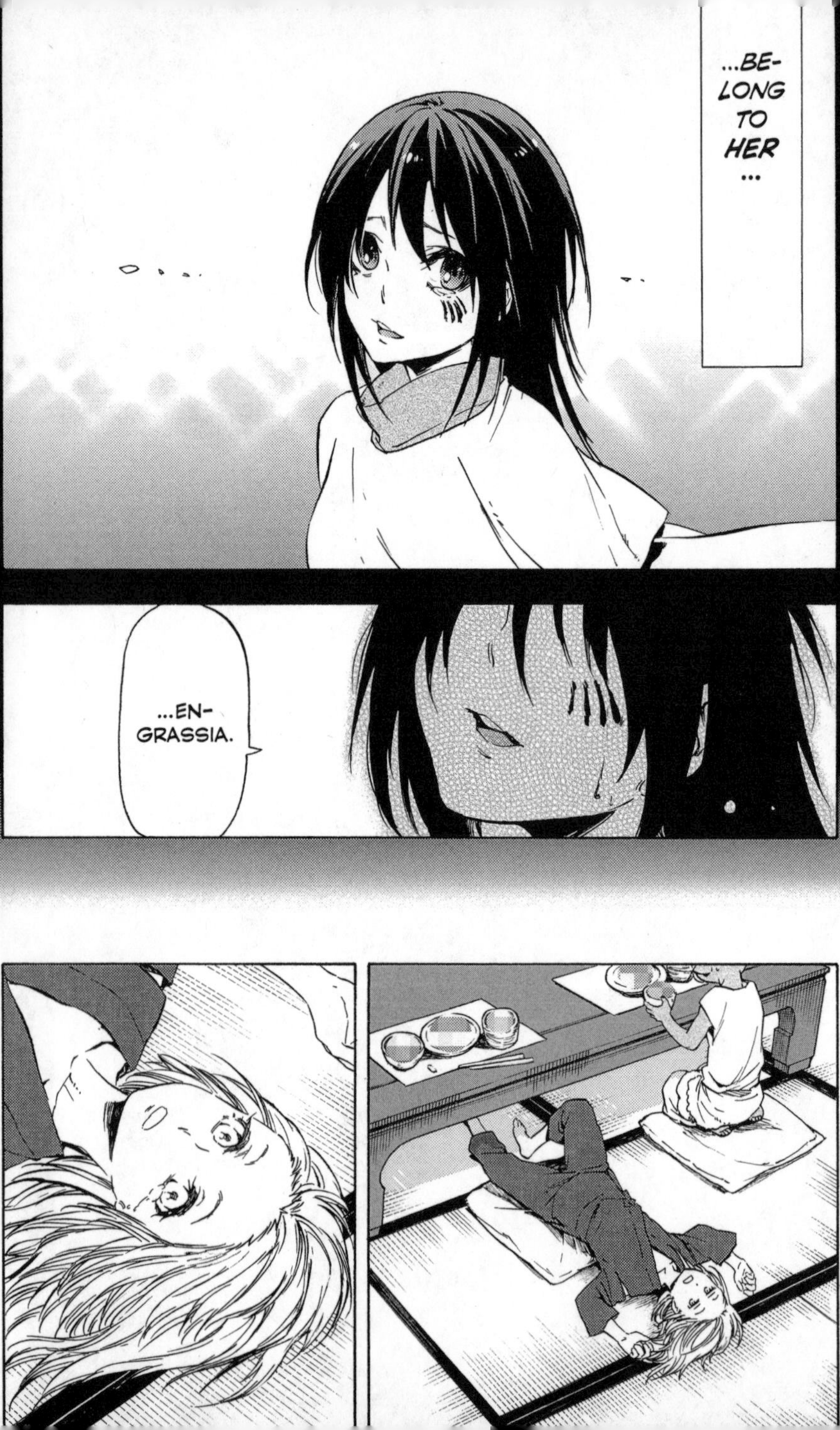
...BE-LONG TO HER ...
...EN-GRASSIA.

CHAPTER 43 To the Human Kingdom

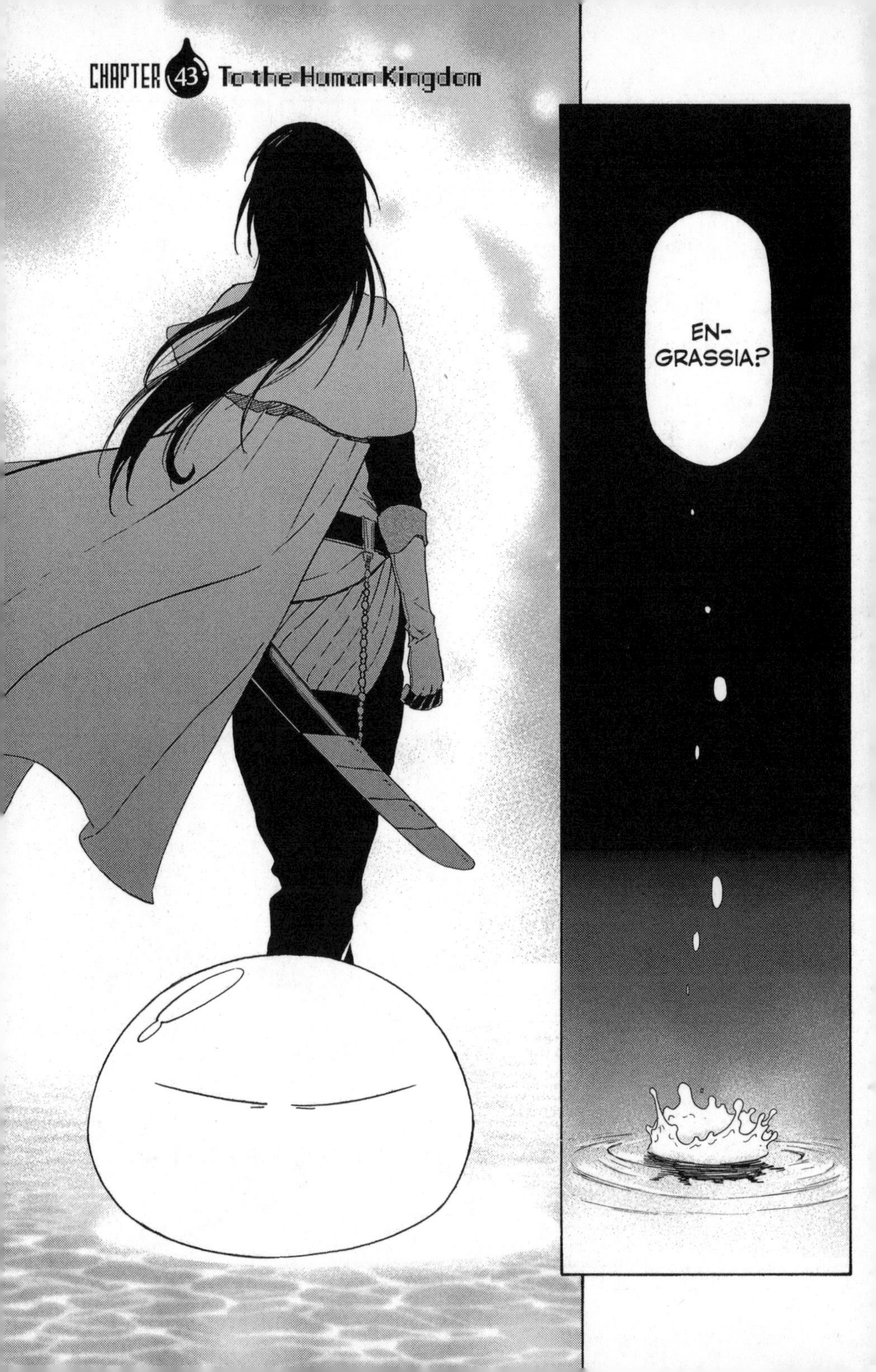
EN-
GRASSIA?

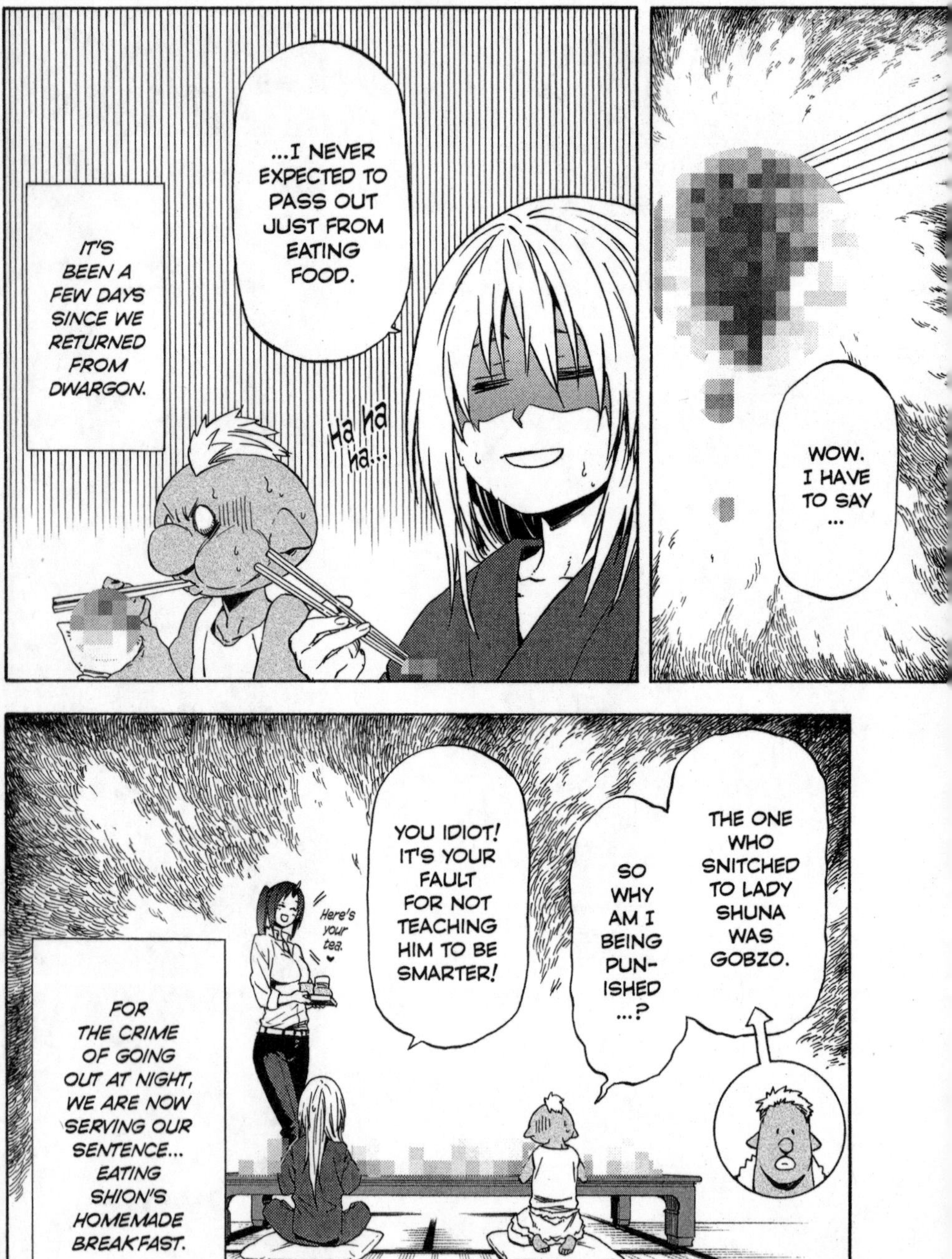
WOW. I HAVE TO SAY ...
...I NEVER EXPECTED TO PASS OUT JUST FROM EATING FOOD.
IT'S BEEN A FEW DAYS SINCE WE RETURNED FROM DWARGON.
Ha ha ha...
THE ONE WHO SNITCHED TO LADY SHUNA WAS GOBZO.
SO WHY AM I BEING PUN-ISHED ...?
YOU IDIOT! IT'S YOUR FAULT FOR NOT TEACHING HIM TO BE SMARTER!
Here's your tea. ♥
FOR THE CRIME OF GOING OUT AT NIGHT, WE ARE NOW SERVING OUR SENTENCE... EATING SHION'S HOMEMADE BREAKFAST.

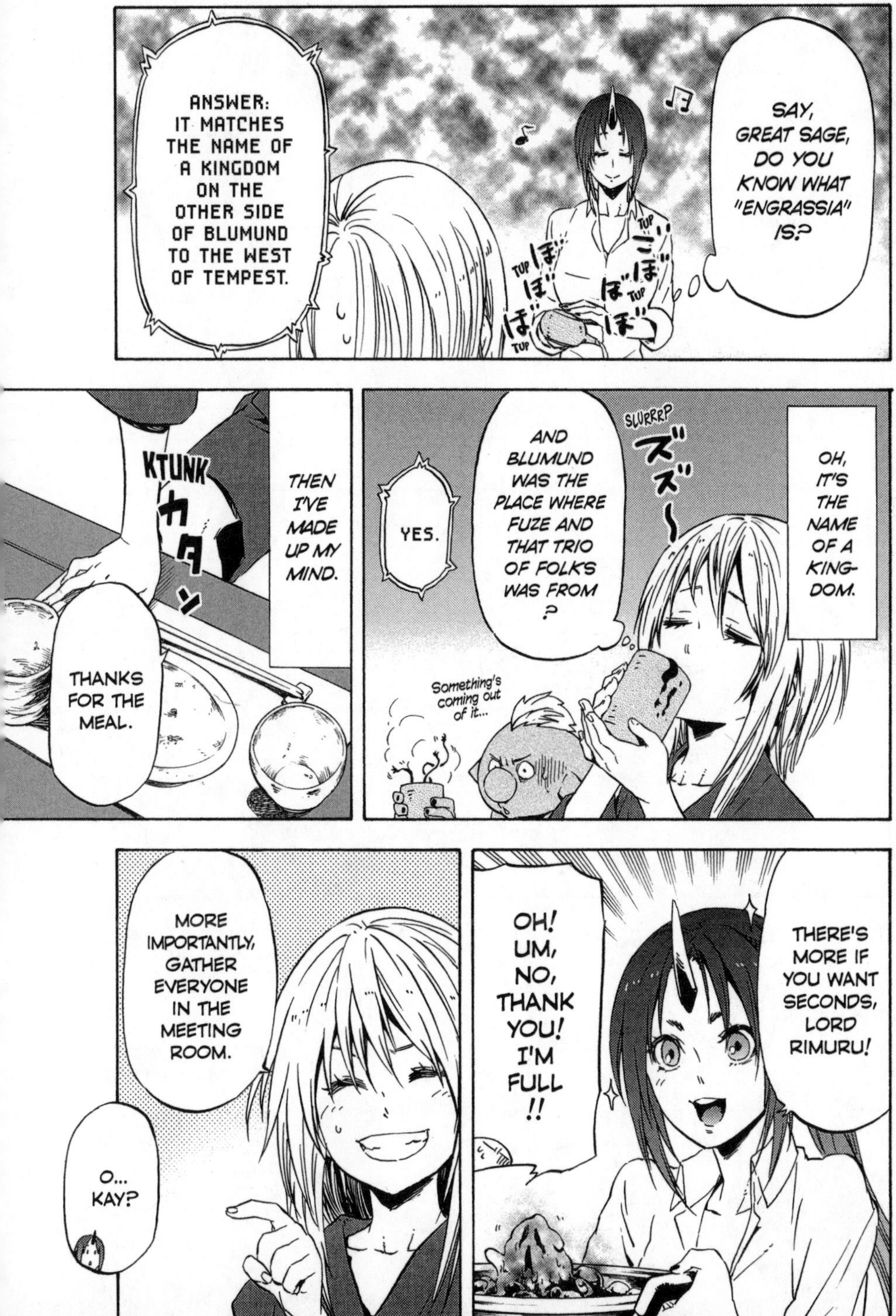
SAY, GREAT SAGE, DO YOU KNOW WHAT "ENGRASSIA" IS?
TUP TUP TUP TUP TUP
ANSWER: IT MATCHES THE NAME OF A KINGDOM ON THE OTHER SIDE OF BLUMUND TO THE WEST OF TEMPEST.
OH, IT'S THE NAME OF A KING-DOM.
SLURRRP
ズズ～
AND BLUMUND WAS THE PLACE WHERE FUZE AND THAT TRIO OF FOLKS WAS FROM?
YES.
Something's coming out of it...
THEN I'VE MADE UP MY MIND.
KTUNK
カタン
THANKS FOR THE MEAL.
THERE'S MORE IF YOU WANT SECONDS, LORD RIMURU!
OH! UM, NO, THANK YOU! I'M FULL!!
MORE IMPORTANTLY, GATHER EVERYONE IN THE MEETING ROOM.
O... KAY?

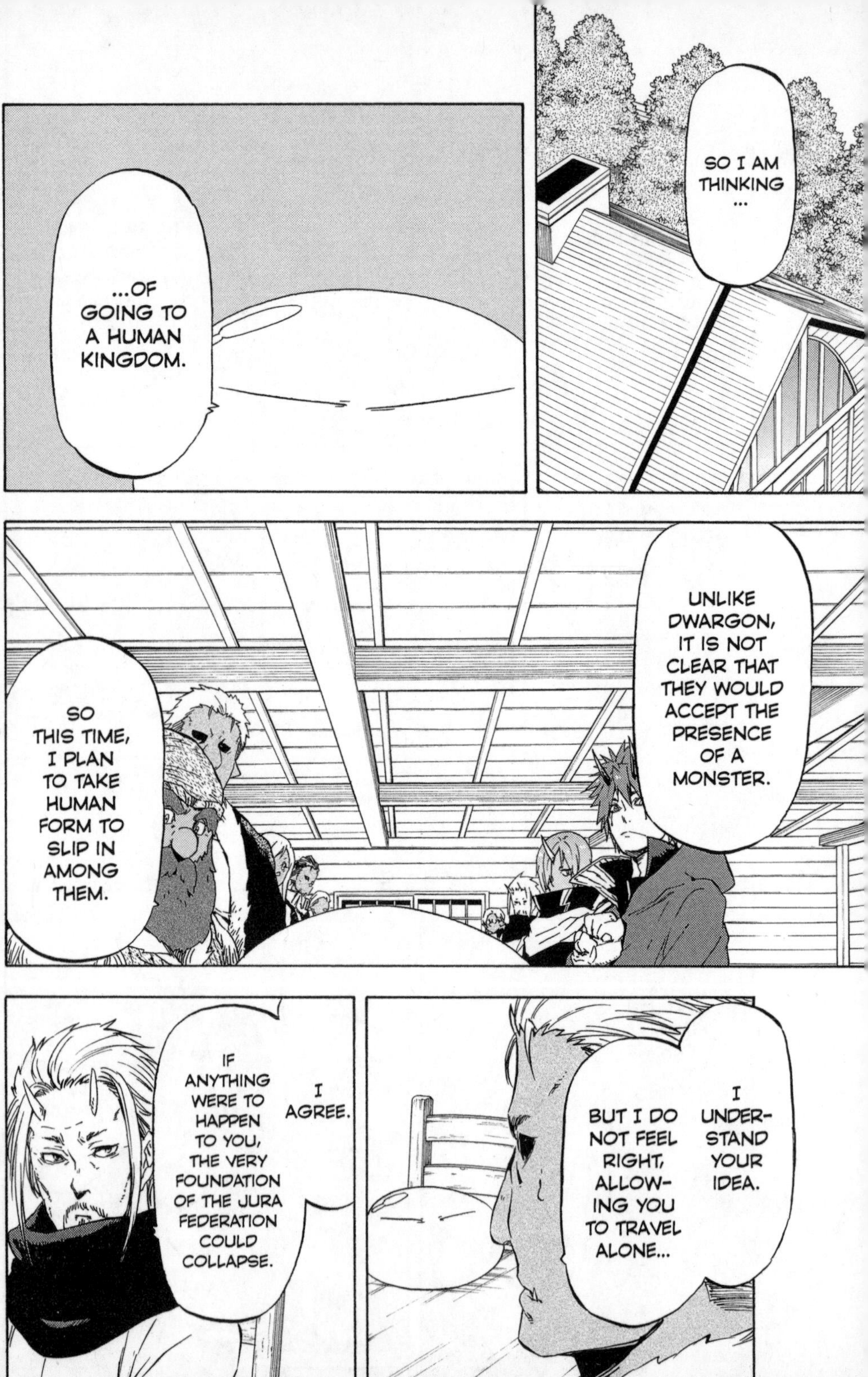
SO I AM THINKING ...
...OF GOING TO A HUMAN KINGDOM.
UNLIKE DWARGON, IT IS NOT CLEAR THAT THEY WOULD ACCEPT THE PRESENCE OF A MONSTER.
SO THIS TIME, I PLAN TO TAKE HUMAN FORM TO SLIP IN AMONG THEM.
I UNDER-STAND YOUR IDEA.
BUT I DO NOT FEEL RIGHT, ALLOW-ING YOU TO TRAVEL ALONE...
I AGREE.
IF ANYTHING WERE TO HAPPEN TO YOU, THE VERY FOUNDATION OF THE JURA FEDERATION COULD COLLAPSE.

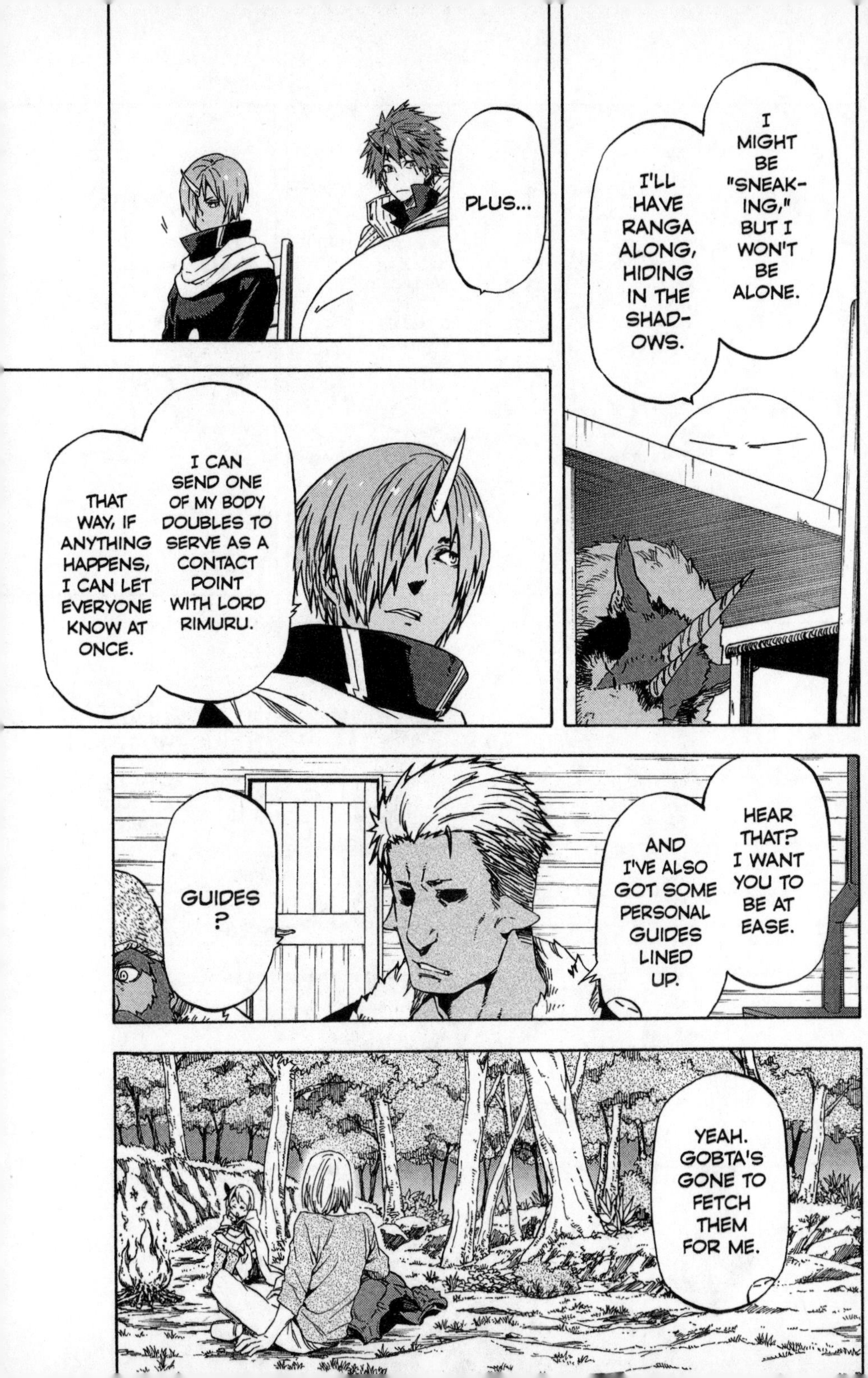
I MIGHT BE "SNEAKING," BUT I WON'T BE ALONE.
I'LL HAVE RANGA ALONG, HIDING IN THE SHADOWS.
PLUS...
I CAN SEND ONE OF MY BODY DOUBLES TO SERVE AS A CONTACT POINT WITH LORD RIMURU.
THAT WAY, IF ANYTHING HAPPENS, I CAN LET EVERYONE KNOW AT ONCE.
HEAR THAT? I WANT YOU TO BE AT EASE.
AND I'VE ALSO GOT SOME PERSONAL GUIDES LINED UP.
GUIDES?
YEAH. GOBTA'S GONE TO FETCH THEM FOR ME.

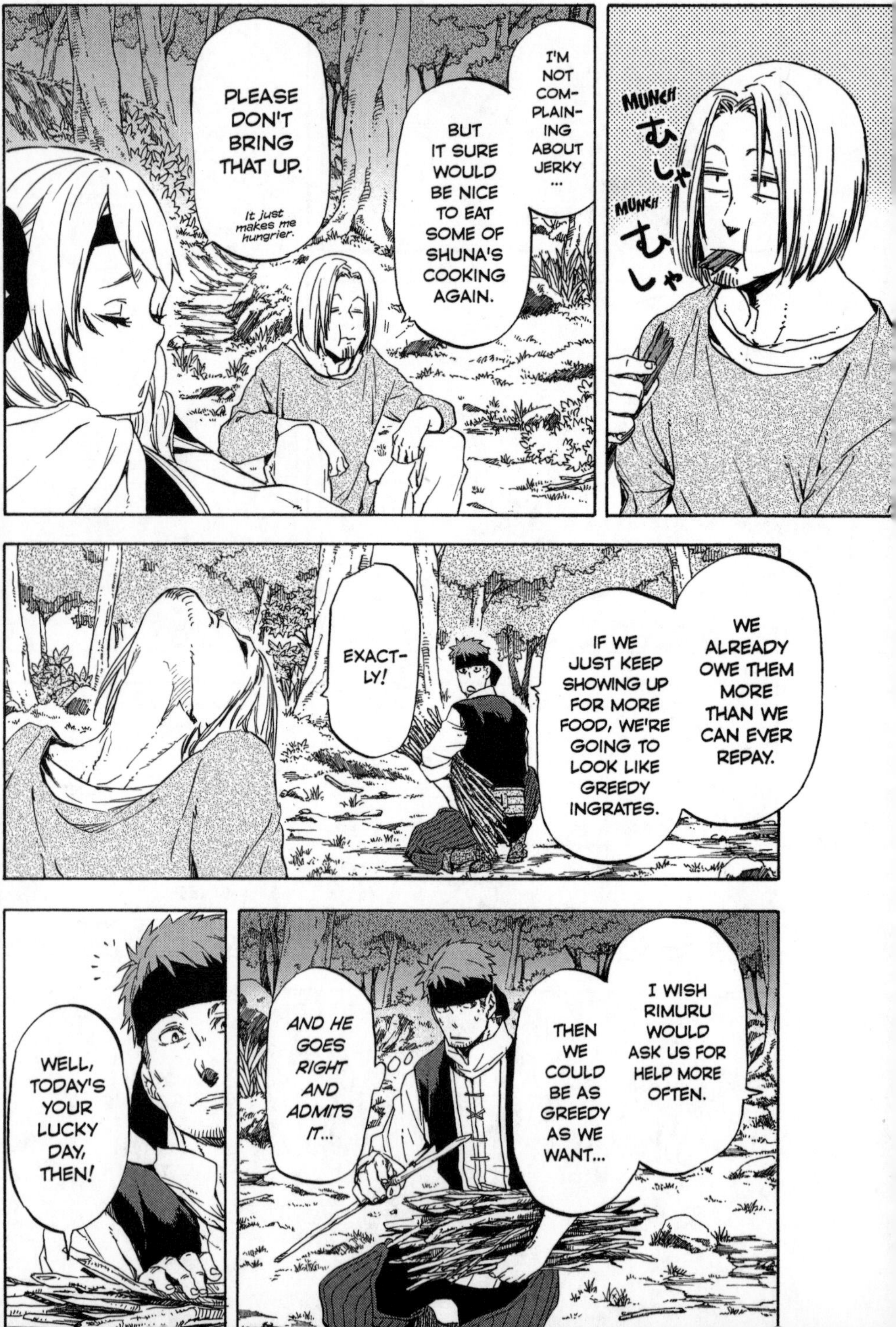
MUNCH むしゃ
MUNCH むしゃ
I'M NOT COMPLAINING ABOUT JERKY...
BUT IT SURE WOULD BE NICE TO EAT SOME OF SHUNA'S COOKING AGAIN.
PLEASE DON'T BRING THAT UP.
It just makes me hungrier.
WE ALREADY OWE THEM MORE THAN WE CAN EVER REPAY.
IF WE JUST KEEP SHOWING UP FOR MORE FOOD, WE'RE GOING TO LOOK LIKE GREEDY INGRATES.
EXACTLY!
I WISH RIMURU WOULD ASK US FOR HELP MORE OFTEN.
THEN WE COULD BE AS GREEDY AS WE WANT...
AND HE GOES RIGHT AND ADMITS IT...
WELL, TODAY'S YOUR LUCKY DAY, THEN!

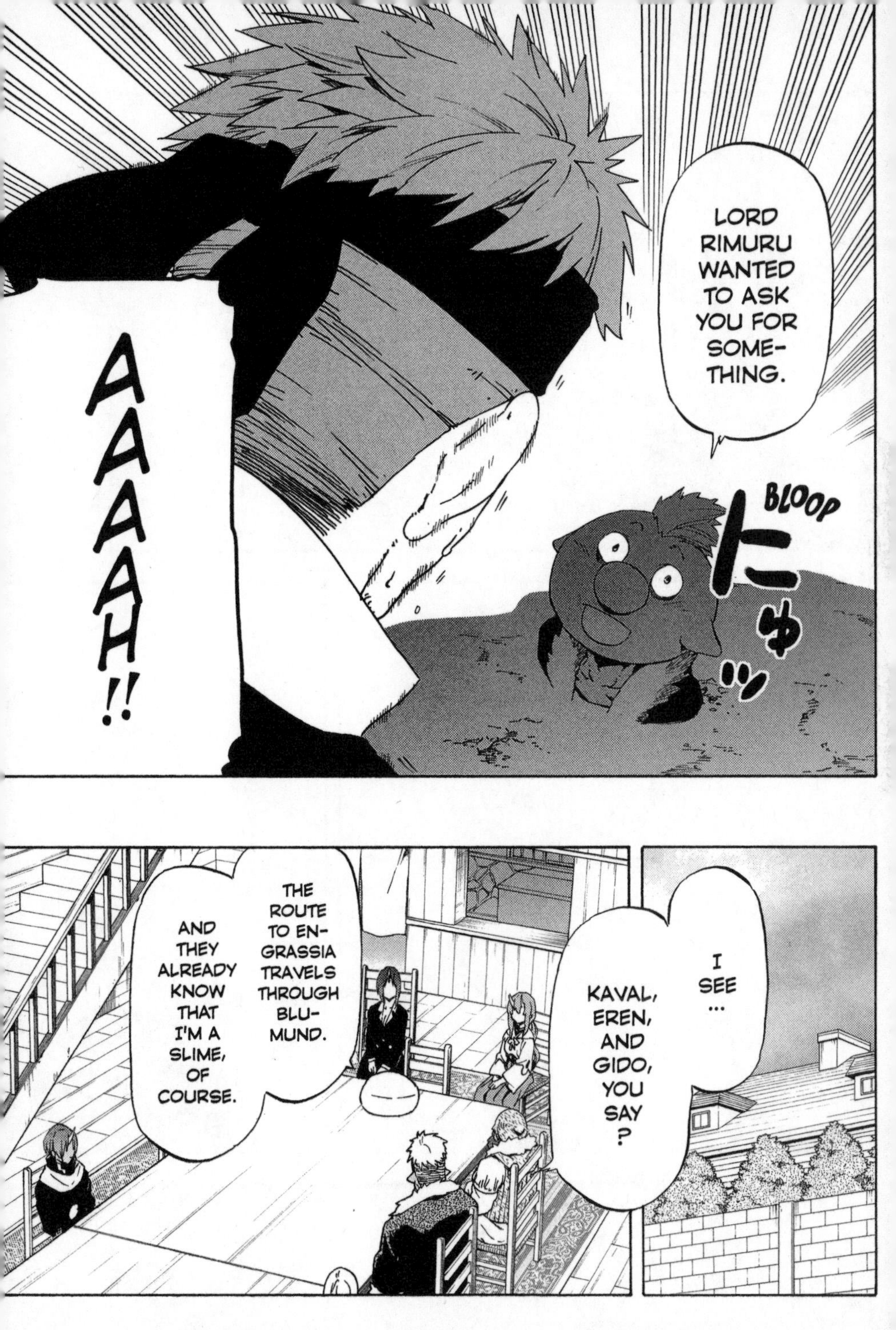
LORD RIMURU WANTED TO ASK YOU FOR SOME-THING.
BLOOP
にゅッ
AAAAAH!!
I SEE...
KAVAL, EREN, AND GIDO, YOU SAY?
THE ROUTE TO EN-GRASSIA TRAVELS THROUGH BLU-MUND.
AND THEY ALREADY KNOW THAT I'M A SLIME, OF COURSE.

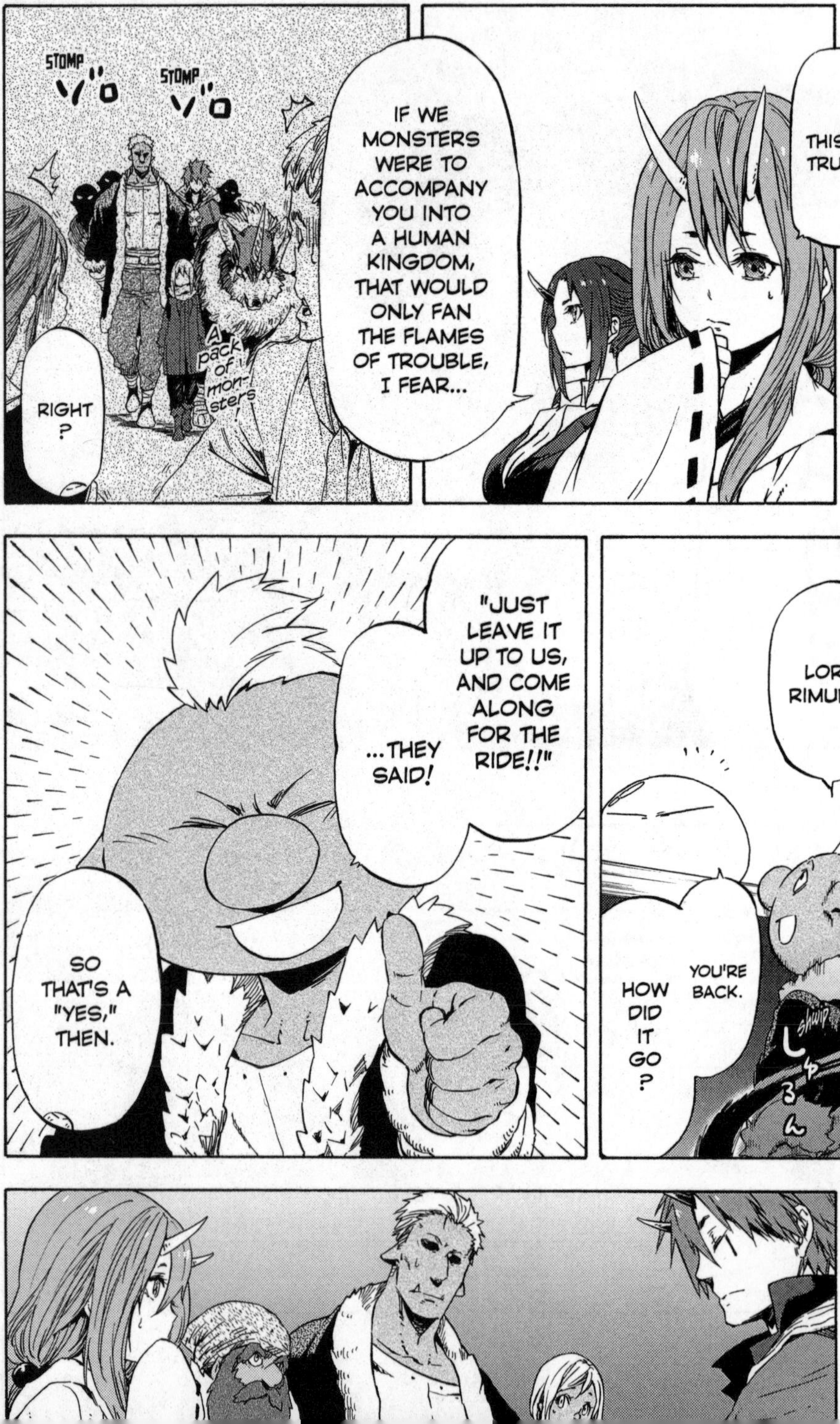
THIS IS TRUE...
IF WE MONSTERS WERE TO ACCOMPANY YOU INTO A HUMAN KINGDOM, THAT WOULD ONLY FAN THE FLAMES OF TROUBLE, I FEAR...
STOMP
STOMP
A pack of monsters!
RIGHT?
LORD RIMURU!
YOU'RE BACK.
HOW DID IT GO?
shwip
"JUST LEAVE IT UP TO US, AND COME ALONG FOR THE RIDE!!"
...THEY SAID!
SO THAT'S A "YES," THEN.

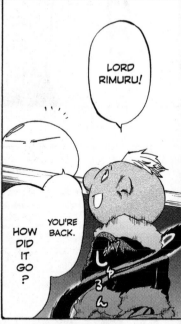

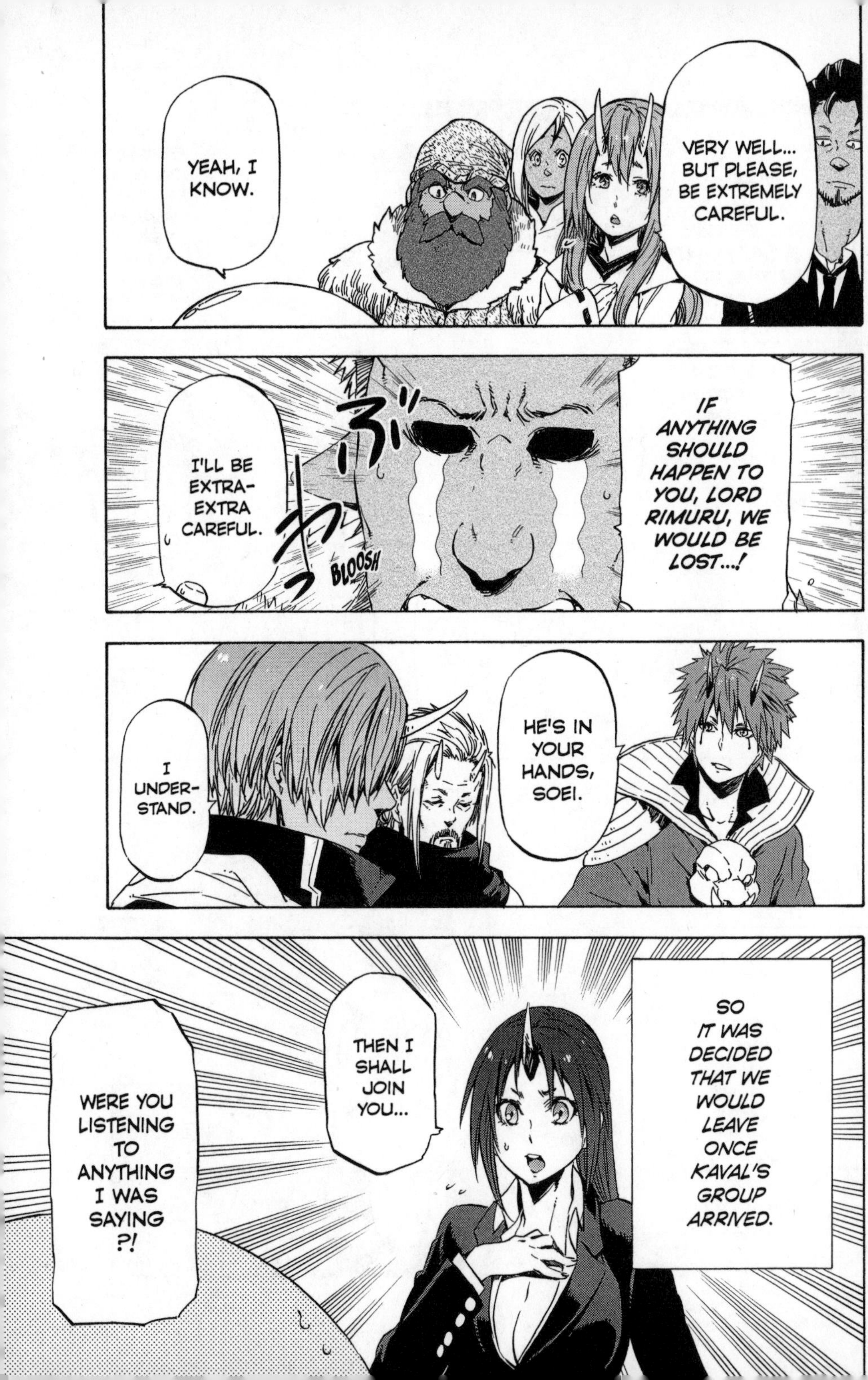
VERY WELL... BUT PLEASE, BE EXTREMELY CAREFUL.
YEAH, I KNOW.
IF ANYTHING SHOULD HAPPEN TO YOU, LORD RIMURU, WE WOULD BE LOST...!
BLOOSH
I'LL BE EXTRA-EXTRA CAREFUL.
HE'S IN YOUR HANDS, SOEI.
I UNDER-STAND.
SO IT WAS DECIDED THAT WE WOULD LEAVE ONCE KAVAL'S GROUP ARRIVED.
THEN I SHALL JOIN YOU...
WERE YOU LISTENING TO ANYTHING I WAS SAYING ?!

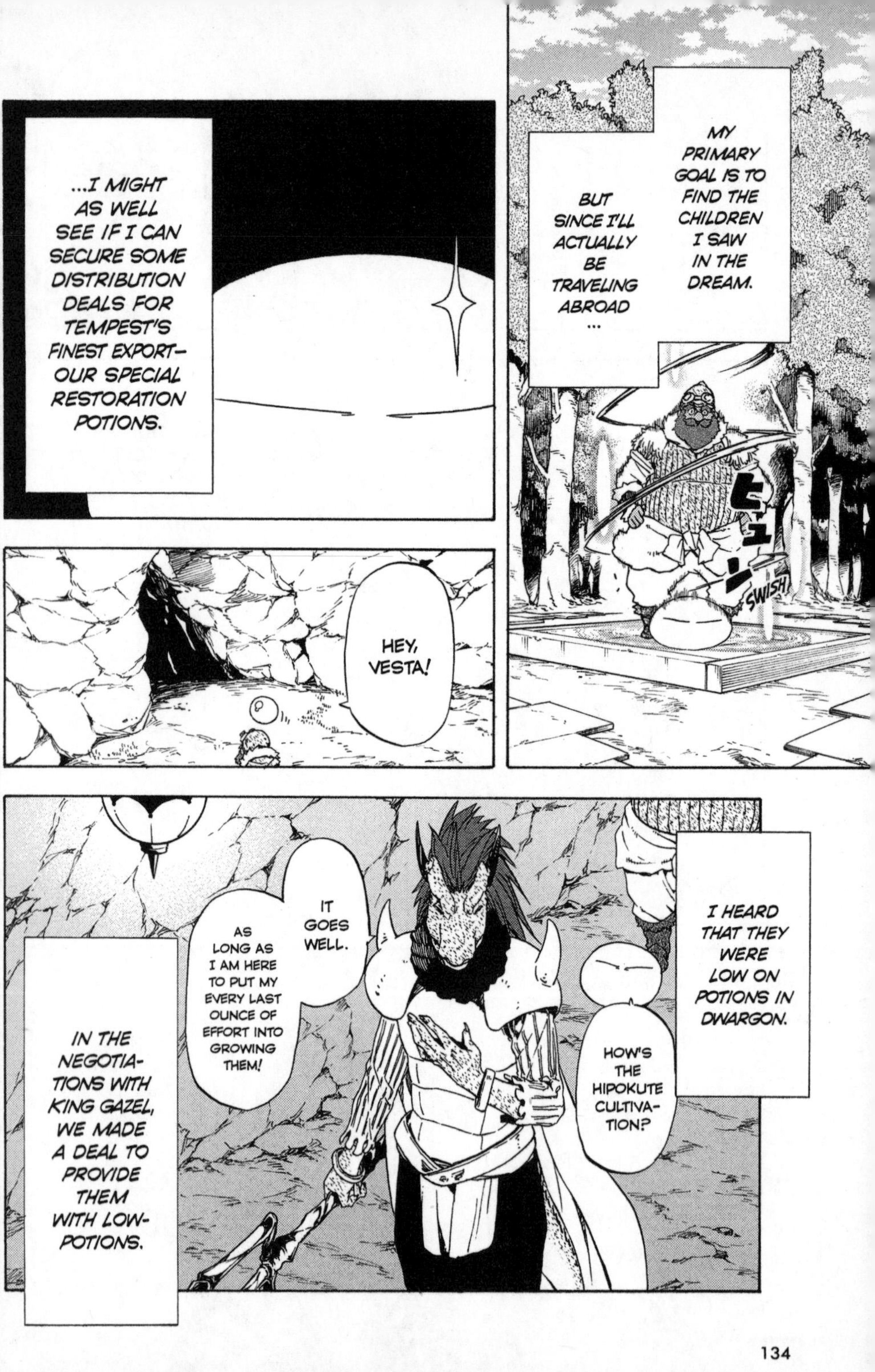
MY PRIMARY GOAL IS TO FIND THE CHILDREN I SAW IN THE DREAM.
BUT SINCE I'LL ACTUALLY BE TRAVELING ABROAD...
SWISH
...I MIGHT AS WELL SEE IF I CAN SECURE SOME DISTRIBUTION DEALS FOR TEMPEST'S FINEST EXPORT—OUR SPECIAL RESTORATION POTIONS.
HEY, VESTA!
I HEARD THAT THEY WERE LOW ON POTIONS IN DWARGON.
HOW'S THE HIPOKUTE CULTIVATION?
IT GOES WELL.
AS LONG AS I AM HERE TO PUT MY EVERY LAST OUNCE OF EFFORT INTO GROWING THEM!
IN THE NEGOTIATIONS WITH KING GAZEL, WE MADE A DEAL TO PROVIDE THEM WITH LOW-POTIONS.

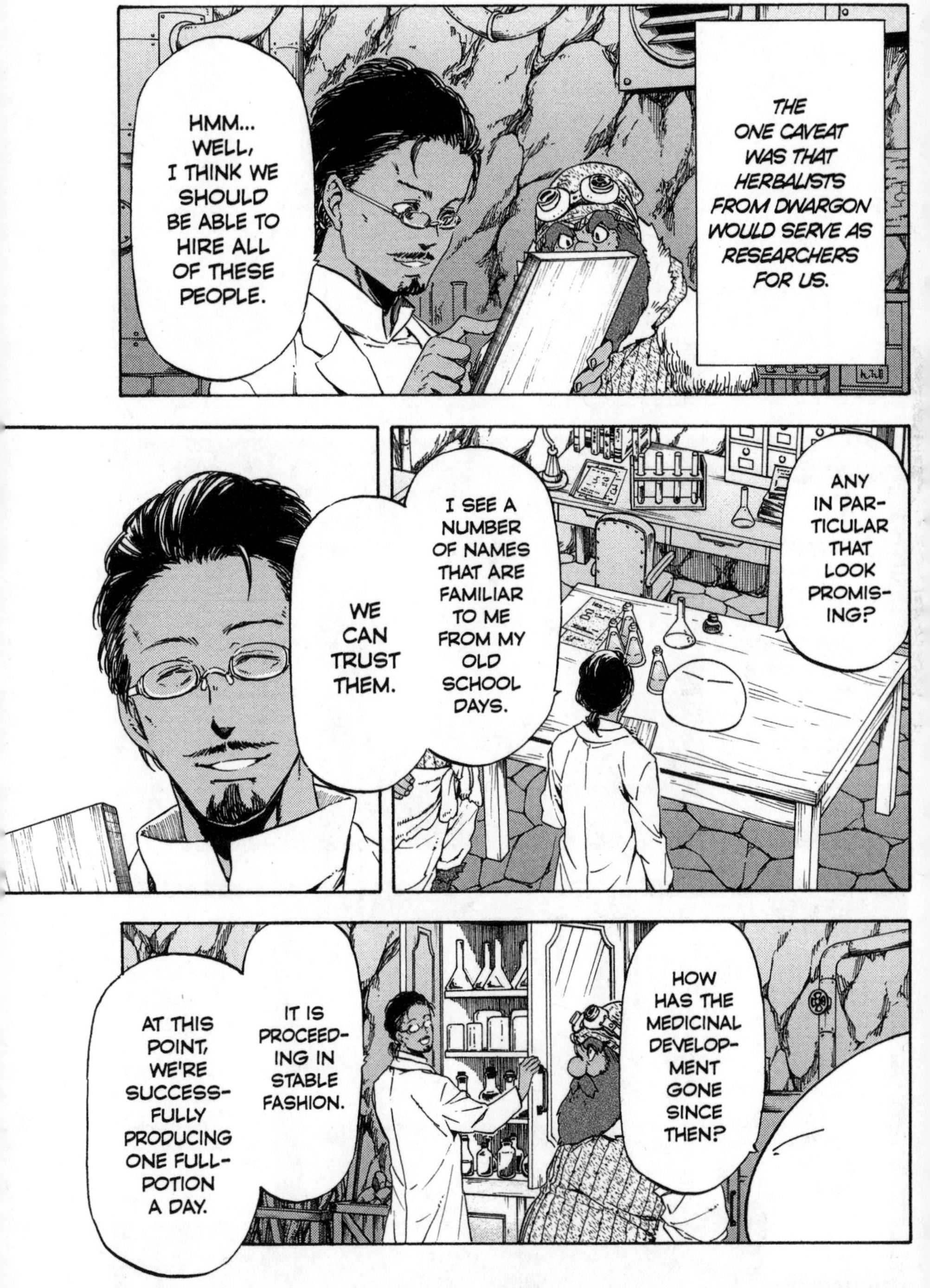
THE ONE CAVEAT WAS THAT HERBALISTS FROM DWARGON WOULD SERVE AS RESEARCHERS FOR US.
HMM... WELL, I THINK WE SHOULD BE ABLE TO HIRE ALL OF THESE PEOPLE.
ANY IN PARTICULAR THAT LOOK PROMISING?
I SEE A NUMBER OF NAMES THAT ARE FAMILIAR TO ME FROM MY OLD SCHOOL DAYS.
WE CAN TRUST THEM.
HOW HAS THE MEDICINAL DEVELOPMENT GONE SINCE THEN?
IT IS PROCEEDING IN STABLE FASHION.
AT THIS POINT, WE'RE SUCCESSFULLY PRODUCING ONE FULL-POTION A DAY.

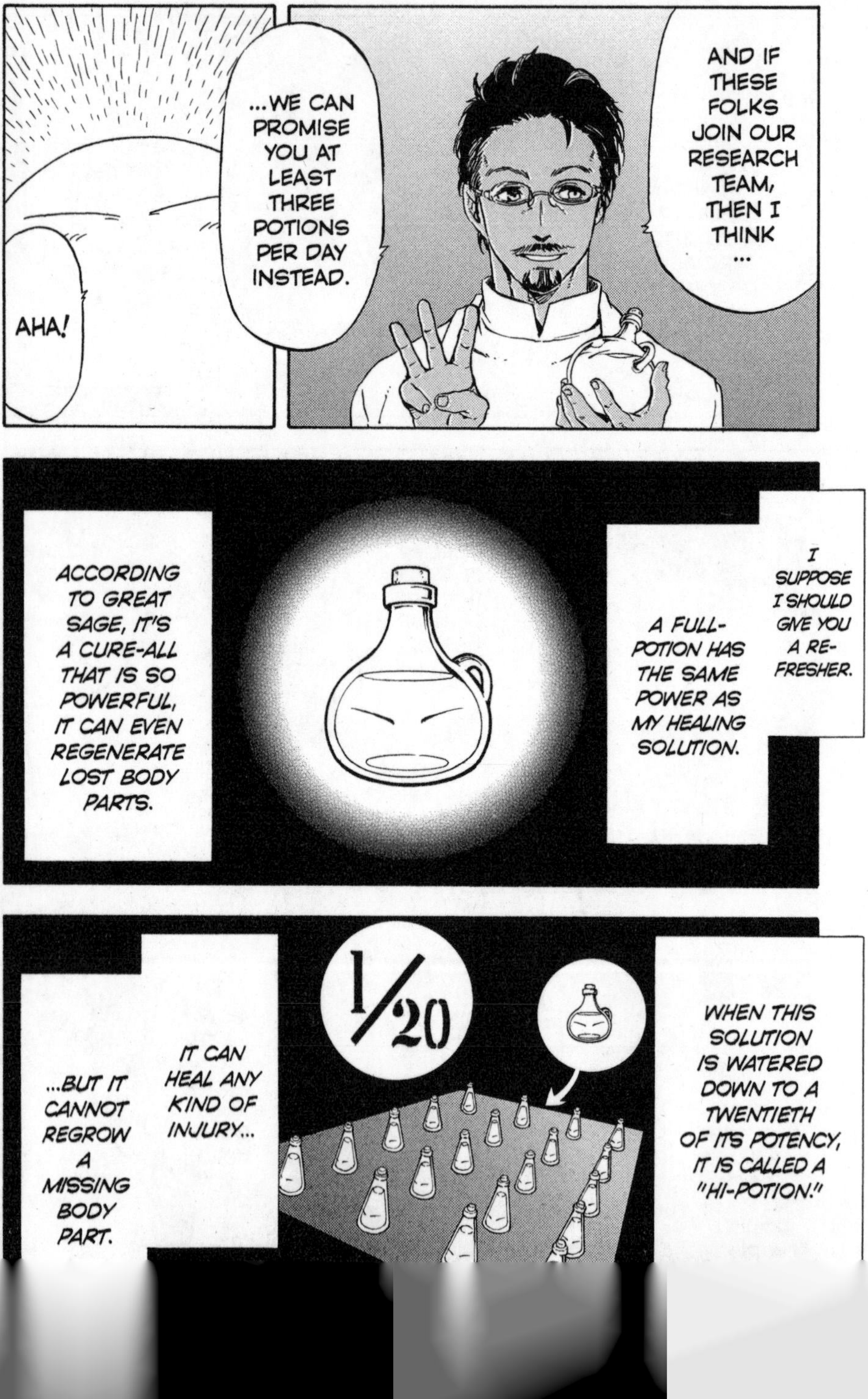
AND IF THESE FOLKS JOIN OUR RESEARCH TEAM, THEN I THINK...
...WE CAN PROMISE YOU AT LEAST THREE POTIONS PER DAY INSTEAD.
AHA!
I SUPPOSE I SHOULD GIVE YOU A RE-FRESHER.
A FULL-POTION HAS THE SAME POWER AS MY HEALING SOLUTION.
ACCORDING TO GREAT SAGE, IT'S A CURE-ALL THAT IS SO POWERFUL, IT CAN EVEN REGENERATE LOST BODY PARTS.
WHEN THIS SOLUTION IS WATERED DOWN TO A TWENTIETH OF ITS POTENCY, IT IS CALLED A "HI-POTION."
1/20
IT CAN HEAL ANY KIND OF INJURY...
...BUT IT CANNOT REGROW A MISSING BODY PART.

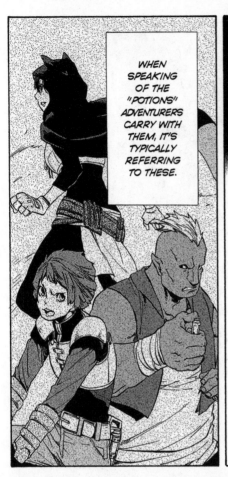

WHEN A FULL-POTION IS WATERED DOWN TO A HUNDREDTH OF ITS ORIGINAL STRENGTH, THAT IS A "LOW-POTION."
IT HAS THE ABILITY TO HEAL WOUNDS TO A CERTAIN EXTENT.
WHEN SPEAKING OF THE "POTIONS" ADVENTURERS CARRY WITH THEM, IT'S TYPICALLY REFERRING TO THESE.
IT'LL BE HARD TO SELL A FULL-POTION, BOSS.
IT'S JUST TOO POWER-FUL, YA SEE.
IT'S NOT MEANT FOR CASUAL USE, AND IF YOU WERE TO ASK A PROPER PRICE, NO ADVENTURER WOULD BE ABLE TO PAY IT.

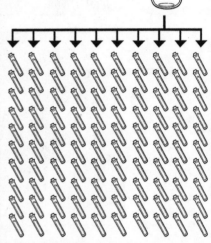

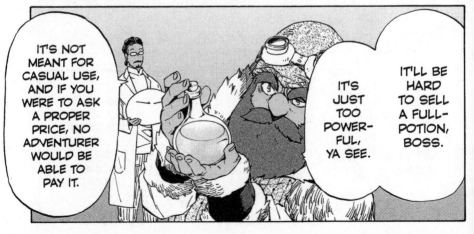

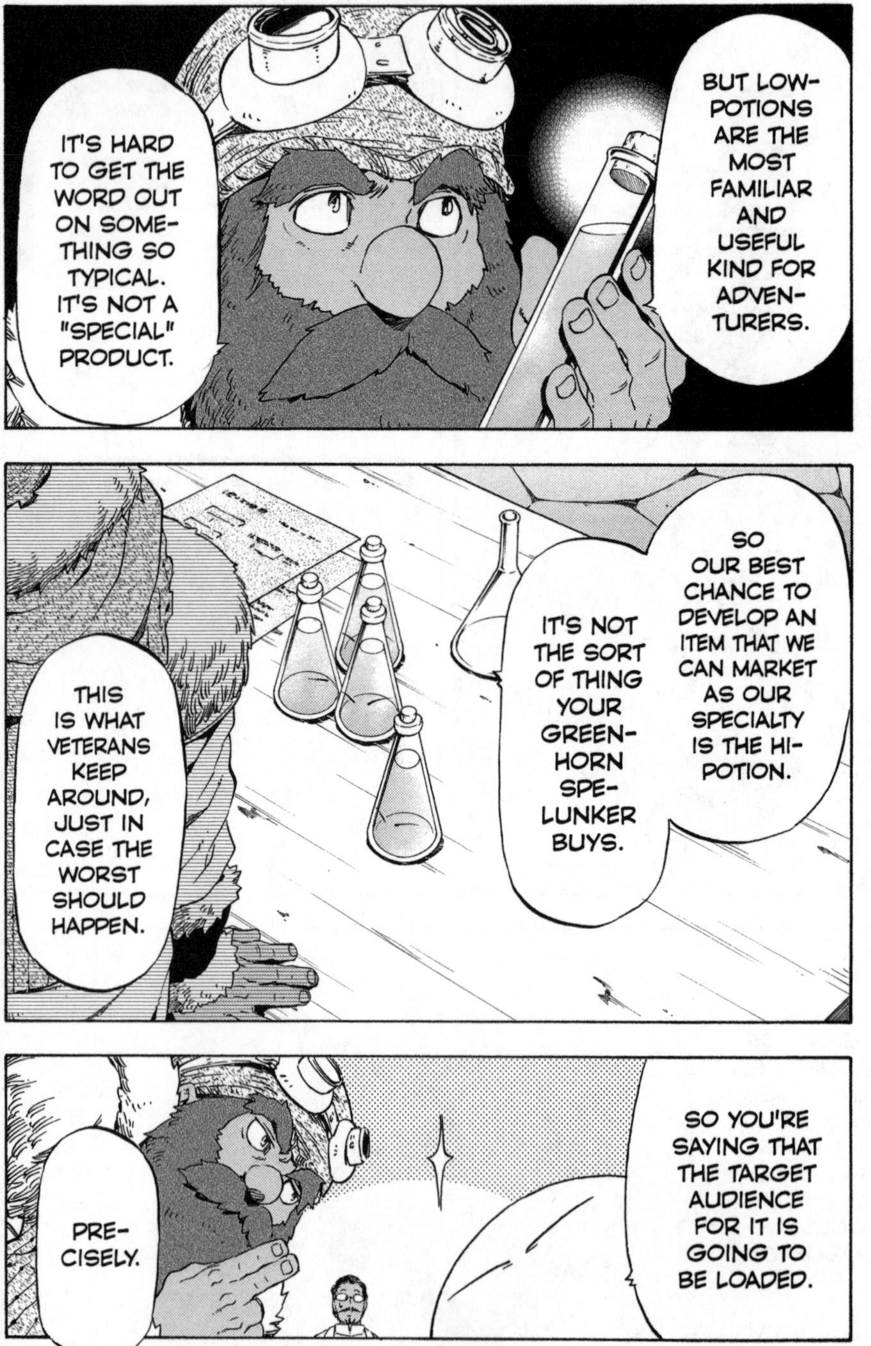
BUT LOW-POTIONS ARE THE MOST FAMILIAR AND USEFUL KIND FOR ADVENTURERS.
IT'S HARD TO GET THE WORD OUT ON SOMETHING SO TYPICAL. IT'S NOT A "SPECIAL" PRODUCT.
SO OUR BEST CHANCE TO DEVELOP AN ITEM THAT WE CAN MARKET AS OUR SPECIALTY IS THE HI-POTION.
IT'S NOT THE SORT OF THING YOUR GREENHORN SPELUNKER BUYS.
THIS IS WHAT VETERANS KEEP AROUND, JUST IN CASE THE WORST SHOULD HAPPEN.
SO YOU'RE SAYING THAT THE TARGET AUDIENCE FOR IT IS GOING TO BE LOADED.
PRECISELY.

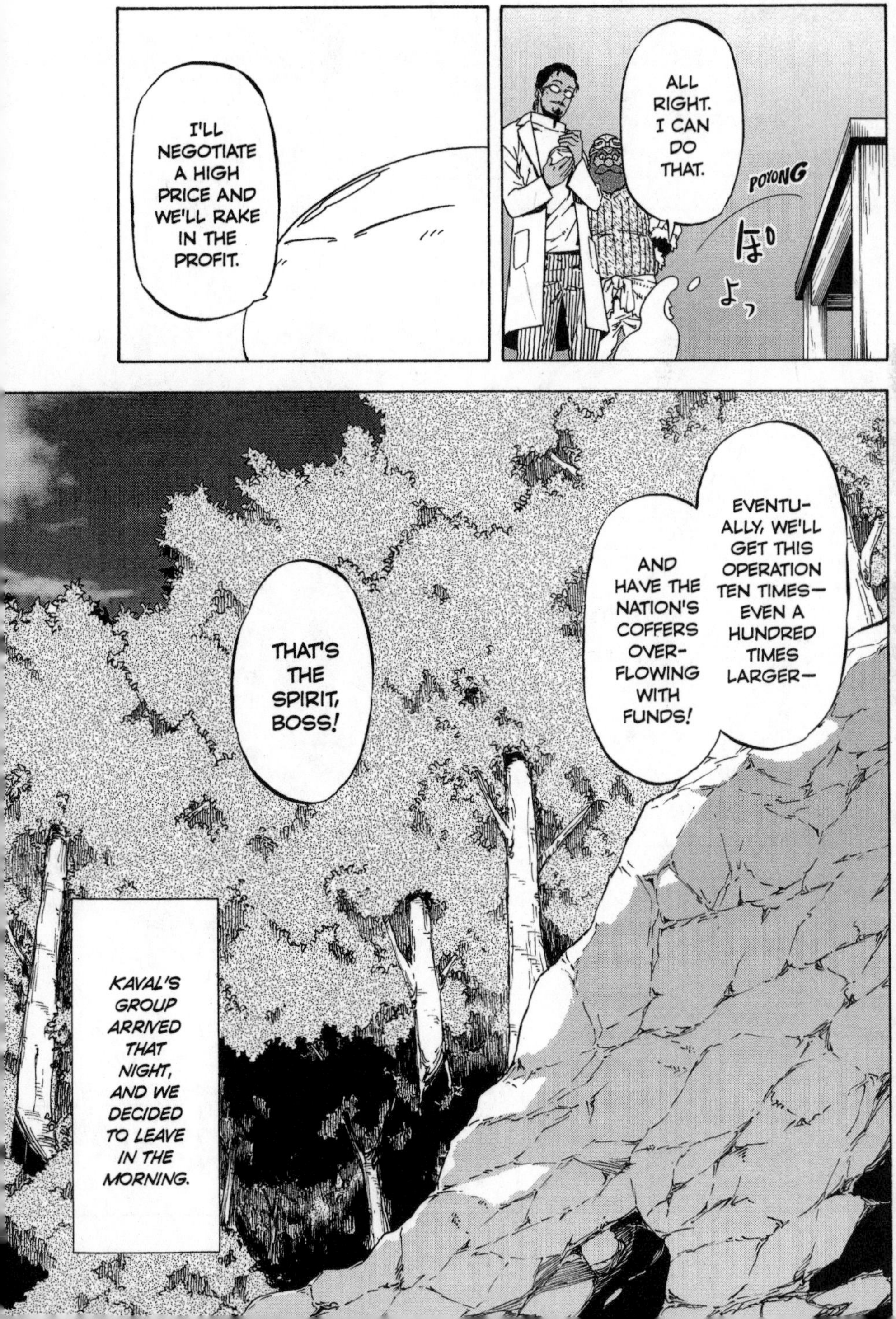
ALL RIGHT. I CAN DO THAT.
POYONG
ぽよっ
I'LL NEGOTIATE A HIGH PRICE AND WE'LL RAKE IN THE PROFIT.
EVENTU-ALLY, WE'LL GET THIS OPERATION TEN TIMES— EVEN A HUNDRED TIMES LARGER—
AND HAVE THE NATION'S COFFERS OVER-FLOWING WITH FUNDS!
THAT'S THE SPIRIT, BOSS!
KAVAL'S GROUP ARRIVED THAT NIGHT, AND WE DECIDED TO LEAVE IN THE MORNING.

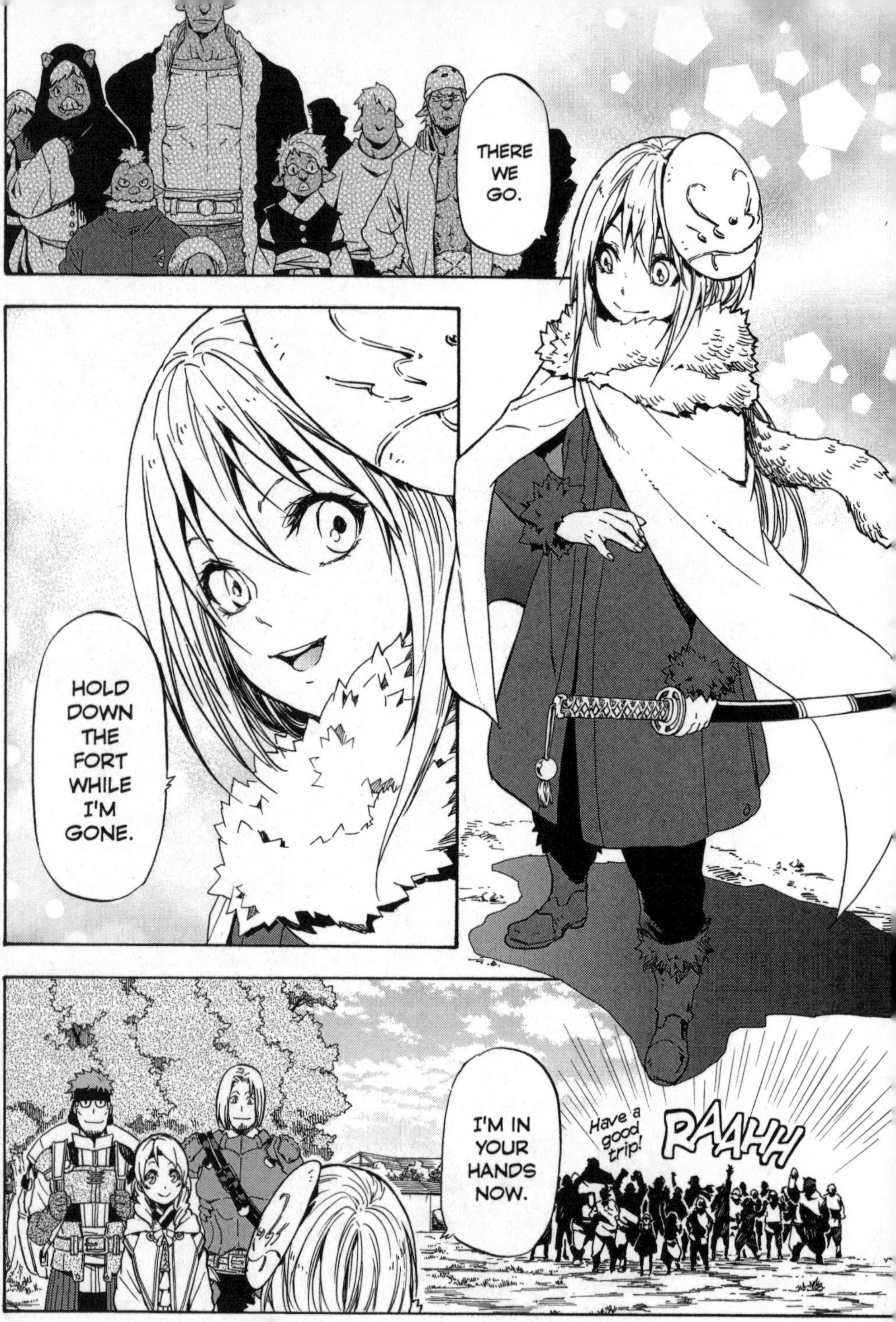
THERE WE GO.
HOLD DOWN THE FORT WHILE I'M GONE.
I'M IN YOUR HANDS NOW.
Have a good trip!
RAAHH

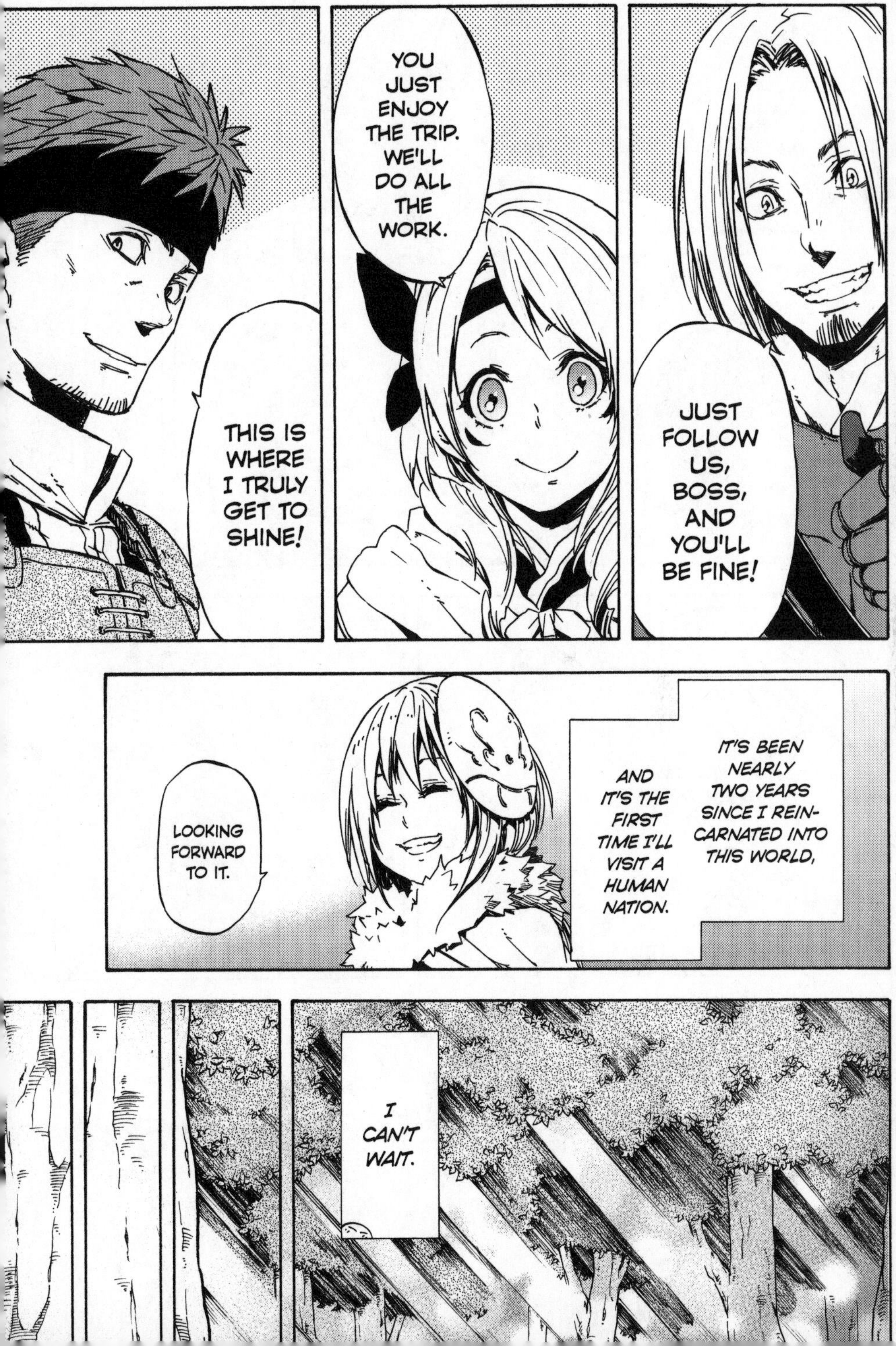
JUST FOLLOW US, BOSS, AND YOU'LL BE FINE!
YOU JUST ENJOY THE TRIP. WE'LL DO ALL THE WORK.
THIS IS WHERE I TRULY GET TO SHINE!
IT'S BEEN NEARLY TWO YEARS SINCE I REIN-CARNATED INTO THIS WORLD,
AND IT'S THE FIRST TIME I'LL VISIT A HUMAN NATION.
LOOKING FORWARD TO IT.
I CAN'T WAIT.

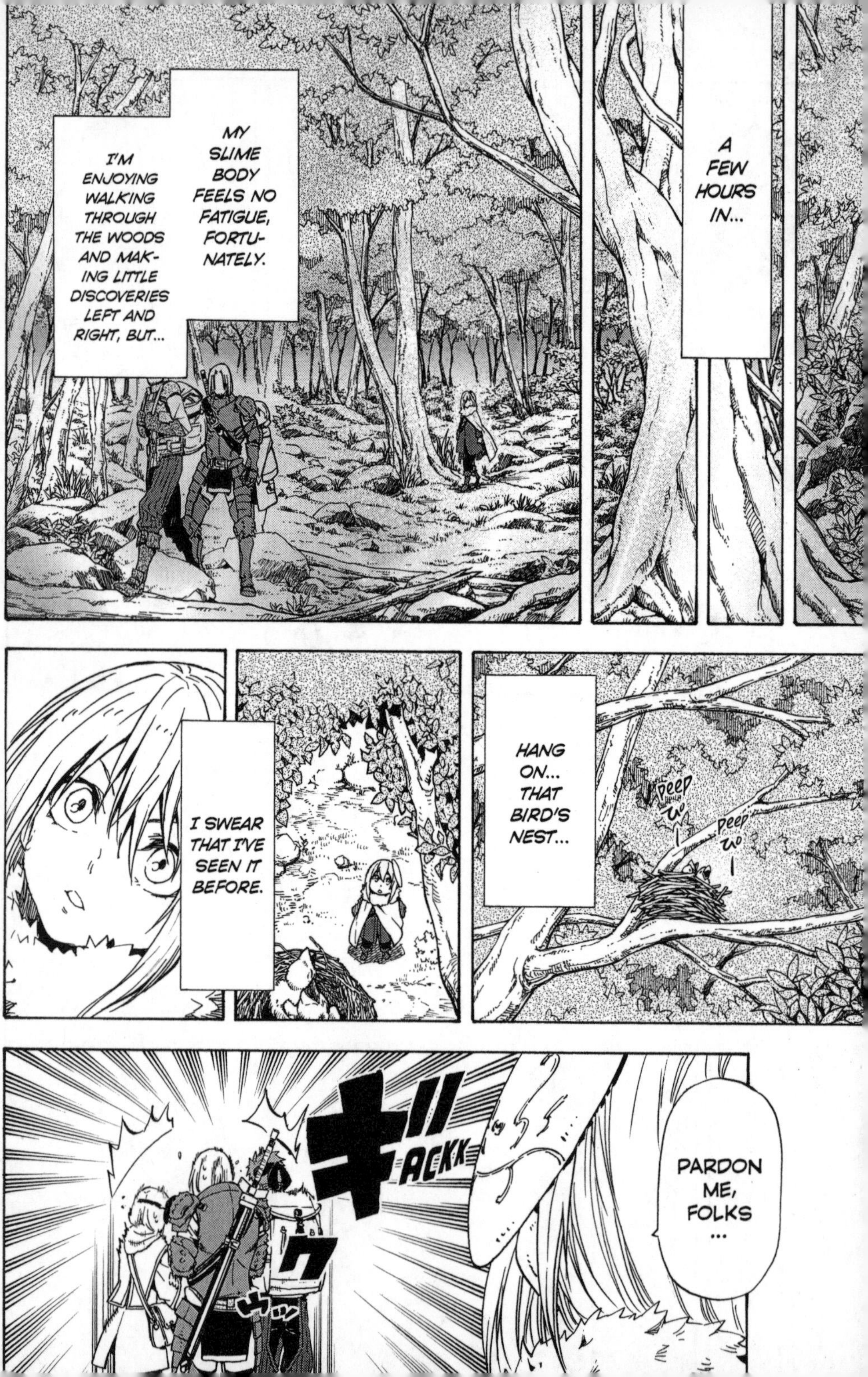
A FEW HOURS IN...
MY SLIME BODY FEELS NO FATIGUE, FORTUNATELY.
I'M ENJOYING WALKING THROUGH THE WOODS AND MAKING LITTLE DISCOVERIES LEFT AND RIGHT, BUT...
HANG ON... THAT BIRD'S NEST...
PEEP
PEEP
I SWEAR THAT I'VE SEEN IT BEFORE.
PARDON ME, FOLKS...
ACKK

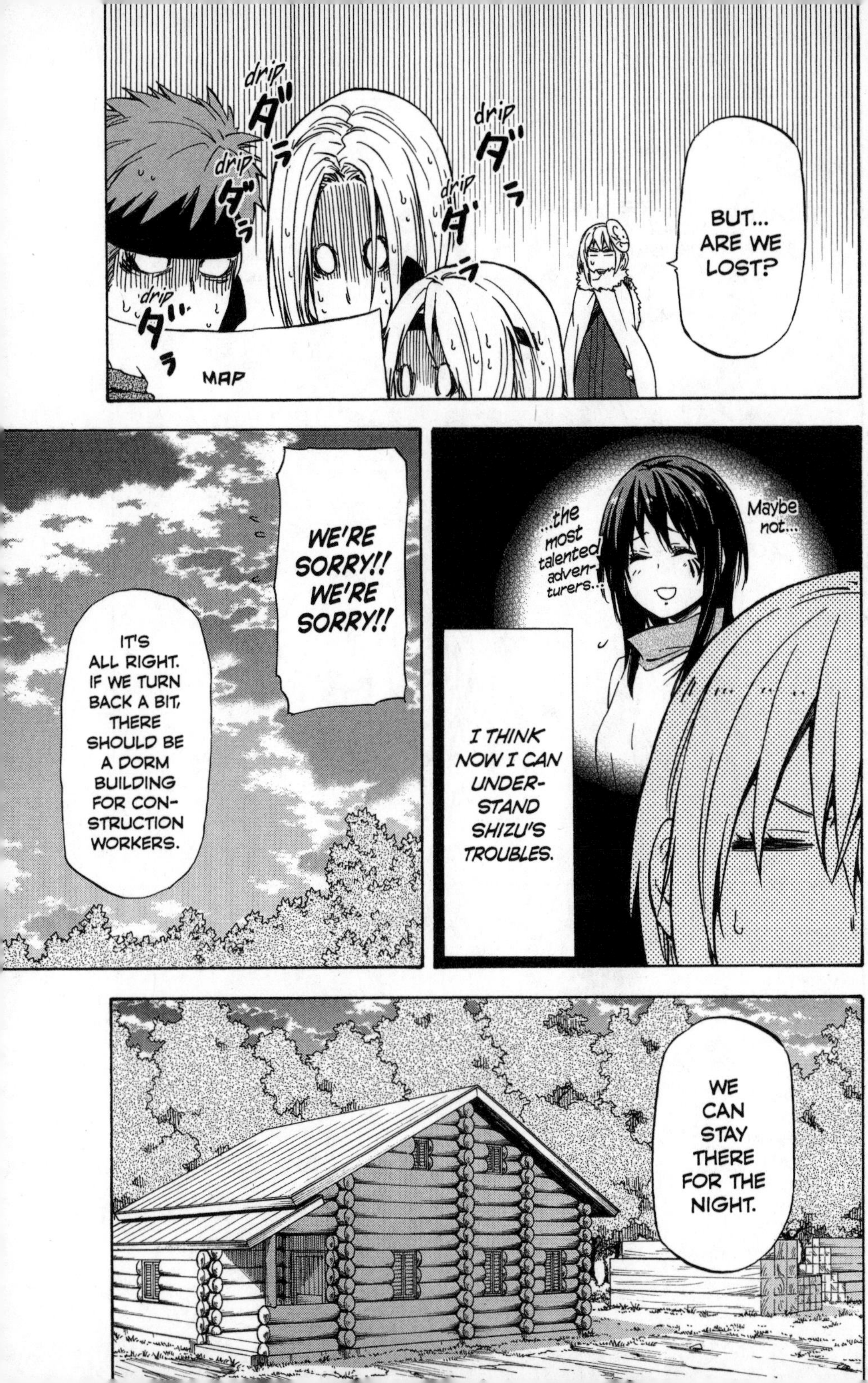
BUT... ARE WE LOST?
drip
drip
drip
drip
MAP
Maybe not...
...the most talented adventurers...
I THINK NOW I CAN UNDER-STAND SHIZU'S TROUBLES.
WE'RE SORRY!! WE'RE SORRY!!
IT'S ALL RIGHT. IF WE TURN BACK A BIT, THERE SHOULD BE A DORM BUILDING FOR CON-STRUCTION WORKERS.
WE CAN STAY THERE FOR THE NIGHT.

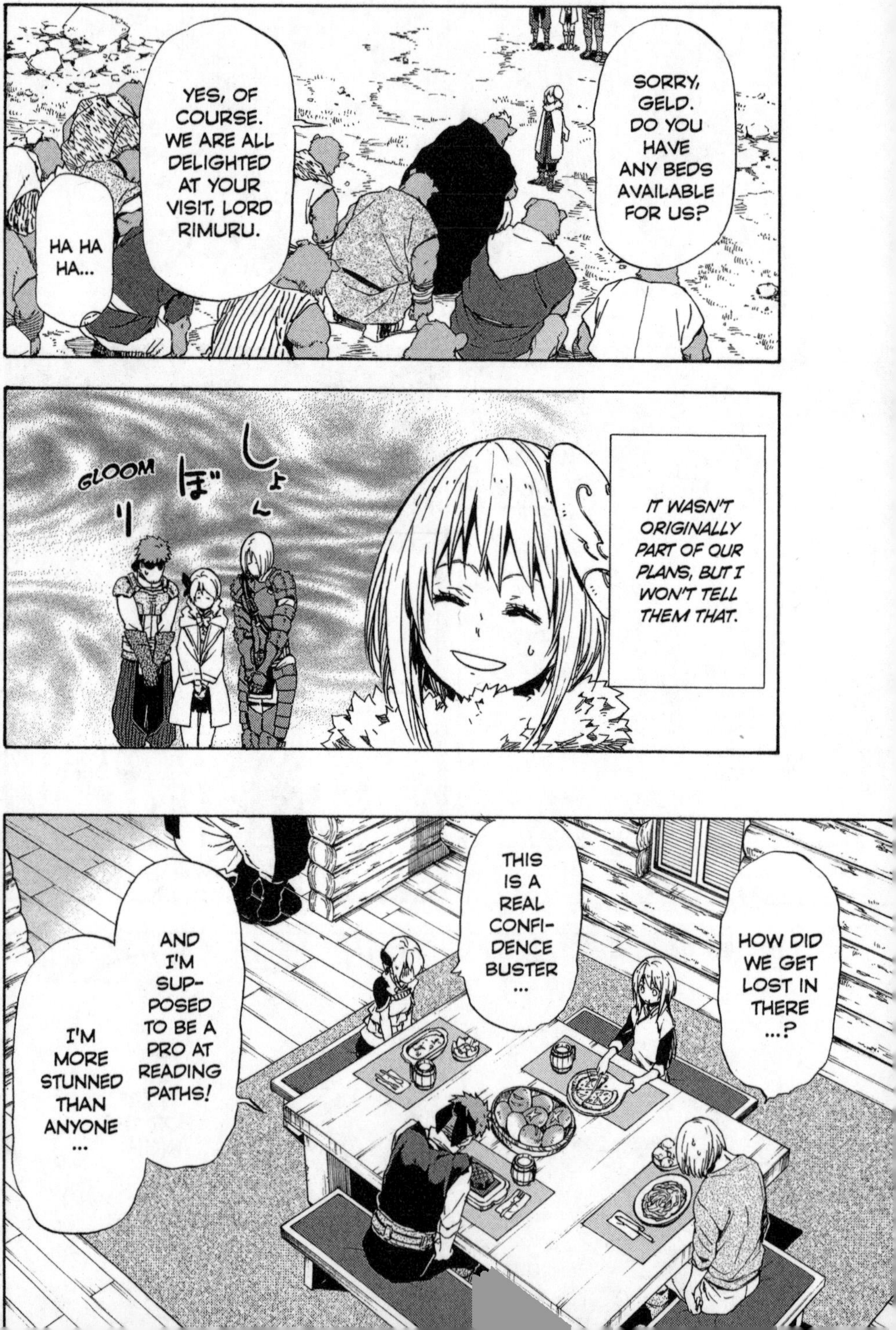
SORRY, GELD. DO YOU HAVE ANY BEDS AVAILABLE FOR US?
YES, OF COURSE. WE ARE ALL DELIGHTED AT YOUR VISIT, LORD RIMURU.
HA HA HA...
IT WASN'T ORIGINALLY PART OF OUR PLANS, BUT I WON'T TELL THEM THAT.
しょんぼり
GLOOM
HOW DID WE GET LOST IN THERE ...?
THIS IS A REAL CONFI-DENCE BUSTER ...
AND I'M SUP-POSED TO BE A PRO AT READING PATHS!
I'M MORE STUNNED THAN ANYONE ...

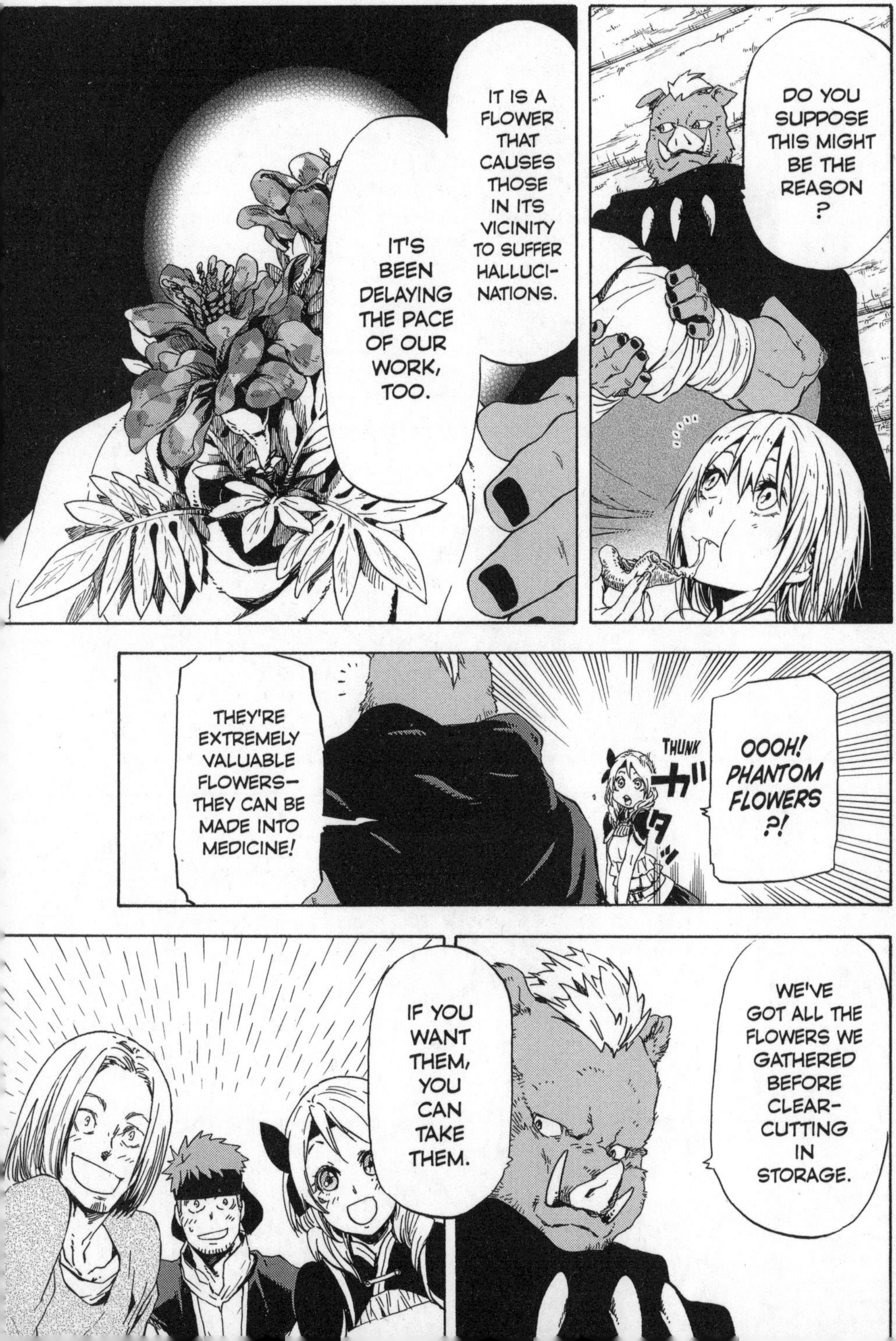
DO YOU SUPPOSE THIS MIGHT BE THE REASON?
IT IS A FLOWER THAT CAUSES THOSE IN ITS VICINITY TO SUFFER HALLUCI-NATIONS.
IT'S BEEN DELAYING THE PACE OF OUR WORK, TOO.
OOOH! PHANTOM FLOWERS?!
THUNK
THEY'RE EXTREMELY VALUABLE FLOWERS—THEY CAN BE MADE INTO MEDICINE!
WE'VE GOT ALL THE FLOWERS WE GATHERED BEFORE CLEAR-CUTTING IN STORAGE.
IF YOU WANT THEM, YOU CAN TAKE THEM.

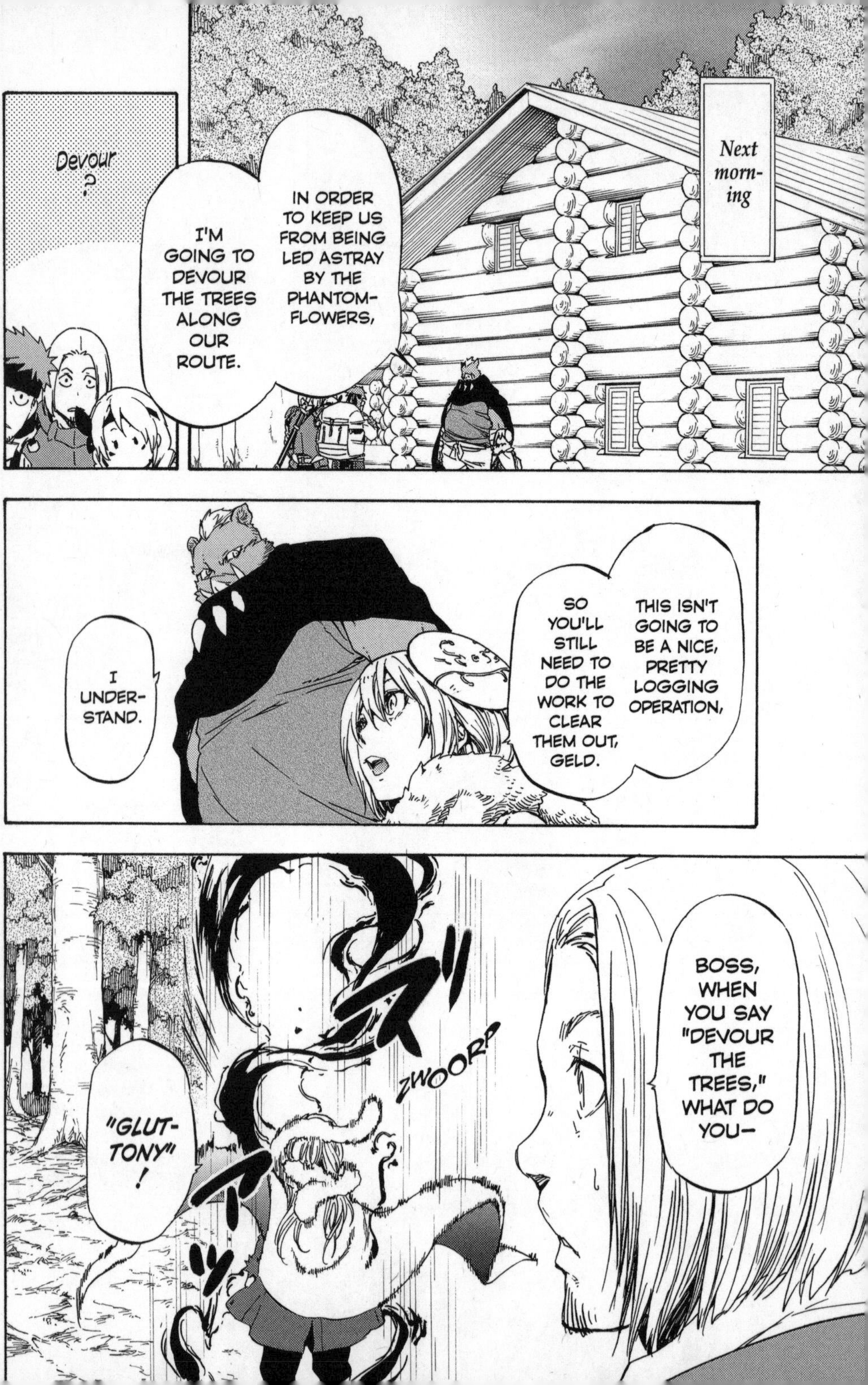
Next morning
IN ORDER TO KEEP US FROM BEING LED ASTRAY BY THE PHANTOM-FLOWERS,
I'M GOING TO DEVOUR THE TREES ALONG OUR ROUTE.
Devour?
THIS ISN'T GOING TO BE A NICE, PRETTY LOGGING OPERATION,
SO YOU'LL STILL NEED TO DO THE WORK TO CLEAR THEM OUT, GELD.
I UNDER-STAND.
BOSS, WHEN YOU SAY "DEVOUR THE TREES," WHAT DO YOU–
ZWOORP
"GLUT-TONY"!

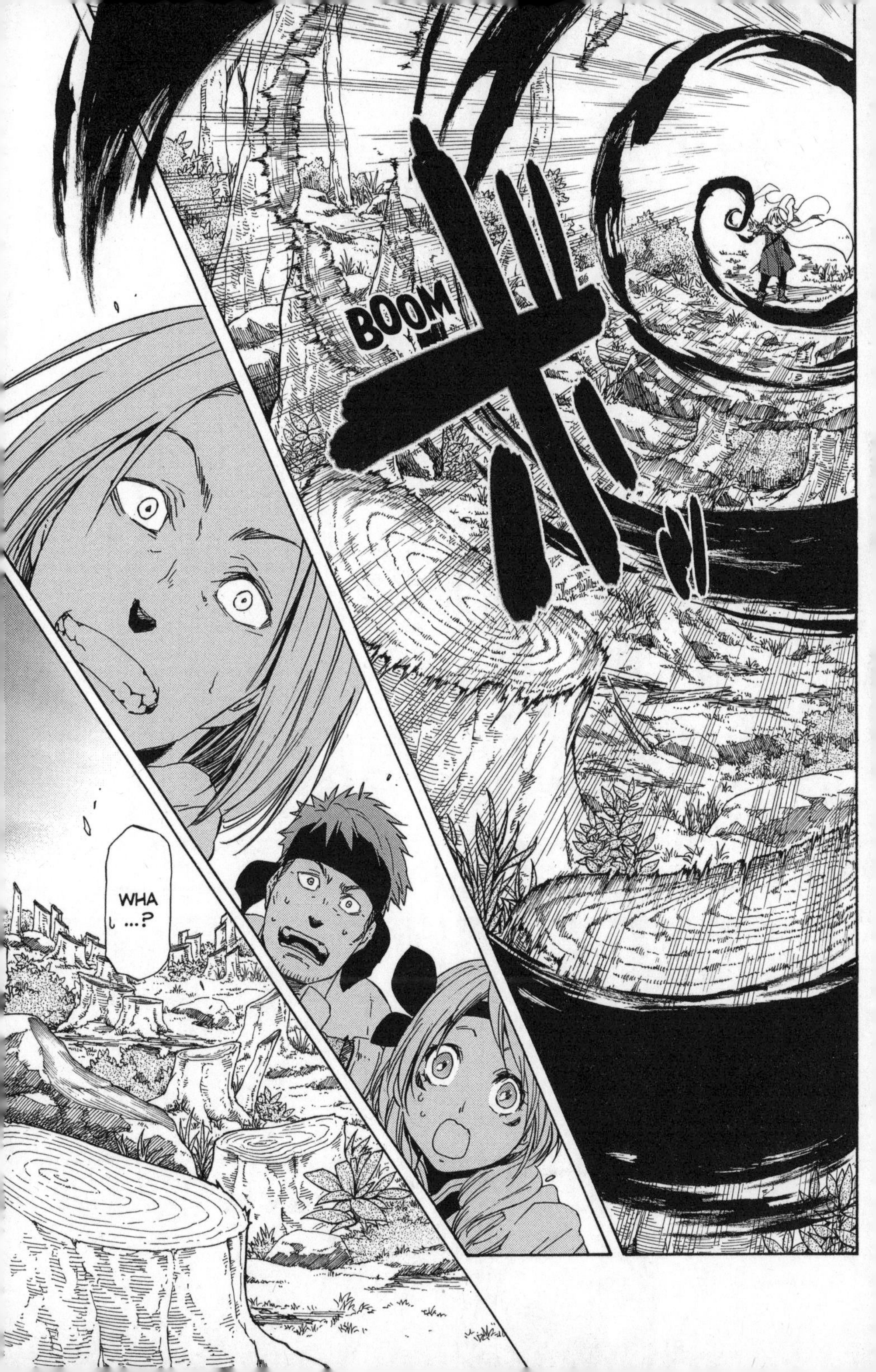
BOOM
WHA ...?

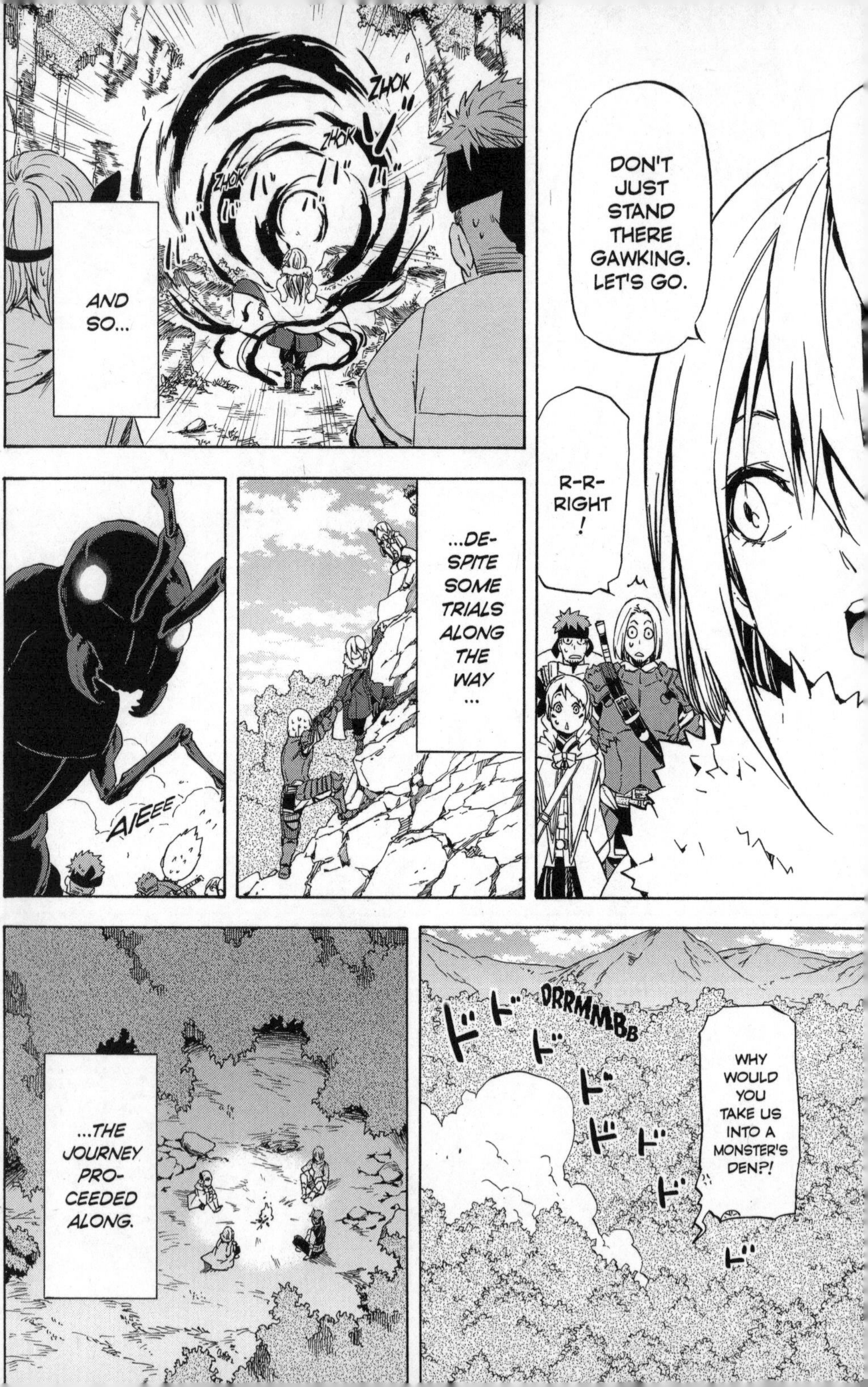
DON'T JUST STAND THERE GAWKING. LET'S GO.
R-R-RIGHT!
ZHOK
ZHOK
ZHOK
AND SO...
...DE-SPITE SOME TRIALS ALONG THE WAY...
AIEEE
DRRMMBB
WHY WOULD YOU TAKE US INTO A MONSTER'S DEN?!
...THE JOURNEY PRO-CEEDED ALONG.

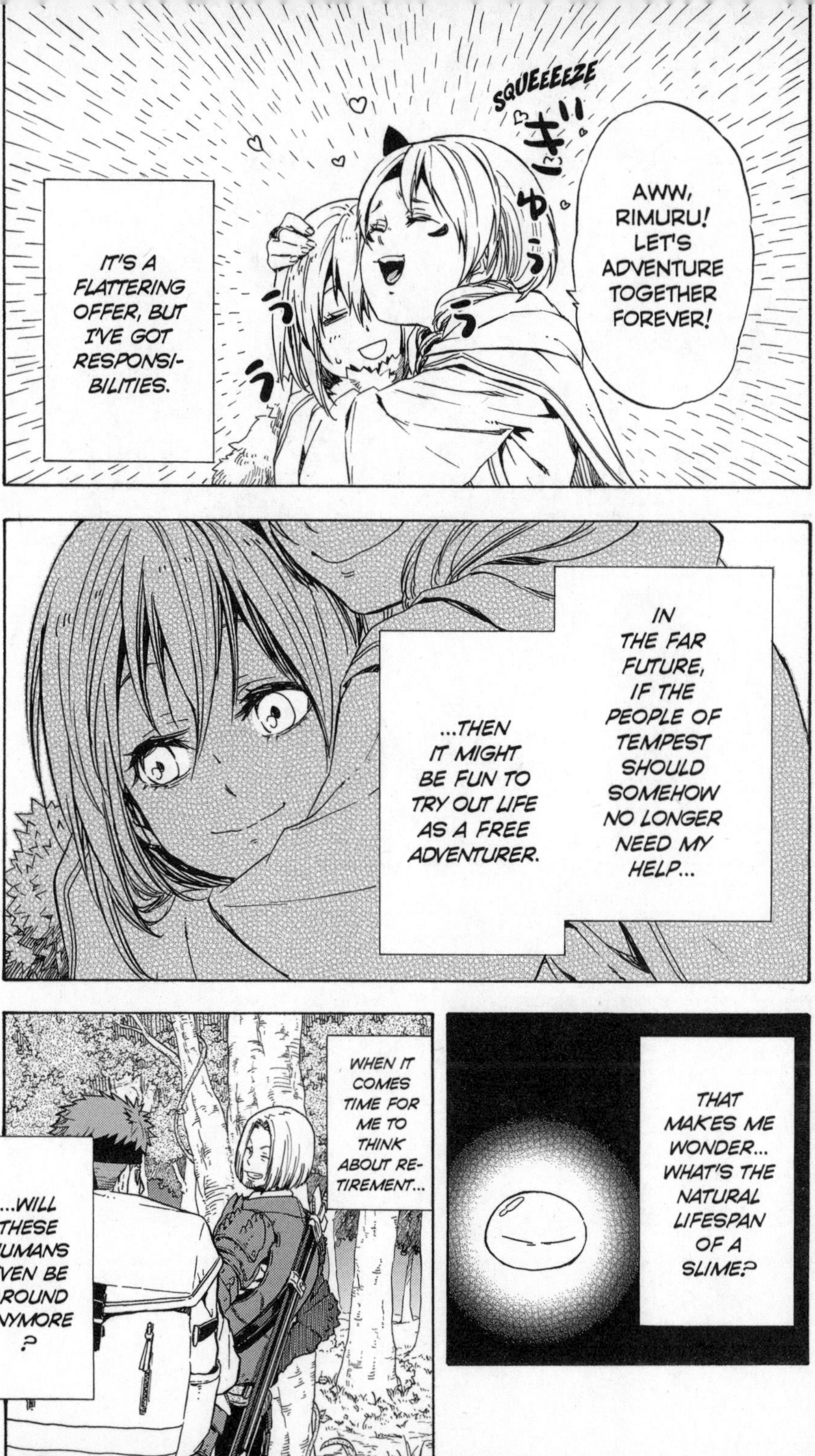
SQUEEEEZE
AWW, RIMURU! LET'S ADVENTURE TOGETHER FOREVER!
IT'S A FLATTERING OFFER, BUT I'VE GOT RESPONSI-BILITIES.
IN THE FAR FUTURE, IF THE PEOPLE OF TEMPEST SHOULD SOMEHOW NO LONGER NEED MY HELP...
...THEN IT MIGHT BE FUN TO TRY OUT LIFE AS A FREE ADVENTURER.
THAT MAKES ME WONDER... WHAT'S THE NATURAL LIFESPAN OF A SLIME?
WHEN IT COMES TIME FOR ME TO THINK ABOUT RE-TIREMENT...
...WILL THESE HUMANS EVEN BE AROUND ANYMORE?

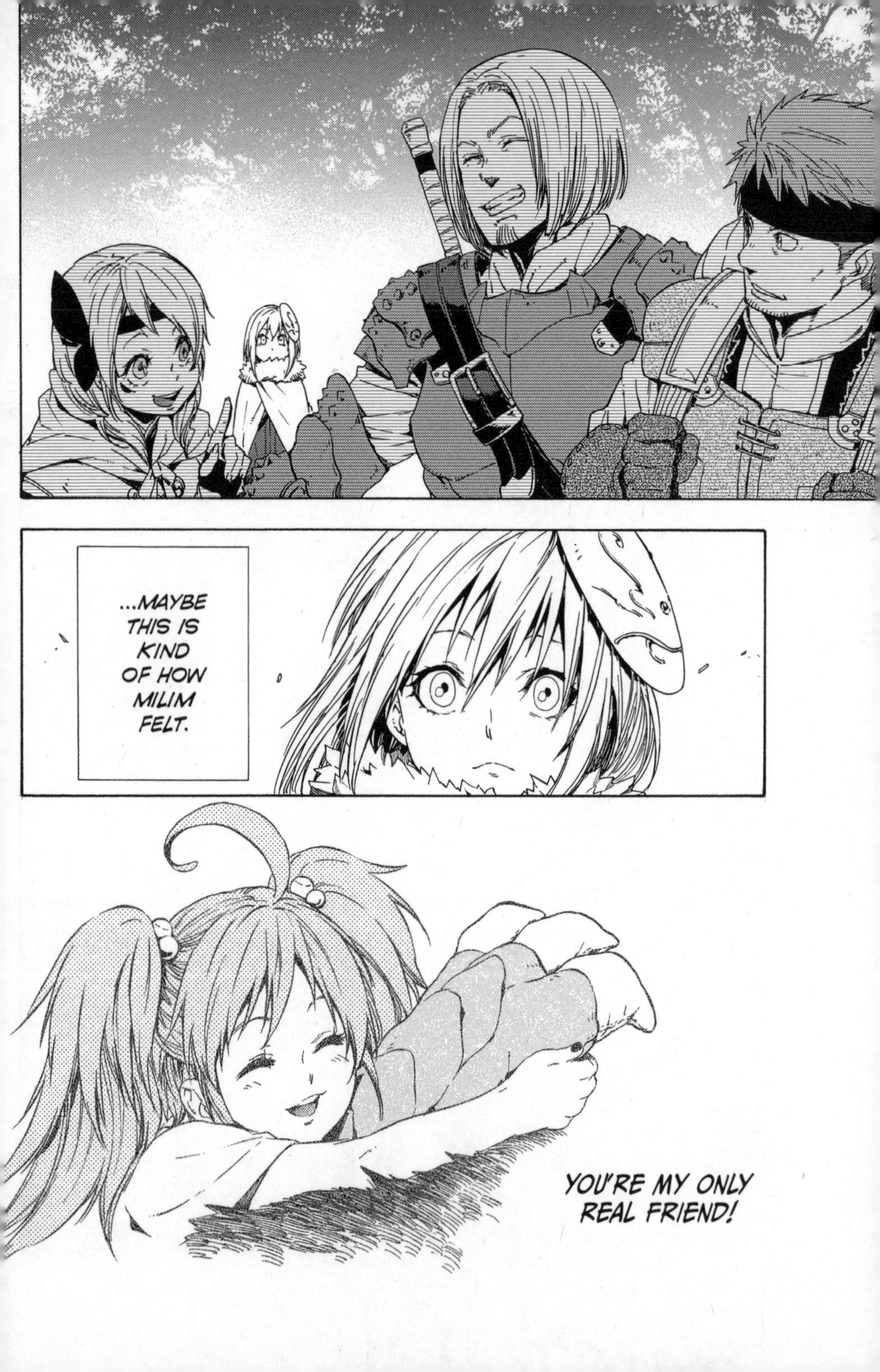
...MAYBE THIS IS KIND OF HOW MILIM FELT.
YOU'RE MY ONLY REAL FRIEND!

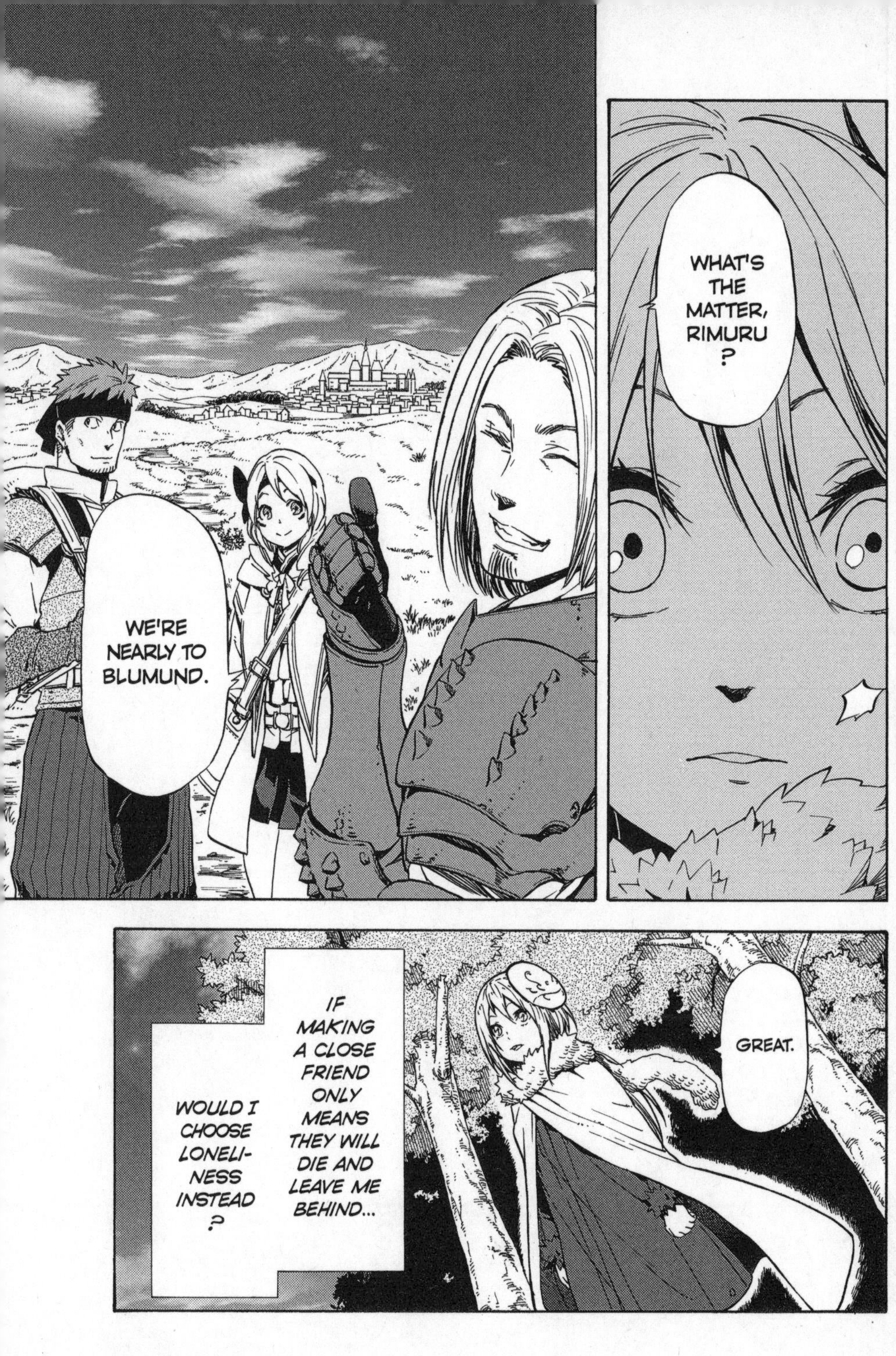
WHAT'S THE MATTER, RIMURU?
WE'RE NEARLY TO BLUMUND.
GREAT.
IF MAKING A CLOSE FRIEND ONLY MEANS THEY WILL DIE AND LEAVE ME BEHIND...
WOULD I CHOOSE LONELI-NESS INSTEAD?

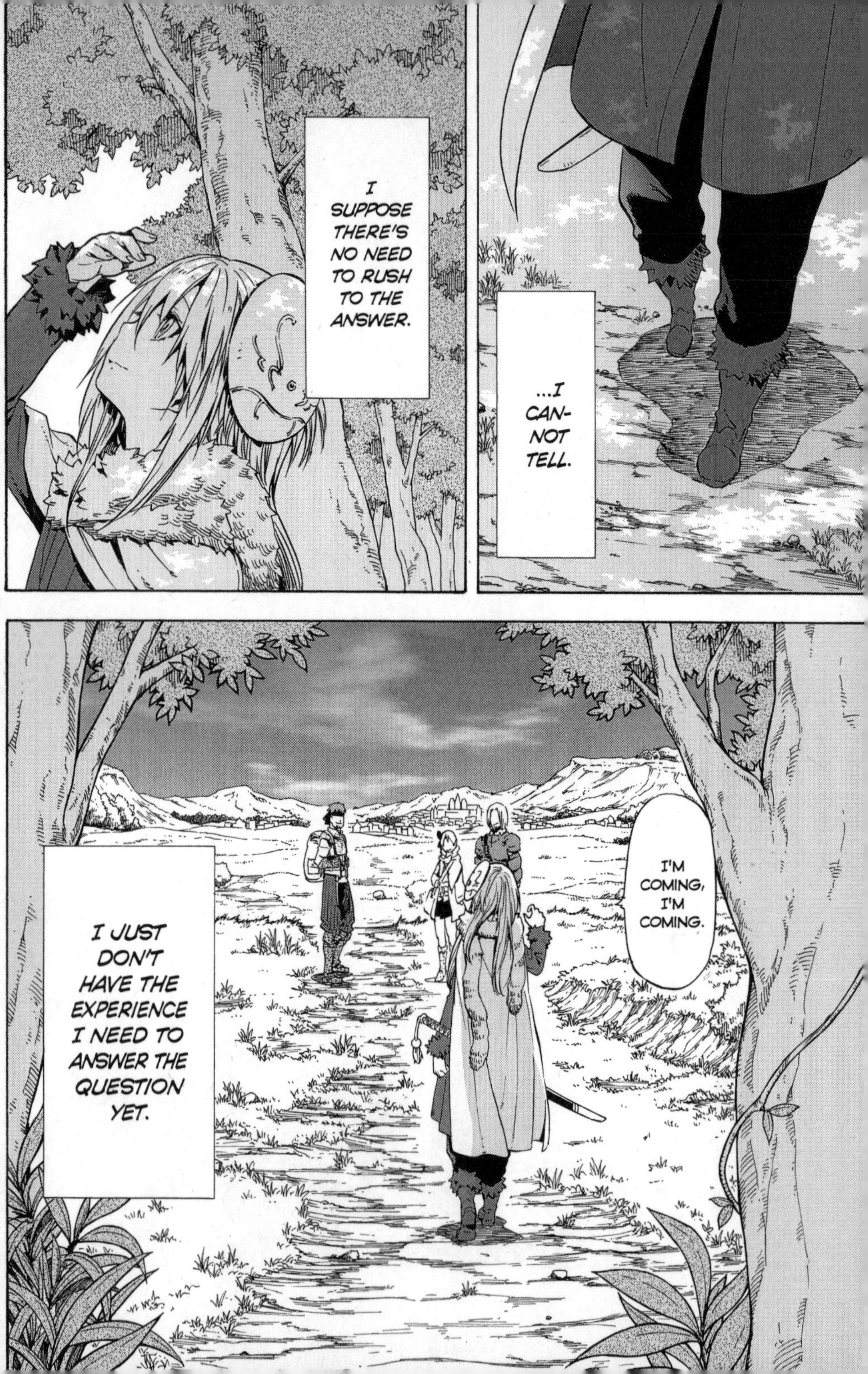
...I CAN-NOT TELL.
I SUPPOSE THERE'S NO NEED TO RUSH TO THE ANSWER.
I'M COMING, I'M COMING.
I JUST DON'T HAVE THE EXPERIENCE I NEED TO ANSWER THE QUESTION YET.

Reincarnate
in Volume 10?

→YES

NO

Bonus
Short Story

Veldora's Slime Observation Journal
~DIPLOMACY~

Veldora's Slime Observation Journal
~DIPLOMACY~

◆ TRADE WITH THE ANIMAL KINGDOM ◆

My hard work continues apace under Rimuru's strict observation. For this reason, I feel as though Rimuru has been slower than usual with his verbal jabs.

I have regained Rimuru's trust!

With that said, sometimes I wish to view the outside world for a change of pace. Would that really be so bad?

I lost a bit of my edge, but this is what I must do to seek the pleasures I desire. Ifrit is in my corner as well, so I have no choice but to keep fighting until I am victorious.

"...Understood. Fruits of effort are acknowledged. Undoing a portion of current limitations."

I have done it!
Victory!! Absolute victory!!

"That took a long time."

"It hasn't been easy for you either, Ifrit."

Ifrit and I were all smiles as we congratulated one another. Now this is friendship. Surely the culmination of all of our hard work is not long in the future.

With bright hope lighting up my chest, I looked to the outside world for the first time in what felt like ages.

Rimuru floats in the air.

What a hardworking little slime he is. Though amateurish, he is slowly learning to utilize the "Gravity Control" skill he gained by devouring Charybdis. With this, he can fight in ways that are practically cheating, enact barriers, and even fly at past the speed of sound. It is an excellent skill. And knowing Rimuru, he will soon have mastered it.

But why is it so noisy outside?

Shuna the kijin princess is calling on Rimuru. There appears to be some kind of event today.

Now that he's been primped up, he's heading up to stand on a stage in the gathering place. Facing him in the front row is a line of individuals dressed in fine clothing, led by Benimaru.

How strange it is, that a simple change of garments can effect such a grand and stylish change in manner.

And now, the time has come for a speech. I am very good at speeches, so show me what you are capable of, Rimuru.

He raised a hand, indicating that he was ready to begin.

"Ladies and gentlemen, I wish you the best of luck, and hope to hear good results!"

…What? That's all? That's the entire speech?

"…Is that all?" smiled Shuna. That was a relief. So I wasn't the only one who felt it entirely insufficient.

So Rimuru proceeded to explain his thoughts. Unlike me, he showed himself to be a poor orator, but at least he does look the part. Rather than hitting the monsters with complex words and statements, he judged it more effective to use honest, direct emotions. I will not claim that it was the "right" choice, but it did get his feelings across to them.

"Speaking of which, are you really that good at speeches, Master Veldora?"

"But of course."

"Pardon me for asking. I just assumed that you would never have the opportunity to give a public speech."

I suppose that I cannot blame Ifrit for assuming so. Because I was so solitary and proud, I never had the chance to speak to a gathering of others. But that is no matter.

"Kwa ha ha ha! Who do you think I am? I am the great Storm Dragon. Of course I practiced my greetings and banter for those foolhardy challengers who attempted to vanquish me. I am never caught unprepared!"

"I-I see… I didn't realize."

Well, at least he gets the picture now. After all, this is a kind of obligation asked of the great and powerful. Ifrit would not understand. But one day, if he continues to better himself, he just might.

In the meantime, Benimaru's delegation left home, but the others were quite busy in their absence. That was not the end of the day's events.

The town was transformed into blocks of neat and pristine buildings. It was a sight to behold. It's amazing how the quality of life around the city has grown so much in a relatively short amount of time.

Shuna is giving cooking lessons. The delectable sight of her dishes lights a fire under my desire to return to life soon.

The man named Vesta, whom dwarven King Gazel left here, has proven himself capable in a variety of ways. His first impression on our travels was awful, but after that, he's exhibited a good heart. He is not stingy with his knowledge and experience.

I had thought that was Rimuru's plan from the start, but this is not true. It is not the sort of change you can expect to happen. It was only Rimuru's sincere and personable treatment that infected Vesta and helped him return to his original nature.

At this time, Vesta is taking a break from his herbal production to teach the residents of this monster town the proper manners for interacting with noble visitors. It suggests to me that the city will soon receive a guest important enough to require such etiquette.

"Probably an envoy from Demon Lord Carrion. After all, Benimaru's delegation was leaving for Eurazania, the animal kingdom."

"Ah, yes. A start to the serious business of trade negotiations. All of this activity in the brief time that I take my eyes off of the action? I cannot do that again."

"Indeed. We have to take our work seriously to ensure that we are never hit with 'Sensory Shutdown' again."

"Aye."

Ifrit is correct, of course. Rimuru's actions are like a bolt of stimulating lightning in this dreary world of boredom. I must not allow myself to grow too fallow, lest my source of stimulation be removed from me again.

I have once again carved that admonishment into my breast.

But before the envoy from Eurazania arrived, we had a visit from Youm. The man whom Rimuru built into a champion has improved since I saw him last. In fact, he seems to be rather powerful, for a human.

Now he is reporting on the latest happenings over drinks with Rimuru. They've got plenty of delicious looking snacks to go with it, too. How I wish I could join them.

The entire scene just seems so mature and refined. Perhaps I should arrange for such accoutrements when I am plotting wicked deeds in the future. For now I can only gaze upon them with jealousy.

When Youm heard of Carrion's agents coming, he spit up his drink in shock. Rimuru nimbly dodged the spray. From the way he reacted, I daresay he had been expecting Youm to do it.

If you ask me, it seems a waste of good drink.

Several days later, the actual delegation arrived. In a carriage pulled by tigers, no less.

"I suppose it is fitting that the kingdom of lycanthropes would have Thunder Tigers in their employ. Those magical beasts are far more powerful than your average or lower elemental."

"Indeed. They eat spiritual lifeforms, in fact. They do not possess enough intelligence to understand human speech, but their ability to discern power through sheer instinct is quite keen. If not, they would be exterminated for the danger they pose."

"Ha ha ha, coming from the dragon locked behind a magical barrier by a hero."

What is your point, Ifrit? I possess ultimate power, coupled with intelligence and intellect. I cannot see how anything I said deserves to be laughed at by a mere fire spirit…

"Oh, look. The envoy is stepping out of the carriage."

Hrmph. I am still curious about Ifrit's implication, but I shall have to let it go. Now is the time to focus on the agents from the animal kingdom.

"It is a pleasure to make your acquaintance, Chancellor of the Great Forest of Jura. I am one of Lord Carrion's Three Beastketeers. I am known as Albis, the Golden Serpent," said a bewitching beauty with long hair of streaked gold and black. The Three Beastketeers, as I recall, are the group that included Phobio among them.

"I remember hearing that the Three Beastketeers were considered supreme among the Animal King's Brigade. If it were not Demon Lord Milim he'd faced, Phobio would not have been bested nearly so easily."

Perhaps. When Ifrit was just an upper elemental, the majin named Phobio would have been more powerful. And this woman Albis is even stronger than Phobio.

"You know, it occurs to me…"

"What is it?"

"If he had just sent this Albis woman originally, Demon Lord Carrion might have been able to achieve an alliance much faster and with less trouble."

"What?!"

"At the very least, this Albis does not seem the type to be so easily swayed into playing the role of Charybdis' bodily vessel."

"…"

Ifrit could not believe what he was hearing. My intellect is terrifying. If anything, it seemed I had just proven myself several times more clever than Carrion.

"Do you have any issue with my brilliance?"

"N-no, Master Veldora. I am overwhelmed by your sagacity."

Of course he is. It has been too long since I came up with such an insightful comment.

My mood was elevated by the feeling of well-deserved respect, only to be disrupted by a coarse shout of, "Is that supposed to be a joke?!"

Who is this uncouth individual?

The second member of the delegation goes by the name of Suphia. From the way she spoke, I assume she is another one of these Beastketeers. But her insolence cannot be overlooked.

She might be powerful, but she seems, shall we say, less intelligent than I. Why else would she refer to my bosom companion Rimuru as a "wimpy little slime"…?

"But Lord Rimuru himself does not seem upset by it at all, does he?"

Hmm?

Upon closer examination, neither he nor Suphia seem to be exuding any true anger. She hurls invective, but there seems to be no actual emotion behind it. Which only leaves one possibility.

"It could be an act."

"An act?"

"Yes. Meaning…"

I can feel how crisp and sharp my mind is today. I mean, it always is—but especially so on this day.

So I confidently stated, "She is attempting to anger Rimuru, to ascertain his true ability."

"Ahh. But Lord Rimuru is not the type to fall for such provocations. Just look at how self-possessed he is, despite her attempt at manipulation!"

"Precisely. As evidence of that, behold! He has named Youm the human as his stand-in!"

"You're right!"

Rimuru responded to Suphia's taunts by allowing Youm to fight for him. The difference between Suphia and Youm is stark. Youm has made great strides, and has excellent, custom-made weapons and armor, but such things cannot fill the vast gap between them.

Instead, this is a means for Rimuru to observe how the enemy intends to act. A reversal of roles.

If Suphia fights Youm to the best of her ability, the result will prove her to be immature. Rather than being a show of her power, it will only lower the standing of the Three Beast-keteers as a group. On the other hand, if she acts lazily, the pragmatic lycanthropes she is with will not take kindly to a poor display. She will lose the faith they put in her, and perhaps even her role in that vaunted trio.

"So, Suphia, how do you react to Rimuru's crafty move?"

Ifrit and I watched the outcome of this tense negotiation with great anticipation. But to our surprise, it was none other than Rimuru's secretary, Shion, who rescued Suphia from her dilemma.

"I've been listening to you insulting Lord Rimuru, one statement after another. While I exercised great patience and control, it seems that will no longer be necessary," she said, utterly ruining Rimuru's crafty strategy—and let us set aside the question of when she exercised patience, exactly.

Naturally, Suphia happily accepted this challenge. And no wonder, for her relative balance with Shion's power meant that she could achieve her goal.

"Her goal?"

"Precisely. Suphia probably expected that she would lose to Rimuru. For if she should actually end up winning, that would lead to a rather unfortunate state of affairs."

"I suppose I can see that. As an official delegate of Demon Lord Carrion, she has a duty to ensure that good relations between the two nations are forged in a safe and stable manner."

"Yes. Therefore, I suspect she intended to make it clear that she had attempted her best and lost to Rimuru anyway."

"In other words, displaying Lord Rimuru's power to the subordinates in a way intended to help them accept the negotiations. It would be a dangerous gamble against any demon lord, but Lord Rimuru would not simply take a life for the sake of it. This strategy seems much more logical than I realized. But then, what was the point of Lord Rimuru choosing Youm to be his stand-in?"

"Perhaps it was a prank."

Despite his appearance, Rimuru does enjoy a cheeky bit of fun now and then. I took his decision to be another example of that. And perhaps to achieve another end as well.

"As a prank, Master? It might be a nasty word, but it does seem to fit the situation."

"Doesn't it? And see the result. With Shion fighting Suphia, the battle is pitched and close. And it's gotten Youm to battle with another majin named Grucius. I suspect that this, in fact, was Rimuru's true intention!" I explained to Ifrit, my brilliance on full display.

Youm is a human, but not a weak one. Rimuru wants to be on good terms with the humans as well, and he chose to make this fact clear to the beastmen.

It was a big gamble against Suphia, but he was probably hoping for Youm to at least put up a good fight. This outcome, however, presents probably the best outcome he could have hoped for.

"Perhaps Lord Rimuru even anticipated how Shion was going to react."

Hrmm? Is that really the case?

I cannot assume that it would all be that easy, but this is Rimuru we are talking about. I suppose it cannot be ruled out.

"That's enough," commanded Albis, which pulled me out of this logical quandary and back to reality.

As I anticipated, Shion and Suphia engaged in a truly spectacular duel, while Youm and Grucius acquitted themselves well. Thanks to this, Suphia was able to make a declaration of friendship, to the approval of the lycanthropes. They did not mock Youm for being human, but accepted him warmly, as a worthy friend.

Everything turned out entirely in Rimuru's favor. I suppose it is indeed possible that Shion's reaction might have been part of his plan. And in fact, what happened next was so decisive that it surpassed anything I could have imagined.

Shion's refined projectile of magical power was so inflated that she was losing control of it. The Three Beastketeers panicked; Suphia was at a loss, and Albis took the opportunity to retreat to safety.

On the issue of Shion's magical energy level, she is either the same as Benimaru, or occasionally even higher, based on her mental state in that moment. From the perspective of Carrion's Beastketeers, this was a state of affairs too dangerous to ignore.

If Shion's magical shot were unleashed, great damage to the surrounding area would be unavoidable. But this ended up being the perfect demonstration of Rimuru's capabilities.

With "Gluttony," the evolved form of the unique skill "Predator," even expelled energy is just another target to be eaten.

He eliminated Shion's massive blast as if nothing ever happened. It was the end of the trouble. The party from the animal kingdom was silent, stunned.

"I suppose Lord Rimuru must have known that all of this would happen."

"But of course. At this point, we must admit that he foresaw Shion's lack of control and incorporated it into his strategy. I do not think that I would dare to take such a bold course of action."

"Indeed. One wrong step, and it would result in disaster. Yet he went ahead and saw it through… I have nothing but praise for the abilities of Lord Rimuru."

We couldn't help but admire his handiwork.

After that, they matter-of-factly headed right into a welcoming celebration. There, Rimuru and the lycanthropes found common agreement and began official trade negotiations in earnest.

Meanwhile, I gnash my teeth at the frustration of watching everyone drinking and enjoying their alcohol. I shall have to make certain that I am able to consume great quantities of it by the time I return to physical form. But for now, it is back to work.

◆ KING GAZEL'S INVITATION (PART ONE) ◆

After a stay of several days, Albis and Suphia returned to their kingdom. The others of their delegation remained behind in Rimuru's Jura Tempest Federation. It seems they decided to learn of this country's benefits before they go home.

Naturally, such studiousness is a good example for me to follow.

"Ifrit, you have made great strides. What nearly killed you just the other day, you now accomplish with ease."

"I am honored by your compliment, Master. But this is entirely thanks to Lord Rimuru's guidance. I've learned how to utilize energy in the most efficient way possible. Or, put another way, I was scolded whenever I wasted my time…"

Ah, yes. Energy efficiency is a crucial matter. No matter how great one's energy store is, it does no good if used wastefully.

"Well, I've noticed that Lord Rimuru doesn't scold you anymore either, Master Veldora. It seems like your progress on the analysis is humming along. That's very good to see."

Heh heh heh. Oh, yes.

"Do you understand, Ifrit? What's important is to accomplish one's work effectively. You cannot take too much time off. If you do, it will stand out, and earn you a rebuke, like it did a while ago. So I learned a valuable lesson."

Indeed, I did learn. From consulting Rimuru's memory, I learned of the concept of "unscrupulous companies." It is not clear what "illegal labor" means, but I do recognize what forced labor and abuse of authority are.

After all, there is one such being close at hand that strikes fear into my heart, despite all of the diligent effort that I expend.

"…"

Aiiie!

Oh, dear. I feel as though my thoughts were being read.

Because Rimuru has started to think using his deeper mental levels, it is much harder than before to read his thoughts— and yet, my thoughts are being read more and more often. It is unbearable.

Careful, careful. I must act carefully, lest my inactivity be detected.

"Effectively? I believe I see what you mean. I understand that working hard to complete a job sets a precedent that becomes the standard for future jobs. I suppose the ideal method is to complete an appropriate amount for one's means in a standard length of time."

Y-yes, precisely. That is correct, Ifrit. But read the room first!

When you detect the presence of a watchful eye, return to work at once. This is an ironclad rule for survival! So let us conclude this conversation before Rimuru notices us.

"Warning. Increase in Ifrit's ability detected. Raising difficulty level of training to encourage progress to the next stage."

Too late.

"Gwaaaaah!!" screamed Ifrit.

The fool. When one fails to adjust to the proper level, the results inspire pity.

"Question. The pace of analysis is extremely steady. Are you operating at less than full capacity?"

I…I am not.

"Suggestion. Could you try harder?"

Not at all. I am at full power.

I made certain to show off my efforts, and make clear that I was working hard. There was a long silence, provided you didn't count the screaming of Ifrit.

"Understood. Continue working hard in pursuit of higher goals."

"Wh-why, yes. That is what I always do," I said with apparent sincerity. In the next moment, I sensed that the observer had left.

"Ifrit, are you alive?"

"Y-yes, I am. Before I had the wherewithal to enjoy the outside scenery, but now all I can manage is to converse with you…"

"Next time, when I go silent, you must stop talking as well. Until you learn to detect Rimuru's presence, you *must* obey this rule."

"Understood."

And so a silent understanding was shared between me and Ifrit.

Many tribulations followed in the days to come, until Rimuru's delegation returned home. The first thing that became apparent was the wide variety of fruit they brought with them.

"Those fruits look delicious."

"I myself have never eaten food, but it seems a shame to me now. If only I had enjoyed some meals while I was fused with Shizue Izawa…"

"Indeed. I feel the same way. If only I had taken human form much earlier, rather than assuming it was all just a lot of fuss. Then I might have discovered new forms of delight in life."

Food would be one of them.

Through a flood of Rimuru's thoughts, I learned that the fruits were called apples, mangos, and melons, and that they were high in sugar, and very sweet and delicious.

Rimuru feels that they are "more delicious than what he ate in Japan," so that should speak to the value of these fruits.

On that topic, the domains of the demon lords are all rich in one way or another, packed with mineral deposits that provide the soil with nutrients to support excellent natural harvests.

In Eurazania, the kingdom under Carrion's rule, fruit is the primary export. If we can succeed in importing their fruit, as Rimuru says will happen, it should mean a big expansion of our food options.

Well, I should certainly hope that happens, for my sake.

According to Rimuru and Benimaru's conversation, the kijin attempted to pick a fight with Demon Lord Carrion, and was soundly beaten. If it were me, I would have been the one doing the beating, I can tell you that!

"Then I shall be the leader of the next delegation!"

"No, Master. They were just talking about how Rigur will take over the position."

"…"

I couldn't help but be disappointed in Ifrit's very serious answer to my japery.

Ah, but now it is Rimuru who is preparing to leave the country.

"They are heading for the Armored Nation of Dwargon, Master. Tempest has been recognized as a worthy nation in its own right, and will attract attention from all over."

"Why do you speak of 'Tempest,' Ifrit? What is this?"

"Oh, it's just an abbreviation of 'Jura Tempest Federation.' It's easier to call it Tempest."

Ahh, an abbreviation. I like that, and it rolls off the tongue, so I will call it that in the future.

But more interesting to me now is the incredible technique that Shion just exhibited. To me, this is of the utmost importance and priority.

"By the way, Ifrit, did you see Shion's grand statement just now, as I did?"

"I did. It was quite a surprise."

Of course it was. Shion's achievement was exhibiting such incredible poutiness that Rimuru's steadfast spirit was broken.

"In the future, I too shall have to try shouting, 'It's not fair, it's not fair!!' Then perhaps Rimuru will feel sorry for me, and do what I want him to do!" I said. Ifrit looked thoughtful. "What is it? Does something bother you?"

"No, it is not quite on the level of a bother…"

But when he says it that way, I cannot help but worry. "Go on, speak."

"Very well. Then I must admit that I wonder what should happen if you attempt this plan, and it fails…"

"If it *fails?*"

I did not consider that. I just assumed I would laugh it off as a simple failure…

"Lord Rimuru is very strict with us, but he is much softer with women, isn't that right? So I believe that assuming he will react the same way is walking right into a trap…"

A very good point! I too have thought for ages that Rimuru was too hard on us.

"Not that you have known him for 'ages.'"

"Don't think about that. My point is, it was worth paying attention to what you just said. Perhaps we need to ascertain—very carefully—just how much pouting one can do before it is no longer indulged, through observation of others."

"Yes, sir!"

And so our strategy was put on hold for the time being.

On the road, Rimuru brought Geld and his orcs a present of beer as a reward and motivation for their good work. Ifrit and I had to share a look and sigh that he could not favor us with the same sort of kindness.

There is nothing special in particular to write about regarding the private conversation between King Gazel and Rimuru. The king was mistaken about the way Milim eradicated Charybdis, thinking that it was the work of some secret weapon of Rimuru's...but when the slime explained the truth, he accepted it quite easily.

This is thanks to Rimuru's character, naturally. He also revealed that Beastmaster Carrion agreed to forge trade, which seems likely to only increase the profile of Tempest in the future. I should not be surprised that the king of a great nation would see such possibilities from this event.

But it is of no interest to me. I am more interested in the catastrophe Shion turned out to be.

King Gazel is a valuable trading partner for Rimuru. And now Shion is falling-down drunk in his vicinity. And what kind of secretary drinks herself into a stupor at such an important event?

"It is simply unthinkable. If such an individual worked for Demon Lord Leon, her head would be separated from her body on the spot. If I were there, I would burn her until not even ashes were left."

Is it not so? My expectations were not incorrect, then. So if her actions are overlooked in this case, it merely speaks to the incredible profile Shion has built. It seems the trick lies in creating a character whose actions can be forgiven. Ifrit agreed with my assessment.

"However, this will not be easy," I said.

"Agreed… I suppose the biggest issue is to make others think that you are helpless to change your nature?"

"Well done. That is indeed the truth."

Ifrit and I ended up debating this topic deep into the night.

◆ KING GAZEL'S INVITATION (PART TWO) ◆

The next day, Rimuru gave a speech before a crowd. I found it to be wondrous in content, and gave it rave reviews, but Gazel did not feel the same way.

"I give that speech zero points."

It makes no sense, no sense at all. And yet, I have still come away with a lesson from this—the fact that Rimuru can fail at something. And more important to me was what occurred later that night.

The promised land. Yes, I have returned at last!

"Yes, but Master Veldora, you can only watch the outside from within Lord Rimuru."

"Do not say it, Ifrit. Experience is the key to everything. Is it not important to study what I can for now, so that when I am revived in full, I will not fail at my task?"

"Well, first of all, money is required to patronize this sort of establishment. In my humble opinion, you should be thinking more about how to gain currency."

Grrr… He does have a point.

Despite his appearance, Rimuru has a way with earning money. He comes up with various creative ideas, and puts them to good use. Perhaps I ought to follow his example and learn a trade that might provide me with money.

But…that is something I can decide later. For now, I must prioritize my study, and see the interior of the bar through Rimuru's eyes.

The space is brightly lit and clean. If I could sense the smell, I have no doubt that it would be fragrant. There is a bevy of beauties in all shapes and sizes. Having a discerning eye for quality, I must admit that this establishment is very well-stocked, indeed.

"Pardon the question, Master Veldora. How is it that you are so well-versed in human beauty?"

"Well, you see, Ifrit, the reason lies with my relatives. Are you aware of the story?"

"Are you referring to other kinds of dragons?"

"I am. My elder brother, in fact, fathered Milim with a human woman. As you might surmise from this, we dragons were capable of taking human form. I simply chose not to learn the secrets of humanization because it would have been a dreadful bore. That is all!"

"I see… And that is how you have the knowledge to gauge beauty and ugliness among different human specimens."

"Yes. I had the details of ultimate beauty repeatedly pounded into me… It was a harrowing experience, I can tell you…"

But that was the start of recalling memories I did not wish to dredge up from the muck of time. Ifrit, who has grown skilled in the ways of restraint, was wise enough not to inquire further.

We examined the room again, and found that Gobta was performing tricks.

"What in blazes is he doing…?"

"I do not know. What do you suppose, Master?"

It does not seem like the type of business for exhibiting tricks. Gobta is standing on his hands, with a fancy drink glass balanced on his foot. The clear crystal is quite fine, and obviously very expensive.

"If you break that glass, I think we'll need you to pay it off with…physical labor," whispered one of the more bewitching women into Gobta's ear. It caused blood to shoot from all of his orifices at once.

This, too, was a very impressive trick. I do not know exactly what he imagined, but I can guess.

"Gobta has so much yet to learn. He is too young for this sort of thing."

"I feel the weight of experience from your words, Master Veldora."

"But of course. Heed my advice, Ifrit. In this sort of place, you must treat the woman's stories as half made-up. Accept her lies, and play along with them knowing that they are nonsense. Once you can do that, you are half of a true adult."

"What?! There is a stage even beyond that?"

"Yes. Witness Rimuru."

Upon my command, Ifrit put his attention upon Rimuru. The slime was in negotiations with the proprietress of the bar at that moment. He was scheming to provide the bar with a newly designed type of alcohol as a test product.

He never rests, it seems. But this is just how ambitious he needs to be. For that is what makes him Rimuru.

Meanwhile, the madam accepted his offer, knowing equally well what Rimuru was after. You see, it is using others that makes one a fully-fledged adult.

"There. Do you understand now?"

"It was a very advanced negotiation. This is how Lord Rimuru earns some spending money for himself, I suppose."

That was your takeaway?!

B-but I suppose that, yes, it was part of Rimuru's plan.

"In this case, he considers having a business connection to this place more important than raising a little money. It is frequented by ministers of this nation, and he can find out how his new product is received. It will be more honest appraisal than any he might hear from the monsters under his rule."

"Oh, I see. So that's what he was thinking…"

"You have much to learn yet, Ifrit. Your shogi skills have improved, but you ought to see and hear more of the world, and expand your horizons. Kwaaaa ha ha ha!"

It felt very good to instruct Ifrit in the proper path forward.

If only that were the end of the issue. That night, another bit of chaos awaited.

Kaijin and the dwarves got plenty drunk, and Gobta bled so much out of sheer excitement that he grew lightheaded. So Rimuru had no choice but to carry Gobta back. Then, suddenly, a voice called out, "Would you like a hand?"

It was Shuna, whose smile merely existed to cover the rage she obviously felt.

"Sh-she frightens me…just a little…"

"You too, Master Veldora…? I thought I felt a ferocious spirit approaching. At least it seems I was not mistaken in that impression."

Ifrit and I huddled together, quaking inside of Rimuru. It

is the most generous and warm of people who are the most frightening when angered—a truism that extends to Shuna.

Shion was there too, and shouting various complaints, but in her case, it was simple sulking. It wasn't really worth getting as angry as she was, but calming her down would be no small feat.

If I am to learn from Rimuru's failure, I must be careful not to anger the females in this group.

"I suppose creating a 'forgivable' persona really is the key. It will be difficult, but achieving that feat will be the way to true victory!"

"I believe it is a challenge worth attempting."

"Aye! By the way, Ifrit, I have just one question."

"What is it, Master?"

"What did you think of Gobzo's actions?"

In my opinion, Ifrit would have reacted the same way Gobzo did not too long in the past. I plan to take on Ifrit as my comrade and confidant in the future, but I cannot have him betraying me the way that Gobzo just did.

I need him to be able to sense my way of thinking and take it into account on his own…

"Oh, you mean that?" Ifrit chuckled, despite my consternation. "Yes, I might have revealed that secret out of sheer honesty in the past. But that is the past! Now my fate is bound to yours, Master Veldora, and I intend to keep all of your secrets!"

Ah, yes! Faithful Ifrit, my jolly friend!!

"That is good to hear. And even if Rimuru himself should question you, you would remain on my side?"

"Huh?"

"Mmm?"

"Ha ha ha. I'll try, but I don't know if I can promise that..."

How quickly his bold statements crumble...

"That is clearly the place where you ought to state that you will always be on my side!" I admonished.

"Now, now, just a moment! Then let me ask you, Master Veldora: if you were the one being questioned by Lord Rimuru, would you succeed at keeping secrets from him?"

Huh?

Well, the answer to that would be...

Perhaps not... In fact, almost certainly not?

"I suppose that will be answered in the future."

"Don't try to wriggle out of answering the question, Master!"

"Ha ha ha."

"Don't laugh this off!"

It does one no good to attempt the impossible. Even Rimuru suffers punishment when it is merited, and therefore, I must admit that some things are beyond my means as well.

Learning this fact is the greatest boon of the day, I reflected, as I laughed long and loud to avoid having to answer Ifrit's questions.

◆ TO THE HUMAN KINGDOM ◆

As punishment for spending the night out on the town, Rimuru was forced to undergo the exceedingly cruel punishment of a week of Shion's home cooking. It is times like these that I am grateful my senses are disconnected from Rimuru's.

Normally I am jealous of his ability to eat food, but anything that causes one's mind to leave one's body does not qualify as "food."

"Why, it's worse than any drug. Lord Rimuru passed out just from taking a single bite," noted Ifrit.

"Yes… I wonder what that substance is. No mere poison could achieve such a dramatic effect."

"It speaks very highly of Gobta. He is suffering the same punishment, but he seems to be taking it rather well."

"A worthy example to follow. I shall note to seek his services if I am ever in similar trouble."

It truly is wondrous, however. Shion has tasted many of Rimuru's ideas for various food and dishes, and proclaimed them to be delicious. Occasionally, there were failures and ideas that did not pan out. When she tried those, Shion scowled with displeasure. In other words, she appeared to have a properly functioning sense of taste.

So how is it that she does not realize how atrocious her own cooking is?

"Perhaps she doesn't taste them herself?"

"I dare say she does not."

"That's the part I don't understand…"

"Neither do I."

It just makes sense. Of course you are supposed to taste-test your own creation!

"Is it because Lord Rimuru is too nice to tell her?"

"No, in this situation, Rimuru will express anger. He has in the past, correct?"

"Yes, he has. I remember that Benimaru suffered on account

of it."

"But how is it possible that even her tea is dangerous?"

"I don't know how…but unless someone chooses to be a noble sacrifice and explains it to her, I don't see her ever improving," Ifrit said, correctly.

She cannot be fixed. If I am not paying close attention, I could suffer grievous harm shortly after being revived into my body at last. But that is its own matter.

"Ifrit, do you suppose there is something you might learn from Shion's actions?"

"Meaning?"

"Well," I began, and proceeded to explain.

When the party left for the dwarven kingdom, Shion threw a fit until she succeeded in being taken along. In other words, she is a prime example of a "forgivable character" whose faults are overlooked.

"My point, Ifrit, is that we might avoid Rimuru's anger if we simply act just like Shion. What do you think?" I asked, proud of my logic.

But rather than a shower of praise, the only response I received was a heavy sigh.

"Master Veldora…I told you this before. Please reconsider this idea. Could you act like Shion in Lord Rimuru's presence?"

"Hrrm…"

"You know what would happen if you tried…"

"What would happen?"

"He would hit you."

I should have known. In fact, a small part of me did know it would happen.

"I suppose that would make such a dangerous move ill-advised," I said.

"Almost certainly."

"Then what can be done...?"

"There's no need to rush, Master. We have plenty of time until the seal is broken. We can think of a more clever idea before we reach that point."

"I suppose you are right!"

Ifrit can be a very helpful fellow. Whenever I am in danger of heading down the wrong path, he is there to guide me back to a wiser direction.

I cannot help but realize...

For three long centuries, I viewed this "Unlimited Imprisonment" as a terrible curse that locked me up. But now, I view its eventual undoing as an inevitable thing. I suppose it is thanks to Rimuru that I can be so optimistic.

"Are you sure you weren't overly optimistic the entire time, Master Veldora?"

"Shut up! Do not act like you know things you did not see for yourself!"

"But I was only making a conjecture based on how you've acted around me. I just can't imagine you acting deadly serious."

Why, you...

Just when I was paying him the compliment of being trustworthy and reliable, I find out what he really thought of me.

But I suppose that is fine, on second thought. If anything, it is a sign that Ifrit and I have grown to share a similar mental wavelength.

"Kwaaa ha ha ha!"

"Wh-what are you laughing about?"

"It is nothing. Let the good times continue, I say!"

"H-huh...?" Ifrit babbled. But I only laughed and laughed. Later, Rimuru escaped Shion's cooking by calling a meeting that would cancel the end of breakfast. There, he declared that he would be traveling to a human nation.

Kaval, Eren, and Gido were chosen to be his travel chaperones. When he reaches human lands, Rimuru plans to sell healing potions. He has other plans as well, it is clear, but I will have to wait until later to learn what they are.

What sort of adventures await him in these new lands?

"It's about time, Master Veldora."

"Yes. In the usual pattern, this is where Rimuru comes and scolds us. I suppose I ought to resume working hard at our task."

See how much I have learned?

"..."

This is when I bide my time.

I resumed the hard work ahead of me, letting the anticipation for Rimuru's quest to the human realm bubble away in the back of my mind.

To be reincarnated in Volume 10!

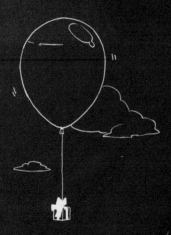

THERE ARE NO REFRIGERATORS OR FREEZERS IN THIS WORLD.
BUT I GOT TO DRINK ALCOHOL ON THE ROCKS IN THE DWARVEN KINGDOM.
THE ICE PROBABLY CAME FROM A WIZARD OR SOMETHING.
ICICLE LANCE!
ZMMF
MAKE MORE! IT'S NOT ENOUGH!
HURRY UP WITH THE ICE!
ICICLE LANCE!
ICICLE LANCE!
ICICLE LANCE!
drip
E... EAT UP.
OKAY!
SHAVED ICE

LIST OF ACKNOWLEDGMENTS

AUTHOR:
Fuse-sensei

CHARACTER DESIGN:
Mitz Vah-sensei

TRAVEL GUIDE:
Sho Okagiri-sensei

REINCARNATED SLIME DIARY:
Shiba-sensei

ASSISTANTS:
Muraichi-san
Daiki Haraguchi-san
Masashi Kiritani-sensei
Taku Arao-sensei

Everyone at the editorial department

AND YOU!!

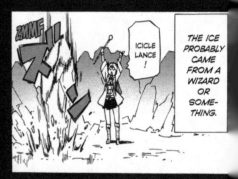

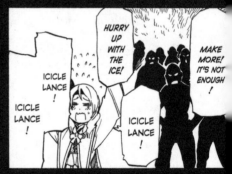

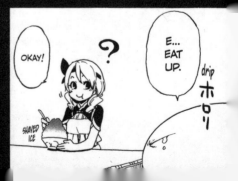

FROM THE VAULT

Storyboard and Illustrations Revealed!!

These are rare storyboard drafts and character pieces done for a pre-series test.

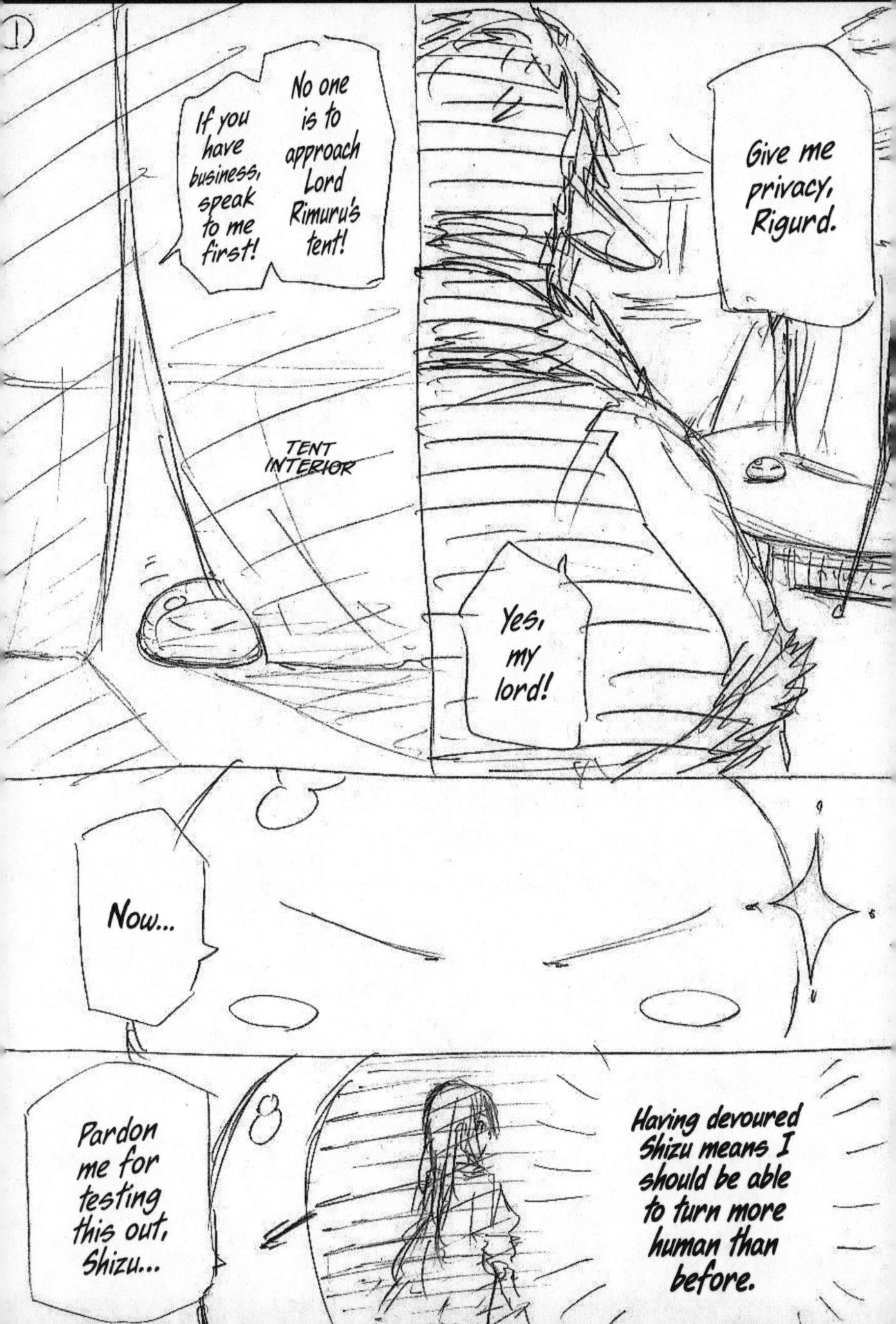
1
Give me privacy, Rigurd.
Yes, my lord!
No one is to approach Lord Rimuru's tent!
If you have business, speak to me first!
TENT INTERIOR
Now...
Having devoured Shizu means I should be able to turn more human than before.
Pardon me for testing this out, Shizu...

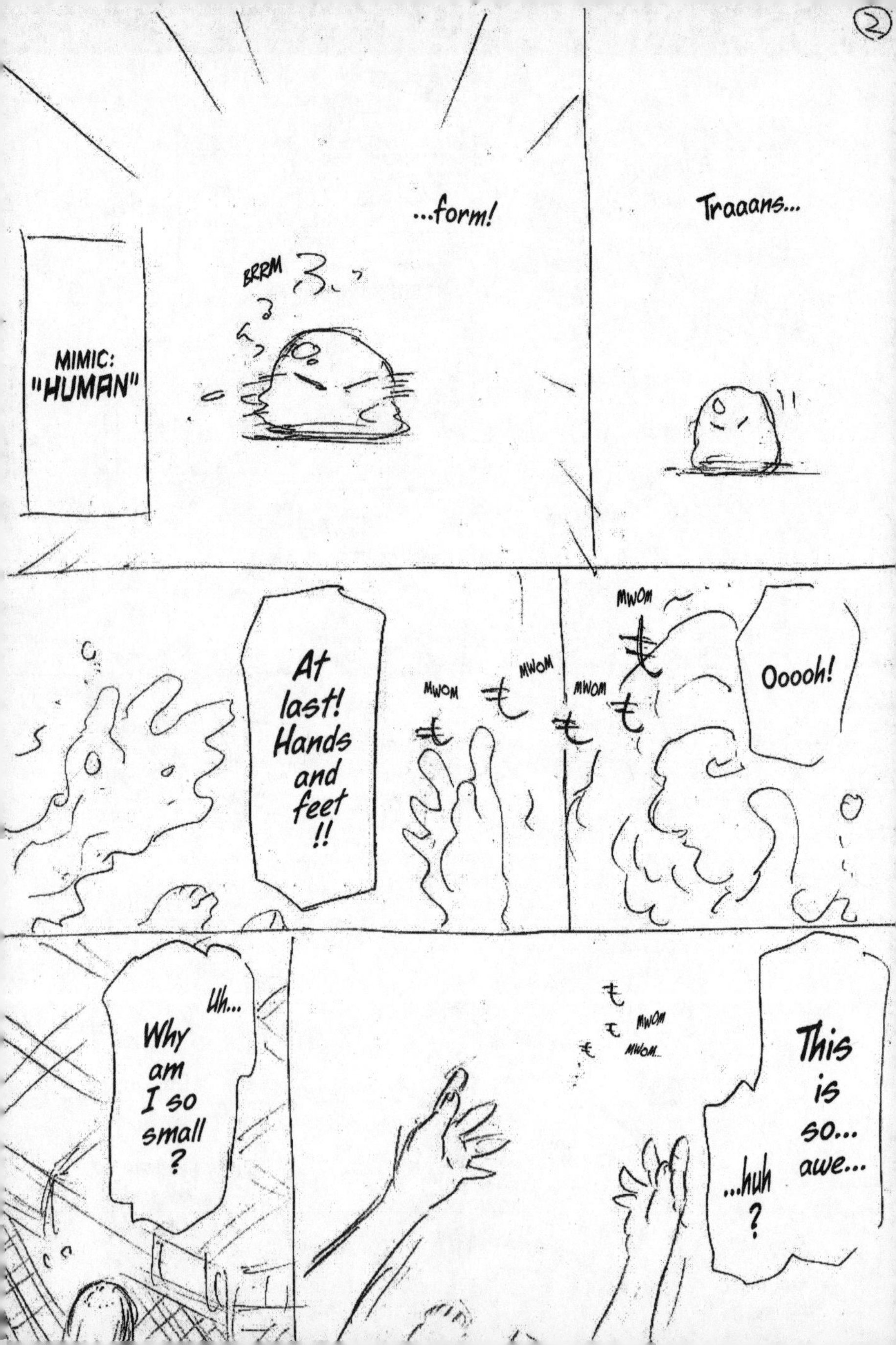

2
Traaans...
...form!
BRRM
MIMIC:
"HUMAN"
MWOM
Ooooh!
MWOM
MWOM
MWOM
At last! Hands and feet!!
This is so... awe...
...huh?
MWOM
MWOM...
Uh...
Why am I so small?

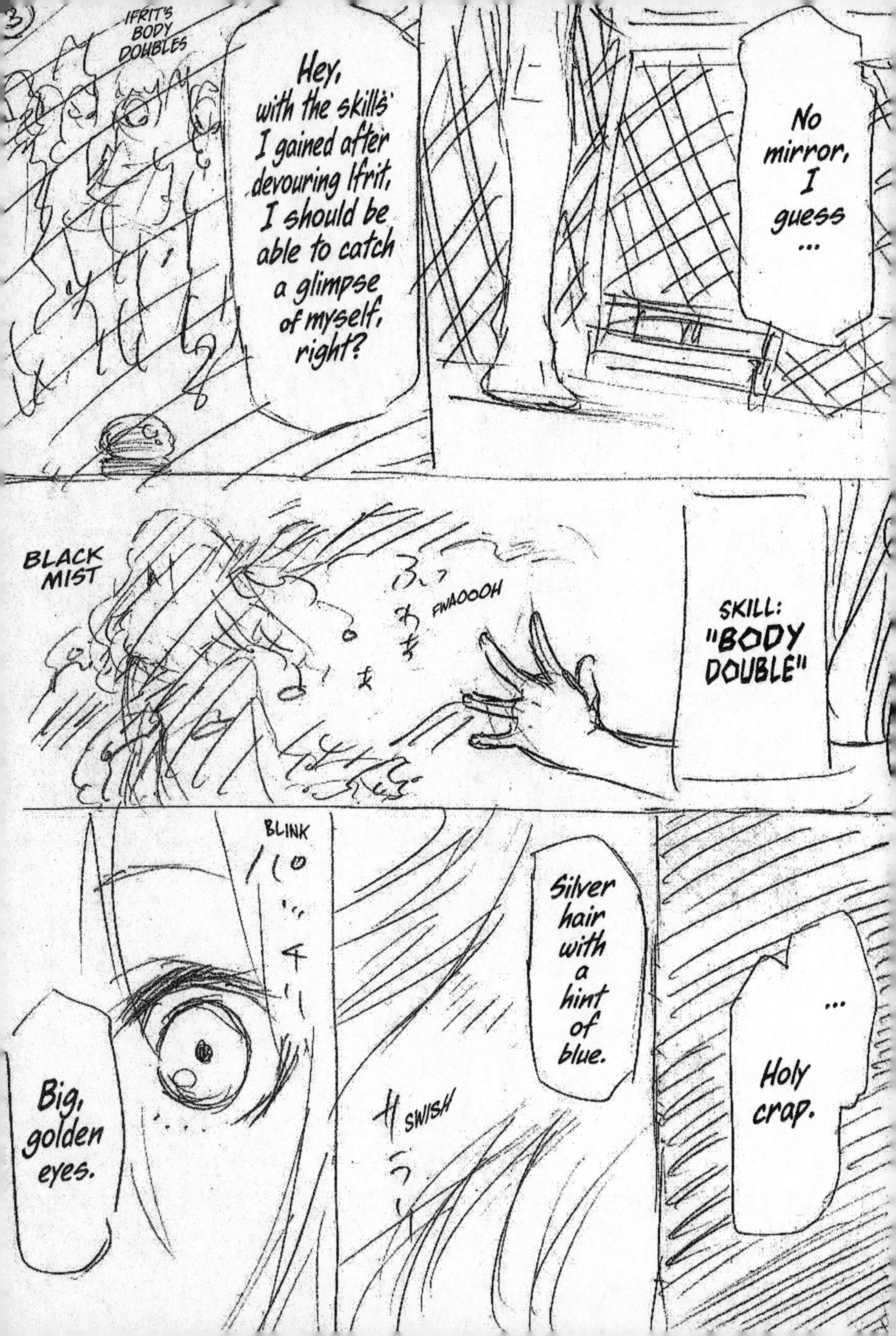
No mirror, I guess...
IFRIT'S BODY DOUBLES
Hey, with the skills I gained after devouring Ifrit, I should be able to catch a glimpse of myself, right?
SKILL: "BODY DOUBLE"
FWAOOOH
BLACK MIST
... Holy crap.
Silver hair with a hint of blue.
SWISH
BLINK
Big, golden eyes.

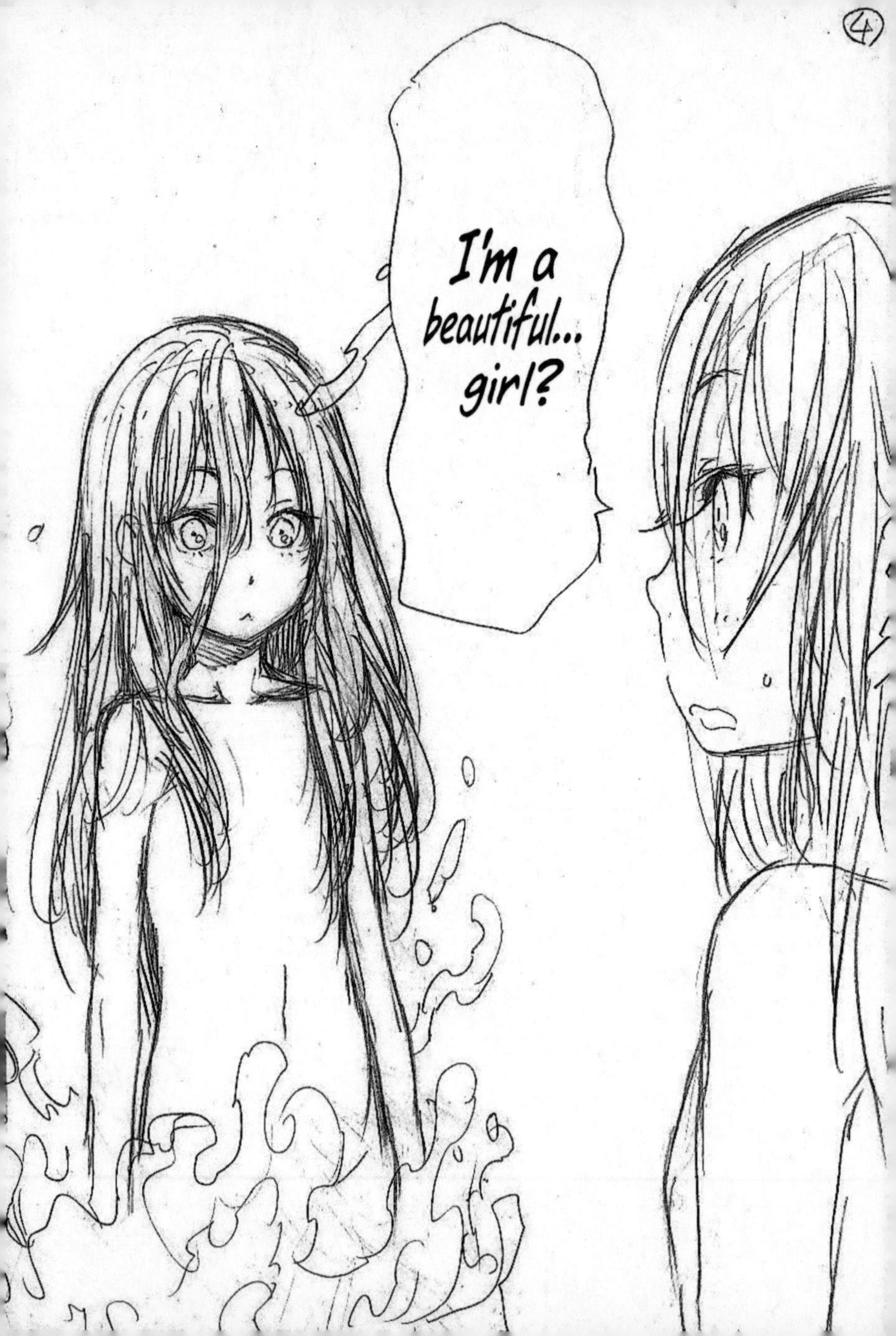
I'm a beautiful... girl?

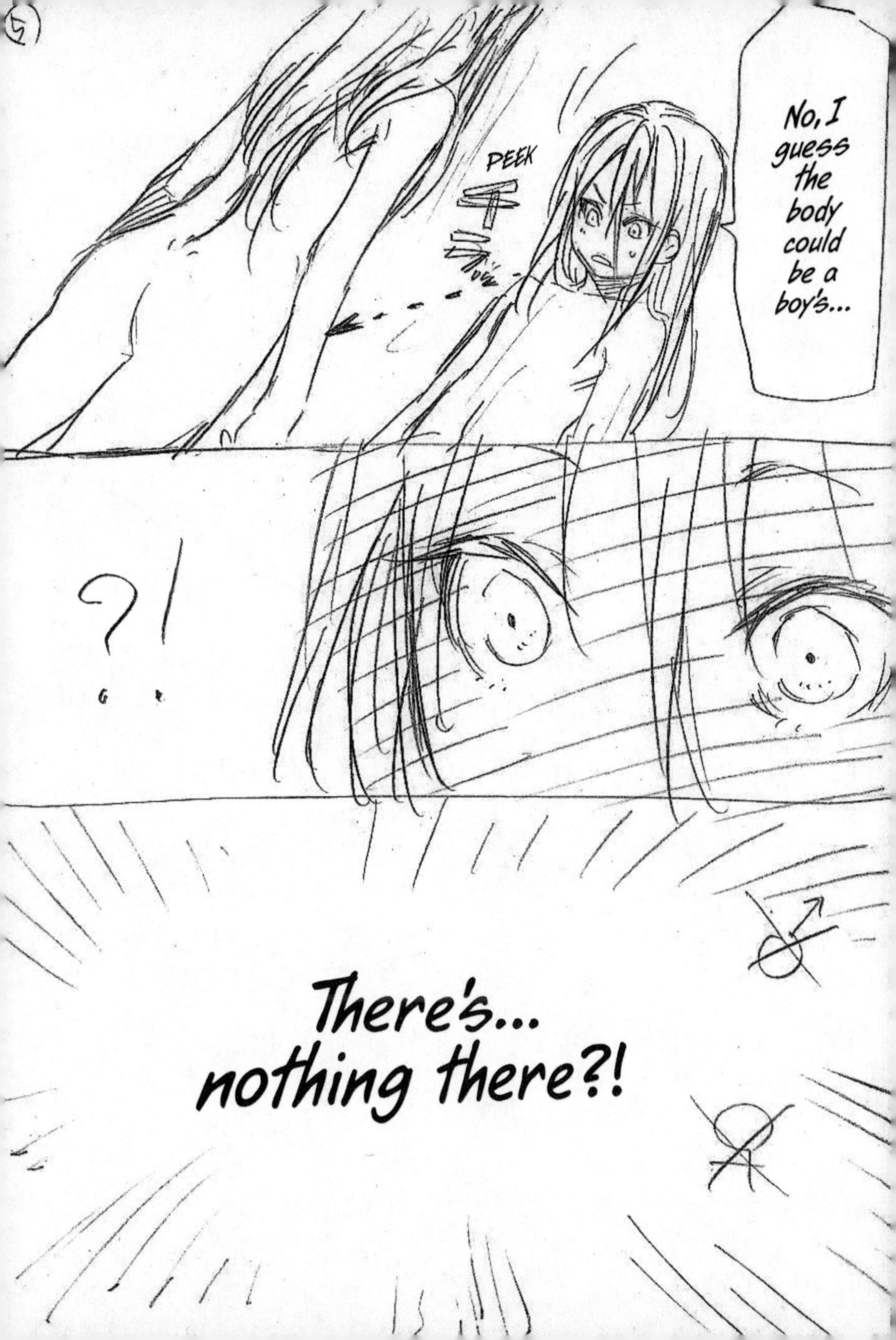
No, I guess the body could be a boy's...
PEEK
?!
There's... nothing there?!

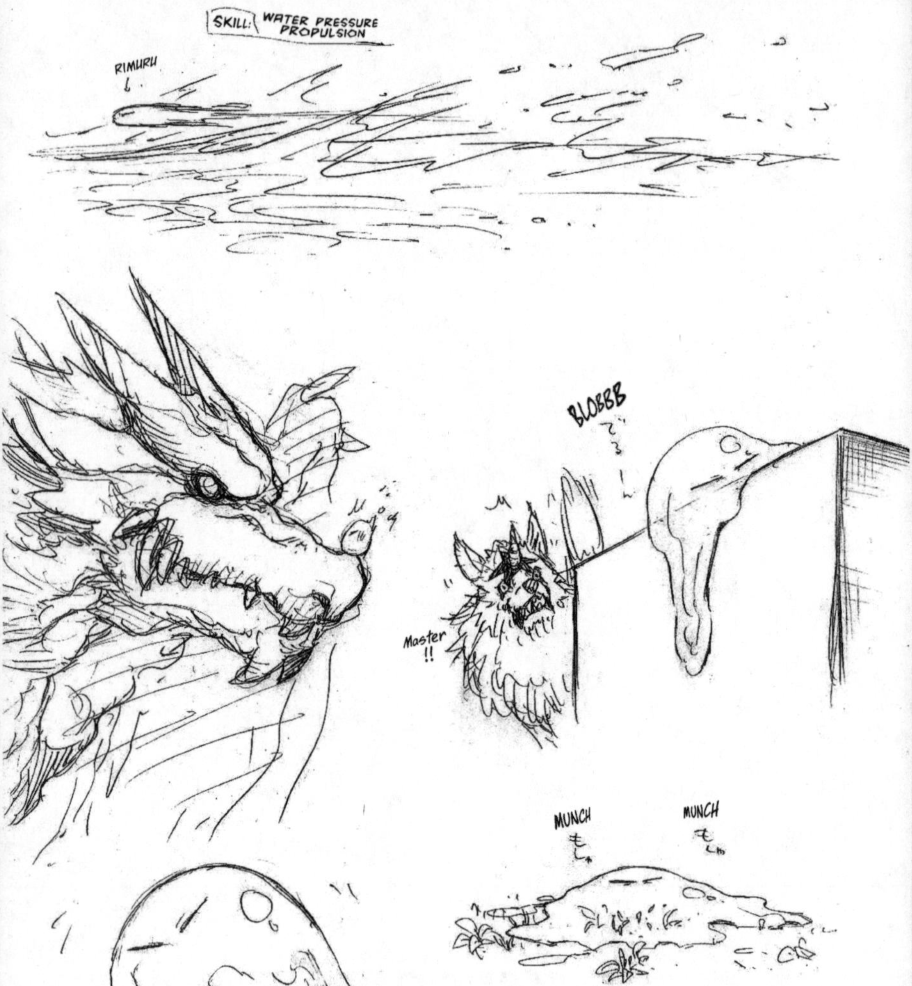
SKILL: WATER PRESSURE PROPULSION
RIMURU
BLOBBB
Master !!
MUNCH
MUNCH
POYOING
ぼよよん

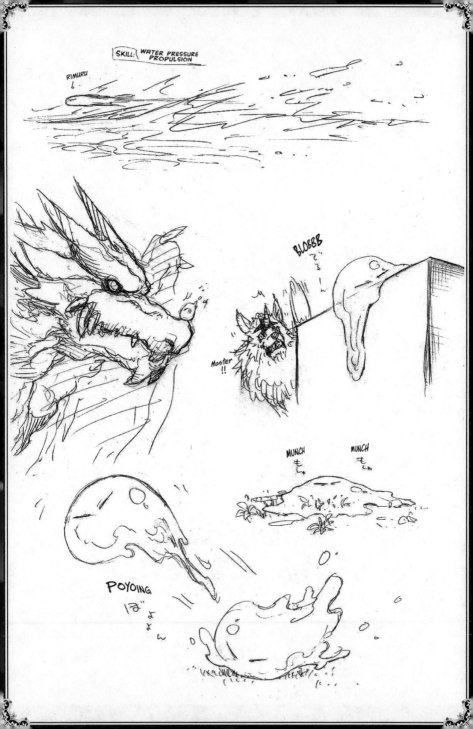

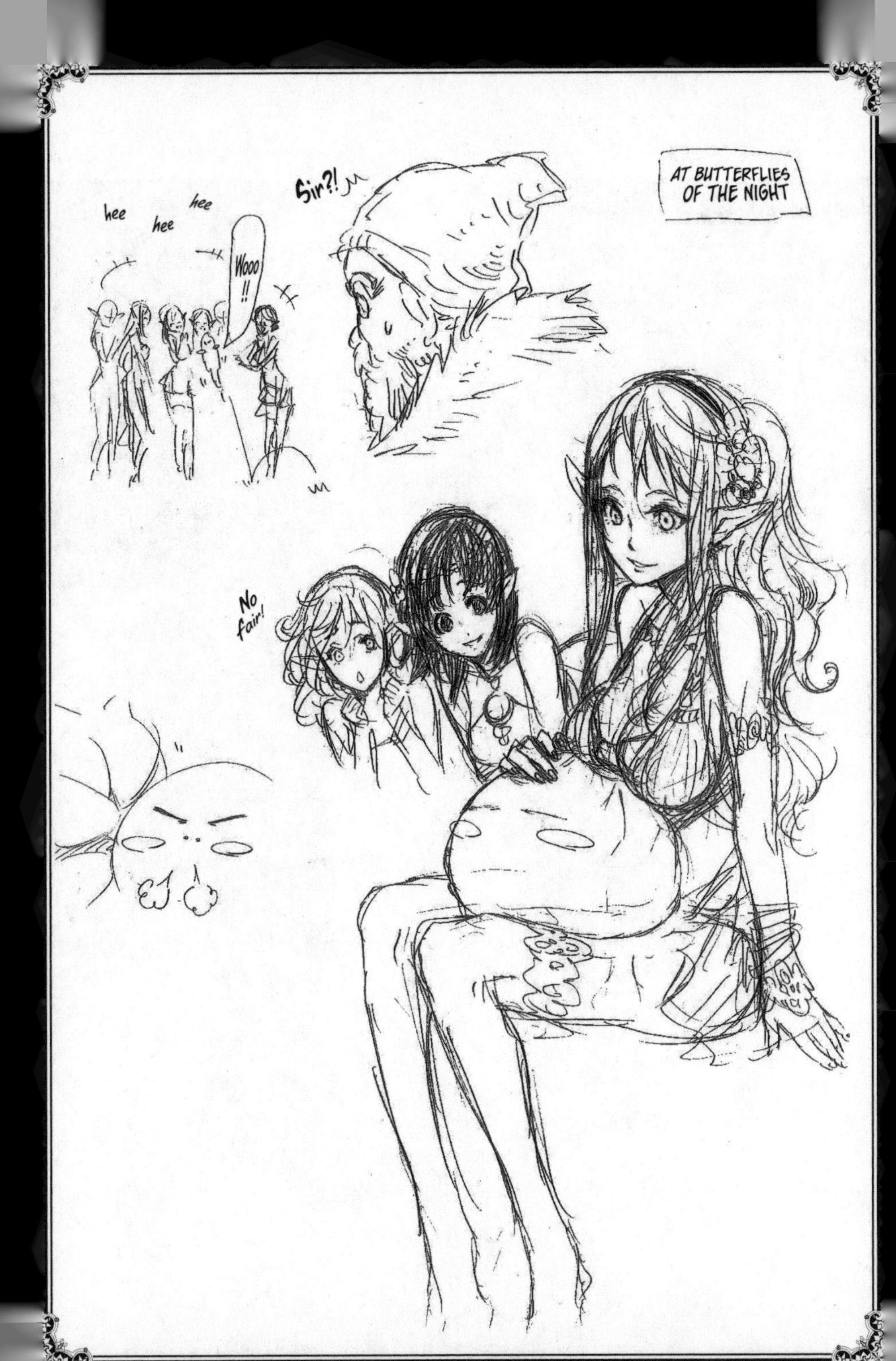
AT BUTTERFLIES OF THE NIGHT
Sir?!
Wooo!!
hee
hee
hee
No fair!

From character designer
Mitz Vah-sensei

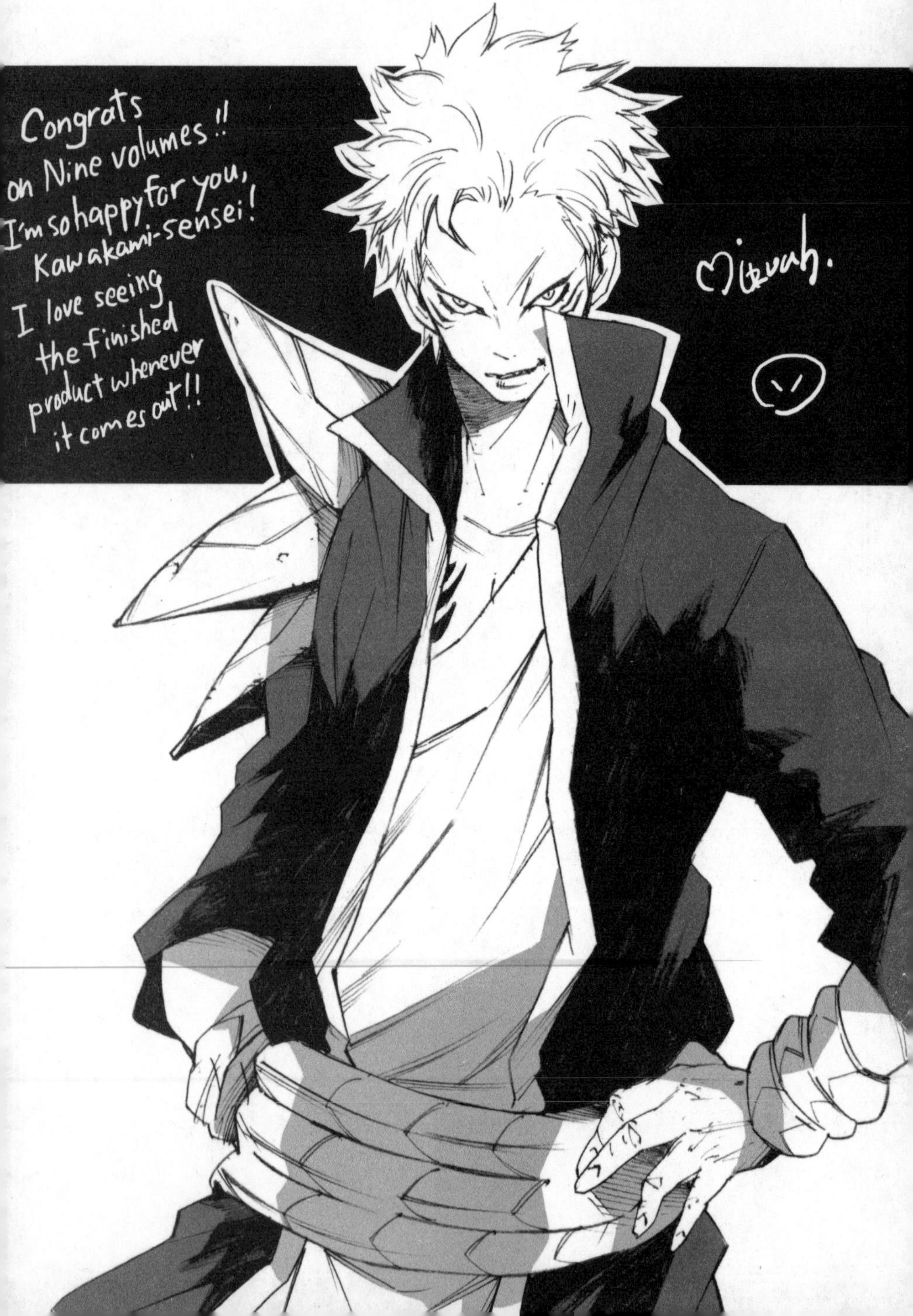
Congrats
on Nine volumes!!
I'm so happy for you,
Kawakami-sensei!
I love seeing
the finished
product whenever
it comes out!!

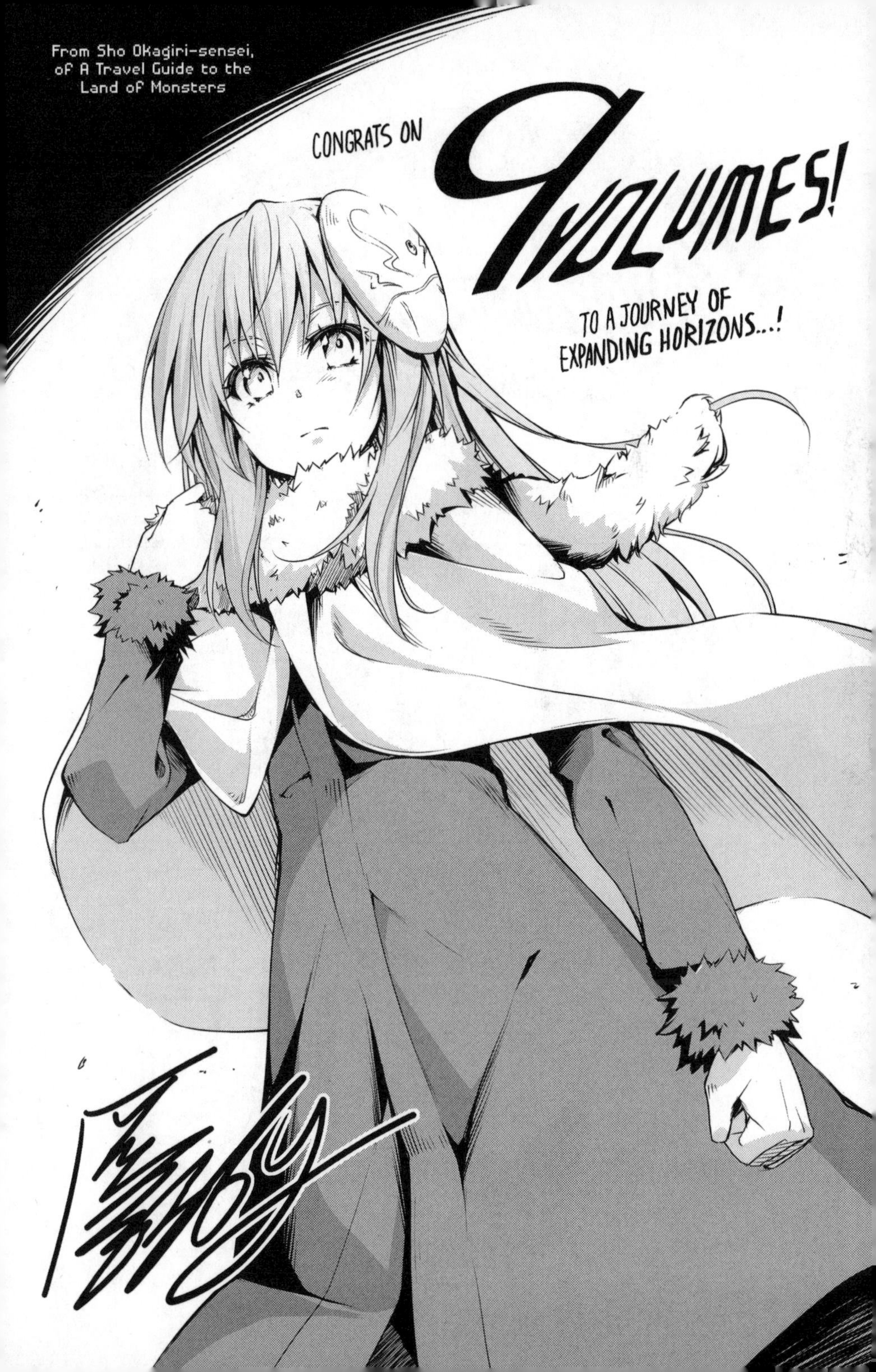

From Sho Okagiri-sensei, of A Travel Guide to the Land of Monsters
CONGRATS ON 9 VOLUMES!
TO A JOURNEY OF EXPANDING HORIZONS...!

From Shiba-sensei, of Reincarnated Slime Diary

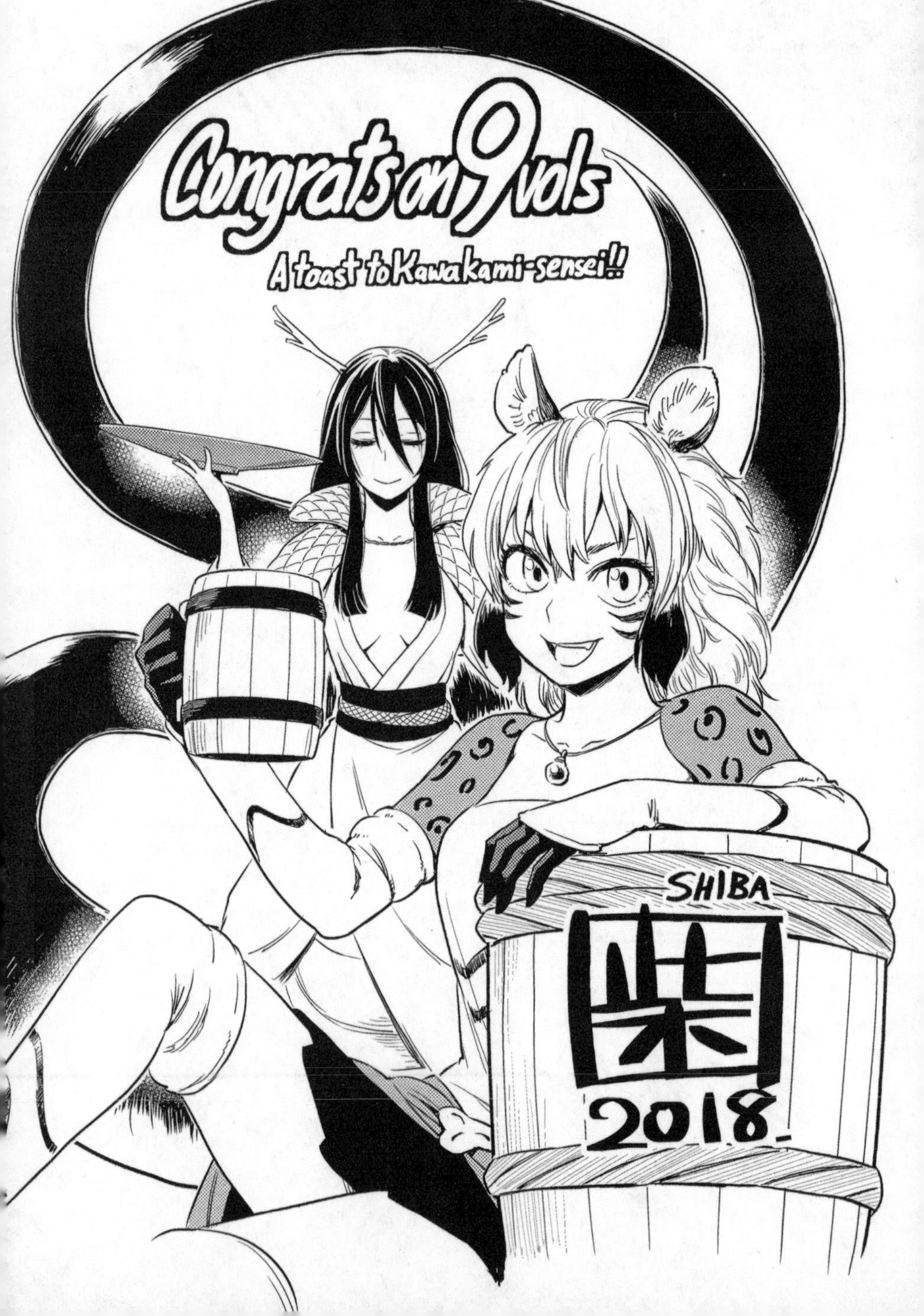
Congrats on 9 vols
A toast to Kawakami-sensei!!
SHIBA
2018

Down in Flames

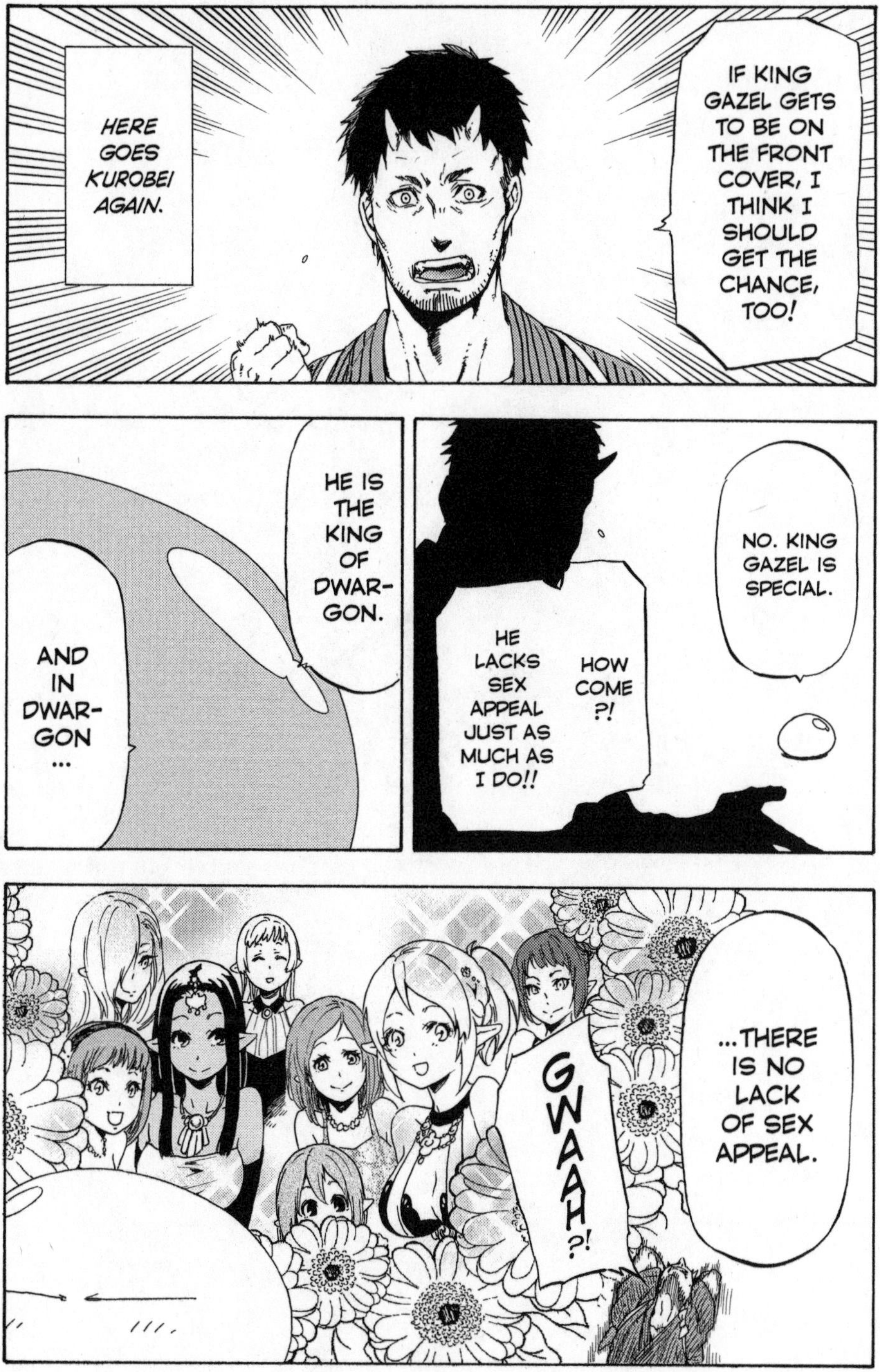
IF KING GAZEL GETS TO BE ON THE FRONT COVER, I THINK I SHOULD GET THE CHANCE, TOO!
HERE GOES KUROBEI AGAIN.
NO. KING GAZEL IS SPECIAL.
HOW COME?!
HE LACKS SEX APPEAL JUST AS MUCH AS I DO!!
HE IS THE KING OF DWAR-GON.
AND IN DWAR-GON...
...THERE IS NO LACK OF SEX APPEAL.
GWAAH?!

The world's simplest
"character bento."

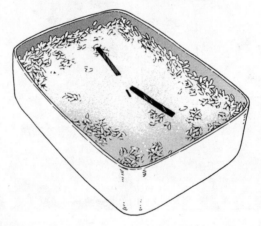

It also works with
rounded onigiri

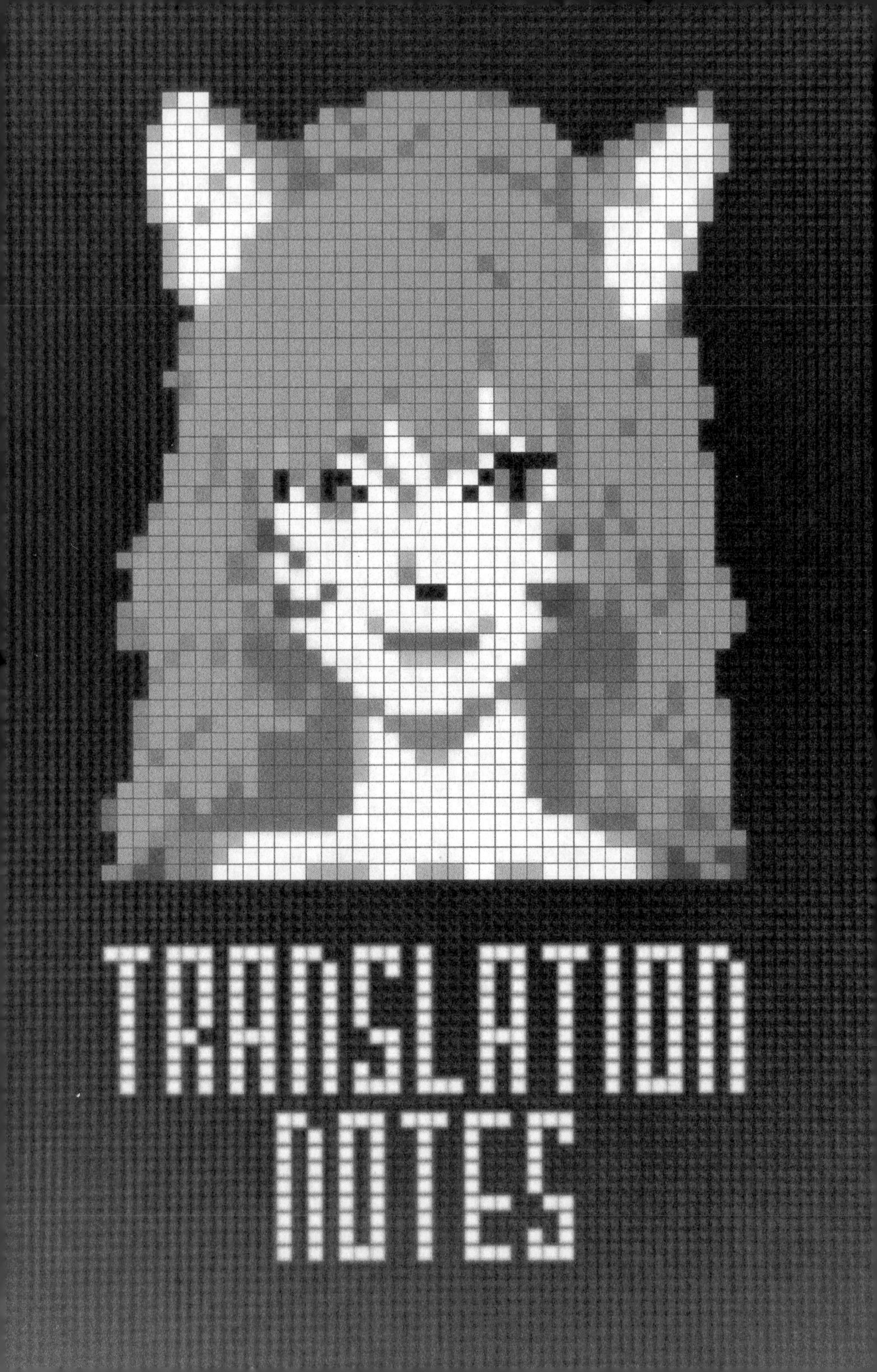

TRANSLATION NOTES

CHARACTER BENTO

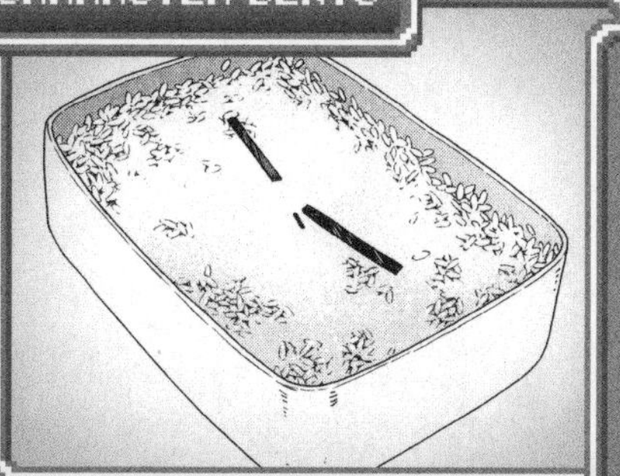

page 194

A popular form of creative cooking. The bento, or Japanese lunch box, is a form of meal based around rice and various sides packed neatly into a special compartmentalized box that in its traditional form is made of lacquer. While a pleasing preparation has always been prized when preparing a bento, the concept of "character bento" has recently come into fashion, in which the food is arranged and designed to resemble a popular character, animal, or other visual feature. The art of character bento is popular enough that there are contests and competitions for it.

The Black Museum — The Ghost and the Lady

By **Kazuhiro Fujita**

Deep in Scotland Yard in London sits an evidence room dedicated to the greatest mysteries of British history. In this "Black Museum" sits a misshapen hunk of lead—two bullets fused together—the key to a wartime encounter between Florence Nightingale, the mother of modern nursing, and a supernatural Man in Grey. This story is unknown to most scholars of history, but a special guest of the museum will tell the tale of The Ghost and the Lady...

Praise for Kazuhiro Fujita's *Ushio and Tora*

"A charming revival that combines a classic look with modern depth and pacing... **Essential viewing both for curmudgeons and new fans alike.**" — Anime News Network

"**GREAT!** The first episode of Ushio and Tora captures the essence of '90s anime." — IGN

New action series from Hiroyuki Takei, creator of the classic shonen franchise Shaman King!

In medieval Japan, a bell hanging on the collar is a sign that a cat has a master. Norachiyo's bell hangs from his katana sheath, but he is nonetheless a stray — a ronin. This one-eyed cat samurai travels across a dishonest world, cutting through pretense and deception with his blade.

By
Hiroyuki Takei

DELUXE EDITION

BATTLE ANGEL ALITA

After more than a decade out of print, the original cyberpunk action classic returns in glorious 400-page hardcover deluxe editions, featuring an all-new translation, color pages, and new cover designs!

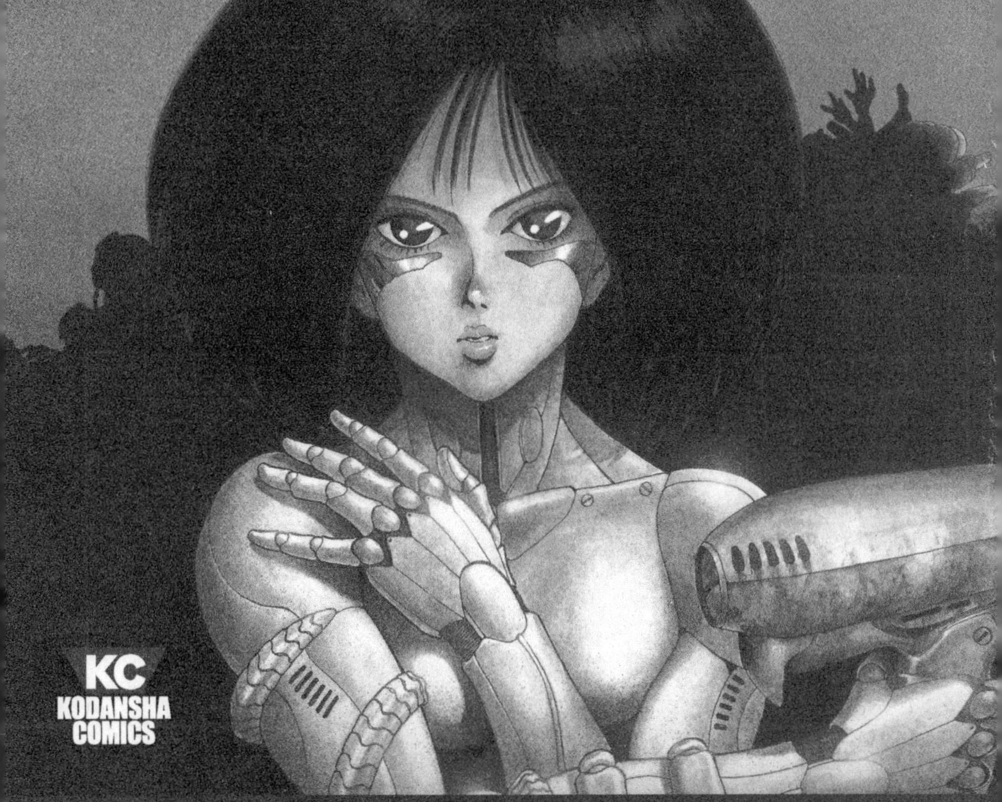

KC
KODANSHA COMICS

Far beneath the shimmering space-city of Zalem lie the trash-heaps of The Scrapyard... Here, cyber-doctor and bounty hunter Daisuke Ido finds the head and torso of an amnesiac cyborg girl. He names her Alita and vows to fill her life with beauty, but in a moment of desperation, a fragment of Alita's mysterious past awakens in her. She discovers that she possesses uncanny prowess in the legendary martial art known as panzerkunst. With her newfound skills, Alita decides to become a hunter-warrior - tracking down and taking out those who prey on the weak. But can she hold onto her humanity in the dark and gritty world of The Scrapyard?

Having lost his wife, high school teacher Kōhei Inuzuka is doing his best to raise his young daughter Tsumugi as a single father. He's pretty bad at cooking and doesn't have a huge appetite to begin with, but chance brings his little family together with one of his students, the lonely Kotori. The three of them are anything but comfortable in the kitchen, but the healing power of home cooking might just work on their grieving hearts.

"This season's number-one feel-good anime!" —Anime News Network

"A beautifully-drawn story about comfort food and family and grief. Recommended." —Otaku USA Magazine

sweetness & lightning

By Gido Amagakure

KC
KODANSHA
COMICS

The award-winning manga about what happens inside you!

"Far more entertaining than it ought to be... what kid doesn't want to think that every time they sneeze a torpedo shoots out their nose?"
–Anime News Network

Strep throat! Hay fever! Influenza! The world is a dangerous place for a red blood cell just trying to get her deliveries finished. Fortunately, she's not alone...she's got a whole human body's worth of cells ready to help out! The mysterious white blood cells, the buff and brash killer T cells, even the cute little platelets—everyone's got to come together if they want to keep you healthy!

Cells at Work!

はたらく細胞

By Akane Shimizu

A new series from Yoshitoki Oima, creator of The New York Times
bestselling manga and Eisner Award nominee *A Silent Voice*!

An intimate,
emotional drama
and an epic story
spanning time and
space...

TO YOUR
ETERNITY

An orb was cast unto the earth. After metamorphosing
into a wolf, It joins a boy on his bleak journey to find
his tribe. Ever learning, It transcends death, even when
those around It cannot...

Japan's most powerful spirit medium delves into the ghost world's greatest mysteries!

Story by Kyo Shirodaira, famed author of mystery fiction and creator of *Spiral, Blast of Tempest,* and *The Record of a Fallen Vampire.*

Both touched by spirits called yôkai, Kotoko and Kurô have gained unique superhuman powers. But to gain her powers Kotoko has given up an eye and a leg, and Kurô's personal life is in shambles. So when Kotoko suggests they team up to deal with renegades from the spirit world, Kurô doesn't have many other choices, but Kotoko might just have a few ulterior motives...

IN/SPECTRE

STORY BY **KYO SHIRODAIRA**
ART BY **CHASHIBA KATASE**

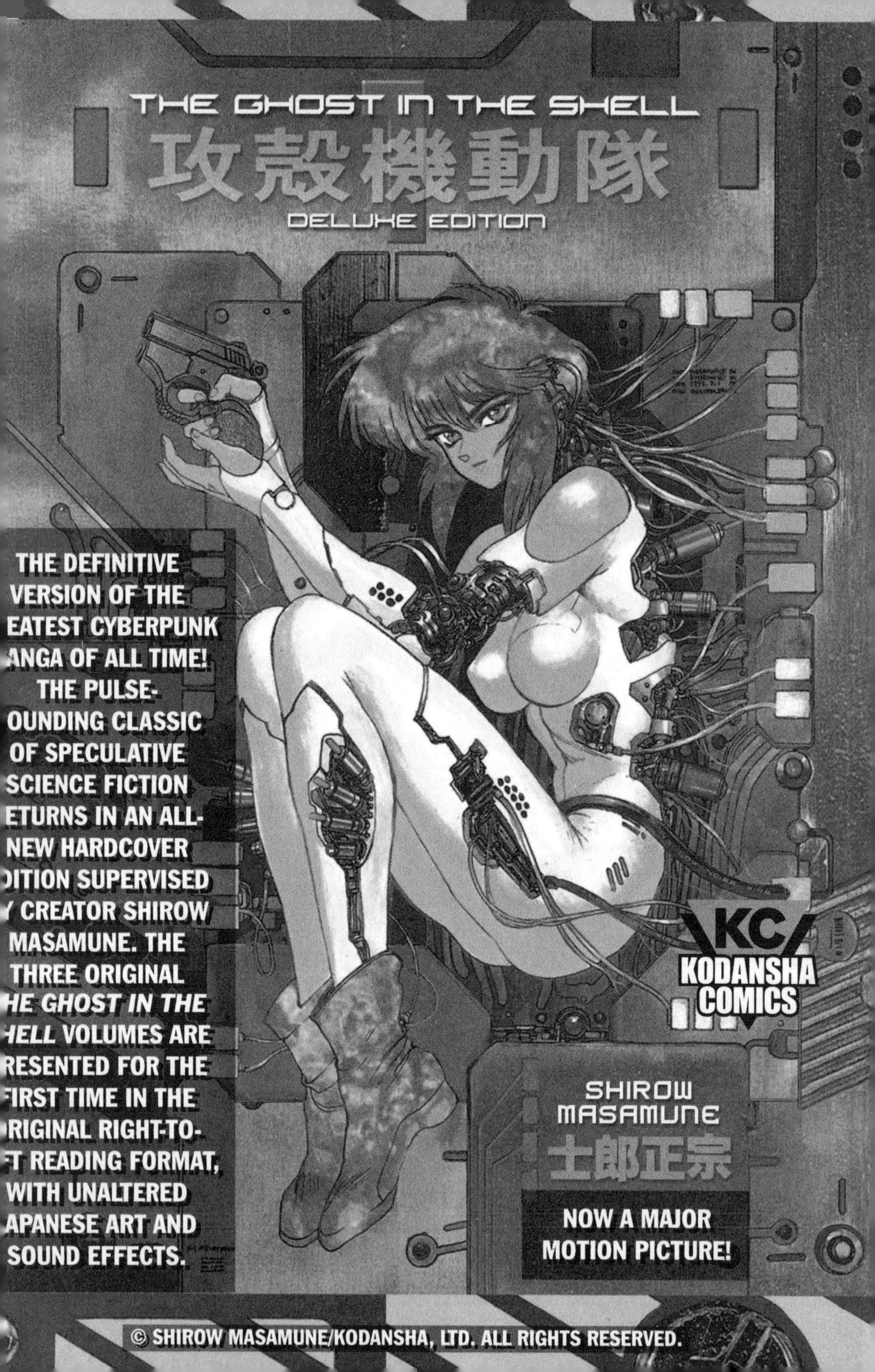
THE GHOST IN THE SHELL
攻殻機動隊
DELUXE EDITION
THE DEFINITIVE VERSION OF THE EATEST CYBERPUNK ANGA OF ALL TIME! THE PULSE-OUNDING CLASSIC OF SPECULATIVE SCIENCE FICTION ETURNS IN AN ALL-NEW HARDCOVER DITION SUPERVISED Y CREATOR SHIROW MASAMUNE. THE THREE ORIGINAL HE GHOST IN THE HELL VOLUMES ARE RESENTED FOR THE FIRST TIME IN THE RIGINAL RIGHT-TO-T READING FORMAT, WITH UNALTERED APANESE ART AND SOUND EFFECTS.
KC
KODANSHA COMICS
SHIROW MASAMUNE
士郎正宗
NOW A MAJOR MOTION PICTURE!
© SHIROW MASAMUNE/KODANSHA, LTD. ALL RIGHTS RESERVED.

OTOMO
大友克洋

A GLOBAL TRIBUTE TO THE MIND BEHIND AKIRA

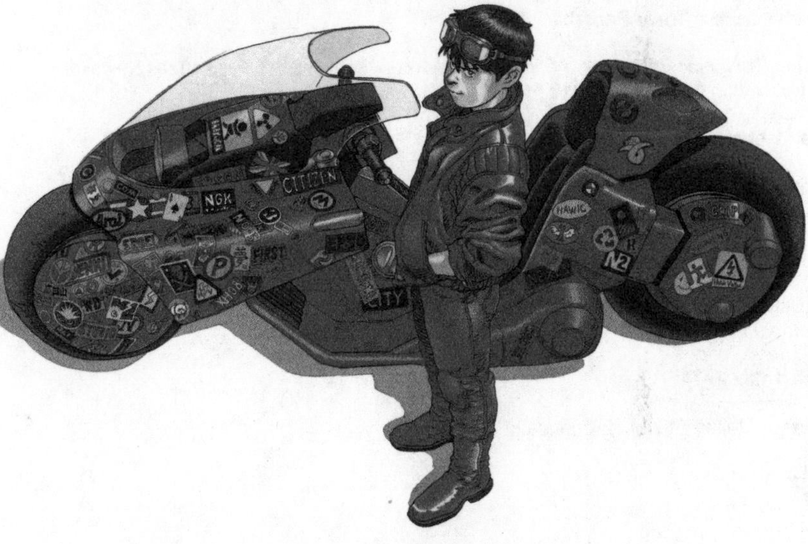
CITIZEN
NGK

A celebration of manga legend Katsuhiro Otomo from more than 80 world-renowned fine artists and comics legends

With contributions from:

- Stan Sakai
- Tomer and Asaf Hanuka
- Sara Pichelli
- Range Murata
- Aleksi Briclot

And more!

168 pages of stunning, full-color art

KC KODANSHA COMICS

That Time I Got Reincarnated as a Slime volume 9 is a work of fiction. Names, characters, places, and incidents are the products of the author's imagination or are used fictitiously. Any resemblance to actual events, locales, or persons, living or dead, is entirely coincidental.

A Kodansha Comics Trade Paperback Original.

That Time I Got Reincarnated as a Slime volume 9 copyright © 2018 Fuse / Taiki Kawakami
English translation copyright © 2019 Fuse / Taiki Kawakami

Published in the United States by Kodansha Comics,
an imprint of Kodansha USA Publishing, LLC, New York.

Publication rights for this English edition arranged through Kodansha Ltd., Tokyo.

First published in Japan in 2018 by Kodansha Ltd., Tokyo, as *Tensei Shitara Suraimu Datta Ken* volume 9.

ISBN 978-1-63236-747-1

Printed in the United States of America.

www.kodansha.us

9 8 7 6 5 4

Translation: Stephen Paul
Lettering: Evan Hayden
Editing: Ajani Oloye
Kodansha Comics edition cover design: Phil Balsman